PROGRAMMING IN C
WITH NUMERICAL METHODS
FOR ENGINEERS

K. B. ROJIANI

Charles E. Via Jr., Department of Civil Engineering
Virginia Polytechnic Institute and State University

PRENTICE HALL, UPPER SADDLE RIVER, NEW JERSEY 07458

Library of Congress Cataloging-in-Publication Data

Rojiani, Kamal B.
    Programming in C with numerical methods for engineers / K.B.
Rojiani.
        p.   cm.
    Includes index.
    ISBN 0-13-726498-4
    1. C (Computer program language)   2. Engineering mathematics--Data
processing.   I. Title.
QA76.73.C15R65 1996
005.13 ' 3--dc20

95-33723
CIP

Acquisitions editor: **MARCIA HORTON**
Editorial/production supervision
and interior design: **SHARYN VITRANO**
Copy editor: **SALLY ANNE BAILEY**
Cover designer: **BRUCE KENSELAAR**
Manufacturing buyer: **DONNA SULLIVAN**
Editorial assistant: **DELORES MARS**
Supplements editor: **BARBARA MURRAY**

©1996 by Prentice-Hall, Inc.
Upper Saddle River New Jersey 07458

The author and publisher of this book have used their best efforts in preparing this book. These efforts include the development, research, and testing of the theories and programs to determine their effectiveness. The author and publisher make no warranty of any kind, expressed or implied, with regard to these programs or the documentation contained in this book. The author and publisher shall not be liable in any event for incidental or consequential damages in connection with, or arising out of, the furnishing, performance, or use of these programs.

Printed in the United States of America

10 9 8 7 6 5 4 3 2 1

ISBN 0-13-726498-4

Prentice-Hall International (UK) Limited,London
Prentice-Hall of Australia Pty. Limited, Sydney
Prentice-Hall Canada Inc., Toronto
Prentice-Hall Hispanoamericana, S.A., Mexico
Prentice-Hall of India Private Limited, New Delhi
Prentice-Hall of Japan, Inc., Tokyo
Pearson Education Asia Pte. Ltd., Singapore
Editora Prentice-Hall do Brasil, Ltda., Rio de Janeiro

To my wife, Rhoda,
and my children,
John, Rehanna, and Navid

CONTENTS

PREFACE

The purpose of this book is to provide a comprehensive description of the C programming language and to demonstrate its use in the solution of engineering problems. Although C was originally designed as a systems programming language to be used with the Unix operating system, it has proven to be a powerful general-purpose programming language and is rapidly replacing FORTRAN as the language for developing programs for engineering applications. The advantages of C over other programming languages include its flexibility, efficiency, and portability. C compilers are available for a wide range of hardware platforms and operating systems. Although there are a number of books on programming in C, they are mostly of a general nature and do not present the subject from the perspective of the engineer. Our specific objectives in this text are the following:

1. To acquaint students with the fundamentals of computer programming and problem solving on a computer.
2. To teach students the C programming language.
3. To present problem-solving techniques and demonstrate the application of these techniques for developing computer-based solutions to engineering problems.
4. To present methods for good program development including programming style, program documentation, program organization, algorithm development, debugging, and testing.
5. To provide students with a background in numerical analysis methods and the implementation of these methods in C and demonstrate the application of these methods by using them to solve practical engineering problems.

DISTINGUISHING FEATURES

A number of features distinguish this book from other books on C programming. These include:

Engineering and Science Applications. The examples and applications presented are taken from a wide range of disciplines including engineering, science and mathematics. The level of mathematics used is that normally taught in freshman and sophomore engineering courses.

Programming Practice and Style. The importance of good programming style is emphasized throughout the text. The student is encouraged to write programs using structured programming techniques. In Chapter 3, there is full treatment of the problem solving and program development process. The role of algorithms, pseudocode, and structure charts in program development is discussed. The essential concepts of structured programming, top-down design, stepwise refinement, modularization, program testing, and debugging are presented. The text stresses the importance of the modular approach to developing programs. After the introduction of functions in Chapter 8, the remaining chapters use functions consistently as a program organization tool.

Comprehensive Coverage of the C Language. A comprehensive coverage of the C programing language is presented. The first eight chapters provide an introduction to the C language. Chapters 9 - 17 present more advanced topics such as file operations, two-dimensional arrays, advanced input and ouput, structures, dynamic memory allocation, and data structures such as linked lists, queues, and stacks. This text is intended to be useful for the beginning student as well as a valuable reference for those experienced in the C language.

Typographic Conventions. Special typographical conventions are used throughout the text to enhance readability and understanding. All C language elements such as keywords, symbols and operators, variable names, and function names are presented in a monospace typeface (as in `x_value`). All program listings are presented in the same monospace typeface. Function names are followed by round brackets (as in `main()`) and all array names have square brackets [] (as in `xarray[]`). All file names are written in italics (as in *stdio.h*).

Numerous Illustrative Examples. The book contains numerous illustrative examples. A number of small examples illustrate basic concepts. Wherever a new C statement or construct is introduced, it is followed by several examples that illustrate its use in a program.

Programming Projects. Most chapters contain programming projects. The programming projects demonstrate the detailed development of a complete program. In each of the programming projects, there is a discussion of the problem analysis, data requirements, algorithm development, and program development. Sample data for several example problems is given at the end along with the results obtained by hand calculations. These sample problems make it possible to test the program developed in the section.

Program Style, Common Errors, and Debugging Guide. In Chapters 2 - 17 (with the exception of Chapter 3), there is a section on program style, common errors, and debugging at the end of the chapter. This section presents techniques for writing better programs, and describes many of the more common programming errors. It also offers suggestions for debugging.

Review Questions and Programming. Each chapter contains a number of short review questions which test the understanding of the basic concepts presented in the chapter. These are followed by programming exercises that require writing programs or modifying or enhancing programs contained in the chapter. The exercises at the end of each chapter are designed to reinforce concepts presented in the chapter.

Numerical Methods. The numerical analysis methods presented in Chapters 18–23 cover most of the important techniques used in engineering analysis. The implementation of these methods on a computer is discussed. Also, code is provided for implementing these methods in C.

Applications of Numerical Methods. The application of numerical methods to the solution of practical engineering problems is illustrated by means of problems from various engineering disciplines. The objective is for the reader to be able to apply these procedures to solve practical problems.

ORGANIZATION

The book is divided into three sections. The first nine chapters cover the essential elements of the C programming language. Chapter 1 presents an introduction to computing and programming languages. Problem-solving techniques are discussed in Chapter 3. This chapter also describes the total software development process. Chapters 10 through 17 cover additional topics such as two-dimensional arrays and matrices, string operations, file and input/ output operations, the C preprocessor, and data structures.

The third section of the book, Chapters 18 through 23, presents numerical analysis methods and the application of these methods in engineering. Topics include roots of nonlinear equations, solution of linear simultaneous equations, regression analysis and curve fitting, interpolation, numerical integration and differentiation, statistical analysis, and simulation.

ACKNOWLEDGMENTS

I would like to acknowledge the efforts of Professors Mark D. LeBlanc (University of New Hampshire), Leonard R. Marino (San Diego State University), Shoichiro Nakamura (Ohio State University), and Michael M. Skolnick (Rensselaer Polytechnic Institute). Their thorough and helpful reviews of an earlier draft of this text were extremely valuable in improving the accuracy and completeness of the presentation. I am also indebted to many students for reading preliminary drafts of this text and suggesting improvements.

The support and encouragement of Marcia Horton, Editor-In-Chief of Prentice Hall's College Technical Division, is gratefully acknowledged. This book may not have happened had it not been for Marcia's persistence and enthusiasm. Special thanks is also due Delores Mars, who was always very helpful and cooperative. Her cheerful disposition helped smooth many a rough moment.

Finally, I would like to thank my family for their patience, support, and understanding. Their encouragement and love sustained me throughout this project.

I would greatly appreciate your comments and suggestions for improving the text. Please address all correspondence to the following e-mail address:

krojiani@vt.edu

You may also write me at the following address:

Kamal B. Rojiani (Author)
c/o Computer Science Editor
College Book Editorial
Prentice Hall
Upper Saddle River, New Jersey 07458

Kamal B. Rojiani

1

INTRODUCTION TO COMPUTERS AND PROGRAMMING

In this chapter we describe the major components of a computer system and explain how information is represented in a computer. We provide an introduction to programming languages and discuss some of the features of the C programming language. We also outline the steps involved in creating a C program.

1.1 COMPUTER HARDWARE

A typical computer system consists of two parts: (1) hardware and (2) software. *Hardware* is the physical equipment that constitutes the computer system. *Software* is a set of instructions to the hardware that is used to solve a problem or perform a specific task. Although the focus of this book is on writing software, it is essential to have a good understanding of the hardware.

A digital computer is essentially a device that accepts data and a set of instructions which tell it how to manipulate these data to produce a set of results. Although they vary tremendously in size, cost, and capabilities, all computers are

1

similar in that they have four components or functional units. These are

1. Central processing unit (CPU)
2. Primary storage
3. Secondary storage
4. Input and output (I/O) devices

The *central processing unit* controls the flow of data and performs the necessary manipulation of data. *Primary storage* is used to store information for immediate access by the central processor. *Secondary storage* devices provide permanent storage of large amounts of data. Input/output devices provide an. interface between the computer and the user. Figure 1.1 shows the basic components of a computer system.

Central Processing Unit

The central processing unit is the heart of the computer system. It monitors and controls the operation of the other devices and the flow of information to and

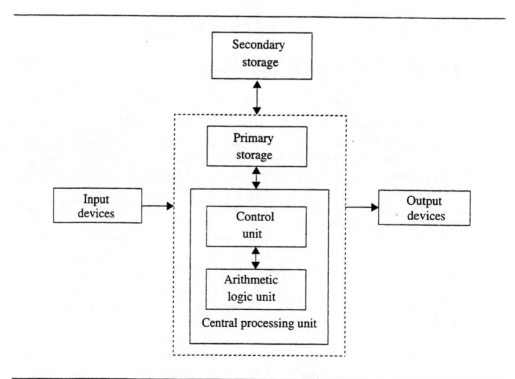

Figure 1.1   The components of a computer system.

from these devices, and it performs all the necessary manipulations of the data. The central processing unit can be subdivided into two submodules: the *control unit* and the *arithmetic logic unit* (ALU).

The control unit is responsible for controlling the flow of data from one section of the CPU to another, for interpreting the instructions stored in memory, and for directing the arithmetic unit to perform the required operations. It is also responsible for moving the results back to primary storage and controlling input and output operations.

The arithmetic logic unit performs the basic arithmetic operations such as addition, subtraction, multiplication, and division. It also has the ability to perform logic operations which involve the comparison of two data items to determine if they are less than, equal to, or greater than each other. The arithmetic logic unit has temporary storage for saving the results of operations.

Primary Storage

Primary storage, also called *main memory*, is used to store information for immediate access by the central processing unit. Memory can be visualized as an organized series of storage locations called *memory cells*. Each memory cell has its own individual *address* which indicates its relative location. Addresses start with the number 0 and go up by one for each successive cell. The information that is contained in a memory cell is called the *contents* of the cell. Memory cells can be used to store both data, such as characters and numbers, and program instructions.

The central processing unit can directly access data stored in main memory. The interchange of data between the CPU and main memory occurs very rapidly. It is important to note that accessing a memory cell does not destroy the contents of that cell. When a memory cell is accessed, an exact copy of the contents of that cell is made, and it is this copy that is used in subsequent processing. When new information is placed in a memory cell, any information already there is destroyed.

Information is stored in a computer using electronic signals. There are two possible states which are identified by the presence or absence of an electronic signal. We use the digits 0 and 1 to represent these two states. Since there are only two digits (0 and 1), all information is stored in *binary* (base 2) form using strings of zeros and ones. The computer interprets these strings of zeros and ones as letters, numbers, or instructions according to certain codes.

The smallest unit of computer storage is called a *bit*, which is an acronym for *bi*nary digi*t*. Each bit can represent a 0 or a 1. A computer uses a series of bits to store information. These bits are organized into groups. Most computers use a group of 8 consecutive bits called a *byte*. Figure 1.2 shows a section of computer memory. A byte can be used to store the binary code for a single letter of the alphabet, or a digit, or a special symbol. Since each bit can take on two possible

Address

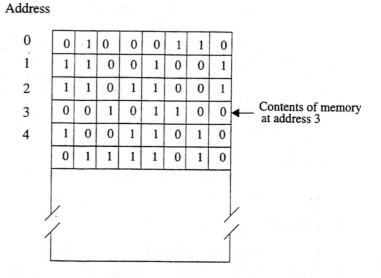

Figure 1.2   A section of computer memory.

values and there are 8 bits in a byte, we have a total of 2^8, or 256, unique combinations, so a byte can hold any of 256 different values depending on how the 0's and 1s are ordered. We can use each one of these combinations to represent any one of 256 characters, such as letters of the alphabet, numbers, or special characters. A byte can also be used to represent unsigned numbers in the range 0 through 255, or signed numbers in the range −128 through 127.

Computers can only store and process numbers. For a computer to store and process characters such as letters, punctuation marks, and other symbols, these characters first have to be converted to numbers. This conversion from characters to numbers is performed in accordance with a code known as the *ASCII code*. ASCII stands for American Standard Code for Information Interchange. Each character is assigned a numeric value called the ASCII code; for example, the ASCII code for the capital letter "A" is 65, the ASCII code for the letter "B" is 66, and the ASCII code for a lowercase "a" is 97. Punctuation marks and other symbols are also assigned ASCII codes. For example, the ASCII code for the greater than (>) symbol is 62, and the code for a semicolon (;) is 59. Appendix B lists the ASCII code for the various characters.

The unit of information that is transferred to and from main memory is called a *word*. Personal computers typically use 16 to 32 bits while minicomputers and mainframe computers use 32- to 64-bit words. Word size is important for several reasons. Since information is transmitted between different locations inside a computer one word at a time, a larger word size results in faster operation. Also, a machine with a larger word size has more primary storage, a larger set of available instructions, and greater precision.

The storage capacity of a computer is usually expressed in kilobytes (K), which is equal to 1024 bytes. Thus a computer with a storage capacity of 512K has 512*1024 = 524,288 bytes of storage. Another unit of storage is the megabyte (MB). One megabyte is equivalent to 1024K or 1,048,576 bytes.

Most computers have two types of memory: ROM and RAM. ROM, which stands for *read-only memory* is designed to hold permanent programs and data needed by the computer. The computer can read only the information contained in ROM. It cannot change the contents of ROM. The contents of ROM are permanently "burned in" and do not change even when the power is turned off. The ROM chips contain special programs which are critical to the operation of the computer. Examples of such programs include programs that control the transfer of information between the central processor and other input/ouput devices and the self-test program which checks out the computer when the power is first turned on.

The other kind of memory inside a computer is called RAM which stands for *random-access memory*. This is memory that is directly available to the user. Our programs and data are stored in random access memory. One problem with random-access memory is that it is "volatile"; that is, the contents of RAM are erased when the electrical current is turned off.

Secondary Storage

Most computer systems have secondary storage devices which are used to provide additional data storage capability. Secondary storage is necessary because of the limitations of primary storage. As mentioned earlier, information contained in primary storage is not permanent. A sudden loss of power from primary storage can destroy all data. Also, primary storage is relatively expensive so most computer systems have only a limited amount of primary storage. This makes it impractical to store our information in primary storage. Secondary storage provides permanent storage for programs and data that is not currently being used. With secondary storage devices it is possible to store large amounts of data.

The data in secondary memory is not directly accessible by the CPU but must be first transferred to main memory before processing. Secondary memory storage is considerably less expensive than main memory but requires significantly longer access times.

Two of the most common secondary storage media are *floppy disks* and *hard disks*. The floppy disk drive writes information on a flexible disk called a diskette or *floppy disk*. A diskette is a circular piece of soft Mylar plastic coated with a magnetic film. This circular piece of plastic is enclosed in a stiff protective jacket. The diskette fits into a slot in the disk drive. The disk drive mechanism grips the flexible plastic disk and spins it inside the jacket. The read/write head accesses the data on the disk through a slot cut in the jacket. This makes it possible to directly access the data on the diskette. Diskettes come in several standard sizes, the two most common sizes being 5¼ in., and 3¼ in.

A hard disk consists of several rigid aluminum platters coated with magnetic material. The size of these platters varies from 3 in. to 5¼ inch. The platters rotate on a spindle at very high speeds, typically around 3600 rpm. A stepper motor positions the read/write heads at the appropriate track. The clearances between the media and the read/write heads are extremely small. The read/write heads float on a cushion of air and do not actually come in contact with the magnetic material. Hard disks are sealed to protect the components from being contaminated by dirt.

The main advantages of hard disks is their speed and greater storage capacity. Hard disks can transfer information many times faster than floppy disks. Hard disks are especially useful for applications which are disk intensive, that is, those applications that require the processing of large amounts of data.

Hard disks have several disadvantages. The major disadvantage is that hard disks use a sealed medium which cannot be removed. A second disadvantage of a hard disk is that the data on the hard disk can be rendered useless if a problem with the hard disk occurs. Thus, it becomes necessary to have some means of backing up the data on a routine basis, which can be a time consuming task.

Other secondary storage devices include *removable cartridge drives*, *tape drives*, and *optical disks*. A removable cartridge drive is similar in many ways to a hard disk with the exception that the platter is placed inside a cartridge which can be removed from the drive unit. Tape drives are used mostly for backing up the contents of a hard disk. They can store large amounts of information on relatively inexpensive tape cartridges. With optical disks a laser beam is used to write data on the surface of a glass or plastic disk containing a coating of metal. The laser beam makes microscopic pits (or bubbles) on the metal coating, and each pit represents a bit of data which can be read by the same laser. Optical disks have storage capacities significantly larger than hard disks.

Input and Output Devices

Input and output devices allow us to communicate with the computer system. They include devices that enter information into the computer and devices that display information stored in the computer's memory. The primary input device is the *keyboard*. The arrangement of keys on most computer keyboards is similar to that on a conventional typewriter. However, in addition to the standard typewriter keys, most computer keyboards have a number of other keys that perform various functions. Other input devices include a mouse, digitizer, joy stick, light pen, and voice and bar code recognition units.

The primary output device is the display *monitor*. The monitor also displays any characters typed on the keyboard. The images on a computer monitor are formed by directing a beam of electrons on the screen. The screen is composed of hundreds of discrete elements called *pixels,* which is an acronym for *picture elements.* The pixels glow momentarily when struck by an electron beam, thus producing the image that we see on the screen. The quality of the image depends on the resolution of the screen, that is, the number of pixels per square inch. The higher the resolution, the better the quality of the image.

Although video displays are used most often for output, they do have a few limitations. Only a small amount of output can be displayed at any one time, and the output is not permanent. When a permanent record is required, a printer is used to generate an image of the output on paper. *Dot matrix printers* create type by printing a collection of dots which approximate the shape of the character. The print head consists of a series of pins or wires. The dots are produced by the impact of these pins striking on a ribbon. The printer selects the specific pins within the matrix needed to create the pattern of dots corresponding to the shape of the character. The quality of the letters printed is determined by the number of pins in the print head: the more pins used, the better the letter printed. Some of the better dot matrix printers use a larger number of pins in the print head which results in a higher density of dots per square inch.

Ink jet printers produce type by spraying liquid ink drops through channels in the print head. There are two major categories of ink jet printers. In *drop-on-demand* ink jet printing the ink jets are routed through several ink channels. The drops are deposited on paper by selectively applying pressure in each channel. *Continuous stream* printers use a single ink channel. An electrical charge is used to break up this stream of ink into separate drops and to route the drops. Color ink jet printers use different color inks on a single cartridge to produce multicolored images.

Thermal printers use heat to form characters on paper. Characters are created by selectively heating pins on a thermal print head. A specially coated, heat-sensitive paper is used. The heat from the pins darkens the paper and creates the images which are composed of dots. *Laser printers* create type by exposing paper to a laser beam. The process used is similar to that used in electrostatic copier machines.

Plotters are used extensively for drawing high-quality images on paper or transparency film. Plotters use pens controlled by the computer to draw images. Plotters are vector devices and have a much higher resolution than printers. Plotters are capable of extremely small pen movements, typically of the order of one-thousandth of an inch. For multicolored drawings, plotters with multiple pens are available.

1.2   PROGRAMMING LANGUAGES

Machine and Assembly Languages

For a computer to perform any task it has to be given a series of specific instructions in a language that it can understand. The fundamental language for any computer is *machine language* which essentially consists of strings of zeros and ones. Writing programs using a series of zeros and ones is extremely tedious and time consuming, and few people program in machine language. To relieve the frustration of programming in machine language *assembly language* was developed. Assembly language allows the programmer to represent machine language instructions by means of *mnemonic* words and symbols. To use assembly language the programmer must have a thorough understanding of the internal architecture of the computer. Although assembly language is a significant improvement over machine language programming, it is still a *low-level* language in that it is oriented more toward the computer than toward the people who are programming the computer. Some of the disadvantages shared by both machine language and assembly language programming are the following:

1. Programs are machine dependent and cannot be easily transferred from one computer system to another. Programs written in these languages can be executed only on computers of identical design.
2. Programming is very time consuming to learn. It requires considerable experience to become proficient.
3. Most of the program is occupied with internal details which have very little to do with the actual task to be accomplished.
4. Programs are difficult to alter due to their complexity.
5. It is very easy to introduce errors.

Machine language and assembly language do have a few advantages. Machine language programs run much faster and require less memory. There are some tasks, particularly those that require direct access to hardware features, that can be done with machine language and assembly language which are difficult and sometimes even impossible to do with high-level languages.

High-Level Languages

High-level languages are geared more toward the people writing the programs rather than the computer. These languages provide the interface between the user and the machine. They are closer to English but are sufficiently rigorous to permit the computer to translate the programs written in the high-level language into machine language. This simplifies the task of programming and saves time.

Most programs today are written in high-level languages.

The advantages of high-level programming languages include the following:

1. These languages are problem oriented. Their structure and operations closely resemble the language in which the problem is formulated rather than the structure and organization of the computer.
2. The programmer does not need to know about the organization or the internal architecture of the computer.
3. Learning to program in a high-level language is easy since the programs are written in a language that the programmer is accustomed.
4. High-level programs require fewer statements. A single source statement generates many machine language statements.
5. Theoretically, high-level programs are machine independent, and programs can be run on a great many different computers. In practice, however, there are considerable variations among different computer systems, and this causes them to be machine dependent and less easily transportable from one computer system to another.
6. High-level languages have extensive error diagnostics. These help the programmer in locating and correcting errors in the programs and generally result in a more friendly environment.

The translation of programs written in a high-level language into machine language is accomplished by means of a special computer program called a *compiler*. The compiler analyzes a program written in a high-level language and translates it into a form that is suitable for execution on the particular computer system. The statements written in the high-level programming language are called *source code*. The compiler's output is called *object code* (see Figure 1.3). Since each computer system has its own machine language, a different compiler is required for each make of computer. The source code typically remains the same though the object code many be different.

A number of high-level languages are in use today. Each has its own special features which make it more suitable for some disciplines and fields. Among the

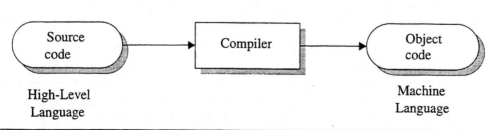

High-Level Language   Machine Language

Figure 1.3   Relationship between compiler, source code, and object code.

major high-level languages are FORTRAN, BASIC, COBOL, Pascal, and C. Other high-level languages are Ada, PL1, and Forth.

FORTRAN was the first high-level language. It was also the first compiled language. FORTRAN was introduced commercially by IBM in 1957. The name FORTRAN stands for *FOR*mula *TRAN*slation. FORTRAN is an algebraic programming language which uses notation similar to that used for solving scientific and engineering problems. FORTRAN is the most widely used language among scientists and engineers, and there is a large collection of engineering programs written in FORTRAN. In the business field COBOL (*C*ommon *B*usiness *O*riented *L*anguage) is widely used since it has features which enable large files of data to be manipulated readily.

BASIC is a powerful programming language that is rather easy to learn, since it was designed specifically for teaching programming to beginners. It was developed in the early 1960s by Professors John G. Kemeny and Thomas E. Kurtz and was designed as an easy-to-learn-and-use, interactive language for general purpose programming. BASIC is an acronym for *B*eginners *A*ll-purpose *S*ymbolic *I*nstruction *C*ode. The BASIC language is quite versatile. The original version of BASIC was somewhat limited, but it has evolved to the point where it is suitable for a wide variety of programming applications.

Pascal was develop by Nicklaus Wirth in the 1970s and is named after the French scientist and philosopher Blaise Pascal. Pascal is a newer, more structured programming language. It is well suited for developing large complex programs since its structured orientation results in programs that are easier to develop and maintain.

1.3   THE C PROGRAMMING LANGUAGE

The C programming language was developed in the early 1970s by Dennis Ritchie, a systems software engineer at AT&T Bell Laboratories. C evolved from a language named B that was developed by Ken Thomson. Around the time of C's creation, Ken Thomson was working on developing the Unix operating system. The earlier versions of Unix were written using assembly language and had a number of shortcomings. Dennis Ritchie developed C to overcome some of the shortcomings of B. He salvaged some of the best features of B, added a number of significant features such as data types and storage classes, and removed many of the hardware-dependent aspects. Although C was originally designed as a systems programming language to be used with the Unix operating system, it soon proved itself to be a powerful general-purpose programming language. C has been used for every type of programming project imaginable from operating systems to expert systems and is the programming language of choice for most professional programmers.

The popularity of the C programming language has increased steadily since its creation. This has been partly due to the increase in popularity of the Unix operating system and the close association between Unix and C. C is the native programming language under Unix. A large part of the Unix operating system is written in C, and most of the software running under Unix is written in C. However, C's success is primarily due to the fact that although it is a simple and elegant language, it is also a very powerful and efficient language. The C programming language has many features that give it an advantage over other procedural languages such as FORTRAN, BASIC, and Pascal. Some of these features include flexibility, efficiency, portability, and speed.

C is already a dominant language on minicomputers and workstations running the Unix operating system. However, C has also become a popular language on personal computers. There appears to be little doubt that C will be one of the more important programming languages of the 1990s. C compilers are now available for a wide range of hardware platforms and operating systems. A knowledge of C programming is also essential for developing applications under many of the newer graphical windowing environments such as Microsoft Windows, OS/2 Presentation Manager, Motif, and X-Windows. C is the preferred language for these environments, and all reference materials, documentation, and development tools assume that the developer has a knowledge of C programming.

1.4 ADVANTAGES OF C

The C programming language has a number of advantages over other procedural languages such as FORTRAN, Pascal, and BASIC. These include flexibility, efficiency, speed and portability. C is a very powerful and flexible language. This is evident from the fact that C is being used extensively for developing a wide variety of applications. C is also a very efficient language. C programs tend to be compact and run faster than programs developed using other languages except assembly language. Also, since C is a small language (C has only about 40 keywords), it encourages concise code.

C enjoys a rather unique position in the hierarchy of computer languages, and it is sometimes described as a "middle-level" language. It has the capabilities of both the high-level problem-oriented languages such as Pascal and FORTRAN, as well as many of the features of the low-level machine-oriented languages such as assembler. With C it is possible to build complex data structures found in other high-level languages. However, it is also possible in C to manipulate individual bits and bytes of that data.

C was written by one man and reflects his area of expertise. Dennis Ritchie was a systems programmer and C was designed to be used for systems programming. However, its wide diversity of operators and commands make it suitable as a general-purpose programming language. Some of the advantages of the C programming language are listed in the paragraphs that follow.

Powerful

C is a very powerful language. This is evident from the fact that C is being used extensively for developing programs for a wide range of applications. Most of the powerful Unix operation system and large parts of the DOS and OS/2 operating system are written in C. C has also been used for writing compilers and interpreters for other languages (include C itself), text editors, typesetting and desktop publishing programs, database management, communications, graphics and CAD applications, expert systems and other artificial intelligence tools, spreadsheets, and a number of engineering applications.

Although C is a small language, it provides a complete set of tools for developing all types of applications. It has a wide diversity of commands and has all the statements necessary to write well-structured programs. It has a powerful set of operators. Another useful feature of C is its use of modular components to create more powerful constructs. By using the basic elements of the language, it is possible to develop powerful functions that can perform complex tasks.

Efficient

The code generated by the better C compilers is extremely fast. C programs run faster than programs written in other high-level languages such as Pascal and FORTRAN. In fact, the code is so efficient that C programs can run almost as fast as those written in assembly language. In the past, most systems programs were written in assembly language. Since assembly language is a low level language, writing programs in assembly language is tedious work, and the possibility of making errors is high. Most systems programmers now use C for writing systems software. C code can be written more quickly than assembly code and is easier to debug and to update.

In addition to being more efficient, C programs also tend to be more compact in size and require less memory.

Flexible

C is a flexible programming language. It provides the programmer with a great deal of control and freedom. Since it was originally designed as a systems programming language for use by programmers, it does not have many of the restrictions of some of the other programming languages. It is relatively easy to manipulate bits, bytes, and addresses in C. C allows you to look at addresses, perform arithmetic on addresses, and manipulate memory directly using pointers.

C also allows you to write code that takes full advantage of the computer hardware to achieve maximum efficiency. Most operations that could only be performed using assembly language can be performed in C and usually more conveniently. Thus C provides the convenience of high-level languages while allowing a degree of control over hardware and peripherals that is only possible in a low-level language such as assembler.

The wide diversity of operators and statements that are available in C make it suitable as a general purpose programming language. It fact, there are many applications that can easily be handled in C that would be difficult, if not impossible, to implement in other languages such as FORTRAN and BASIC.

The freedom and flexibility provided by C is one of its main strengths. However, along with this freedom comes the responsibility of using it wisely since undisciplined use of this freedom can result in errors.

Structured

C is a structured language and is well suited to structured programming. Structured programming is a discipline whose goal is to develop programs that are easy to read and write, and whose logic is easily understood. C has all the features needed to develop structured programs. It has many of the control structures that are considered necessary for a modern structured programming language such as the block structured **if/then/else, for, while, do/while,** and **switch** constructs. Its syntax makes it easy to understand and easy to maintain. C supports the concept of writing programs as independent blocks of code. All C programs are written as a series of subroutines (called functions in C) that are independent and can be easily moved or replaced. C also supports the concept of local variables. Local variables are variables that are known only to the function in which they are defined.

Once you are familiar with the structure and syntax of the C language, you will find that the flow and logic of a well-written C program is easy to follow. For the most part, C programs tend to be clear, compact, and concise. However, as is the case with any programming language, it is the programmer's responsibility to ensure that the program is written in a manner that makes it readable and easy to follow.

Modular

C encourages the development of modular programs. A modular program consists of a number of smaller subprograms or modules. Each module is independent of the others. Modular design has a number of advantages. The most important advantage is that it limits complexity and simplifies the design of the program. It allows us to break up a large and complex task into a series of smaller and more manageable tasks. A modular program is easier to write and debug, because each module of the program can be written and tested separately. A modular program is also easier to maintain; since the modules are independent, they can be changed, rewritten, or even replaced without affecting other parts of the program. Another advantage is that the program can be developed by several people since different people can work on different modules.

The C language has many features especially designed to help us develop modular programs. Programs can be built from separately compiled modules. Also previously developed and tested modules can be combined into a library that can be used by different programs. All C compilers provide files called "include files" and a library of commonly used functions that can be incorporated into your programs. You can also create your own customized include files and libraries containing definitions and functions needed by your program. Most experienced programmers use libraries of modules developed either by them or by others. Because of the modular nature of C programs, numerous libraries of modules are available commercially for a variety of tasks such as creating menus, user interfaces, graphics, and communications. This makes it possible for even novice programmers to develop professional programs with little effort. These libraries can easily be integrated into your programs and can save considerable time when developing programs.

Portable

C is a very portable language. Portability means that software written for one type of computer can be easily adapted to run on another type of computer. C programs written on one system can be run with little or no modifications on other systems. Generally all that is required is that the program be compiled again using a C compiler on the new system. Since C is a small language and has very few statements, it is reasonably easy to write C compilers. C compilers are available for a wide variety of hardware platforms, including personal computers, workstations, minicomputers, and mainframes. It is thus very easy to move a C program from one hardware platform to another.

A feature of the C programming language that helps in portability is its modularity. C supports modular design, which makes it possible to write programs in which hardware dependent features are isolated by placing them in separate include files and modules. If modifications are necessary due to changes in hardware, they can often be made by simply changing the include files or replacing those modules that are hardware dependent.

Another important feature that helps in making C programs more portable is that the C language itself does not have any statements for input/output operations. Instead all C compilers provide a standard library of functions for handling these tasks and take care of the hardware dependent aspects of input and output operations. C programs that use the standard library functions for performing input and output should be able to run on other computer systems with only minor changes.

The ease with which C programs can be moved from one environment to another has been an important factor in the adoption of the C programming language by many professional programmers. Many software developers are now writing programs using C since this results in considerable savings in development costs and provides them access to a wide variety of hardware platforms.

1.5   DISADVANTAGES OF C

C does have a few disadvantages. It is a terse language. Since C is a free-form language and does not impose strict style rules, C programs can be difficult to understand, especially if the programmer has not made the effort to make the program readable.

C gives the programmer a great deal of flexibility. While this flexibility is what gives C its power, it can also result in programming errors that are difficult to find. C places a greater burden on the programmer for ensuring the correctness of the program. It is not a strongly typed language as Pascal. C does not have automatic array bounds checking. Thus it is the programmer's responsibility to make sure that all array references are within the limits of the array.

C also allows a programmer direct access to memory through the use of pointers. Pointers are a very useful feature of the language, but if not used correctly, they can have a disastrous effect on not only the program and data, but also other parts of the computer such as the operating system. Invalid pointers can result in a system crash.

There are some aspects of the language that can result in ambiguity. For example, C compilers have considerable flexibility in determining the order of evaluation within expressions and parameter lists. Also, C makes multiple use of some symbols such as * and =. The * symbol is used in C for both multiplication as in the expression **x** * **y** as well as for pointers as in *x. The equal symbol (=) is used for assignment as in **x** = **y** as well as for testing equality as in **x** == **y**.

In summary, the C programming language is a very powerful language that has many features that make it well suited for developing a wide range of applications. Its speed and flexibility are two of its most well liked features. The C language does have a few disadvantages. Its compact nature makes it possible to write programs that are difficult to understand. Also, since the language imposes few constraints it is possible for inexperienced programmers to write C programs that contain many errors. However, these can be minimized by following a few fundamental rules. It should be pointed out that regardless of which programming language you use, it is important that you pay considerable attention to the design of your program and that you employ sound programming principles. This will minimize errors in your programs and localize the scope of these errors and will result in programs that are easier to read, maintain, and debug. Throughout this book, we will be paying close attention to program design and will encourage good programming style.

1.6   ANSI C STANDARD

Until recently, there was no official standard for the C language. The unofficial standard of the C language was the version described in the book *The C Programming Language* by Brian Kernighan and Dennis Ritchie (1978). This version of C is known as "K & R," C and most C compilers implemented the language as specified in this book.

With the increasing popularity of the language, many firms developing C compilers made a number of enhancements to the language. Although these versions were compatible with the original Kernighan and Ritchie specification, they were often incompatible with each other.

In 1983, the American National Standards Institute (ANSI) formed a committee whose goal was to develop a standard definition of the C language. The committee's task was to resolve the ambiguities and to produce a machine independent definition of the C language. The ANSI C standard (American National Standards Institute, 1989) contains several additions to the language such as a new form of function declaration that reduces errors, several new data types, and specifications for a standard library with an extensive set of functions. Most C compilers conform to the ANSI standard. The presentation in this book is based on the ANSI standard.

1.7   CREATING A C PROGRAM

The translation of programs written in a high-level language such as C into machine code is accomplished by means of a special computer program called a *compiler*. The compiler analyzes a program written in a language such as C and translates it into a form that is suitable for execution on the particular computer system. There are several steps that you have to perform to create a C program (see Figure 1.4):

1.   Use a text editor to write your program (source code) in C.
2.   Compile your program using a C compiler. Correct any errors pointed out by the compiler. Steps 1 and 2 are repeated until there are no errors in the program.
3.   Link your program with library functions using a linker.
4.   Execute and test your program.

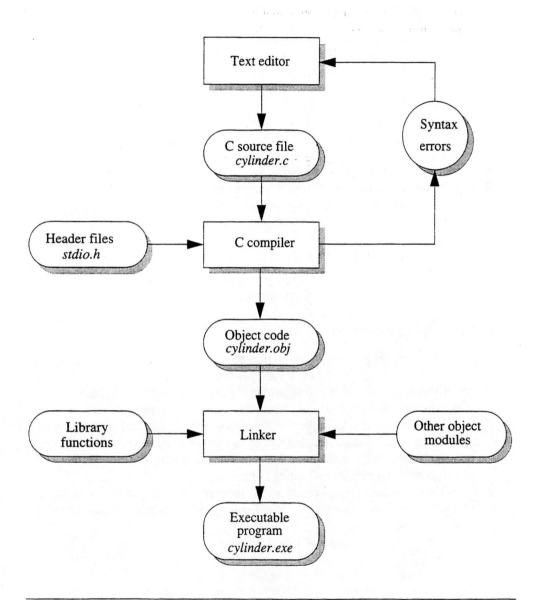

Figure 1.4   Steps involved in creating a C program.

On most systems, the second step may be subdivided into several intermediate steps. On other systems, the second and third steps are combined into one. We will explain each of these steps in detail in the sections that follow.

Creating the Source Code

The first step in creating a C program is to type the C language statements into a file. A text editor is required to accomplish this task. To be able to type in, modify, and correct your C programs, you will need to become familiar with the use of a text editor. There are a number of text editors that can be used for this purpose. Examples of text editors include the *vi* and *emacs* editors that are provided with the Unix operating system and *edit*, which is available on the MS-DOS operating system. All the integrated C programming environments also contain a text editor. An integrated environment is a menu driven system for developing C programs that includes an editor, compiler, linker, and debugger.

After the source code has been entered, it is saved in a file. The C program file is saved as a text file. By convention, C program files have names ending in *.c*, for example,

> *cylinder.c   binomial.c   roots.c*

You should give your program files meaningful names to remind you of what the program does. The second part of the file name (*.c*) identifies it as a C program.

Compiling the Program

The C compiler checks your source code for errors. If there are errors in the program, the compiler issues error messages or warning messages. It also identifies the location within your program where these errors may have occurred. You have to enter the editor and correct all these errors before you can proceed.

The compiler checks for both syntax errors such as unmatched parentheses in expressions and semantic errors such as the use of variables that have not been defined. It is not at all unusual to have to compile your program several times until all errors have been removed from the program.

The commands needed to compile a program on a computer system depends on the compiler being used. You should consult your compiler documentation for additional information.

If the compiler does not detect any errors in your program, it creates a machine language version of your program called *object code*. The compiler will give the newly created file containing the object code an extension of *.obj*. Thus, if the file name of the source code is *cylinder.c*, the compiler will create a file called *cylinder.obj*.

Linking

Although the object code produced by the compiler is in machine language, it is not in a form that can be directly executed by the computer. The last step is to "link" the object code using a program called the *linker*. The linker takes the object file produced by the compiler and combines this with other object files and library functions to produce an executable program.

The linker performs a number of very important functions. First, it allows us to combine several separately compiled object files into a single program. If we have functions that we use frequently in our programs, we can place these functions in separate files and compile these files separately. This saves a considerable amount of time since these functions do not have to be compiled again during program development. This also makes a complex program more manageable since we can break up a large program into a number of smaller modules, save these in separate files, and compile only those modules that have changed or are under development.

The linker also provides a way to incorporate library functions into our programs. Most compilers provide a standard library of functions for performing many of the more common programming tasks such as, for example, functions for performing input/output operations, mathematical functions, and functions for performing operations on strings of characters. Most C programs make use of these library functions. When you link your program, the linker combines your object code with the object code contained in the standard library provided with the compiler. Thus, for example, if your program uses the library function **sqrt()** to compute the square root of a number, the linker takes the already compiled and ready-to-link object code for the **sqrt()** function from the standard library and combines it with your object code to produce the executable file.

The exact command for linking a program depends on the compiler. On many systems, the compile and link steps are integrated into one step, which means that the compiler automatically calls the linker if there are no errors in your program. For example, the Unix C compiler, the Microsoft C compiler, and the Borland C compiler all automatically call the linker if the compilation step is successful.

The linker produces an executable program. You can now run the program by simply typing in the name of the program.

1.8 THE STANDARD C LIBRARY

All C compilers have a standard C library. This library contains functions for performing many of the more common programming tasks. The exact functions provided by the compiler's developer will vary. This is because the C language itself does not define what functions should be in the library or how these functions should work. However, most C compilers provide the standard Unix library functions. The ANSI C standard does specify a set of functions that must be a part of the standard library of a C compiler. All C compilers that conform to the ANSI C standard will have these functions as part of their standard library.

We will use many of the standard library functions in this text. You should study your compiler documentation so you are aware of what functions are available in the standard library. As you write your programs, you will find that many of the functions that you need have already been developed by the compiler's developers. Also, if you develop functions that you use frequently, you can place these in your own library. These functions can be linked with your programs as needed. There are several advantages to doing this. Once the functions have been written, you can save time by reusing them in your programs. You do not have to compile these functions each time you compile your program, since the functions have already been compiled. By using pretested functions, you also increase the reliability of your programs. In fact, many C programmers use precompiled libraries of functions.

1.9   SUMMARY

In this chapter we presented an introduction to computer hardware and programming languages. All computers have four components. They are the central processing unit, primary storage, secondary storage, and input and output devices. The smallest unit of computer storage is a bit, which can represent a 0 or a 1. Computers use a series of bits to store information. These bits are organized into groups. Most computers use a group of 8 consecutive bits called a byte. The unit of information transferred to and from main memory is called a word. Word sizes range from 16 to 64 bits.

Computer memory can be visualized as an organized series of storage locations called memory cells. Each memory cell has its own address, which indicates its relative location. The information contained in a memory cell is called the contents of the cell. The contents of a memory cell are destroyed whenever new information is placed in that cell.

The fundamental language for any computer is machine language which essentially consists of a series of zeros and ones. Assembly language allows programmers to represent machine language instructions by means of mnemonic words and symbols. High-level languages such as FORTRAN, Pascal, and C are geared more toward the people writing the programs than to the computer. They are closer to human languages but are sufficiently rigorous to permit the computer to translate programs written in a high-level language into machine language. The program that performs this translation is called a compiler.

The C programming language is a very powerful language that has many features that make it well suited for developing a wide range of applications. Its speed and flexibility are two of its most well liked features. C is also a very portable language and is available on a wide variety of computer systems. The C language does have a few disadvantages. Its compact nature makes it possible to write programs that are difficult to understand. Also, since the language imposes few constraints, it is possible for inexperienced programmers to write C programs that contain many errors. However, these can be minimized by following a few basic rules regarding program design and good programming style.

In this chapter we also outlined the steps involved in creating a C program. These include writing the source code using a text editor, compiling the program and correcting any errors indicated by the compiler, linking the program and finally executing the program.

Key Terms Presented in This Chapter

ANSI C standard	input/output devices
arithmetic logic unit	linker
ASCII code	low-level language
assembly language	machine language
bit	object code
byte	primary storage
central processing unit	programming languages
compiler	software
computer word	standard C library
control unit	secondary storage
hardware	source code
high-level language	

EXERCISES

Review Questions

1. What are the fundamental components of a computer system? Describe the function of each component.

2. Define the function of the arithmetic logic unit .

3. How is information stored in memory? What is the difference between a bit, byte, and word?

4. Explain the difference between ROM and RAM.

5. List some mass storage devices that are used in computers.

6. List the various types of printers. Which type of printer is most suitable for general

engineering work? Why?

7.   Obtain the following information for the computer system on which you will be programming:

    a.   The amount of main memory

    b.   The amount of disk storage capacity

    c.   The name of the central processing unit

    d.   The number of instructions the CPU can execute per second

    e.   The name and version number of the operating system running on the computer

    f.   The name of the text editor that you will be using

    g.   The name of the C compiler available on the computer.

8.   What is the difference between machine, assembly, and high-level languages?

9.   List some high-level programming languages.

10. What is the function of a compiler?

11. Describe what is meant by "object program" and "source program."

12. What is the function of a linker?

13. What are some of the strengths of C as a programming language? What are some of its weaknesses?

2

BASIC ELEMENTS OF C PROGRAMS

In this chapter we show you what a C program looks like and present the basic elements of a C program. We discuss the various building blocks that form a C program and present two simple C programs to illustrate these basic building blocks.

2.1 STRUCTURE OF A C PROGRAM

The structure of a typical C program is shown in Figure 2.1. Most C programs contain the following basic elements:

1. Preprocessor statements
2. Global declarations
3. Function prototypes
4. Functions

A brief description of these basic elements follows. Detailed explanations are given in later sections.

Preprocessor statements represent instructions to the C preprocessor. The C preprocessor is a program that analyzes source code before passing it on to the

```
preprocessor statements
```

```
global declarations
```

```
function prototypes
```

```
main()
{
...
...
}
```

```
function1()
{
...
...
}
```

```
function2()
{
...
...
}
```

Figure 2.1   The basic elements of a C program.

compiler. All preprocessor statements begin with the **#** symbol. Although preprocessor statements can appear anywhere in a program, they are usually placed near the beginning of a program. Global declaration statements define global variables. Global variables are variables that are accessible to all parts of a C program. Function declarations (also called function prototypes) are statements that provide the compiler with information regarding the type of value returned by a function and also the type and number of function arguments. Functions are groups of statements or instructions that the computer can execute. C functions are similar to subroutines in other programming languages. All C programs consist of a set of functions. There are three functions in the skeleton program shown in Figure 2.1, `main()`, `function1()`, and `function2()`.

2.2   A SIMPLE C PROGRAM

We begin by looking at a simple program *cylinder.c* that computes the volume and surface area of a cylinder (see Figure 2.2). The program is shown in Figure 2.3 along with the input and output for a trial run. We recommend that you enter and run the program since it will help you better understand and remember the concepts we will discuss. In this section we will present a brief description of the various elements of the program so you can get an overview of what a C program looks like. Detailed descriptions of the these elements will be appear in later sections. A brief line-by-line explanation of the program follows.

The first few lines of the program which begin with /* and end with */ are comments. Comments are remarks which help clarify a program. Comments are ignored by the compiler. The line

```
#include <stdio.h>
```

is a preprocessor statement. The C preprocessor is a program that reads the source code and modifies it before passing it on to the C compiler. All preprocessor statements begin with the # symbol. The preprocessor directive just introduced tells the preprocessor to read in the contents of the file *stdio.h* into the program. The file *stdio.h* contains information needed by the input and output functions that are a part of the standard C library. The line

```
#define PI 3.14159265
```

is another preprocessor statement. It defines a symbolic constant called `PI`

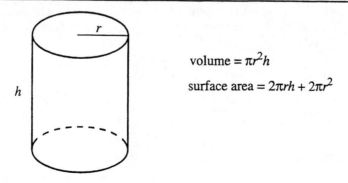

volume $= \pi r^2 h$

surface area $= 2\pi r h + 2\pi r^2$

Figure 2.2   Volume and surface area of a cylinder.

representing the constant π.

The next line

```
void main(void);
```

is a function prototype. Function prototypes are statements that provide the C compiler with useful information about a function. They inform the compiler about

```
/******************************************************************/
/*    cylinder.c                                                  */
/*    Computes the volume and surface area of a cylinder          */
/******************************************************************/
#include <stdio.h>
#define PI 3.141592654    ◄──────────── preprocessor statements

void main(void);  ◄──────────── function prototype

void main(void)  ◄──────── function header
{  ◄──────────────────────────────────── begin body of function main()
    float radius,height,volume,surface_area;  ◄────── variable declarations

    /* print heading */
    printf("\n Cylinder.c");  ◄──────────────── call printf() library function
    printf("\n Computes volume and surface area of a cylinder.");

    /* read in radius and height */
    printf("\n\n Enter radius of cylinder: ");
    scanf("%f", &radius);  ◄──────────────── call scanf() library function
    printf(" Enter height of cylinder: ");
    scanf("%f", &height);

    /* compute volume and surface area */
    volume = PI * radius * radius * height;                    ◄── assignment
    surface_area = 2.0 * PI * radius * (radius + height);         statements

    /* print results */
    printf("\n Volume of cylinder is:      %10.4f",volume);
    printf("\n Surface area of cylinder is:%10.4f",surface_area);
}  ◄──────────────────────────────────── end body of function main()
```

Sample input and output

```
Cylinder.c
Computes volume and surface area of a cylinder.

Enter radius of cylinder: 10
Enter height of cylinder: 20

Volume of cylinder is:      6283.1860
Surface area of cylinder is: 1884.9558
```

Figure 2.3   Program for computing the volume and surfacea area of a cylinder.

the type and number of inputs (also called arguments) that the function expects and the type of value that the function returns. The foregoing statement tells the compiler to expect a function called `main()`. It also tells the compiler that the function `main()` does not return a value and that it does not have any arguments. Note the semicolon at the end of the statement. *All C statements end with a semicolon.* (Preprocessor directives do not end with a semicolon since they are not C statements but rather instructions to the preprocessor.)

In the programs shown in this chapter, each statement appears on a separate line. However, this will not be the case in the programs that appear in later chapters. It is possible in C to place more that one statement on a line as long as each statement is separated by a semicolon. It is also possible to put one statement over several lines.

The line

```
void main(void)
```

marks the beginning of the function `main()` and is called the *function header*. The function header specifies the name of the function, the type of value returned by the function, and any information needed by the function. Note that there is no semicolon at the end of the function header. The `void` preceding `main` specifies the type of value that is returned by the function `main()`. In our example, function `main()` does not return a value, so we use the keyword void to indicate this to the compiler. The parentheses following `main` enclose information being passed along to the function. In our example, we are not passing any information to `main()`, and so we again use the special keyword `void` to indicate this to the compiler.

The opening brace

```
{
```

marks the beginning of the function body which contains the statements that make up the function.

The statement

```
float radius, height, volume, surface_area;
```

is a declaration statement that tells the compiler that we will be using four variables, `radius`, `height`, `volume`, and `surface_area`, and that these variables will be used for storing floating point numbers. When the compiler executes this statement, it allocates memory storage for these four variables as shown here. The question marks indicate that the variables have not been assigned any values.

Variable	Contents
`radius`	?
`height`	?
`volume`	?
`surface_area`	?

The line

```
printf("\n Cylinder.c");
```

is an example of a function call. It calls the library function `printf()` to print the string of characters

```
cylinder.c
```

The `printf()` function is part of the standard C library that comes with the C compiler. A detailed description of the `printf()` function is given in Section 2.7. The `\n` is the code for the newline character and tells the computer to start a new line. The statement

```
printf("\n Computes volume and surface area of a cylinder.");
```

prints the phrase

```
Computes volume and surface area of a cylinder.
```

Again, the `\n` tells the computer to start a new line. The line

```
printf("\n Enter radius of cylinder:");
```

prints the phrase

```
Enter radius of cylinder
```

The line

```
scanf("%f", &radius);
```

calls the library input function `scanf()` to read in a floating point value and store this value in the variable `radius`. The line

```
printf("\n Enter height of cylinder:");
```

prints the phrase

```
Enter height of cylinder:
```

and the line

```
scanf("%f", &height);
```

calls the library input function **scanf()** to read in a floating point value and store this value in the variable **height**.

The statement

```
volume = PI * radius * radius * height;
```

is an arithmetic assignment statement. It computes the volume of the cylinder and assigns the result to the variable **volume.** The statement

```
surface_area = 2.0 * PI * radius * (radius + height);
```

is another assignment statement. It computes the surface area of the cylinder and assigns the result to the variable **surface_area**. If the values entered for **radius** and **height** are 10 and 20, then the values stored at the memory locations representing **radius**, **height**, **area**, and **surface_area** after the above assignment statement is executed are

Variable	Contents
radius	10.0
height	20.0
volume	6282.1860
surface_area	1884.9558

The line

```
printf("\n Volume of cylinder is: %10.4f, volume);
```

prints the volume of the cylinder. The **%10.4f** is a format specifier which tells the **printf()** statement to print the floating point value with a minimum field width of ten characters and with four digits after the decimal. The line

```
printf("\n Surface area of cylinder: %10.4f", surface_area);
```

prints the surface area of the cylinder.
The closing brace

```
}
```

marks the end of the function **main()**.

2.3 FUNCTIONS

A fundamental aspect of C programs is that all C programs consist of a set of functions. A C function is of a group of statements or instructions that the computer can execute. Every C program has one or more functions. One of the functions must be called **main()**. Program execution begins with **main()**, which normally calls other functions, which may in turn call other functions. The program shown in Figure 2.3 has only one function **main()**.

A C function consists of a header and a body. Figure 2.4 illustrates the basic structure of a C function. The function header defines the name of the function, the type of data returned by the function and the function parameters. The function body contains the C statements that are executed when the function is called.

An example of a function header is

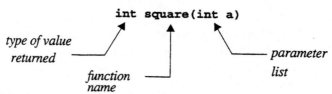

The function **square()** accepts an integer value and returns the square of this value. The parameter list which follows the function name consists of the information that is passed to the function by the calling function. In the example just given, the function **square()** expects one value of type **int** and it returns a value of type **int**. The parameter list is enclosed in parentheses, and the items in the list are separated by commas. The function header for the function **main()** in the program *cylinder.c* is given as

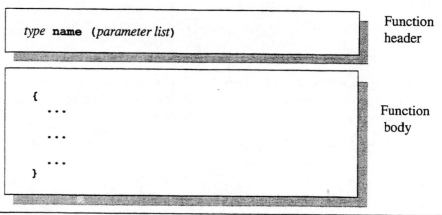

Figure 2.4   The structure of a C function.

```
void main(void)
```

The function **main()** does not have any arguments and this is indicated by the special keyword **void**. The function **main()** does not return any value back to the calling function. This is indicated by the keyword **void**, which precedes the name of the function.

Another example of a function header is

```
float square_root(float x)
```

In this example, the function name is **square_root**. The function has one formal parameter **x**, which is defined to have a data type of **float** (representing a floating point value). The return type of the function is defined to also be of type **float**, which means that the function returns a floating point value. The function computes the square root of **x** and returns this result to the calling function.

The function body consists of a group of statements enclosed in braces **{** and **}**. The left brace **{** marks the beginning of the function body, and the right brace **}** marks the end of the body. The function body contains one or more program statements that are executed when the function is called.

All C functions have equal importance and are visible to all other functions. Any C function can call any other C function (including itself) or be called by another function. Every C program must have a function called **main()**. The function **main()** is somewhat special in that control is passed from the operating system to function **main()** and program execution begins with the first statement in **main()**. Statements are executed sequentially beginning with the first statement in **main()**. However, it is possible to change the order of execution. C provides several statements which allow us to select which statements will be executed and in what order. We will discuss these statements in Chapters 6 and 7. The function **main()** typically calls other functions in the program that may in turn call other functions. Functions can appear in any order in a C program. Also, **main()** does not have to be the first function in a program. However, since execution begins with **main()**, it is traditional for **main()** to be the first function in a C program.

2.4   STATEMENTS

A C statement consists of keywords, variables, function names, and operators. A C statement always ends with a semicolon. Examples of C statements are

```
float x;                      /* declaration             */
y = 10;                       /* assignment              */
z = x + y;                    /* arithmetic assignment    */
printf("\n Volume = %f",volume); /* function call         */
```

The semicolon marks the end of a C statement. Omitting the semicolon at the end of a program statement is a common mistake made by beginning C programmers.

Although the statements in the foregoing examples all appear on a separate line, it is possible, as noted earlier, to have more that one statement on a line, provided they are separated by semicolons. C also lets you write statements that appear over several lines.

We will be using many different types of statements in our programs. Each of these statements will be described in detail in later chapters in the text. In this section we present a brief description of some of the more commonly used statements in C programs.

Declaration Statements

All C programs work with data. There are two kinds of data: *constants* and *variables*. The value of a constant remains fixed throughout the execution of a program. Variables, on the other hand, are symbolic names to which we can assign a range of values. The value of a variable can, thus, change during program execution. In C, unlike BASIC and FORTRAN, all variables must be declared before we can use them.

Declaration statements are used to declare variables and the type of data that will be stored in the variable. For example, the declaration statement

    int count;

declares that we will be using a variable named `count` and that this variable will be of type integer; that is, it will be used for storing a whole number. When the compiler executes the above statement it allocates a storage location in memory named `count`:

count | ? |

We can now use the variable name `count` to access the contents of the memory location. The question mark indicates that the variable has not been assigned a value. We can use an assignment statement of the form

    count = 10;

to assign a value of 10 to the storage location named `count`:

count | 10 |

Another example of a declaration statement is

    float radius, height, volume, surface_area;

This statement causes storage to be allocated for four variables: `radius`, `height`, `volume`, and `surface_area`, all of type `float`, which will be used for storing floating point numbers.

Keywords

The words **int** and **float** are C *keywords*. C keywords are the words that form the language. All C keywords are in lowercase. The C language keywords are

auto	break	case	char	const	continue
default	do	double	else	enum	extern
float	for	goto	if	int	long
register	return	short	signed	sizeof	static
register	return	short	signed	sizeof	static
struct	switch	typedef	union	unsigned	void
volatile	while				

Keywords cannot be used for any other purpose in a C program, that is, they may not be used as variable names or function names.

Assignment Statements

Assignment statements are used to assign values to variables. The assignment statement consists of a variable name followed by an equal symbol (=) and the value to be assigned to the variable. Examples of assignment statements are

```
y = 10;
z = x + y;
```

The first statement assigns the value 10 to the variable **y**. The second statement is an example of an arithmetic assignment statement. The expression on the right side of the equal (=) symbol, **x + y**, is evaluated using the current values of the variables **x** and **y**, and the result is assigned to the variable **z** on the left side of the equal symbol.

2.5   COMMENTS

In the program shown in Figure 2.3 there are several lines that begin with **/*** and end with ***/** for example,

```
/* Cylinder.c                                          */
/* Computes the volume and surface area of a cylinder  */
```

These lines are comment lines. Comments are remarks that describe the program. Comments are nonexecutable, which means that the compiler ignores everything between the **/*** and ***/**. Comments are an invaluable part of a program, and their importance cannot be overemphasized. Comments document what the program does. They serve to define program variables, assist users in understanding the logic of the program, and facilitate future modifications to the program. We strongly urge you to use comments in your programs. Although it does require more effort to type in the comments, the extra effort is justified because of the benefits involved.

Most C programs have several comments lines at the beginning of the program. The type of information contained in these comment lines generally consists of the name of the file containing the source code and a brief description of the program. Most programmers also precede functions with comments describing the task performed by the function and the arguments that are passed to the function when it is invoked.

There are a number of different styles that can be used for comments. Some examples are

```
/*    This is comment line one      */
/*    This is comment line two      */

/*    This is comment line one
      This is comment line two      */

/* This is comment line one
 * This is comment line two
 * This is comment line three    */
```

It is not possible to have nested comments, that is, a comment line within a comment line, as in

```
/*    This is comment line one
/*    This is a nested comment line */
      This is comment line three      */
```

The reason why you cannot nest comments is that the C compiler ignores everything after the first /* including another /* until it sees a */.

2.6   PUNCTUATION AND STYLE

C is a free-form language, which means that it does not care what style or format you use, as long as it is syntactically correct. The position of the statement itself is not important. You can break lines of code almost anywhere and insert extra spaces between program elements. For example, it is perfectly legal in C to write the statement

```
volume = PI * radius * radius * height;
```

as

```
volume = PI * radius *
                    radius * height;
```

The extra spaces between program elements is called "white space." In addition to spaces, tabs and carriage returns are also treated as white space. In general, the C compiler ignores all white space in the program. However, you cannot split a function name, and you cannot break a quoted string such as **"Welcome to C Programming"** between two lines.

Unlike some other programming languages such as BASIC and Pascal, C is case sensitive. This means that C distinguishes between uppercase and lowercase letters. Thus, the functions **PRINTF()**, **Printf()**, and **printF()** are not the same as **printf()**. A convention followed by most C programmers is to use lowercase letters for everything except symbolic names and constants. Thus, all functions and variable names are written in lowercase letters, while symbolic constants such as **PI** are written in all uppercase letters. However, many programmers now also use mixed case when naming functions and variables. Some examples of function names written using mixed case are

SquareRoot	**squareRoot**	**absValue**	**quickSort**
Bisection	**drawCircle**	**PlotValues**	**doSaveMenu**

Making programs readable is good programming practice. It is essential that you write your programs in such a manner that they are easy to understand and follow since this will make it easier for other programmers (and for you) to read and revise your programs. Since C is a free form language and is somewhat cryptic, it is especially important that you use spacing and alignment of code to make your programs easier to use. We will present style guidelines at the end of each chapter that will help to make your C programs easier to read. We will also present some of the more common errors that beginning C programmers make and discuss ways of debugging your programs.

2.7   THE C PREPROCESSOR

The C language has a built-in preprocessor. The C preprocessor is a C program that examines your source code before passing it on to the compiler. The preprocessor changes the source code and adds new source code based on directives contained in your program. The C preprocessor is a very useful feature of the language since it provides a means of modifying a C program in a number of ways before the actual compilation takes place. The C preprocessor is always included with the C system, and the C compiler automatically calls the preprocessor prior to compiling your program.

Although it is possible to write programs that do not use the facilities of the C preprocessor, you will find that the functionality and convenience are so great that all C programmers use it. Some of the features of the C preprocessor include string replacement, macro expansion, file inclusion, and conditional compilation.

All preprocessor statements begin with the # character. There may be one or more blank spaces before the #, but the # character must be the first nonblank character on the line. Some applications require that preprocessor statements begin in column 1. Unlike C statements, preprocessor statements do not have a semicolon at the end of the statement.

The #define Directive

One of the C preprocessor's valuable functions is handling macro substitutions. A macro substitution is simply the replacement of a string of characters with another. We can define a macro substitution with the **#define** directive. The syntax of this statement is

> **#define** *token_string   replacement_string*

When the preprocessor encounters this statement, it replaces every subsequent occurrence of *token_string* in the file with *replacement_string*. As with all other preprocessor statements, the # character must be the first character on the line. Also, there is no space between the # and **define**.

One of the primary uses of the **#define** directive is for assigning symbolic names to program constants. For example, a program that computes the area of a circle would need to use the constant π. We can define a symbolic constant **PI** by placing the following **#define** statement near the beginning of the program

```
#define PI 3.141592654
```

We can then use the symbolic constant **PI** throughout the program, as for example, in the statement

```
area = PI * radius * radius;
```

When the program is compiled, the preprocessor replaces every occurrence of the symbolic constant **PI** with the character string **3.141592654**. Thus the statement that is actually passed on to the compiler reads as

```
area = 3.141592654 * radius * radius;
```

Some other examples of **#define** statements are

```
#define CM_TO_INCHES  0.393701
#define DEGREES_TO_RADIANS  0.017453293
#define TRUE  1
#define FALSE 0
#define ERROR_FLAG TRUE
#define MESSAGE "An invalid value was entered."
```

It is a convention in C to write symbolic constants using all uppercase letters. This makes it easy to distinguish symbolic constants from variable names.

Although **#define** statements can occur anywhere in a program, they are usually placed near the beginning of the file. This is because **#define** statements can affect only lines that follow. It is important to note that the preprocessor does not change the value of symbolic constants that are embedded within a string enclosed in double quotation marks. For example, in the statement

```
printf("Value of PI computed by integration = %f", PI);
```

only the second **PI** will be changed. The first **PI** is embedded in the string enclosed by double quotation marks.

There are a number of advantages to using symbolic constants. Symbolic constants make it easier to develop a program, since we do not have to remember the value of the constant every time. Symbolic constants make a program more readable and easier to maintain. It is very easy to change the value of a symbolic constant. All we need to do is change the **#define** statement. When the program is compiled, the preprocessor will automatically change each occurrence of the symbolic constant in the program. The **#define** statement can also assist in making a program more portable, since some hardware specific values such as machine addresses, can be defined as symbolic constants. These values can then be easily changed for each different hardware platform.

Besides defining symbolic constants, the **#define** directive can be used for defining macros. In fact, macro substitution is one of the more powerful features of the **#define** directive and is used quite extensively by professional C programmers. Macro substitution is discussed in some detail in Chapter 16.

File Inclusion and Header Files

Another feature of the C preprocessor that is used quite extensively is the **#include** directive. The syntax for this statement is

```
#include "filename"
```

The **#include** statement causes the contents of the named file to be placed in the source program at the location where the **#include** statement was found. For example, the statement

```
#include "mydefs.h"
```

causes the contents of the file *mydefs.h* to be included into the program. The statements in the file *mydefs.h* are thus treated as if they had been typed into the program at that point.

The **#include** directive allows us to place all definitions and constants in a separate file and then include these in one or more program files, thus ensuring that all programs receive the same values. Include files are also called "header" files since they are usually included near the beginning of the program. It is traditional for C programmers to use the extension ".*h*" for header files.

There are a number of advantages to using header files. We can create different versions of a program simply by using different header files and compiling the same program. We can make our programs more portable by placing hardware dependent definitions in separate header files. Header files are also useful for developing programs as a series of separate modules. In addition to **#include** statements, header files also contain structure definitions, variable declarations, and function prototypes, all of which may be common to the various modules in the program. We will discuss many of these features of header files in later chapters.

There is another form of the **#include** statement in which the file name is enclosed in angle brackets

```
#include <filename>
```

An example of this form of **#include** statement is

```
#include <stdio.h>
```

The difference between this form of the **#include** statement and the form presented earlier has to do with where the compiler searches for the included file. When the file name is enclosed in angle brackets, the compiler searches for the file in a prearranged list of directories. This form of the **#include** statement is most useful for including standard definition files provided by the developers of the compiler. When the file name is enclosed in double quotes, the compiler searched for the included file in the current directory. If it cannot find it in the current directory, it searches in the prearranged list of directories. This form of the command is generally used for files that you have created.

All compilers provide a set of header files. These files contain definitions for many of the system-dependent variables and constants. They also contain function prototypes for the library functions. An example of such a file is the header file *stdio.h*. The file *stdio.h* (which stands for standard input and output) contains system dependent information needed by the input/output library functions such as **printf()** and **scanf()**. You should place the preprocessor directive

```
#include <stdio.h>
```

near the beginning of each program file that uses any of the standard input/output functions. This makes the information contained in *stdio.h* available to the compiler. It also ensures that the function prototypes and macro definitions are entered exactly right and saves you from having to retype them.

Another useful include file is the file *math.h*. This file contains definitions required by many of the mathematical functions provided in the standard C library.

2.8 THE `print()` FUNCTION

In the program *cylinder.c* the statement

```
printf("\n Computes volume and surface area of a cylinder.");
```

prints the message between the double quotation marks on the screen. This statement is an example of a function call. The function being called is the `printf()` function. You will notice that the code for `printf()` is not in our program. This is because `printf()` is part of the standard C library. When we use a function that is not within our program, the compiler makes a note of this when it compiles the program and leaves a message for the linker. When the linker links the program it searches for the code for the function in the standard library or in any other libraries that we specify and links this code with our program.

The `printf()` function is a powerful output function that allows us to display information on the standard output screen. The general format of the `printf()` function is

> `printf("`*control string*`",` *argument list*`);`

The *control string* which is enclosed in double quotation marks consists of two type of items: the characters that will be displayed on the screen and *format specifiers*. Format specifiers define the way in which the items in the argument list are actually displayed. The argument list consists of the list of items whose values are to be displayed. Figure 2.5 illustrates the various elements of the `printf()` statement.

Format Specifiers

A format specifier begins with a percent sign (**%**) and is followed by a *type conversion character*, which is a one character code indicating the type of data to be printed. Table 2.1 lists the type conversion characters and the data types that they represent.

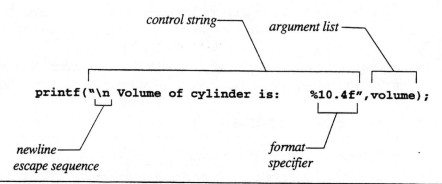

Figure 2.5   A `printf()` statement in program *cylinder.c.*

Table 2.1: Type conversion characters in the `printf()` control string

Format Specifier	Data Type
`%c`	character
`%d`	decimal integer
`%i`	decimal integer
`%f`	floating point, decimal notation
`%e`	floating point, exponential notation
`%g`	floating point, use `%f` or `%e` whichever is shorter
`%o`	octal integer
`%s`	string of characters
`%x`	hexadecimal integer
`%u`	unsigned decimal integer

Some examples of calls to the `printf()` function are

```
printf("An integer number %d",100);
printf("A floating point number %f", 100.232);
printf("A character %c",'c');
```

In the first statement the `%d` specifies that the number 100 is to be treated as an integer value. In the second statement the `%f` specifies that the number 100.232 is to be treated as a floating point value. In the third statement the `%c` indicates that a character value is to be printed.

The format specifiers have modifiers that appear before the type conversion character (see Figure 2.6). These modifiers control the field width, number of

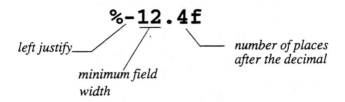

%-12.4f

left justify ⟋   ⟍ *number of places*
               after the decimal
minimum field
width

Figure 2.6   Field width, justification, and decimal places in the format specifier.

decimal places and justification. An integer placed between the percent sign and the type conversion character defines the field width. For example, the format specifier **%4d** specifies a field width of four characters, which means that the number will be printed with a minimum of four characters. If the item to be printed has fewer than four characters, then the output is padded with blanks. If the item to be printed is larger than the field width, it will be printed in full regardless of the field width. For example, the statement shown below

```
printf("|%4d|  |%4d|  |%4d|  |%4d|  |%4d|",1,10,100,1000,1000);
```

will result in the following output:

```
0         1         2         3         4
01234567890123456789012345678901234567890
|   1|  |  10|  | 100|  |1000|  |10000|
```

The number of decimal places printed for a floating point number is specified by placing a decimal point followed by the number of places. For example, the format specifier **%.5f** specifies that the number should be printed with five decimal places. The field width and the decimal places modifiers can be combined. For example, the format specifier **%10.3f** causes **printf()** to display the number at least 10 characters wide with three decimal places. For example, the statement

```
printf("|%10.3f|  |%10.3f|  |%10.3f|",1.234,10.2346,100.34567);
```

will result in the following output:

```
0         1         2         3         4
01234567890123456789012345678901234567890
|     1.234|  |    10.235|  |   100.346|
```

You should note that the **printf()** function automatically rounds the result to the number of decimal places specified.

By default, all output is printed right justified. If the field width is larger than the item printed, the item is placed on the right edge of the field. However, if a "-" sign is placed directly after the percent sign then the item is left justified. For example, **%-f** left justifies a floating point value as in the statement

```
printf("|%-f| |%-10.3f| |%-12.5f|",1.234,10.2346,1000.34567);
```

The output from this example is

```
0         1         2         3         4
01234567890123456789012345678901234567890
|1.234000| |10.235    | |1000.34567   |
```

There are two additional modifiers that can be applied to the type conversion character. The **1** modifier specifies that a long data type follows. For example, the format specifier **%ld** indicates that a long integer is to be printed. The **h** modifier indicates that a short data type follows.

Escape Sequences

The control string in the **printf()** function can also contain *escape sequences*. These escape sequences are used for representing nonprinting characters. Nonprinting characters are characters that perform special functions such as backspace and tab. All escape sequences begin with the backslash (\) character. Table 2.2 lists the predefined escape sequences and the corresponding characters. Examples of **printf()** statements containing escape sequences are given below.

```
printf("\n Begin printing on next line");
printf("\t Tab character");
printf("\t \t Two tab characters");
```

The output from the preceding examples is .

```
0         1         2         3         4
01234567890123456789012345678901234567890
 Begin printing on next line
         Tab character
                 Two tab characters
```

Table 2.2: Escape sequences

Escape Sequences	Characters
\a	bell
\b	backspace
\f	formfeed
\n	newline
\r	carriage return
\t	horizontal tab
\v	vertical tab
\'	single quote
\"	double quote
\\	backslash
\ddd	octal notation
\xddd	hexadecimal notation

The newline character \n causes output to be printed on the next line. The tab \t character causes output to be printed beginning at the next tab stop. A character that does not have a predefined escape sequence can be represented by specifying its ASCII code in either octal or hexadecimal notation (see Appendix A for a discussion of the binary, octal, and hexadecimal number systems). In octal notation the backslash is followed by one to three octal digits. Examples are

```
'\007''\016''\053'
```

In hexadecimal notation the backslash is followed by an **x** or an **X** and one to three hexadecimal digits as in

```
'\x007''\x5e''\x3f'
```

2.9   THE scanf() FUNCTION

The scanf() function is a general purpose input function that is provided as part of the standard C library. The format of the scanf() function is similar to the printf() function:

```
scanf("control string", argument list);
```

The *control string* contains format specifiers, white space characters, and nonwhite space characters. The format specifiers are similar to those for the `printf()` function. They begin with the percent (%) character and are followed by a type specifier. The type specifiers for the `scanf()` function are essentially the same as those for `printf()`. For example, `%d` reads a decimal integer number, and `%f` reads a floating point number. The statement

```
scanf("%f", &radius);
```

in program *cylinder.c* reads in a floating point number and assigns the value to the variable `radius`.

The control string in the `scanf()` function can contain white space characters. When the `scanf()` function encounters a white space character in the control string, it skips over *all* white space characters in the input stream up to the first nonwhite space character. Thus, to read in several variables we can separate the format specifiers in the control string with spaces. For example, the statement

```
scanf("%f %f %f", &length, &width, &height);
```

reads in three floating point numbers and stores them in the variable `length`, `width`, and `height`.

An important difference between the `printf()` and `scanf()` functions is that in the `scanf()` function we must provide `scanf()` with the addresses of the variables defined in the argument list. This is done by preceding the variable name with an ampersand (`&`). The ampersand is the *address of* operator. The expression

```
&length
```

represents the address of the variable `length` in memory. By passing `scanf()` the address of the variable, we are providing the `scanf()` with a way to access the variable and to change its value.

As mentioned in Chapter 1, every memory location has an address associated with it. This is similar to addresses on mail boxes. Figure 2.7 shows a section of computer memory with the associated addresses. The expression `&length` represents the address of the variable length in memory, which is 2000, and the expression `&width` represents the address of the variable width, which is 2004. In our example, the addresses increase by four, since on our system floating point numbers are allocated four bytes of storage.

The concept of addresses is one of the more powerful and interesting features of the C language. We will be discussing addresses in considerable detail in Chapter 10 when we discuss pointers. In later chapters you will find that it is not always necessary to use the address of operator when passing arguments to the `scanf()` function (for example, when working with strings and arrays). However, for the present, you should remember to precede the variable name with an

Variable	Contents	Address
length	10.0	2000
width	20.0	2004
height	15.0	2008
	...	
	...	

Figure 2.7   Variables and addresses.

ampersand when using the **scanf()** function. Forgetting to do this will most certainly result in errors and may even cause abnormal termination of your program. A common error made by beginning C programmers is failing to precede the variable name with an ampersand. We suggest that if your program crashes during execution, you check all **scanf()** statements in your program.

Example 2.1   Linear Interpolation

PROBLEM STATEMENT: The equation of a straight line is (see Figure 2.8):

$$y = mx + c \qquad\qquad (2.1)$$

where m is the slope and c the intercept. If the coordinates of two points P_1 and P_2

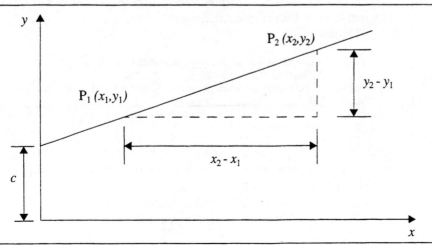

Figure 2.8   Straight-line equation.

are (x_1,y_1) and (x_2,y_2), the slope Of the line is

$$m = \frac{y_2 - y_1}{x_2 - x_1}$$ (2.2)

$$c = \frac{y_1 x_2 - y_2 x_1}{x_2 - x_1}$$ (2.3)

Write a program to compute the slope and intercept of a straight line given the coordinates of two points on the straight line. The program should also compute the y coordinate of a point on the straight line, given the x coordinate of the point.

SOLUTION: The program listing and input and output for a sample run is shown in Figure 2.9. A brief description of the program follows:

The first few lines are comments and provide the name of the source file and a brief description of the purpose of the program. The statement

```
#include <stdio.h>
```

includes the header file *stdio.h*. We have to include this file since we will be using the **printf()** and **scanf()** function from the standard C library.
The statements

```
float x1,y1,x2,y2;  /* coordinates of two points on line  */
float m,c;            /* slope and intercept of line         */
float x,y;       /* coordinates of point to be interpolated */
```

declare several variables of type **float**. These variables will be used in the program to store floating point numbers.
The statements

```
printf("\n\nEnter x and y coordinates of first point ");
scanf("%f %f", &x1, &y1);
printf("\nEnter x and y coordinates of second point ");
scanf("%f %f", &x2, &y2);
printf("\nEnter x coordinate of point to be interpolated");
scanf("%f", &x);
```

obtain the necessary input from the user. The **printf()** function is used to prompt for the type of information required, while the **scanf()** function reads in the values and assign these to the variables given in the argument list. Note that in all the calls to **scanf()**, the address of the variable is passed.
The slope and intercept are computed in the following lines

```
m = (y2 - y1)/(x2 - x1);          /*   slope of line    */
c = (y1 * x2 - y2*x1)/(x2 - x1);  /*   intercept        */
```

```
/***************************************************************/
/*   interplt.c  --   Linear Interpolation                     */
/*                                                             */
/*   Computes the slope and intercept of a straight line       */
/*   given the coordinates of two points on the line. It       */
/*   also computes the y coordinate of a point given the x     */
/*   coordinate.                                               */
/***************************************************************/
/* preprocessor statements */
#include <stdio.h>

main()
{
    float x1,y1,x2,y2;   /* coordinates of two points on line  */
    float m,c;               /* slope and intercept of line    */
    float x,y;       /* coordinates of point to be interpolated */

    printf("\n\tLINEAR INTERPOLATION");

    /* input */
    printf("\n\nEnter x and y coordinates of first point ");
    scanf("%f %f", &x1, &y1);
    printf("\nEnter x and y coordinates of second point ");
    scanf("%f %f", &x2, &y2);
    printf("\nEnter x coordinate of point to be interpolated ");
    scanf("%f", &x);

    /* computations */
    m = (y2 - y1)/(x2 - x1);          /* slope of line         */
    c = (y1 * x2 - y2*x1)/(x2 - x1);  /* intercept             */
    y = m * x + c ;                   /* y coordinate of point */

    /* print results */
    printf("\n\nSlope of line = %f", m);
    printf("\nIntercept of line = %f", c);
    printf("\nY coordinate of point = %f", y);
}
```

Sample input and output

```
         LINEAR INTERPOLATION

Enter x and y coordinates of first point 10.0 10.0

Enter x and y coordinates of second point 20.0 20.0

Enter x coordinate of point to be interpolated 15.


Slope of line = 1.000000
Intercept of line = 0.000000
Y coordinate of point = 15.000000
```

Figure 2.9   Linear interpolation program.

while the y coordinate of the point to be interpolated is computed by

```
y = m * x + c ;                    /*  y coordinate of point */
```

The results are printed by the following statements, all of which call the `printf()` function

```
printf("\n\nSlope of line = %f", m);
printf("\nIntercept of line = %f", c);
printf("\nY coordinate of point = %f", y);
```

The output from the program is also shown in Figure 2.9. The program prints the slope of the line, the intercept of the line, and the y coordinate of the point corresponding to the given value of x.

2.10 SUMMARY

In this chapter we described the basic elements of a C program. Most C programs consists of the following basic elements: preprocessor statements, global declarations, function prototypes, and functions. All C programs consist of one or more functions. A C function is a group of statements or instructions that the computer can execute. One of the functions in your program must be called **main()**. The function **main()** is a special function in that program execution begins with the first statement in **main()**. A C function consists of a header and a body. The header defines the name of the function, the type and number of inputs expected by the function, and the value returned by the function. The function body consists of C statements that are executed when the function is called. An opening brace marks the beginning of the function body, and a closing brace marks the end.

C statements represent instructions to the computer. All C statements end with a semicolon. We can place one or more statements on a line, provided that the statements are separated by semicolons. C statements can also be split up across several lines. Some of the statements presented in this chapter included declaration statements for declaring variables, comments which begin with /* and end with */, and assignment statements which are used for assigning values to variables.

Function prototypes are statements that provide the C compiler with useful information about a function. They inform the compiler about the type and number of inputs (also called arguments) that the function expects and the type of value that the function returns. Function prototypes must appear before any statements that call the function.

The C preprocessor is a program that examines and changes the source code before passing it on to the compiler. C preprocessor directives are instructions to the preprocessor. All preprocessor directives begin with the # symbol. The **#define** directive allows us to define symbolic constants. The **#include** directive instructs the preprocessor to place the contents of a file in the source program at the location where the **#include** directive was found. This directive allows us to include header files in our programs. All C compilers provide a set of header files. Examples of such files are the *stdio.h* file, which contains system-dependent information needed by the input and output functions, and *math.h*, which contains the definitions needed for using the mathematical library functions.

In this chapter we also presented an introduction to two C library functions. The **printf()** function is a powerful output function that allows us to display information on the screen. The **scanf()** function is a general-purpose input function.

Key Terms Presented in This Chapter

argument list	function body
assignment statement	function header
comments	function **main()**
declaration statement	function prototypes
#define directive	header files
escape sequences	**#include** directive
file inclusion	keywords
format specifiers	macro substitution
functions	parameter list
preprocessor	symbolic constants
printf() library function	**void** keyword
scanf() library function	white space

PROGRAM STYLE, COMMON ERRORS, AND DEBUGGING GUIDE

Programs should be written so that they are readable and understandable. This makers it easier for you and others to revise and maintain your programs. In this section we suggest guidelines for good programming style and point out some of the common errors that occur when writing C programs. We also offer suggestions for debugging your programs.

1. Choose meaningful names for variables and functions. For example, the variables **root1** and **root2** are more meaningful than the variables **r1** and **r2** for representing the roots of a quadratic equation. Also, the function name **Compute_roots()** is more meaningful than the function name **roots()** for a function that computes the roots.

2. Use lowercase letters for variables and function names. You many use the underscore character (_) to separate words in a compound word as in `mean_value`, `first_root`. Some programmers prefer to use mixed case and use uppercase for the first character of a compound word as in `meanValue` and `firstRoot`.

3. Align opening and closing braces vertically. Braces group programs statements together and mark the beginning and ending of functions. Aligning the opening and closing braces vertically makes your program easier to follow and helps you avoid errors since it is easier to match beginning and ending braces if they are vertically aligned.

4. The statements that form the body of a function should be indented. This makes it easier to see where the function begins and ends. In fact, all blocks of code enclosed in braces such as statements that form the body of a loop, or other control structures, should be indented. Indentation is an important way to increase the readability of programs. Indentation is especially important when there are many sets of nested statements in a program.

5. The use of blank spaces and blank lines can significantly enhance the readability of a program. You should a blank spaces after a comma and before and after operators such as +, -, /, *. You should also use blank lines to separate one conceptual section of a function from another. For example, use a blank line to separate the declaration section from the rest of the function and to separate the input, output, and computational segments of a program.

6. Preprocessor statements should normally be placed near the beginning of a file.

7. You should use symbolic constants instead of regular constants whenever possible. Symbolic constants make your programs more readable and also have the advantage that you do not have to remember the value of the constant each time you use it. They also make it much easier to modify your program if it becomes necessary to change the value of the constant.

8. You should use all uppercase letters for symbolic constants. This makes it possible to differentiate between variable names and symbolic constants.

9. You should be very liberal in the use of comments in your program. Comments serve to document your programs. Every program should contain comment lines near the beginning of the program describing the purpose of the program, a brief description of the program and the name of the file containing the program. You may also want to indicate the name of the programmer, the version of the program, and the name

of the compiler on which this program was compiled and document any major revisions made to the program. Within the program, you should explain the meaning of important variables and the purpose of key program segments.

10. Every C statement should end with a semicolon. Forgetting to place a semicolon at the end of a C program is a very common error made by beginning C programmers.

11. Every variable in a C program must be defined before you can use it. The compiler will generate a syntax error whenever it encounters a variable name that is undefined.

12. You should not use the C keywords for variable names.

13. C is case sensitive, which means that C distinguishes between upper-case and lowercase letters. You should be aware of this when typing variable names. For example, the variables **maxx** and **maxX** are not the same in C. If you type **maxx** in place of **maxX**, the C compiler will generate an error indicating that the variable **maxX** has not been defined. Also, if you use the statement

```
y = Sqrt(x);
```

to compute the square root, you will get an error message since the C library square root function is called **sqrt()** and not **Sqrt()**.

14. Most C compilers require that preprocessor statements begin in column 1.

15. Preprocessor statements do not end with a semicolon. For example, the statement

```
#define PI 3.141593;
```

is wrong since the preprocessor will substitute the entire string (including the semicolon) in any statement that uses the symbolic constant PI. For example, the statement

```
area = PI * r * r;
```

will appear to the compiler as

```
area = 3.141593; * r * r;
```

which will result in a syntax error.

16. Your programs should include the *stdio.h* header file if you are using any of the C library input/output functions with the statement

```
#include <stdio.h>
```

This header file provides the compiler with the system dependent information necessary for using these functions

17. When using the **printf()** statement, you should make sure that the type conversion character in the format specifier matches the type of data to be printed. For example, if you use a **%d** format specifier to print a floating point value, the output from **printf()** will be wrong.

18. When using **scanf()**, you must use the address of operator (**&**) to pass the address of the variable; otherwise, the results could be disastrous. For example, the statement

    ```
    scanf("%lf",length);
    ```

    is wrong since the address of the variable length was not passed to **scanf()**. The correct statement is

    ```
    scanf("%lf",&length);
    ```

19. As with **printf()**, you should make sure that the type conversion character in the **scanf()** call matches the type of value to be read. Also, most compilers expect a format specifier of the form **"%lf"** for reading double precision numbers. For example, if the variable **radius** is defined to be of type double, then the **scanf()** call should be

    ```
    scanf("%lf", &radius);
    ```

    and not

    ```
    scanf("%f",&radius);
    ```

20. String constants should be enclosed in double quotes. A common error is forgetting the closing quotation mark at the end of a string especially in the **printf()** and **scanf()** control string.

EXERCISES

Review Questions

1. Answer true of false for each part:
   a. A C statement must end in a semicolon.
   b. All preprocessor statements must end in a semicolon.
   c. A C statement must be written on a single line.
   d. C statements can be split across several lines.
   e. The symbol **/*** marks the beginning of a comment.
   f. In every C program there must be an equal number of left and right braces.

2. Explain the significance of the following in a C program:

    a. Braces

    b. Semicolons

3. What is a preprocessor?

4. What are header files? Why is it important that you include header files in your program when using the C library functions?

5. Use your text editor to look at the header files *stdio.h* and *math.h*. Write down the values of three symbolic constants defined in these files and the function prototypes for three functions.

6. Write a C program to print your name, address, and telephone number. Compile, link, and execute the program.

Programming Exercises

7. Type in the program shown in Figure 2.3. Compile the program. You should not be surprised if you get some error messages from the compiler, since it is difficult to type in programs without making mistakes. Run the program and compare the output from your program with that given in Figure 2.3.

8. The following program contains several syntax errors. Identify the errors. Type in and run the corrected program to make sure that you have correctly identified the mistakes.

```
#include <stdio.h>
main()
{
    FLOAT resut;

    /* compute result
    result = 20.56 + 300.34

    /* display result */
    printf("The sume of 20.56 and 300.34 is %f",result ;
}
```

9. The program given below computes the area and circumference of a circle using the following equations

    $$area = \pi \, r^2$$

    $$circumference = 2\pi r$$

    The program contains several errors. Type in the program *exactly* as shown (but do not type in the line numbers). Try to compile the program and note the error messages that your compiler gives.

```
1.  /*******************************************************/
2.  /*  circle.c  --    Area and Circumference of a Circle  */
3.  /*                                                       */
4.  /*  Computes area and circumference of a circle for a    */
5.  /*  given radius.                                        */
6.  /*******************************************************/
7.  #include <stdio.h>
8.  #define PI 3.241592654
9.  main()
10. {
11.   float radius;                /* radius of circle */
12.   float area, circumference   /* area and circumference */
13.
14.   printf("\n\tAREA AND CIRCUMFERENCE OF A CIRCLE");
15.
16.   /* input */
17.   printf("\n\nEnter radius of circle: ");
18.   scamf("%f", &radius);
19.
20.   /* computations */
21.   area = PI * radus * radius;
22.   circumference = 2. * PI * radius;
23.
24.   /* print results */
25.   printf("\n\nArea of circle  = %f", araa);
26.   primtf("\n\nCircumference of circle = %f",circumference);
28. }
```

Now make the following changes to the program:

a.   In line 8, change **3.241592654** to **3.141592654.**

b.   In line 12, add a semicolon at the end of the statement (before the comment).

c.   In line 18, change **scamf** to **scanf.**

d.   In line 21, change **radus** to **radius.**

e.   In line 25, change **araa** to **area.**

f.   In line 26, change **primtf** to **printf.**

Run the program using several values of **radius**. Compare the results with those obtained by hand calculation.

10. Write a C program to read in and convert temperatures from degrees Celsius to degrees Fahrenheit using the following formula

$$F = (9/5) \ C + 32$$

where F is the temperature in degrees Fahrenheit and C is the temperature in degrees Celsius. This can be written in C as

f = (9./5.) * c + 32. ;

11. According to the straight line method the yearly depreciation in value for an item is given by the following formula:

$$\text{depreciation} = \frac{\text{purchase price - salvage value}}{\text{number of years of service}}$$

Write a C program that reads in the purchase price of an item, the expected salvage value, and the number of years of service and prints the yearly depreciation for that item.

12. The power loss in an electrical cable is given by

$$P = I\,R^2$$

where P is the power loss in watts, I is the current in amperes and R is the resistance in ohms.

Write a C program that reads in the current and resistance and prints the power loss in the cable.

13. The volume of a mass of air is given by

$$V = \frac{2.83\,m(T + 273)}{P}$$

where V = volume in liters, P = pressure in atmospheres, T = temperature in degrees Celsius, and m = mass of air in kilograms.

Write a C program to determine the volume if the pressure, temperature, and mass are given.

3

PROBLEM SOLVING ON
A COMPUTER

The ability to solve problems is an essential component of computer programming. In fact, the main reason that people learn programming languages is to use the computer as a problem solving tool. In this chapter we present an introduction to problem solving on the computer. The steps involved in developing sound and logically correct programs are described. The technique of top-down design is presented as an approach to developing algorithms, a series of instructions for solving the problem. Strategies for testing programs and for improving program efficiency are also presented.

3.1 PROBLEM-SOLVING STEPS

Solving a problem on a computer requires steps similar to those followed when solving the problem manually. The engineer must still formulate a correct solution to the problem, acquire the necessary data for the solution, and assess the validity of the results. The basic steps involved in solving a programming problem are the following:

1. Problem definition
2. Problem analysis

3. Algorithm design
4. Program development
5. Program verification
6. Documentation
7. Maintenance and modification

These steps are illustrated in Figure 3.1.

1. Problem definition. The first and most important step in problem solving is to define the problem. Before we begin to formulate a solution, it is important that we have a clear understanding of the problem to be solved. The problem statement should be carefully examined to determine what information is given and what needs to be found. The initial description of the problem may be somewhat vague and imprecise. It may be necessary to reformulate the original problem statement so that it is clear and concise.

2. Problem analysis. The second step is to analyze the problem and develop a mathematical formulation. This process requires that we have a clear understanding of the underlying concepts and principles inherent to the problem. In this step the information needed to solve the problem is assembled. This involves identifying what information is given (input) and what results should be computed and displayed (output). The relationships between the input and output variables are obtained. These relationships may be expressed in the form of mathematical equations. If it is found that additional information is required to obtain a solution, we have to determine how this information is to be obtained, and we have to state any modeling assumptions that are made.

3. Algorithm design. The third step is to formulate the *algorithm*. An algorithm is a series of step-by-step instructions for solving a problem. The development of an algorithm is considered in some detail in a later section. The technique that we will use for algorithm development is called top-down design and is described in Section 3.7. It should be emphasized that the algorithm must be completed before the computer program is actually written.

4. Program development. The fourth step in the problem solving process is conversion of the algorithm into the desired programming language. The process of writing computer instructions in a programming language such as C is called *coding.*

5. Program verification. The next step is program verification. Almost all programs contain errors or "bugs." The term *debugging* is used to describe the process of correcting known errors in a program, such as syntax errors. After a program has been debugged, it is tested. Testing is conducted to determine the reliability of the program, that is, to determine whether the program does indeed perform its intended function. Testing usually involves running the program using data for which the correct answers are known beforehand and also using different data sets to test the different computational paths of a program. The main objective

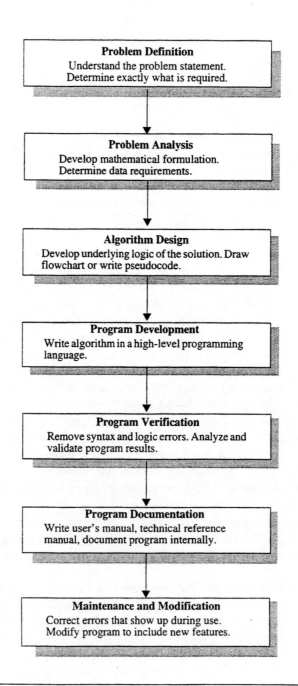

Problem Definition
Understand the problem statement.
Determine exactly what is required.

Problem Analysis
Develop mathematical formulation.
Determine data requirements.

Algorithm Design
Develop underlying logic of the solution. Draw
flowchart or write pseudocode.

Program Development
Write algorithm in a high-level programming
language.

Program Verification
Remove syntax and logic errors. Analyze and
validate program results.

Program Documentation
Write user's manual, technical reference
manual, document program internally.

Maintenance and Modification
Correct errors that show up during use.
Modify program to include new features.

Figure 3.1   Problem-solving steps.

of testing is to uncover unknown errors in the program.

The life cycle of a program developed by students normally ends with the fifth step. Once the program has been developed and tested, the assignment is complete. For programs developed for real-world applications there are two additional steps that have to be completed. These steps are program documentation; maintenance, and modification.

6. Program documentation. Program documentation is an important step in program development, but one that is neglected much too often. Documentation should be included so that the intended users can understand the program and use it effectively. Internal documentation of computer code is needed to facilitate understanding of the solution's logic. External documentation consists of a user's manual and a technical reference manual. Some programmers prefer to write a large part of the documentation before the program is actually coded. This can be helpful since it forces them to decide on the details of the program before the program is actually written.

7. Maintenance and modification. The last step is maintenance and modification. Programs for real-world applications will likely be used for a number of years. As a program is used, its limitations become apparent. Typically, more errors are also discovered. A good program usually undergoes a number of revisions. Maintenance involves correcting errors as they are discovered as well as making modifications to the program to incorporate additional features. Software maintenance is a major component of the life cycle of a program and may account for as much as 80 percent of the total cost of the program.

Beginning programmers incorrectly assume that once they have mastered a programming language they can solve almost any problem. This could not be further from the truth. Coding is only a small part of the entire process. Most experienced programmers spend over 80 to 90 percent of their time working on the logic of the program. Although it is tempting to rush to the computer and start entering your program as soon as you have some idea of how to write it, you should resist this temptation. You should give careful thought to the problem and its solution and develop the algorithm before writing any code. If you follow the steps just outlined, you will find that the extra effort spent in developing the solution to the problem will often save many hours of frustration later and your programs will have fewer errors and will be easier to follow.

3.2 ALGORITHMS

As stated earlier, step 3 of the problem solving process is to develop an algorithm. This consists of a series of step-by-step instructions for the solution of the problem. The design of a good algorithm is an important factor in program development. Once an algorithm has been designed, the writing of the program in a programming language is a relatively simple and straightforward task.

Instructions given to people are often imprecise, and incomplete and assume a certain amount of intelligence and reasoning ability on the part of the recipient. Don't, however, make the same assumption when solving a problem on a computer. Procedures written for a computer must be explicit, precise, and unambiguous. For an algorithm to be usable on a computer, it must have the following attributes:

1. Each step in the algorithm must be unambiguous, explicit, and precise.
2. The order in which the instructions are performed must be precisely defined. Each possible point of decision must be considered and the steps defined for all possible outcomes.
3. It must lead to an answer in a finite number of calculations. That is, the algorithm must eventually terminate.

Example 3.1   Average of Three Numbers

PROBLEM STATEMENT: Write an algorithm to read in three numbers and to compute and print the average.

SOLUTION: The steps to solve the problem are as follows:

1. Input the data items into the variables a, b, and c.
2. Compute the sum of a, b, and c and save the result in the variable sum.
3. Divide sum by 3 and save the result in the variable average.
4. Print the values of a, b, c and average.

Example 3.2   Arc Length and Sector Area

PROBLEM STATEMENT: Write an algorithm to compute the arc length and area of a sector of a circle, where θ is the angle (in degrees) between the radii.

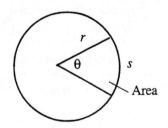

SOLUTION: The arc length s is given by

$$s = 2\pi r\left(\frac{\theta}{360}\right) = \pi r\left(\frac{\theta}{180}\right)$$

and the area of the sector is

$$\text{area} = \frac{\pi r^2}{360} = \frac{rs}{2}$$

The algorithm is given as follows:

1. Define constants, **PI** = 3.141593.
2. Read radius and angle theta.
3. Compute arc length from $s = \pi r \theta / 180$.
4. Compute area from area = $rs/2$.
5. Print radius, theta, arc length, and area.

Algorithms are usually more complicated that the ones just given. Many algorithms contain branches where the solution may follow alternate paths depending on the situation. In such cases the steps to be performed for each alternate path have to be clearly defined.

Example 3.3   Square Root of a Number

PROBLEM STATEMENT: Write an algorithm for computing the square root of a number. Since it is not possible to compute the square root of a negative number, your algorithm should check for a negative value and print a message to that effect. Assume that a function for computing the square root is available on your system.

SOLUTION: The algorithm is as follows:

1. Read in the number.
2. Check the sign of the number.
3. If the number is negative, then print a message and stop; otherwise, proceed to step 4.
4. Compute the square root of the number.
5. Print the number and the square root.

Note that most computer programming languages have built-in functions for computing various functions such as square roots.

3.3   FLOWCHARTS

For complex problems step-by-step English descriptions are inadequate for describing algorithms. Two common methods for describing algorithms are *flowcharts* and *pseudocode*. A flowchart is a pictorial description of an algorithm. The flowchart outlines the structure and logic of the algorithm and the sequence of operations to be followed in solving the problem. A flowchart is composed of a set of standard symbols, each of which is unique in shape and represents a particular type of operation (see Figure 3.2). The symbols are connected by straight lines called *flowlines*. These usually contain arrows to indicate the order in which the

Symbol	Name	Meaning
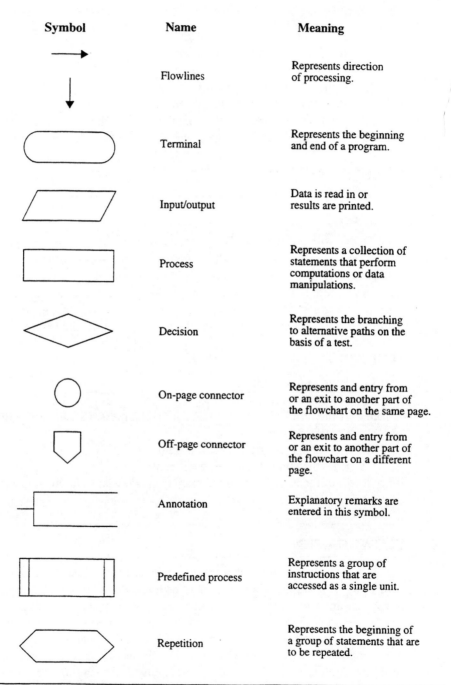	Flowlines	Represents direction of processing.
	Terminal	Represents the beginning and end of a program.
	Input/output	Data is read in or results are printed.
	Process	Represents a collection of statements that perform computations or data manipulations.
	Decision	Represents the branching to alternative paths on the basis of a test.
	On-page connector	Represents and entry from or an exit to another part of the flowchart on the same page.
	Off-page connector	Represents and entry from or an exit to another part of the flowchart on a different page.
	Annotation	Explanatory remarks are entered in this symbol.
	Predefined process	Represents a group of instructions that are accessed as a single unit.
	Repetition	Represents the beginning of a group of statements that are to be repeated.

Figure 3.2   Flowchart symbols.

operations are performed. A flowchart provides a means of organizing our thinking about a problem solution. Because flowcharts provide pictorial representations of the steps that are to be followed, they assist in both the development and communication of the logic of the problem solution. They are also helpful in detecting and correcting errors in logic and developing more efficient structures.

A flowchart is useful for complicated programs which contain numerous branches, since it can depict the interrelationships between the various branches and loops. Flowcharts also allow us to quickly test several alternative solutions to a problem since it is much easier to draw the flowchart than to write the program. Once a flowchart has been developed, the task of writing the program is greatly simplified.

Finally, a flowchart is an excellent vehicle for documenting a program. It provides a convenient means of communication between both programmers and nonprogrammers. This is important during the development of a program, especially when several people are working on the same project. Since a flowchart is not dependent on a particular programming language, it can be understood by another programmer and by people who have limited knowledge of programming. This can be of great benefit during later maintenance and use of the program.

In summary, a flowchart is an analytical tool and is useful for documentation and as a communication device.

Flowchart Symbols

The symbols used in flowcharts have been standardized by the American National Standards Institute. Arrows are used on the connecting flowlines if the direction of flow is not clear. A flowchart should have one start and one or more stop points and should be arranged so that the direction of processing is from top to bottom and from left to right. Although flowlines can cross, the crossing flowlines are independent of each other. Whenever possible, crossing of flowlines should be avoided, since it makes the flowchart difficult to read. Figure 3.2 shows the various flowchart symbols and the operation that they represent. These symbols are described in the paragraphs that follow.

Terminal symbol. The terminal symbol, which is oval shaped, represents start and end points of an algorithm. The words START and STOP are usually placed as narratives within the start and end symbols, respectively. Typically, there is only one starting point, but there may be more than one end point, one to indicate the end of normal processing and others to indicate an exit resulting from one or more unrecoverable error conditions.

Input/output symbol. Both input and output operations are represented by a parallelogram tilted to the right. The nature of the operation to be performed is indicated by including the terms READ and INPUT to denote input operations and the terms PRINT and WRITE to denote output operations.

Processing symbol. The rectangular processing symbol is used to indicate operations involving arithmetic and data manipulation. This symbol is also used to represent a collection of statements that perform computations.

Decision symbol. The diamond-shaped decision symbol is used to indicate a point in the algorithm at which a branch to one or more alternative paths is possible. The condition upon which each of the exit paths will be executed is identified within the diamond-shaped symbol. Also, flowlines leaving the corners of the diamond are labeled with the decision results associated with each path.

On-page connector. A small circle is used to indicate a connection between two points on the same page in a flowchart. For complex programs containing numerous branches and loops, the number and direction of flowlines can result in confusion. In such situations connectors are used to replace flowlines. Whenever possible, connectors should be used instead of flowlines. Connectors are used in pairs, one indicating an exit from and the other an entry to a point in a flowchart. The connector pairs are identically labeled.

Off-page connector. Off-page connectors are used to connect flowcharts that are too large to fit on one page. They represent an entry, or an exit from, a point in a flowchart on a different page. As with on-page connectors, they appear in identically labeled pairs.

Annotation symbol. The annotation symbol is used to add explanatory remarks. Since no operations are performed, the remarks are connected to other flowchart symbols by means of dashed lines and can be placed at any point in the flowchart. Annotation symbols are used to explain special features of the program or to explain certain concepts of the solution.

Predefined process. This symbol is used to represent a group of instructions that are to be accessed as a single unit.

Repetition. The hexagon symbol is used to indicate the beginning of a loop structure.

3.4   Pseudocode

An alternate scheme for describing an algorithm is pseudocode. Pseudocode is a highly informal language for describing algorithms. There are no strict rules for writing pseudocode and most programmers develop their own version. Pseudocode consists of a series of statements and instructions that, when followed, will solve the problem. Pseudocode uses a mix of English, mathematical notation, and a set of special words (called keywords) to describe the operations of the algorithm. Some of the more commonly used keywords are BEGIN, END, READ, PRINT, IF, ELSE, ELSEIF, ENDIF, WHILE, DO, ENDWHILE, and ENDDO. Keywords are capitalized whereas processing steps and conditions are written in lowercase. A separate line is used for each distinct step of the algorithm, and the statements between the keywords are indented to clarify the structure of the algorithm.

There are a number of advantages to designing algorithms using pseudocode. The most important advantage of using pseudocode is that it shows the logic of the algorithm immediately. Pseudocode is language independent; that is, it depends on the problem being solved and not the particular programming language. Thus it can be understood by nonprogrammers or by programmers who use a different programming language. As such, it is also a valuable tool for documentation. Algorithms expressed in pseudocode can be readily converted into any variety of programming languages. It is easier to develop a program from pseudocode than from a flowchart because pseudocode is much closer to the actual computer code. There is a direct correspondence between pseudocode statements and statements in a programming language. Another advantage of pseudocode is that it is more easily modified than is a flowchart. Most programmers prefer to use pseudocode instead of flowcharts because of their flexibility and ease of use.

3.5   FUNDAMENTAL CONTROL STRUCTURES

All algorithms, no matter how complex, can be reduced to combinations of three fundamental control structures. These basic structures are independent of the programming language and can be used to develop algorithms for any problem. They are

1. **Sequence structure.** One operation, or a group of operations, is performed after the other, that is, sequentially. All the programs considered so have been sequential.
2. **Selection structure.** This structure tests a condition to determine which steps are to be performed next. Different operations are selected depending on whether the condition tested is true or false.
3. **Repetition.** A series of steps is repeated. In a *conditional loop* the steps are repeated as long as a certain condition is true. In a *counting loop* the steps are repeated for a predetermined number of times.

Sequence Structure

The sequence structure consists of steps that are performed one after another. The flowchart and pseudocode representations of a sequence structure are shown in Figure 3.3. In the pseudocode for the sequence structure, the words BEGIN and END are used to define the beginning and end points of the structure. The operations that are performed in sequence structure primarily consist of computations, input, and output.

Computations are indicated in pseudocode by an arrow pointing to the left ($\leftarrow$) as in the example

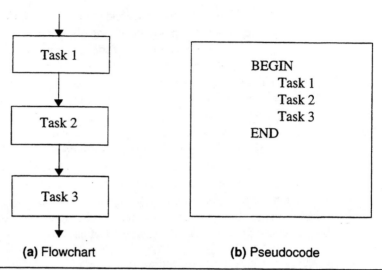

(a) Flowchart **(b)** Pseudocode

Figure 3.3 Sequence structure.

area ← PI * radius * height

This statement assigns the result of the computation to area. The flowchart representation of a computation is a rectangle. We write the specific instructions to be executed within the rectangle. The flowchart statement for the previous computation is

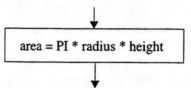

Input statements are specified in pseudocode by the word READ followed by the list of variables to be read. For example, to read the radius and height we would use the following pseudocode

READ radius, height

As shown here the flowchart for input is a parallelogram. We write the specific input operations to be conducted inside the parallelogram. Thus the flowchart statement to read the radius and height would be

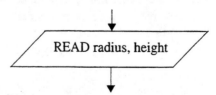

We specify output in pseudocode by the word PRINT followed by a list of constants, variables, or a string of characters. The following pseudocode prints a message followed by the value of the variable area

PRINT "Area = ", area

The flowchart symbol for output is the same as for input. Thus the flowchart representation of the preceding pseudocode statement is

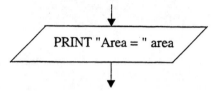

Selection Structure

The selection structure tests a condition to determine which steps are to be performed next. Depending on whether the condition is true or false, different operations are selected. For example, a step of this structure might be "if the data value is positive, compute the square root of the value; otherwise print an error message."

The selection structure is most commonly described in terms of an IF structure. We will consider three forms of the IF structure for selection. The flowchart and pseudocode for the simple IF structure is shown in Figure 3.4. This

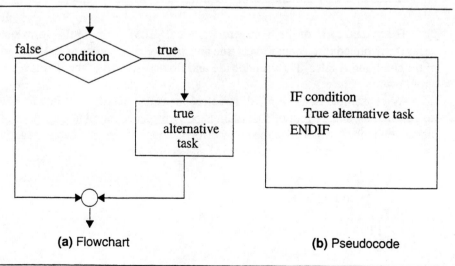

(a) Flowchart   (b) Pseudocode

Figure 3.4   The IF structure.

structure is also called the single-alternative IF structure. The simple IF structure tests a condition: if the condition is true, a certain step or group of steps is performed. No action is performed if the test is false.

Suppose that in the algorithm we are developing we need to obtain the absolute value of a data value. One step in our algorithm might be "if the data value is negative multiply it by -1." We can write this in pseudocode and flowchart form as

IF x < 0
    x ← (-1) * x
ENDIF

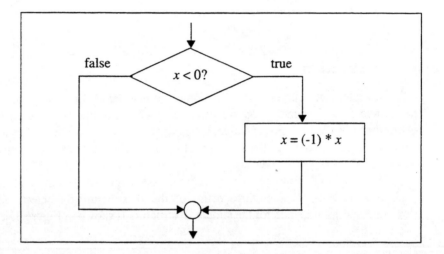

The second form of the IF structure is the IF-ELSE form. In this form a series of tasks is performed if the condition is true and an alternative series of tasks is performed if the condition is false. The pseudocode and flowchart form of the IF-ELSE structure are shown in Figure 3.5.

As an example of an IF-ELSE structure, consider an algorithm in which we need to compute the square root of a number. Since we cannot compute the square root of a negative number, we need to print an error message if the number is negative. The pseudocode and flowchart forms of these statements are

IF x >= 0
    y ← sqrt(x)
ELSE
    PRINT "Number is negative"
ENDIF

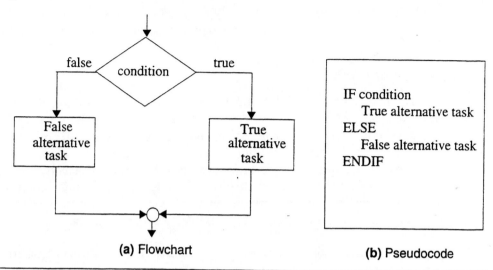

IF condition
    True alternative task
ELSE
    False alternative task
ENDIF

(a) Flowchart   **(b)** Pseudocode

Figure 3.5   The IF-ELSE structure.

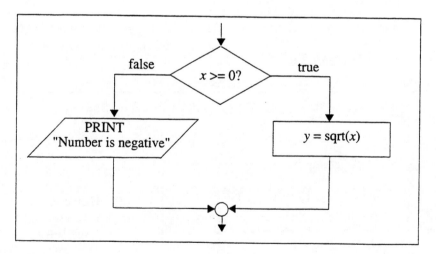

In the pseudocode for the selection structure, the IF and ELSE are vertically aligned. The ENDIF explicitly marks the end of the structure. The true and false alternative statements are indented. This makes it easier to follow the logic of the program. In the IF-ELSE structure each of the two paths lead to a common merge point, so that the flow of program control continues in a forward direction regardless of which of the two paths is taken.

There is also a third form of the IF structure, called the IF-ELSEIF structure, which allows us to test for multiple conditions. A newer construct is the CASE

SELECT structure, which is specifically designed to handle complex selection operations with multiple conditions. We will discuss these structures in detail in Chapter 6.

Repetition or Loop Structure

The third fundamental control structure is the loop or repetition structure, which allows repeated execution of one or more steps. Loops have a selection operation built into it to control how many times the loop executes. There are two basic types of loops, the conditional loop and the counting loop. In a conditional loop, the exact number of repetitions is not known in advance. The loop executes until some particular condition is satisfied. An example of a conditional loop is a loop that is repeated until all data values have been read and processed. In a counting loop, a series of statements is repeated for a predetermined number of times.

In the WHILE loop, a test condition is evaluated. If the test condition is true, a series of steps is executed, and the test condition is evaluated again. This iterative process continues as long as the condition tested is true. When the condition becomes false, there is an exit from the loop. Note that the value of the variable affecting the test condition should change within the series of statements being repeated; otherwise, the test condition will always remain true, and the loop will not terminate. The flowchart and pseudocode representation of a WHILE loop is shown in Figure 3.6.

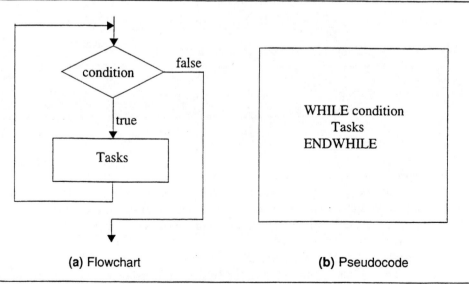

(a) Flowchart   (b) Pseudocode

Figure 3.6   Pseudocode and flowchart for the WHILE loop.

In the pseudocode for the WHILE loop the end of the loop is explicitly marked by the keyword ENDWHILE. This helps to emphasize the logic of the structure and clearly indicates which statements are included in the structure. The statements forming the body of the loop are indented to emphasize the range of the loop.

As an example of a WHILE statement consider the algorithm for computing the average of N test scores, where N is the number of students in the class. One of the steps in the algorithm would be to read each test score and compute the sum of these scores. This step can be implemented with the WHILE loop as shown:

count ← 0
sum ← 0
WHILE count < N
    READ score
    sum ← sum + score
ENDWHILE

The first two statements are not actually part of the WHILE loop but are necessary for initializing the variables sum and count. The flowchart representation is shown in Figure 3.7.

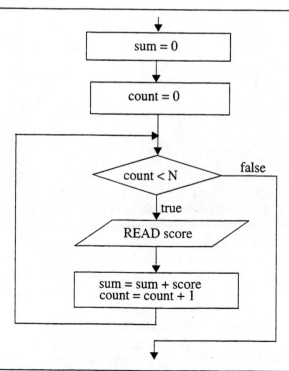

Figure 3.7   Flowchart for computing the sum of test scores.

Another loop structure is the DOWHILE loop. The DOWHILE loop differs from the WHILE loop in that the test condition is evaluated after the series of steps that are to be repeated has been executed. Thus in a DOWHILE loop the statements that are to be repeated will always be executed at least once regardless of the result of the test condition. The pseudocode and flowchart representation of a DOWHILE loop is shown in Figure 3.8. The DOWHILE loop is not used as often as the WHILE loop.

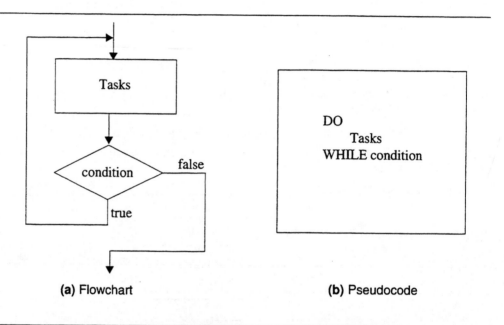

(a) Flowchart   (b) Pseudocode

Figure 3.8   The DOWHILE loop.

Each of the fundamental control structures presented in this section has only one entry point and one exit point. This means that in the context of the algorithm these control structures can themselves be considered as a series of sequence structures. Thus the entire algorithm can be considered to be a series of sequence structures. The three basic structures can be combined with each other as required to perform any operation. Figure 3.9 shows how two selection structures can be combined. Again, there is only one entry point and one exit point for the combination. Thus by combining these three basic structures it is possible to develop complex programs. In fact, it has been demonstrated that any program, no matter how complex, can be constructed using the three basic control structures.

One of the advantages of using only the basic structures just described is that program control flows from top to bottom. Program statements are executed in the order in which they appear in the program. Of course, some statements will be

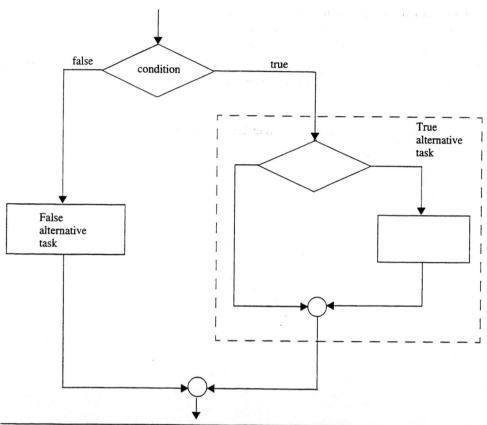

Figure 3.9   Combination of two selection structures.

repeated (as in the case of the loop structure), but the general flow of control will always be from top to bottom. This makes the program easier to read and easier to understand.

Example 3.4   Average of Three Numbers

PROBLEM STATEMENT: Write pseudocode and flowchart statements to describe the algorithm of Example 3.1 for computing the average of three numbers.

SOLUTION: The pseudocode representation of the algorithm is

    BEGIN
        READ a, b, c
        sum ← a + b + c
        average ← sum/3

    PRINT a, b, c, average
END

The arrows (←) shown in the pseudocode represent assignment operations.

The flowchart representation of the algorithm is shown in Figure 3.10. Note that this is an example of a sequential structure.

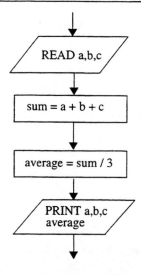

Figure 3.10　Flowchart for computing the average of three numbers.

Example 3.5　Largest of Three Numbers

PROBLEM STATEMENT: Write the pseudocode and flowchart representation of the algorithm for computing the largest of three numbers, a, b, and c.

SOLUTON: The pseudocode representation is given as

    BEGIN
        READ a, b, c
        xmax ← a
        IF xmax < b THEN
            xmax ← b
        ENDIF

```
        IF xmax < c THEN
            xmax ← c
        ENDIF
        PRINT a, b, c, xmax
    END
```

The solution consists of comparing a and b, discarding the smaller, and then comparing the larger with c. The larger of the last two values compared is the desired answer. The flowchart version is shown in Figure 3.11.

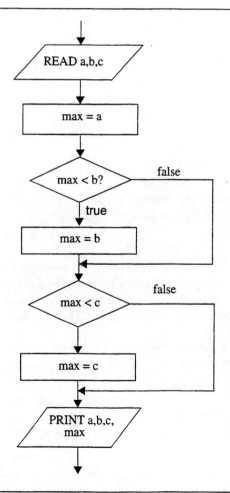

Figure 3.11   Flowchart for computing the largest of three numbers.

Example 3.6   Average Maximum and Minimum Temperatures

PROBLEM STATEMENT: Write the pseudocode and flowchart representation for the problem of computing the average maximum and minimum temperatures for a period of N days. The available data consist of the minimum and maximum temperature for each day.

SOLUTION: The pseudocode representation is given as

```
BEGIN
      sum_max ← 0
      sum_min ← 0
      count ← 1
      Read n
      WHILE count <= n
            READ max_temp, min_temp
            sum_min ←  sum_min + min_temp
            sum_max ← sum_max + max_temp
            count ← count + 1
      ENDWHILE
      ave_min ← sum_min/n
      ave_max ← sum_max/n
      PRINT ave_max, ave_min
END
```

The procedure consists of reading the maximum and minimum temperatures in the variables max_temp and min_temp and adding these to the variables sum_max and sum_min. Thus sum_max and sum_min contain the sum of the maximum and minimum temperatures read so far. This process is repeated until all data has been read.

The variable count is used to count the number of times the loop has been performed. The value of count is incremented by one with each pass through the loop. At the beginning of each pass a test is made. If count is not less than or equal to n, all data has been read and the averages are computed by dividing sum_max and sum_min by n. The result is saved in the variables ave_max and avg_min. The flowchart representation is shown in Figure 3.12.

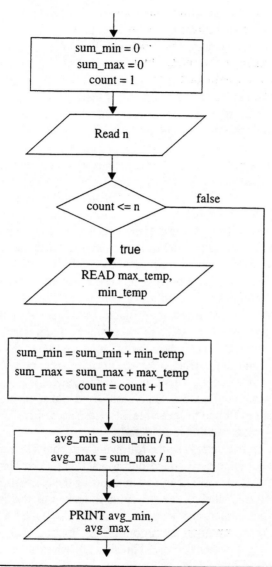

Figure 3.12 Flowchart for computing average minimum and maximum temperatures over an *n*-day period.

3.6 TOP-DOWN DESIGN

The previous sections presented some tools for developing algorithms. They also described some desirable characteristics of algorithms and presented the basic control structures that are the building blocks of algorithms. This section will describe one method of designing algorithms, *top-down design*.

Algorithms for simple problems can be developed without any formal techniques. However, many of the problems that are routinely encountered by engineers tend to be quite large and complex. For such problems it becomes necessary to follow a systematic procedure of algorithm design because of the complexity of the problem and the need to manage large amounts of detail. Top-down design is a systematic procedure for breaking a large problem into smaller, more manageable, subproblems that can be dealt with separately. Top-down design consists of two techniques: *decomposition* and *stepwise refinement.*

The first step in the algorithm development process is a statement of the problem in general terms. The next step consists of decomposing the original problem into a series of smaller subproblems and addressing each subproblem individually. The solution is written in English and each part of the overall problem is described in general terms. It is not necessary to present a detailed solution at this stage of the design. In fact, any decisions regarding details should be postponed.

Problem decomposition delineates the major steps to be performed in solving the problem so that they are not obscured by details. It is the most important part of the algorithm development process since the decisions made at this stage will influence the form of the final solution.

In the stepwise refinement technique, we start with the general English language description of the steps to the problem solution and successively refine each step in greater detail. With each iteration, one step of the algorithm is chosen for refinement and more detail is added. For large programs there will usually be many levels of refinement. This process of refinement is continued until all steps are detailed enough so that they can be converted into computer instructions. Thus, the program is developed in several levels. Each successive level is obtained from the previous level by adding more detail.

When refining a step, keep the following two points in mind: (1) Only a small amount of detail should be added during each iteration. This will assist you in postponing the details until later, and in ensuring the correctness of the expansion. And (2) at each step, analyze the algorithm to make sure that it is correct.

Many programmers use a structure chart (also called a hierarchy chart) to assist in the development of a program. The structure chart is a block diagram similar to an organizational chart. The structure chart gives an overview of the various tasks and their relationship to one another. The structure chart is very helpful in developing solutions to complex programming problems. It allows the programmer to concentrate on defining *what* need to be done before deciding *how* it is to be done.

The general form of a structure chart is shown in Figure 3.13. The boxes indicate the tasks, and the line connecting the boxes shows the relationship of these tasks to one another. The major decisions are made at the first level. The second level consists of the following major tasks:

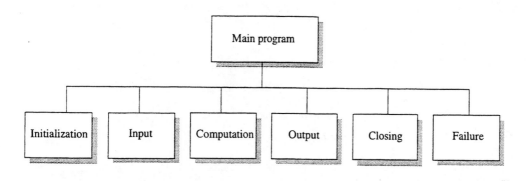

Figure 3.13   A structure chart.

1. Initialization
2. Input
3. Computation and processing
4. Output
5. Closing
6. Failure path

Usually these tasks are still quite complex, and in the refinement process they are divided into subtasks. Figure 3.14 shows the structure chart to which a third level has been added. These tasks may require further division in to still smaller subtasks as shown in Figure 3.15. The successive refinement continues until each subtask is sufficiently simple to allow a direct translation to computer instructions (C statements).

Top-down design has a number of benefits. It provides us with a procedure for developing well-designed modular programs. It enables program development on various levels, each level being obtained from the previous level. It helps to reduce the complexity of the problem since decisions about the program are made at the appropriate level in the development. Major decisions are made first, and decisions regarding specific details of the program are made later. It focuses the designer's attention to one aspect of the problem without having to manage all the other details of the solution. It helps in the development of logical, sound, and correct algorithms.

3.7 MODULAR DESIGN

One of the consequences of top-down design is that the problem is decomposed into smaller and simpler subproblems and each problem is considered independently. The program is thus broken up into a number of smaller subprograms or modules. This approach of designing programs as a series of modules is called *modular design* and is a natural consequence of top-down design.

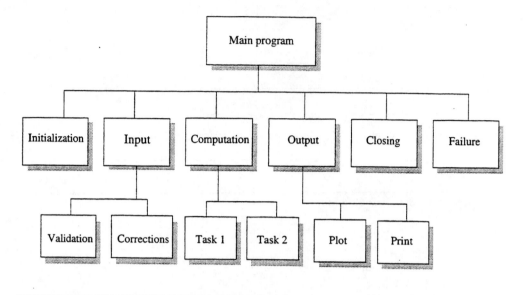

Figure 3.14   A structure chart with three levels.

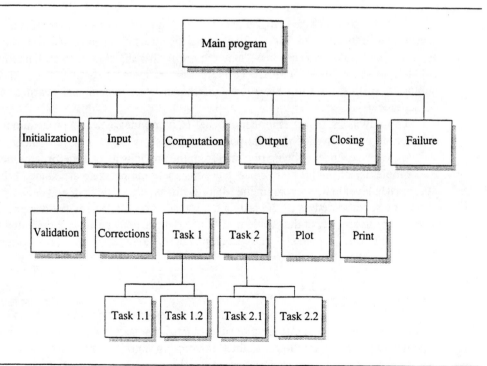

Figure 3.15   A structure chart with four levels.

Depending on the size and nature of the problem, the modules are usually broken down into even smaller modules. The idea is to keep the modules small and self-contained so that they can be developed and tested separately.

In a modular program each module is independent of the others. Ideally, each module performs a specific, well-defined function. A module is a small self-contained section of an algorithm. Some of the desirable attributes of modules are the following:

1. A module should be relatively small. Although there are differing opinions on exactly what the size of a module should be, a good rule of thumb is to limit the size of a module to no more than one or two pages. If the module is too large it should be broken up into smaller modules.

2. A module should have only one entry point. This makes is possible to access the module as a single unit and also to modify it or replace it without having to replace other segments of the program.

3. A module should be independent and self-contained so that it can be developed and tested separately.

4. Changes in a module should not affect other modules.

5. A module should perform a single well-defined function. Simply breaking a program into modules does not by itself guarantee that the program will be modular. The key factor in achieving modularity is that each module should have a specific function. Developing modules on the basis of function enhances the possibility of the modules being used in other programs.

6. A module should have a well-defined interface. The interface defines what input is required by the module and the result returned by the module. In a well-defined interface, these values are clearly specified in the module.

Modular design has a number of advantages. A modular program is easier to write and debug, because each module of the program can be written and tested separately. A modular program is also easier to maintain and change: since the modules are independent, they can be changed, rewritten, or even replaced without affecting other parts of the program. Another advantage is that the program can be developed by several people since different people can work on different modules. Also, previously developed and tested modules can be used in different programs. In fact, most experienced programmers have a library of modules which they can incorporate into programs. All this reduces program development time and enhances program reliability. The most significant advantage of modular design is that it limits complexity and simplifies the design of the program. The logic of the program is thus easy to follow and to understand.

3.8   STRUCTURED PROGRAMMING

The importance of good planning and organization when developing a program cannot be overemphasized. Many inexperienced programmers begin by writing programs without giving enough thought to the overall structure and organization of the program. The result is programs that are difficult to understand and modify. Such programs usually contain a large number of unconditional transfers which have been used to correct errors and omissions resulting from poor planning. The excessive jumping around in the program makes it difficult to trace the flow of control. Modifying or making even minor changes to such programs usually results in disastrous consequences.

Typically, more time and effort are expended in locating and correcting errors in programs than in the development of the program. The structure of a program (or lack of it) is a significant factor in determining the ease with which it can be read and understood. A well-written program is easier to debug and modify since it is easily read and understood by another person. In a well-ritten program the purpose and sequence of each statement are clear, and it is easy to follow the logic of the solution.

In recent years, considerable attention has been given to developing better programs. Many computer scientists have recognized the importance of structure in the development of logical programs and have arrived at a number of rules for writing better programs. The application of these concepts to program development and design is called *structured programming*. The goals of structured programming are to avoid bad program structure and to produce programs that can be read, maintained, and modified easily by programmers. Some of the rules that have been proposed for accomplishing this are as follows:

1. Programs should employ only the three fundamental control structures.
2. Each of these structures should have one entry point and one exit point.
3. The use of unconditional transfer statements (gotos) should be avoided.
4. The program should be written as a series of modules, with each module performing a single well-defined function.
5. The program should be written so that it is easy to read and employs logic that is easy to follow. Some of the steps that can improve a programs readability include using comments to explain the program, indenting sections of code, including a description of variables, and using meaningful variable names.

Structured programming is an aid in the logical development of programs. Experience has shown that the application of structured programming techniques results in logically sound programs, as well as in significant improvements in programmer efficiency.

Some of the benefits of structured programming are:

1. Increased programmer productivity
2. Reduction in time taken to compose, debug, and test program
3. Improved program readability
4. Easier program modification and maintenance
5. Improved program reliability

Once the structured programming approach is mastered, programs will have fewer errors and will be easier to understand and modify. While the benefits of structured programming are more evident in large, complex programs, all programs, regardless of their size, can benefit from the application of these principles.

3.9 PROGRAM ERRORS

Errors are always present in a newly written program. In fact, it is safe to assume that a program contains errors until it is proven otherwise. A considerable amount of time should be set aside for locating and correcting errors. When testing computer programs, two basic principles should always be kept in mind:

1. The program is wrong until proven right under all possible conditions.
2. Any errors produced are due to faults in the program rather than in the computer hardware. Machine failures are extremely rare and are usually recognizable as such.

There are three types of errors (see Figure 3.16) that might be present in a computer program: (1) syntax errors, (2) run-time errors, and (3) logic errors.

Syntax Errors

A syntax error is any violation of the grammatical rule of the language. Syntax errors are very common and relatively easy to correct. Examples of syntax errors include omitting a semicolon or a closing parenthesis or brace. Syntax errors are produced during the compilation stage.

Syntax errors are easier to correct than other errors because the compiler will usually find these errors and provide diagnostic error messages indicating where and what the errors may be. Some compiler messages are clear. But there may be many error messages that are not easy to understand. This is because the error has prevented the compiler from determining the type of statement we wanted. In many cases the error message does not accurately describe the location of the error and may even point to a statement with no errors. If this occurs, you should check the statement or statements immediately preceding the one supposedly in error.

There is usually not a one-to-one correspondence between compiler error messages and the number of errors. Usually a single error results in several error

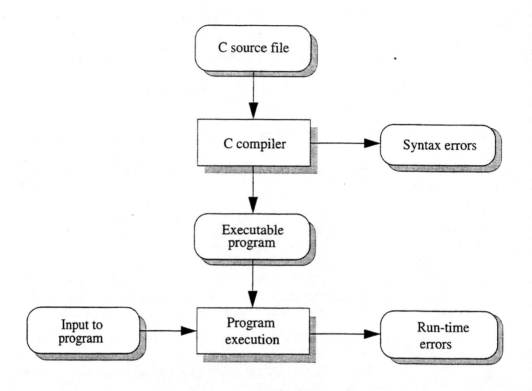

Figure 3.16   Syntax and run-time errors.

messages. Occasionally the computer may overlook a syntax error because of other syntax errors on the same line. Thus it may be necessary to compile the program several times to correct all syntax errors in a program.

Some of the more common syntax errors include the following:

1. Missing or misplaced semicolon.
2. Illegal variable names — use of invalid characters in a variable name.
3. Misspelled keywords — typing `floot` instead of `float.`
4. Unmatched parentheses — there should be the same number of left and right parentheses in arithmetic expressions.
5. Undefined variable names — all variables have to be declared in C prior to their use.
6. Missing subscripts in arrays.
7. Declaring function arguments and return values of the wrong type.

If you are unable to locate an error based on the compiler error message, you should check all statements that are related in any way to the one in error. You should also check all variable declarations, check for matching begin and end brace pairs, and check all **then** and **else** clauses of **if** statements.

Run-time Errors

These are errors that occur during the execution of a program. Run-time errors can be detected only when the program is run since these are not syntax errors. They are usually caused by incorrect or incomplete algorithms that produce unexpected numbers or fail to allow for all possible input data. Most run-time errors occur during the evaluation of arithmetic expressions. Some of the more common run-time errors are:

1. Indefinite result, which occurs when a division by zero is attempted. For example, the following statement will result in an overflow if the value of **y** is zero

   ```
   z = x/y;
   ```

2. Complex result, which can occur when attempting to raise a negative number to some power or attempting to take the square root of a negative number.

3. Overflow and underflow, examples of which include expressions that result in values greater than the maximum value that can be stored in the variable of a given data type, raising numbers to very large positive or negative powers, and evaluating e^x with a large positive or negative value of x.

4. Using invalid subscripts in arrays, which is a common error when using arrays.

5. Using variables that have not been assigned a value; for example, in the statement

   ```
   a = b * c;
   ```

   the value of **a** will be incorrect if either **b** or **c** have not been previously assigned a value. This type of error may be difficult to detect.

Most compilers will detect run-time errors and provide a message describing the nature of the error. Many run-time errors cause execution to be terminated. However, some errors may be passed. For example, on some computer systems the result of an underflow may be set to zero. Run-time errors are harder to find than syntax errors because they only occur under certain conditions. Also, run-time errors often cause system crashes that destroy any information about the cause of the error.

Logic Errors

Logic errors are a result of faulty program design. Errors in logic can be insidious because the output from a program that contains logic errors may appear to be deceptively correct. Such errors are very difficult to diagnose and correct since no error messages are printed. Logic errors are usually easy to fix once they are found. However, they are very difficult to find since the computer does not give any error message. Some of the logic errors you should check for include

1. Incorrect conditions in `if` statements
2. Incorrect conditions in `while` or `do` statements
3. Uninitialized or incorrectly initialized variables
4. Mistakes in the placement of semicolons
5. Failure to modify the loop controlling variable within a `while` or `do` loop
6. Unexpected end of data.

Detecting the exact cause and location of logic errors requires some detective work and a considerable amount of patience. When searching for logic errors the logic of the algorithm as well as the code itself must be checked. It is usually helpful to print out intermediate values and to check these values against those obtained from manual calculations. Other techniques include tracing program execution, letting another person study the program, and isolating and testing each module separately.

There is an endless number of errors that can occur in a program. The best protection against logic errors is a carefully designed and written program.

Other Errors

In addition to the three types of errors just described, there may be some other sources of error. The computed results may not provide an accurate solution to the original problem because of faults in the mathematical model used or in the numerical analysis technique. For example, an iterative method of solution may not converge as the number of iterations is increased.

3.10   DEBUGGING TECHNIQUES

Debugging is the process of locating and correcting errors. Debugging is a slow, tedious, and time-consuming process. One of the reasons why debugging is such a time-consuming process is that debugging has not been taught systematically and students rarely receive formal instruction on what to do when a program fails.

One approach to debugging that is habit forming and wrong and should be avoided is trying something mindlessly because you do not know what else to do. Making random changes to a program and trying quick fixes without giving careful thought makes the program confusing and seldom corrects the original bug. Program errors can be tracked down in a logical manner. There is little sense in changing or rerunning a program until you have spotted a likely cause of the error.

You should also ignore any desire to rerun a program because the problem may have been due to a machine error. Machine errors are rare. Although it is comforting to blame the computer for the error, it is almost always a waste of time and will not result in solving the problem.

A number of techniques can be used for debugging a program:

1. **Tracing.** Tracing is an excellent way to determine the exact location of an error. To trace a program you will need to add several `printf()` statements at strategic locations within your program and output the values of certain key variables. `printf()` statements can also be placed immediately after `scanf()` statements to assure that the input values are correct.

2. **Hand Simulation.** Another method that may help in locating errors is hand simulation. This involves pretending that you are the computer and executing each statement in sequence and recording the value of all variables. This approach is suitable for small programs or small sections of code. It may not be practical for large or complex programs.

3. **Checking Loops.** Incorrectly set up loops are one of the more common causes of program errors. If you have an infinite loop, you can insert `printf()` statements within the loop body to print the values of the loop control variables. You should also check the conditions that must be satisfied (1) for the loop to be entered, (2) for the loop to be continued, and (3) for an exit from the loop to occur.

4. **Isolating sections of code.** A useful technique for debugging complex programs is to isolate sections of the program and to check these sections separately. This can be done only for sections that are independent such as functions. If you know that the error is within a specific function, you may want to remove the function and test it separately.

It is possible that none of these techniques may work. If this occurs, it may be a good idea to discuss the problem with someone else. It is entirely possible that you will discover the error while describing the problem to another person. Also, another person may be able to locate the error immediately, since he or she will have a new and different perspective from you.

We again want to emphasize the importance of structured programming and good programming style. One of the reasons why debugging is so time consuming is that most programmers expect that programs will be free of errors when run the very first time. You will find that if you carefully design your programs and write programs that are readable and easy to understand and whose logic is clear to follow, then you will save considerable time and effort in debugging. A program that consists of well defined modules each of which performs a single well-defined task and is independent is considerably easier to debug, test, and maintain.

3.11 PROGRAM TESTING

Program testing or verification is the process by which a program is validated. The purpose of testing is to demonstrate that the program is working properly. Except for very small programs, it is not practical to perform exhaustive testing of programs. To be effective testing must be done systematically.

The most important factor in testing is the careful selection of data that thoroughly tests the program. The data should be selected so that it exercises all parts of the program. When testing, it is the quality of the test data that is more important that the quantity. For example, testing a program numerous times with similar test data that exercises the same parts of a program tell us that particular part of the program works. However, it does not say anything about the rest of the program. We should select test data that will cause execution of as many flow paths as possible.

Unless a program is small, it is usually not possible nor is it practical to test all flow paths in a program. The number of flow paths in a large program is usually so large that exhaustive testing is impractical. As programs grow larger, the number of flow paths increases exponentially. This suggests that we keep program modules small and thoroughly test each module as it is developed.

The most practical strategy of program testing consists of testing programs in short units. The importance of keeping our modules small and thoroughly testing each module cannot be overemphasized. In addition to testing each individual module, it is also necessary to test the combined program. Testing a module by itself does not guarantee that the overall program will work correctly. This is because there may be errors in the interface between the modules. Thus additional testing is necessary to ensure that the modules interact with each other and the main program as expected.

When selecting test data the following points should be kept in mind:

1. You should choose data for which you know or can easily calculate the answer with a minimum of effort.
2. You should choose a variety of different types of data.
3. You should select a number of boundary cases. These are data sets that fall at the extremes or fall exactly at the crossover point from one case to another. You should also include any special values of data to which

the program is sensitive.

4. You should choose illegal data, that is, data that violates the specifica-
    tions of the problem. Some examples of illegal data include zero values
    or negative values when only positive values are expected. Another test
    possibility is to choose data which leaves the program with nothing to
    do (the so-called null case).

5. When choosing test data you should always keep in mind that the
    objective behind selecting test data is to make the program fail and to
    uncover errors, not to show that the program works.

The following items should be considered when testing a program:

1. Programs should be tested with a wide variety of data sets which
    attempt to exercise many different paths of the program since it is
    possible that some errors cause incorrect results only under certain
    circumstances.

2. Each module should be completely tested before it is linked with the
    main module.

3. All boundary cases should be tested.

4. Null and illegal cases should be tested.

5. The modules should be combined and the entire program, especially
    the interface between the modules, should be tested.

6. Whenever a program is modified, all modules that have been changed
    should be tested. Also, the entire program should be tested.

3.12 PROGRAM DOCUMENTATION

Program documentation is an important step in program development, but one
that is neglected much too often. Documentation should be included so that the
intended users can understand the program and use it effectively. Internal
documentation of computer code is needed to facilitate understanding of the logic
of the solution. External documentation is also needed. Some programmers prefer
to write a large part of the documentation before the program is actually coded.
This can be helpful since it forces them to make decisions regarding the details of
the program before the program is actually written.

External documentation consists of (1) user documentation and (2) technical
documentation.

User Documentation. This is intended for end users only. The end users may or
may not be familiar with programming or with computers or the program. They are
mostly interested in entering some data into the program and getting back correct
results. They may not be in the least bit interested in the inner workings or technical
details of the program. User documentation should focus primarily on the input and

output characteristics of the program and should present an overview of the program. Details about implementation or specific procedures or data structures are usually not included. The user's manual should provide end users with everything that is needed to prepare the necessary input data, execute the program, and interpret the results.

Technical Documentation. The technical documentation is intended for programmers who will be responsible for maintaining the programs. It contains material needed by the programmer to change, correct, and understand the program. The technical documentation should describe both the high level structure of the program and the low-level coding details.

The program listing is the primary documentation of the low-level details. Thus it is important to write programs that are easy to understand and that follow the rules of programming style. To facilitate understanding, your programs should (1) include good descriptive comments, (2) use clear and well chosen variable names, (3) provide helpful indentation, (4) use clear and understandable control structures. A program that has good documentary comments embedded in it will save you and others considerable time and effort in the future when modifications or changes become necessary.

In addition to the program listing it will be necessary to provide separate technical documentation that gives an overview of the overall program structure. This should contain the name of the program, its purpose and current status, its overall program structure, a description of each module and the interface for each module, a description of important data structures, and any debugging or maintenance aids incorporated in the program.

3.13   MAINTENANCE AND MODIFICATION

The last step in the program development cycle is maintenance and modification. As a program is used, its limitations become apparent, and typically, more errors are discovered. A good program usually undergoes a number of revisions. Maintenance involves correcting errors as they are discovered as well as making modifications to the program to incorporate additional features.

Maintenance may be required for a number of reasons. These include newly discovered bugs, specification changes, expansion of the scope of the program, and hardware changes. The costs involved in maintaining programs are considerable and are usually underestimated.

3.14   PROGRAM EFFICIENCY

The efficiency of a program is determined by the amount of time and storage that the program uses. For small programs, efficiency is not an important factor. However, for large programs that require long execution times, it can be important.

Some of the factors that contribute to inefficiency include

1. Performing operations within a loop which produce the same result each time. Such operations should be performed outside the loop and used as a constant value within the loop.

2. Calculating a value two or more times when it can be calculated once and stored.

3. Evaluating each term of a series from scratch when calculating the sum of a series. It is usually possible to calculate the next term of a series from the preceding term rather than starting from scratch.

4. Sometimes using too many small functions can cause inefficiency. This is because the overhead associated with function entry and exit may be relatively high. In such cases it is usually more efficient to include the code of the function directly within the loop from which the function was called in place of the function call.

It is sometimes possible to improve the efficiency of a program significantly by making a few simple changes. Most of the time spent by all programs is in loops. Even more time is spent in loops within loops. By making some changes in an inner loop, it may be possible to speed up the program considerably.

Before rewriting a program to make it more efficient you should be aware of some of the hidden costs involved. Making a program more efficient usually results in a more complex program structure. This can make it more difficult to maintain the program. Also, there is always the possibility of introducing additional errors.

At the present time, execution speed and storage are not as important as programmer time. This is due to the fact that computer hardware has become cheaper. In the microcomputer environment there is little or no cost involved in executing a program. Also, with the decreasing cost of memory chips and the availability of more powerful microprocessors that are capable of addressing large amounts of memory, there is little advantage to spending huge amounts of time making a program more efficient. Thus it is more important to have a well-written, understandable, and readable program that provides correct answers than to have a program that is complex and difficult to debug and maintain but that runs fast.

3.15 SUMMARY

In this chapter we described the seven part process involved in solving a problem on the computer. These are problem definition, problem analysis, algorithm design, program development, testing, documentation, and maintenance. We will follow the first five steps in all the programming projects that are presented in this text.

An essential step in the problem-solving process is the development of an algorithm which is a series of step-by-step instructions for the solution of the problem. We presented two techniques for describing algorithms: flowcharts and pseudocode. A flowchart is a pictorial description of an algorithm. Pseudocode is an highly informal language for describing algorithms. It uses a mix of English, mathematical notation, and a set of keywords to describe the steps of an algorithm.

All algorithms can be developed from combinations of three fundamental structures: the sequence structure in which a group of operations is performed one after another, the selection structure in which different operations are selected depending on the result of a test condition, and the repetition structure in which a series of steps is repeated. We also described a method for developing algorithms called top-down design. Top-down design consists to two techniques, decomposition and stepwise refinement. In decomposition, the major steps required to solve the problem are described in general terms. In stepwise refinement, we successively refine each step in greater detail.

Another tool that is useful for program development is the structure chart. The structure chart is a block diagram similar to an organizational chart. It gives an overview of the various tasks to be performed and their relationship to each other. We also presented the concept of modular design in which a program is broken up into a series of smaller independent subprograms or modules. Modular design is a natural consequence of using the top-down design technique.

In this chapter we also discussed the importance of good planning and organization when developing a program and presented a number of rules for writing better programs. The application of these concepts to program development and design is called structured programming.

A considerable amount of time is spent in finding and correcting errors in a program. There are three types of errors that can occur in a program: syntax errors, run-time errors, and logic errors. We presented a number of techniques for debugging your programs. These include tracing, hand simulation, checking loops, and isolating sections of code. We also presented techniques for testing your programs and for selecting test data.

We also discussed the various types of program documentation, including both internal and external documentation and some issues related to program maintenance and efficiency.

Key Terms Presented in This Chapter

algorithm	counting loop
conditional expression	control structures
conditional loop	debugging

decomposition	run-time errors
documentation	selection structure
DOWHILE loop	sequence structure
flowchart	stepwise refinement
IF structure	structure chart
IF-ELSE structure	structured programming
logic errors	syntax errors
maintenance	testing
modular design	top-down design
pseudocode	WHILE loop

EXERCISES

Review Questions

1.   List the steps involved in the development of a computer program.

2.   What is an algorithm? List the attributes of algorithms? Why is an algorithm so important in the development of a program?

3.   List advantages and disadvantages of using flowcharts.

4.   What is pseudocode? List advantages of using pseudocode.

5.   Explain the difference between a WHILE loop and a DOWHILE loop.

6.   What is meant by the following: (a) structured programming, (b) top-down design?

7.   What are some of the benefits of top-down design?

8.   Explain stepwise refinement. How do you know when you have gone far enough in the refinement process?

9.   Write an algorithm to compute the largest and smallest of a set of N numbers. Save these values in the variables XMAX and XMIN.

10.   Write a flowchart for the following steps:
    1.   Read x.
    2.   If x is negative then set sign $= -1$.
    3.   If x is positive then set sign $= 1$.
    4.   If x is equal to zero then set sign $= 0$.
    5.   Print x, sign.
    6.   Stop.

11. Construct a flowchart for the following steps:
    1. Set SUM = 0.
    2. Set COUNT = 0.
    3. Read N.
    4. Read X.
    5. Set SUM = SUM + X.
    6. Set COUNT = COUNT + 1.
    7. If COUNT less than or equal to N, then go to step 4.
    8. Print SUM.
    9. Stop.

12. Write a flowchart to determine whether three lengths a, b, and c can form a triangle. The three lengths can form a triangle if the following conditions are satisfied

    $$|a - b| < c$$
    $$c < a + b$$

13. Modify the flowchart of the previous problem so that it also determines whether the triangle is isosceles or equilateral. The triangle is isosceles if any two of its sides are equal; that is,

    $$a = b$$

    or

    $$a = c$$

    or

    $$b = c$$

    The triangle is equilateral if all three sides are equal; that is,

    $$a = b$$

    and

    $$a = c$$

    and

    $$b = c$$

14. Write a pseudocode algorithm to read in 100 values and count the number of positive values, the number of negative values, and the number of zero values.

15. Write a pseudocode algorithm which will read in a integer number N and determine if the number is prime. To do this, divide the number N by each of the numbers 2 through $N/2$. If any remainder is zero, then the number is not prime; otherwise, the number is prime.

16. The efficiency of the foregoing algorithm can be improved by dividing the number N by 2 and then using only odd-valued test divisors up to the integer value closest to, but below, the square root of N. Write a pseudocode algorithm to accomplish this.

17. The equivalent resistance of n resistors in parallel can be computed from

$$RT = \frac{1}{1/R_1 + 1/R_2 + 1/R_3 + \ldots + 1/R_n}$$

Draw a flowchart for a procedure to read a number n; then read n resistances $R_1, R_2, \ldots,$ R_n and compute and print the equivalent resistance.

18. Write a flowchart to compute the sum of the squares of n numbers

The binomial coefficients $\binom{n}{x}$ are given by the following expression

$$\binom{n}{x} = \frac{n!}{x!(n-x)!} \qquad x = 0, 1, 2, \ldots, n$$

These coefficients also correspond to the number of combinations of x objects taken from a group of n. Write pseudocode statements to read a value of n, compute the binomial coefficients, and print the results. Note that the first term is equal to 1 and that each succeeding term can be determined by multiplying the previous term by

$$\frac{n - x + 1}{x} \qquad x = 1, 2, \ldots, n$$

This approach avoids some of the overflow problems that can occur if the factorials were evaluated directly.

19. What is modular design? Give a brief description of a modular program.

20. What are the advantages of modularization based on function?

21. What factors determine the size of a module?

4

VARIABLES, CONSTANTS, AND DATA TYPES

In this chapter we describe the concepts of variables and constants and present some of the basic data types that are available in C for storing information. C programs use variables to store objects whose values change during the execution of a program. Many C programs also use constants whose values do not change during program execution. The C language provides a variety of data types for storing the different types of values that a program needs.

4.1   VARIABLES AND CONSTANTS

One of the most important features of a computer is its ability to manipulate data. The computer stores this data in memory. Since our programs are going to make use of this data, we must have some way of accessing the data in computer memory. C permits access to data stored in the memory through the uses of symbolic names, also called *variable names* or *variables*. A variable represents a memory location that is assigned a name. The content of the memory location is the current value of the variable. Variable names allow us to make use of these values without having to keep track of where the values are stored. Each time we want to retrieve the value or perform calculations using the value, all we have to do is to refer to the value by its name. We can visualize variable names and their contents as shown here

Variable Name   **Contents**

  `root1` | 4.53 |

  `rate` | 11.0 |

  `sum` | 1000 |

Here, `root1`, `rate`, and `sum` represent three storage locations. The contents of these storage locations are 4.53, 11.0, and 1000 respectively. Thus, the current value of the variable `root1` is 4.53, the current value of `rate` is 11.0, and the current value of `sum` is 1000.

Suppose we want to compute the area of a rectangle using the expression

area = width * height

We can create three variables `area`, `width`, and `height` in our program. When C encounters the declaration statement for creating these variables in our program, it allocates memory storage for each of these three variables. It uses this memory storage to save the current values of the area, width, and height. To compute the area, we could use a statement such as

```
area = width * height;
```

When the computer executes the statement, it obtains the current values of `width` and `height`, multiplies them, and then places the result in the storage location defined by `area`. The program data area before and after the statement is executed is shown in Figure 4.1. The question mark in the memory cells representing `area` indicates that the variable is undefined.

You should note that the *name* of a storage location is different from the *contents* of that location. The variable name simply points to the storage location, while the contents of this location store the current value of the variable.

The value of a variable need not remain constant throughout a program and may change repeatedly during the execution of a program. Each time the program assigns a new value to a variable, the old value is replaced with this new value. The current value is always used in all computations involving the variable.

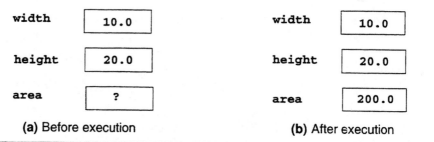

(a) Before execution   **(b)** After execution

Figure 4.1   Program data area before and after execution of statement `area = width * height`.

Naming Variables

There are a few rules that we must follow when forming variable names. These rules are necessary so that the compiler can distinguish between variable names and other elements of the C language.

1. A variable name must be made up of the letters a to z, the digits 0 to 9 and the underscore character (_). No other character can be used.
2. The first character of a variable name must be a letter or underscore (_).Variable names cannot match any of the C reserved words such as `float`, `int`, and `static`. Reserved words can, however, be imbedded in a variable name. Here are some examples of variable names containing imbedded keywords

    float_var   exit_flag   staticva   intvalue

Although there is no restriction on the total number of characters that can be used in a variable name, the number of characters that are significant in a variable name differs on different systems. For example, on some systems only the first eight characters are significant, while on others the first 31 characters are significant. On a system that considers only the first eight characters to be significant, the variables `tempvalue1` and `tempvalue2` would not be distinguishable since the first eight characters are the same.

Unlike BASIC and Pascal, C is case sensitive, which means that upper- and lowercase letters are distinct in C. Thus the variables `count`, `Count`, and `COUNT` each refer to a different variable. It is conventional to use lowercase for variable names. However, in some programming environments mixedcase is also used. We will be using lowercase throughout this text.

In addition to following the foregoing rules, we should select variable names that are meaningful and that help us remember what is being stored in the location assigned to that variable. For example, the variables `r1` and `r2` can be used to represent the roots of a quadratic equation, or the variable names `root1` and `root2` could be used. The second choice is obviously much better since it gives a better indication of what the variables represent. Following are some examples of legal variables

number	value	radius	count
area	first_root	sum	integral
mean_value	std_deviation	second_root	temp1
r2d2	r1	x23y33	last_one

In some programming environments is becoming popular to used mixedcase for variable names comprised of compound words. The first character of the compound word is written is uppercase as in

firstRoot   stdDeviation   secondRoot   surfaceArea

The following variable names are illegal:

2times	first character must be a letter
x.value	contains illegal character.
float	float is a reserved word
x+y	contains illegal character +
real val	contains blank space
ab*12c	contains illegal character *

Constants

The solution of many engineering problems involve the use of numerical constants. For example, in the equation for the area of a circle

$$\text{area} = \pi r^2$$

the quantity π is a constant that has a value of 3.141593. The area of circles of varying radii can be computed by substituting different values for the radius r in the equation. However, the value of π remains fixed. A C statement for computing the area of a circle can be written as

```
area = 3.141593 * radius;
```

In this statement, **area** and **radius** are variables, and the number **3.141593** is a constant. Thus, constants are numbers used directly in C statements whose value do not change during the course of program execution. The difference between variables and constants is that the value of a variable can change during the course of a program, but the value of a constant remains fixed (unchanged).

4.2   DATA TYPES

Computers work with many types of data such as letters, strings of characters, and numbers. All C programs need a way to identify and work with these different types of data. The C language recognizes several fundamental data types. The fundamental data types in C are **char**, **int**, **float**, and **double**. The data type **char** is used for letters of the alphabet and other characters such as **#, %, $,** and **&**. The data type **int** is used to represent integers which are positive or negative whole numbers. The data type **float** is used to represent single-precision floating point numbers, and the data type **double** is used to represent double-precision floating point numbers. The ANSI C standard also provides for the type **void** which is valueless.

In addition to these fundamental data types, C provides several modifiers. These modifiers when applied to the fundamental data types change the meaning of the fundamental data types. The modifiers **signed** and **unsigned** are applied to character and integer types, and the modifiers **short** and **long** are applied to integers. Some compilers also allow the use of the modifier **long** to type **float**. The ANSI standard has eliminated the **long float** since it is redundant and has the same meaning as **double**. Also, some compilers allow the type **long double**.

4.3   INTEGERS

Integers are whole numbers. They may have a positive or negative value. Negative integers must be preceded with the minus sign, but positive integers may not include the + sign, as this symbol is reserved for addition. The size and range of integers depend on the architecture of the machine and may vary from machine to machine. An integer usually has the same length in bits as the word size of the processor. The word size of microcomputers is typically 16 bits, and the range of integers is -32767 to +32768. Some examples of valid integers are

```
5021      1586      -655      -100
   0     -1100     30200    -32000
 532       -12      4000     16000
```

If the number is positive, it is not necessary to put a + sign in front of it. No embedded spaces are permitted between digits, and commas cannot be used to separate successive groups of digits in an integer. Here are some examples of invalid integers and reasons for their invalidity

```
8.85    contains a decimal point and fraction
5 60    contains an embedded space
20,000  contains imbedded comma
```

Declaring Integer Variables

All variables in a C program have to be declared before they can be used. The declaration statement has the following general form

where *type* is the data type of variable (such as **int**, **long**, **float**, **double**) and

> *type variable_ list*

variable_list is a list of variables. The variables in the list are separated by commas. The keyword **int** is used to declare integer variables as in the statements

```
int count;
int i;
```

These statements declare two integer variables, **count** and **i**. The declaration statements cause storage to be set aside for the variable. We can use a separate declaration for each variable or combine it in one statement as in

```
int count, i;
```

The effect of this declaration statement is to create storage space for two integer sized variables and to associate a name with each variable.

It is also possible to initialize a variable, that is, to assign it an initial value in the declaration statement. For example, the statement

```
int count = 20;
```

creates an integer variable **count** and assigns it an initial value of 20. Here is another example:

```
int i, j = 5;
```

In this example, two integer variables **i** and **j** are created. Note that only **j** is assigned an initial value of 5.

Type long int

Most C compilers provide for a number of different integer types. These different integer types are useful for storing integers of different magnitudes. In addition to the fundamental integer type, most C compilers provide the **long**, **short**, and **unsigned int** types. The type **long int** is used to store integers that require a larger range than type **int**. Although the storage requirements for **long int** vary from machine to machine, **long int** usually requires twice the amount of storage of an **int**. On mini- and microcomputers, a **long int** is stored using 32 bits and can range in value from -2,147,483,648 to 2,147,483,647. On a VAX the word size is 32 bits, and both **int** and **long int** are stored using 32 bits.

Type short int

The data type **short int** is used in situations where it is important to conserve memory. The compiler may provide less storage for a **short int** than for an **int**, although it is not required to do so. Again, the amount of storage used for a **short int** will depend on the architecture of the machine. On mini- and microcomputers a **short int** requires the same amount of storage as an **int**. On a VAX a **short int** requires less storage (2 bytes) than an **int** (4 bytes).

Type unsigned int

The type **int** is by default a signed type, which means that an **int** variable can be used to represent both positive and negative values. Unsigned integers are integers that can have only positive values. The modifier **unsigned** is applied to type **int** to declare unsigned integers. Variables of type **unsigned int** are used in situations when the integer variable will never be negative. Unsigned integers typically require the same number of bytes of storage as signed integers, and since the sign is not stored, they can assume larger values than signed integers. On mini and microcomputers an unsigned integer typically requires 16 bits of storage and can assume values in the range of 0 to 65,535. The following statement declares two unsigned integer variables:

```
unsigned int counter, abs_value;
```

If the **short, long,** or **unsigned** modifiers are used without a type specifier, the compiler will treat it as an integer type. Thus, the following pairs of declarations are identical:

```
unsigned abs_value;
unsigned int abs_value;

long distance;
long int distance;

short height;
short int height;
```

Also, some compilers allow **short** and **long** integer variables of type **unsigned** as **int**.

```
unsigned short int address;
unsigned long int abs_value;
```

Since C was designed to run on many different types of hardware, the ANSI C standard does not impose specific limits on the range of values that can be stored in the various integer types. However, it does require that the compiler developer provide a file called *limits.h* with each implementation that provides the necessary details, such as the maximum and minimum values of the different integer types. Some of the constants defined in the file *limits.h* are given in Table 4.1. The table also shows the values of these constants for our system.

Table 4.1: Constants defined in the file *limits.h*

Constant	Meaning	Value for Our System
`INT_MIN`	minimum value of **int**	-32768
`INT_MAX`	maximum value of **int**	32767
`UNIT_MAX`	maximum value of **unsigned int**	65535
`LONG_MIN`	minimum value of **long int**	-2147483648
`LONG_MAX`	maximum value of **long int**	2147483647
`ULONG_MAX`	maximum value of **unsigned long int**	4294967295
`SHRT_MIN`	minimum value of **short int**	-32768
`SHRT_MAX`	maximum value of **short int**	32767
`USHRT_MAX`	maximum value of **short int**	65535

Integer Constants

When we write a number without an decimal point or an exponent, the C compiler treats it as an integer constant. Thus, the numbers 20 and 34 are integer constants, while 20.0 and 1e2 are not. Integer constants can be expressed in decimal, octal, or hexadecimal notation. Appendix A contains a discussion of the decimal, binary, hexadecimal, and octal number systems and presents the rules for conversion between these number systems. Examples of decimal (base 10) integer constants are

```
5   100   25000
```

We can use the %d formatting code in the **printf()** statement to print an integer in decimal notation.

If the first digit is a zero, then the integer constant is taken as expressed in octal (base 8) notation. For numbers expressed in octal notation the digits must be from 0 through 7. Examples of octal constants are

```
035   063   0156   0250
```

The decimal values of the octal constants are 29, 51, 110, and 168, respectively. To print an integer in octal notation, we use the %o formatting code in the **printf()** statement.

Hexadecimal constants are written with a preceding **0** and the letter **x** (either lowercase or uppercase). The digits 0 through 9 and the letters a through f (or A thorough F) are used to represent a hexadecimal digit. The letters a through f represent the values 10 through 15, respectively. Examples of integers written in hexadecimal notation are

```
0x5b   0x3f   0x12cb   0x5c1
```

The decimal equivalents of these hexadecimal constants are 91, 63, 4811, and 1473, respectively. To print an integer value in hexadecimal notation, we use the **%x** formatting code in the **printf()** statement. The value will be printed without the leading **0x**.

Example 4.1   Integer Variables and Constants

PROBLEM STATEMENT: Write a program to assign integer values to three integer variables **i**, **j**, and **k** and print these values in decimal, hexadecimal, and octal notation using **printf()**.

SOLUTION: The program is shown in Figure 4.2. The program declares three integer variables with the statement

```
int i, j, k;
```

The assignment statements

```
i = 368;          /* decimal          */
j = 02456;        /* octal            */
k = 0x2ab9;       /* hexadecimal      */
```

assign values to the three variables. The variable **i** is assigned an integer value using decimal notation; the variable **j** is assigned a value that is expressed as an octal number; and the variable **k** is assigned a value using hexadecimal notation.

The program then prints the values of **i**, **j**, and **k** in decimal, octal, and hexadecimal notation using the **%d**, **%o**, and **%x** format specifiers. The output from the program is also shown in Figure 4.2.

Long integer constants are written with a trailing "**L**" or "**l**." Examples of long integer constants are

```
896543L   4432160L
```

Long integer constants can also be written in octal and hexadecimal notation as in

```
/****************************************************************/
/*  integers.c   -   Integer Numbers                           */
/*                                                             */
/*  Prints integers in decimal, octal and hexadecimal          */
/*  formats.                                                    */
/****************************************************************/

#include <stdio.h>


main()
{
    int i, j, k;

    /* assign values */
    i = 368;                    /* decimal                     */
    j = 02456;                  /* octal                       */
    k = 0x2ab9;                 /* hexadecimal                 */

    /* print in all three formats */
    printf(" Decimal    Octal    Hexadecimal");
    printf(" %d         %o       %x", i,i,i);
    printf(" %d         %o       %x", j,j,j);
    printf(" %d         %o       %x", k,k,k);
}
```

Program output

```
Decimal      Octal    Hexadecimal
368          560      170
1326         2456     52e
10937        25271    2ab9
```

Figure 4.2   A program to print integers in various formats.

```
076325L   0xeab501L
```

If an integer constant is written that is too large or too small to fit in type `int`, the compiler will automatically store it as a `long int`.

4.4   REAL NUMBERS

A real number is a number containing a decimal point. Real numbers can be written in several different but equivalent ways. The two most common forms for writing real numbers are *fixed point* notation and *floating point* notation. Examples of some real numbers written in fixed point notation are

```
12.1452    10000.12    300.34563    16.5534
-1400.00   0.000001    -400.30      -0.003452
```

Fixed point notation becomes cumbersome when working with very large or very small numbers, such as 1000000000.1 or 0.00000000001. An especially useful way of expressing very small or very large numbers is to use floating point or scientific notation. The number is expressed as a product of a real number and some power of 10. Examples of some numbers written in floating point notation are

$$1.21452 \times 10^1 \qquad 1.000012 \times 10^4 \qquad 1.65534 \times 10^1$$
$$-2.100034 \times 10^{30} \qquad 4.101678 \times 10^{-20} \qquad -7.9856434 \times 10^{-5}$$

Most computers use *exponential* notation to represent floating point numbers. Exponential notation is similar to scientific notation. A number written in exponential notation consists of three parts: a fixed point number (termed mantissa), followed by the letter e, and a positive or negative exponent:

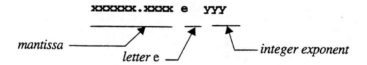

The notation indicates that the mantissa is multiplied by 10 raised to the power of the exponent. Examples of numbers written in exponential notation are the following:

```
1.2345e6    4.43424e-2    0.100e-10
55.5e-30    3.31533e21    1.0e5
```

Examples of some real numbers written in fixed point, scientific, and exponential notation are given in Table 4.2..

Table 4.2: Fixed point, scientific, and exponential notation

Fixed-Point Number	Scientific Notation	Exponential Notation
123.456	1.23456×10^2	1.23456e+02
0.0000124	1.24×10^{-5}	1.24e-05
2005612.0	2.005612×10^6	2.005612e+06
0.00002	2.0×10^{-5}	2.0e-05
32.354	3.2354×10^1	3.2354e01
50000.0	5.0×10^4	5.0e+04
0.0000005	5.0×10^{-7}	5.0e-07

When working with real numbers we are interested in two important characteristics: *precision* and *range*. The precision of a real number relates to the number of significant digits that can be represented. For example, 3.141593 is a more precise approximation of π than 3.142, since it contains more significant digits. The range relates to the maximum and minimum value that can be stored. Both the precision and the range are related to the amount of storage allocated in memory for representing the number. To provide greater flexibility, C provides two data types for storing real numbers — these are type `float` and type `double`

Data Type `float`

The data type `float` is used to represent single-precision floating point numbers. Although the precise number of digits and the range of `float` depends on the implementation, a single-precision floating point number typically has six or seven digits of precision and a range of $\pm(10^{-37}$ to $10^{+38})$. Single-precision floating point numbers are typically stored on mini- and microcomputers using 32 bits: 8 bits are used for the exponent and the remaining 24 bits are used for the mantissa.

Variables of type `float` are declared using the keyword `float` as in

```
float radius, height, width;
```

This statement declares three variables, `radius`, `height`, and `width`, of type `float`.

Data Type `double`

The data type `double` is an extension of type `float` and is used for storing double-precision floating point numbers. A `double` is normally allocated twice as much memory storage as `float`, typically 64 bits. Double-precision numbers have twice the precision of single precision numbers, usually 14 to 15 digits. Also the range is usually one order of magnitude higher, typically around $\pm(10^{-308}$ to $10^{+308})$.

Double-precision variables are declared using the keyword `double` as in the statement

```
double area, volume, circumference;
```

This statement declares three variables, `area`, `volume`, and `circumference`, of type `double`.

Printing Real Numbers

There are several formatting codes that can be used for printing real numbers. These are `%f`, `%e`, and `%g`. These codes apply to both single-precision and double-precision numbers. The `%f` formatting code causes the number to be printed using the fixed point format. The **%e** formatting code prints the number using exponential format. The result obtained with the **%g** formatting code depends on the magnitude of the number being printed. If the number is very large or very small, then the **%g** formatting code prints the number using exponential format; otherwise, it prints the number using fixed point format. Thus the **%g** formatting code uses either **%f** or **%e**, whichever is smaller.

Floating Point Constants

Floating point constants can be written is several ways. Floating point constants may contain an integer part, a fractional part, a decimal point, and an exponent. We can leave out the decimal point or the exponent, but not both. It is not necessary to include the plus sign for positive exponents. Some examples of floating point constants are

```
10.68    0.58    12e05    9e-05    0.001e-09
```

Commas and embedded spaces are not allowed. Examples of invalid floating point constants are

```
205,65.89   contains comma
156.635     contains embedded space
20136       no decimal or exponent
e10         no integer or fractional part
```

All floating point constants are taken to be double precision. For example, in the statement

```
area = 3.141593 * radius * radius;
```

the constant 3.141593 is stored as **double**.

Example 4.2   Printing Floating Point Numbers

PROBLEM STATEMENT: Write a program that assigns values to several floating point variables and prints the values of these variables using the **%f**, **%e**, and **%g** formatting codes.

SOLUTION: The program is shown in Figure 4.4. The statements

```
float a,b;
double c,d;
```

declare four floating point variables, **a**, **b**, **c**, and **d**. The variables **a** and **b** are declared to be of type **float**, and the variables **c** and **d** are of type **double**. The

```
/*****************************************************************/
/* floats.c  -- Floating Point Numbers                           */
/*                                                               */
/* Prints floating point numbers using the %f, %e and %g        */
/* formatting codes.                                             */
/*****************************************************************/
#include <stdio.h>

main()
{
   float a,b;
   double c,d;

   a = 100.123456;
   b = 4.345678e2;
   c = 12.145678903045;
   d = 2.3459012345e-10;

   printf("Formatting codes for floating point numbers");
   printf("\n\n Fixed point format");
   printf("\n a=%f b=%f c=%f d=%f ", a,b,c,d);
   printf("\n\n Exponential format");
   printf("\n a=%e b=%e c=%e d=%e ", a,b,c,d);
   printf("\n\n Fixed point or exponential format ");
   printf("\n a=%g b=%g c=%g d=%g ", a,b,c,d);
}
```

Program output

```
Formatting codes for floating point numbers

Fixed point format
a=100.123459 b=434.567810 c=12.145679 d=0.000000

Exponential format
a=1.00123e+02 b=4.34568e+02 c=1.21457e+01 d=2.34590e-10

Fixed point or exponential format
a=100.123 b=434.568 c=12.1457 d=2.3459e-10
```

Figure 4.3   A program to print floating point numbers.

statements

```
a = 100.123456;
b = 4.345678e2;
c = 12.145678903045;
d = 2.3459012345e-10;
```

assign values to these variables.
The third **printf()** statement

```
printf("\n a=%f b=%f c=%f d=%f ", a,b,c,d);
```

prints the values of the variables using the `%f` format specification. The `%e` format specification is used in the statement

```
printf("\n a=%e b=%e c=%e d=%e ", a,b,c,d);
```

which results in the values being printed in exponential notation. Notice that on our system the numbers are printed with five digits after the decimal for both the `%f` and `%e` format specification.

The statement

```
printf("\n a=%g b=%g c=%g d=%g ", a,b,c,d);
```

prints the variables using the `%g` format specification. This results in **a**, **b**, and **c** being printed in fixed point notation, and **d** is printed using exponential notation.

Range and Precision of Real Types

The precise number of digits and the range of values of variables of type **float** and **double** depends on the specific implementation. The ANSI C standard specifies that these characteristics be defined in a header file called *float.h*. This header file must be provided with each implementation. The header file *float.h* defines several constants related to floating point arithmetic such as the number of significant digits in the **float** and **double** types and the largest and smallest **float** and **double** values. Table 4.3 lists some of the more useful constants defined in *float.h*, the ANSI C minimum and maximum allowed values for these constants, and corresponding values for our system.

Table 4.3: Constants defined in float.h

Constant	Meaning	ANSI	Our System
FLT_MIN	minimum positive value for **float**	$\leq 10^{-37}$	1.1749e-38
FLT_MAX	maximum positive value for **float**	≥ 10-37	2.4082e+38
FLT_DIG	number of digits of precision for **float**	≥ 6	6
FLT_EPSILON	machine precision for **float**	$\leq 10^{-5}$	1.19209e-7
DBL_MIN	minimum positive value for **double**	$\leq 10^{-37}$	2.22507e-308
DBL_MAX	maximum positive value for **double**	$\geq 10^{37}$	1.79769e+308
DBL_DIG	number of digits of precision for **double**	≥ 10	15
DBL_EPSILON	machine precision for **double**	$\leq 10^{-9}$	2.22045e-16

Example 4.3 Machine Dependent Characteristics of Real Types

PROBLEM STATEMENT: Write a program to print the values of the constants defining the characteristics of floating point arithmetic on your system.

SOLUTION: The constants defining the characteristics of floating point arithmetic are contained in the system header file *floats.h*. The program shown in Figure 4.4 prints the values of these constants. The header file *float.h* is included in the program with the following preprocessor directive

```
#include <float.h>
```

The output from the program is also shown in Figure 4.4. On our system the number of digits of precision is 6 for type **float** and 15 for type **double**. The output from the program also shows the minimum and maximum values and the machine precision for types **float** and **double** on our system. You should run the program on your system. Since these constants are machine dependent, you should expect to get different results.

```
/*******************************************************/
/*  fltlimit.c  -- Machine dependent limits on reals  */
/*                                                     */
/*  Prints values of some constants defined in the    */
/*  file floats.h. These constants reflect machine    */
/*  dependent characteristics of floating point        */
/*  arithmetic.                                        */
/*******************************************************/
#include <stdio.h>
#include <limits.h>
#include <float.h>

main()
{
  printf("Float minimum = %lg \n",FLT_MIN);
  printf("Float maximum = %lg \n", FLT_MAX);
  printf("Number of digits of precision for float = %d
      \n",FLT_DIG);
  printf("Machine precision for float = %lg \n\n",FLT_EPSILON);
  printf("Double minimum = %lg \n",DBL_MIN);
  printf("Double maximum = %lg \n",DBL_MAX);
  printf("Number of digits of precision for double = %d
      \n",DBL_DIG);
  printf("Machine precision for double = %lg \n",DBL_EPSILON);
}
```

Figure 4.4   A C program to display the machine dependent characteristics of floating point types.

Program output

```
Float minimum = 1.17549e-38
Float maximum = 3.40282e+38
Number of digits of precision for float = 6
Machine precision for float = 1.19209e-07

Double minimum = 2.22507e-308
Double maximum = 1.79769e+308
Number of digits of precision for double = 15
Machine precision for double = 2.22045e-16
```

FIGURE 4.5   (continued)

4.5   PROGRAMMING PROJECT: WEIGHT OF A HOLLOW CYLINDER

Problem Statement

Write a program to calculate the weight of a hollow cylinder of height, h, outer radius, r, wall thickness, t, and density, γ.

Problem Analysis

The volume V of the cylinder is

volume, $V = \pi (r - t)^2 h$

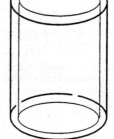

and the weight W of the cylinder is

weight, $W = \gamma V$

Input Variables

height of cylinder, t (**float height**)
outer radius, r (**float radius**)
wall thickness, t (**float t**)
density, γ (**float gamma**)

Output Variables

volume, V (**float volume**)
weight, W (**float weight**)

Algorithm

1.   Read in **height, radius, t**, and **gamma**.
2.   Calculate **volume**.

3. Calculate **weight**.
4. Print **volume** and **weight**.

Program

The program is shown in Figure 4.5. We use a **printf()** statement before each **scanf()** statement to display a prompt message to indicate what input is required. The **scanf()** statements use the **%f** format specifier to read in the values entered. Notice, also, that in the **scanf()** statements we pass the address of the variables as in the statement

```
scanf("%lf", &height);
```

The volume is computed in the statement

```
volume = PI * (r -t) * (r - t) * h;
```

and the weight is computed in the statement

```
weight = gamma * volume;
```

The program prints out the volume and weight with identifying information using the statements:

```
printf("\n The volume of the hollow cylinder is: %f", vol-
ume);
printf("\n The weight of the hollow cylinder is:  %f" ,
    weight);
```

Testing

For $h = 10$, $r = 10$, $t = 1$, and $\gamma = 4.5$ we obtain the following values of V and W:
$V = \pi(10 - 1)2(20) = 5089.38$
$W = 4.5(5089.38) = 22902.20$
The output from the program using these values is shown in Figure 4.5. You should rerun the program using other values to see if the results appear reasonable.

4.6   CHARACTERS

The data type **char** is used to represent single characters such as uppercase and lowercase letters, digits, punctuation marks and nonprinting control characters. A character is stored in one byte. On most C implementations the default is to make **char** a signed type, which means that it can hold values in the range −128 through +127.

A constant of type **char** is written by enclosing the character in single quotes. Examples of characters constants are

'a'   'b'   '*'   '2'   '#'   '%'

```
/**********************************************************/
/*  cylwt.  -- Weight of Hollow Cylinder                  */
/*                                                        */
/*  Computes the weight of a hollow cylinder.             */
/**********************************************************/
#include <stdio.h>
#define PI 3.141592654

main()
{
  double h,r;              /* height, outer radius    */
  double t, gamma;         /* thickness and density   */
  double volume, weight;   /* volume and weight       */

  /* input */
  printf("\n Weight of a Hollow Cylinder \n");
  printf("\n Enter height of hollow cylinder, h: ");
  scanf("%lf",&h);
  printf(" Enter outer radius, r: ");
  scanf("%lf",&r);
  printf(" Enter wall thickness, t: ");
  scanf("%lf",&t);
  printf(" Enter density, gamma: ");
  scanf("%lf",&gamma);

  /* compute volume and weight */
  volume = PI * (r -t) * (r - t) * h;
  weight = gamma * volume;

  /* print results */
  printf("\n Volume of hollow cylinder = %f", volume);
  printf("\n Weight of hollow cylinder = %f", weight);
}
```

Sample input and output

```
Weight of a Hollow Cylinder

Enter height of hollow cylinder, h: 20
Enter outer radius, r: 10.
Enter wall thickness, t: 1.
Enter density, gamma: 4.5

Volume of hollow cylinder = 5089.380099
Weight of hollow cylinder = 22902.210448
```

Figure 4.6   A program to compute the weight of a hollow cylinder.

It is important to note the difference between a character constant and a character string. A character string is an array of characters. Character strings are enclosed in double quotation marks and contain one or more characters. Examples of character strings are

```
"This is a character string"
"This is another character string"
"abcd"
"a"
```

In C, `'a'` and `"a"` are not the same; `'a'` is a character constant, while `"a"` is a character string.

A character is actually stored internally as an integer. The character is converted to an integer before it is stored and is converted back to a character when it is printed. The conversion from characters to numbers is performed in accordance with either the ASCII code or the EBCDIC code. Most microcomputer systems use the ASCII code, which stands for American Standard Code for Information Interchange. Each character is assigned a numeric value called the ASCII code; for example, the ASCII code for the capital letter "A" is 65, the ASCII code for the letter "B" is 66, and the ASCII code for a lowercase "a" is 97. Punctuation marks and other symbols are also assigned ASCII codes. For example, the ASCII code for a semicolon (;) is 59 and for a period (.) is 46.

In the standard ASCII code, characters are assigned values in the range of 0 to 127. Many personal computers use an extended character set which have ASCII codes in the range 0 to 255. The first half of the extended ASCII code, that is, 0 to 127, is the same as the regular ASCII code. The ASCII codes from 128 to 255 are used to represent special characters, Greek symbols, technical symbols such as the square root sign, and graphics characters. We will be using the ASCII code throughout this text. Appendix B lists the ASCII codes for the various characters.

The code segment that follows creates two character variables **ch1** and **ch2**. It assigns the value `'a'` to **ch1** and `'A'` to **ch2**. The program then prints the values of **ch1** and **ch2** using the **%c** format specifier in the **printf()** statement

```
#include <stdio.h>

main()
{
    char ch1, ch2;  /* declare variables of type char */

    /* assign values */
    ch1 = 'a';
    ch2 = 'A';

    /* print these values using %c format specifier */
    printf("\n ch1 = %c ", ch1);
    printf("\n ch2 = %c", ch2);
}
```

Operations on Characters

Since the data type **char** is treated internally as a type of integer, it is possible to assign integer values to characters, provided that the value is smaller than the maximum value for type **char**. For example, the statement

```
char grade = 66;
```

assigns the integer value 66 to the character variable **grade**. Since the character corresponding to the ASCII value 66 is the letter C, this is equivalent to assigning the character constant 'C' to the variable **grade**.

It is also possible to perform arithmetic operations on character variables. The assignment statements is the following program segment are perfectly legal.

```
char ch1, ch2, ch3;
ch1 = 'A';
ch2 = ch1 + 32;
ch3 = 'A' + 'B'- 50;
```

The first assignment statement assigns the character constant **'A'** to the variable **ch1**. The second statement adds 32 to the current value of **ch1**. Since the ASCII code for a lowercase character can be obtained by adding 32 to the ASCII code for the corresponding uppercase character, this statement results in the value **'a'** being assigned to **ch2**. The third assignment statement results in the value 65 + 66 − 50 = 81 being assigned to the variable **ch3**. The ASCII code for the letter 'Q' is 81, so the result is that **ch3** is assigned the character constant **'Q'**.

Example 4.4   Uppercase to Lowercase

PROBLEM STATEMENT: Write a program to read in an uppercase character and convert it to lowercase.

SOLUTION: The program is shown in Figure 4.6. The declaration statement

```
char uc, lc;        /* uppercase and lowercase */
```

creates two variables, **uc** and **lc**, of type **char**. The program reads in a value for **uc** using the following **scanf()** statement.

```
scanf("%c", &uc);
```

The statement

```
lc = uc + 32;
```

adds 32 to **uc** to obtain the corresponding lowercase character. The program then prints the uppercase and lowercase character and their ASCII codes.

```
/**********************************************************/
/*    uprtolwr.c  -- Uppercase to Lowercase               */
/*                                                        */
/*    Reads an uppercase character and converts it to     */
/*    lowercase.                                           */
/**********************************************************/

#include <stdio.h>

main()
{
char lc,uc; /* uppercase and lowercase character */

/* read in uppercase character */
printf("Enter an uppercase character ");
scanf("%c", &uc);

/* convert to lowercase */
lc = uc + 32;

/* print results */
printf("\n The uppercase character is %c ", uc);
printf("\n Its ASCII code is %d ", uc);
printf("\n The lowercase character is %c ",lc);
printf("\n Its ASCII code is %d ", lc);
}
```

Sample output

```
Enter an uppercase character F

The uppercase character is F
Its ASCII code is 70
The lowercase character is f
Its ASCII code is 102
```

Figure 4.7   A program to read in an uppercase character and convert it to lowercase.

Type unsigned char

On most C implementations the data type **char** is a signed type, which means that it can hold values in the range of -128 through 127. Many C compilers allow an **unsigned char** type that provides values in the range of 0 through 255. The **unsigned char** type is useful for representing characters on systems that use the extended ASCII codes. An example of the declaration for the **unsigned char** type is

```
unsigned char ch1, ch2;
```

This statement creates two **unsigned char** variables, **ch1** and **ch2**.

4.7   THE `sizeof` OPERATOR

C has a built-in operator called the `sizeof` operator that returns the size of various data items in bytes. For example, the expression

```
sizeof(float)
```

will return the size of type `float`. The `sizeof` operator can be used to determine the size of the basic data types, such as `char`, `int`, `float`, and `double`, as well as the size of the derived data types, such as arrays and strings. The `sizeof` operator can also be used with a specific data object, such as the name of a variable or a constant. For example, the statements

```
int count;
printf("The size of count in bytes is %d", sizeof(count));
```

print the size of the variable `count`.

Example 4.5   The `sizeof` Operator

PROBLEM STATEMENT: Write a program that uses the uses the `sizeof` operator to print the size in bytes of the basic data types, `char`, `int`, `long int`, `float`, and `double`.

SOLUTION: The program is shown in Figure 4.7. For our system a character requires 1 byte of storage, an integer 2 bytes, long integers and float point values 4 bytes, and double-precision values 8 bytes of storage. Note that the results given by the program will be different for your system since the amount of storage allocated for the various data types is hardware dependent.

4.8   USING THE DIFFERENT DATA TYPES

The reason for having different data types is that each type has specific uses in our programs. The character data types are used for manipulating character data. The three numeric data types `int`, `float`, and `double` provide considerable flexibility and, if used appropriately, can make our programs more efficient. The three numeric data types are stored differently inside the computer. Integers require the least space in memory, double-precision numbers require the most space in memory, and single-precision numbers fall in between. Computations involving integers result in faster execution than do computations involving single- and double-precision numbers. However, integers can store only whole numbers and the range of values that can be stored in an variable of type `int` is limited. Also,

```
/*****************************************************************/
/*   sizeof.c  -- Size of Data Types                             */
/*                                                               */
/*   Prints the size in bytes of the various C data types.       */
/*****************************************************************/

#include <stdio.h>

main()
{
  printf("\n The size of data type char is %d byte",
         sizeof(char));
  printf("\n The size of data type int is %d bytes",
         sizeof(int));
  printf("\n The size of data type long int is %d bytes",
         sizeof(long int));
  printf("\n The size of data type float is %d bytes",
         sizeof(float));
  printf("\n The size of data type double is %d bytes",
         sizeof(double));
}
```

Program output

```
The size of data type char is 1 byte
The size of data type int is 2 bytes
The size of data type long int is 4 bytes
The size of data type float is 4 bytes
The size of data type double is 8 bytes
```

Figure 4.8   Program to print the size of the basic C data types.

operations with integers are always precise, whereas there may be some loss of accuracy when performing computations with floating point values.

The differences in the various data types result from the way in which they are represented internally in memory. All data is represented as binary strings, that is, as strings of zeros and ones. The exact representation of the different data types is machine dependent. Figure 4.8 shows how variables of type **int**, **long**, **float**, and **double** are stored on our system. On our system, the **int** type requires 2 bytes, both the **long** and **float** types require 4 bytes, while doubles require 8 bytes of storage. For all the signed data types 1 bit is reserved for the sign.

Floating point numbers are stored in two parts: the mantissa, which stores the decimal portion of the value, and the exponent. The exponent is a power of 2, and the mantissa and exponent are chosen so that the following relation is satisfied

$$\text{number} = \text{mantissa} \cdot 2^{\text{exponent}}$$

The number of data bits allocated to the exponent determines the range of values

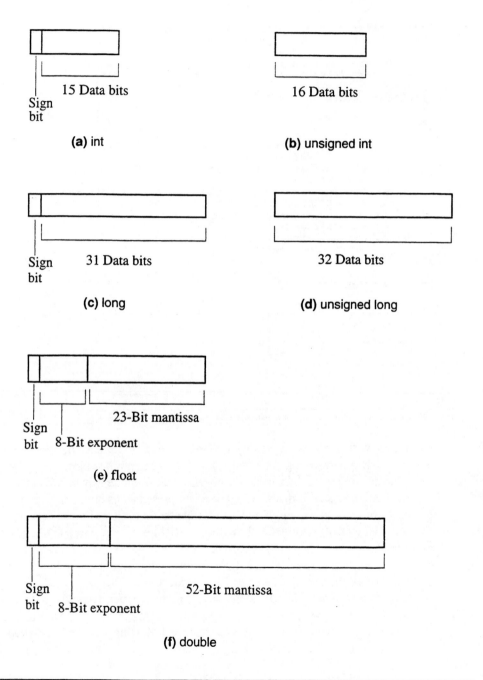

Figure 4.9 Representation of numeric data types in memory.

that can be stored, while the number of data bits in the mantissa affects the accuracy or precision of the values. Table 4.4 lists the various types of numeric data and the minimum and maximum values for each type for our system.

Table 4.4: Storage requirements and range for numeric data types.

Data Type	Size (in bytes)	Range
char	1	$-127 - 128$
unsigned char	1	$0 - 255$
short int	2	$-32,768 - 32,767$
int	2	$-32,768 - 32,767$
unsigned int	2	$0 - 65,535$
long int	4	$-2,147,483,648 - 2,147,483,647$
unsigned long int	4	0 š 4,294,967,265
float	4	3.4e-38 – 3.4e+38
double	8	1.7e-308 – 1.7e+308

Integers are typically used as counters in loops and to represent data that are whole numbers. In most other instances we use type **float** or type **double**. Values of type **double** require more memory storage. Computations with type **double** are slower than computations with type **float**. The advantage of using double-precision numbers lies in the wide range of numbers that can be stored and the high degree of precision they provide. There are many engineering applications where a high degree of precision is essential for obtaining reliable results. Examples of such applications include matrix inversion and solution of simultaneous equations containing a large number of unknowns. For such applications it becomes necessary to sacrifice speed for higher accuracy.

4.9   INACCURACIES IN FLOATING POINT COMPUTATIONS

In the previous section we described the internal representation of the various data types. As shown in Figure 4.9, floating point numbers are stored as binary strings and consist of three parts, a sign bit, a mantissa, and an exponent. The three floating point data types, **float**, **double**, and **long double**, differ in the number of data bits allocated for the mantissa and the exponent. The number of data bits allocated to the exponent determines the range of values that can be stored, while the number of data bits in the mantissa affects the precision of the values. Since variables of type **double** have a larger number of data bits for both the mantissa and exponent, they are capable of storing a larger range of values with greater precision.

One of the problems in working with floating point numbers is that most floating point numbers cannot be stored exactly. Just as there are certain numbers that cannot be represented exactly in the decimal number system (for example, the value 1/3 is 0.33333333...), so there are numbers that cannot be represented exactly in a computer. In fact, many decimal fractions (such as, for example, 0.2 and 0.1) cannot be represented exactly in the internal binary format used for floating point numbers. The magnitude of the error depends on the number of bits used for the mantissa. Since more bits are used for the mantissa for type **double** than for type **float**, the error for type **double** is less than that for type **float**.

Since computers retain only a fixed number of significant digits, almost all computations with floating point numbers can introduce errors. These errors are called *round-off* errors. Although round-off errors are quite small, the effect of round-off errors can become magnified through repeated computations. If the calculation is done only once, the error is usually not substantial. However, if we perform the calculation repeatedly, the error grows with each step. When developing algorithms, we must always be aware of the possibility of propagation of round-off errors, especially since it is not unusual to perform thousands of computations in a program.

4.10   OVERFLOW AND UNDERFLOW

Overflow and underflow occur when the value of a variable exceeds the maximum or minimum value that can be stored in the variable. This usually happens when the result obtained when evaluating an arithmetic expression exceeds the limits for the variable. For example, suppose that we execute the following statements

```
float a = 1.0e+20;
float b = 2.0e+30;
float c;
c = a * b;
```

On our system, the range of values for variables of type **float** is **3.4e-38** to **3.4e+38**, and the values assigned to **a** and **b** are within this range. The result of the multiplication **a * b** is **1.0e+50**. This result is larger than the maximum value that can be stored in a variable of type **float** on our system. When the last statement is executed on our system, the program terminates and the following message is displayed:

```
Floating point error: Overflow
Abnormal termination
```

You should note that the compiler will not give an error message when the program containing these statements is compiled, since all four statements are valid C statements and do not contain syntax errors. The error message appears when the program is executed.

An underflow occurs when the result of an arithmetic operation is smaller than the minimum value that can be stored in a variable. Consider the following statements

```
float a, b, c;
a = 1.0e-30;
b = 2.0e+20;
c = a / b;
```

The result of the division is **5.0e-51**, which is smaller than the minimum value that can be stored in a variable of type **float** on our system. However, in this case no error message is displayed. Instead, the result is set equal to zero, and so the variable **c** will be assigned the value 0. Since different systems handle underflow and overflow differently, you should check out the rules for your system.

If you get an overflow or underflow during program execution, you need to check the magnitude of the values you are using in your program. Some of the more common reasons for overflow and underflow are the following:

1. Variables that have not been initialized
2. Variables that have been initialized to an incorrect value
3. A wrong arithmetic operation is specified
4. A denominator having a zero value is used during a division

Overflow and underflow can also result when a program that worked correctly on one system is run on another system. Since the range of values for the various data types is different for different systems, a program that executes correctly one system may not work on another system if the range of values for a variable of the same type on the new system is smaller. Overflow and underflow usually occur when you are working with very small or very large numbers. In many cases you may be able to run your program on another system by switching to a data type that has a wider range, for example, from a **float** to a **double** or a **long double**.

You can test for overflow and underflow by using the constants in the header files *limits.h*, which defines the minimum and maximum values for the integer data types, and *float.h*, which defines the minimum and maximum values and precision for the floating point data types. For example, the constants **FLT_MAX** and **FLT_MIN** defined in the header file *float.h* represent the largest and smallest number that can be represented by a variable of type **float**. Since variables of type **double** have a wider range, we can use a **double** for temporary storage and test the magnitude of the **double** before assigning it to a variable of type **float**.

Other problems occur when manipulating very large and very small numbers.

When a large number and a small number are added, the larger number may cancel out the smaller number. For example, if **a** is much larger than **b**, **a+b** and **a** may have the same value. For example, if **a** = 1000.0 and **b** = 0.0000001234, the result **a+b** may be equal to 1000.0 on some computers. If the difference in magnitude between the two numbers to be added is larger than the precision of the floating point representation of that type of value, then the smaller number is in effect treated as zero. Similar problems can occur when subtracting two numbers of different magnitude. The constants **FLT_EPSILON** and **DBL_EPSILON** defined in the header file *float.h* contain the value of the machine precision for types **float** and **double**, respectively.

Example 4.6   Integer Overflow and Underflow

The program shown in Figure 4.9 illustrates what happens on our system when we exceed the limits of an integer variable. The program creates two variables **too_small** and **too_big** of type **int** with the declaration statement

```
int too_small,too_big;
```

The statement

```
too_big = INT_MAX + 2;
```

adds 2 to the maximum value for an integer and assigns the result to the variable **too_big**. The constant **INT_MAX** represents the maximum value that can be stored in type **int**. It is defined in the file *limits.h*. The program includes this file with the preprocessor directive

```
#include <limits.h>
```

The statement

```
too_small = INT_MIN + 2;
```

subtracts 2 from the minimum value for an integer and assigns the result to the variable **too_small**. The constant **INT_MIN** represents the minimum value that can be stored in a variable of type **int**. It is also defined in the file *limits.h*.

The output from the program is also shown in Figure 4.9. Note that on our system when the range of a positive value is exceeded, the result is a negative value. When the range of a negative value is exceeded, the result is a positive value. However, the compiler does not give any indication that an error has occurred.

```
/***************************************************************/
/*    overflow.c - Integer Overflow and Underflow             */
/*                                                             */
/*    Illustrates integer overflow and underflow.             */
/***************************************************************/
#include <stdio.h>

#include <limits.h>

main()
{
    int too_small,too_big;

    too_big  = MAX_INT + 2;
    too_small = MIN_INT - 2;

    printf("too_small = %d \n", too_small);
    printf("too_big = %d", too_big);
}
```

Program output

```
too_small = 32766
too_big = -32767
```

Figure 4.10   Integer overflow and underflow.

4.11   PROGRAMMING PROJECT: SOLUTION OF SIMULTANEOUS EQUATIONS

Problem Statement

Write a program to compute x and y for the linear system of equations:

$$a_1 x + b_1 y = c_1$$
$$a_2 x + b_2 y = c_2$$

Problem Analysis

The solutions for x and y are given by

$$x = \frac{b_2 c_1 - b_1 c_2}{a_1 b_2 - a_2 b_1}$$

(4.1)

$$y = \frac{a_1 c_2 - a_2 c_1}{a_1 b_2 - a_2 b_1}$$

(4.2)

It is assumed that the denominator $a_1 b_2 - a_2 b_1$ is not zero. If the denominator were zero, a division-by-zero error would occur resulting in an overflow. A complete program would check to see that the denominator is not zero.

Input Variables

coefficients a_1, b_1, c_1, a_2, b_2, c_2 (`float a1,b1,c1,a2,b2,c2`) .

Output Variables

the computed values of x and y (`float x, y`)

Algorithm

1. Read **a1**, **b1**, and **b2**.
2. Read **a2**, **b2**, **c2**.
3. Compute **x**.
4. Compute **y**.
5. Print **x** and **y**.

Program

The program is shown in Figure 4.10. The declaration statement

```
float a1,b1,c1,a2,b2,c2;
```

declares floating point variables for storing the coefficients of the simultaneous equations. The declaration statement

```
float x, y;
```

declares two floating point variables **x** and **y** to hold the results of the computation.

The first `scanf()` statement reads in the values for **a1**, **b1**, and **c1**, and the second `scanf()` statement reads in the values for **a2**, **b2**, and **c2**. Each `scanf()` statement is preceded by a `printf()` statement that prints a prompt message to indicate the order of variable input.

The value of x is computed and assigned to the variable **x** in the following assignment statement

```
x = (b2 * c1 - b1 * c2)/(a1 * b2 - a2 * b1);
```

and the value of y is computed in the statement

```
y = (a1 * c2 - a2 * c1)/(a1 * b2 - a2 * b1);
```

```c
/*************************************************************/
/*    simulteq.c -- Solution of Simultaneous Equations       */
/*                                                           */
/*    Computes x and y for the linear system of equations    */
/*                      a1x + b1y = c1                        */
/*                      a2x + b2y = c2                        */
/*************************************************************/
#include <stdio.h>

main()
{
    float a1,b1,c1,a2,b2,c2;
    float x,y;

    /* read input data */
    printf("\n \t SOLUTION OF SIMULTANEOUS EQUATIONS\n");
    printf("\n Enter a1, b1 and c1: ");
    scanf("%f %f %f", &a1, &b1, &c1);
    printf(" Enter a2, b2 and c2: ");
    scanf("%f %f %f", &a2, &b2, &c2);

    /* compute x and y */
    x = (b2 * c1 - b1 * c2)/(a1 * b2 - a2 * b1);
    y = (a1 * c2 - a2 * c1)/(a1 * b2 - a2*b1);

    /*  print results */
    printf("\n\nINPUT DATA");
    printf("\n a1 = %f    b1 = %f   c1 = %f", a1, b1, c1);
    printf("\n a2 = %f    b2 = %f   c2 = %f", a2, b2, c2);
    printf("\n\n   The solution is: ");
    printf("\n x = %f", x);
    printf("\n y = %f", y);
}
```

Program output

```
SOLUTION OF SIMULTANEOUS EQUATIONS

 Enter a1, b1 and c1: 1. 2. 3.
 Enter a2, b2 and c2: 4. 5. 6.


INPUT DATA
 a1 = 1.000000    b1 = 2.000000    c1 = 3.000000
 a2 = 4.000000    b2 = 5.000000    c2 = 6.000000

  The solution is:
 x = -1.000000
 y = 2.000000
```

Figure 4.11   Program for the solution of simultaneous equations.

Notice that the numerator and denominator of each of the preceding expressions is enclosed in parentheses to ensure that the compiler evaluates the expressions in the correct order. It should be noted that a division by zero error will result if the denominator `a1*b2-a2*b1` is zero. The program does not check for this condition. A complete program would need to do so.

The program prints the input data and the computed value of `x` and `y`.

Testing

For $a_1 = 1$, $b_1 = 2$, $c_1 = 3$ and $a_2 = 4$, $b_2 = 5$, $c_2 = 6$ we get the following values for x and y:

$$x = \frac{(5)(3) - (2)(6)}{(1)(5) - (4)(2)} = \frac{15 - 12}{5 - 8} = -1$$

$$y = \frac{(1)(6) - (4)(3)}{(1)(5) - (4)(2)} = \frac{6 - 12}{5 - 8} = 2$$

The program output for the input data given is shown in Figure 4.10. You should run the program using other input values.

4.12 SUMMARY

In this chapter we introduced the concepts of variables and constants. Variables represent storage locations in memory that have been assigned a name. The value of a variable can change during program execution. The value of a constant remains the same throughout the program. The fundamental data types that are available in C are `int`, `float`, `double`, and `char`. The data type `int` is used for storing integer numbers, while the data types `float`, and `double` are used for floating point numbers. The data type `char` provides storage for character data.

The C programming language also has several modifiers such as `short`, `long`, `signed`, and `unsigned`. The modifiers `short` and `long` are applied to integers. Variables of `type long int` are used to store integer values that require a larger range than type `int`. The modifier `long` is also applied to type `double`. The modifiers `signed` and `unsigned` are applied to character and integer types. Variables declared with the `unsigned` modifier can only have positive values.

The ANSI C standard does not impose specific limits on the range of values that can be stored in the various integer types. Implementation specific details are given in a file called *limits.h* that must be provided with each implementation. Also, the precise number of digits and the range of the real numbers of type `float` and type `double` depends on the implementation. The header file *float.h* contains definitions of several constants that define these characteristics for each implementation.

The three numeric data types `int`, `float`, and `double` are stored differently in memory. Integers require the least amount of memory storage, double-precision numbers require the most amount of storage, and single-precision numbers fall in between. Operations involving integers result in faster execution than do operations involving floating point numbers. Also, operations with integers are always precise, whereas there may be some loss of accuracy when performing operations with floating point numbers. Since computers retain only a fixed number of significant digits almost all computations with floating point numbers can introduce round-off errors. Also, overflow and underflow can occur when the value of the variable exceeds the maximum or minimum value that can be stored in the variable. Such problems usually occur when working with very large or very small numbers.

Key Terms Presented in This Chapter

constants	**long** type modifier
char data type	overflow
double data type	scientific notation
exponential notation	**short** type modifier
fixed point notation	**unsigned** type modifier
float data type	**sizeof** operator
float.h header file	underflow
int data type	**unsigned** type modifier
limits.h header file	variables

PROGRAM STYLE, COMMON ERRORS, AND DEBUGGING GUIDE

1. You should write your programs so that they are general and solve a class of problems rather than a specific problem.
2. You should be careful in the selection of the data types you use for storing values. Integers should be used only for storing whole numbers and as counters in loops. Single-precision variables are appropriate for routine computations where a high degree of accuracy is not needed. For most engineering applications you should use double precision variables, especially in situations where many computations are being performed and a high degree is accuracy is needed.

3. The header file *float.h* contains useful information regarding the range and precision of the various floating point variables available on your system. You should be familiar with the information contained in this file.

4. Is is better to use symbolic constants in your programs rather than ordinary constants. For example, the following is preferable

    ```
    #define TAX_RATE 0.15
    tax = TAX_RATE * income;
    ```

    to the statement

    ```
    tax = 0.15 * income;
    ```

    If the tax rate changes, it is easier to change the value of the symbolic constant **TAX_RATE** than to search through the entire program and change every occurrence of the constant 0.15.

5. We suggest that you use a lowercase letter for the first character of a variable name and an uppercase letter for the first character of a function name. This will help in distinguishing between variable names and function names.

6. You should echo print the input data that was provided by the program user. This helps to verify that the right information was entered during program execution.

7. You should label all output produced by your program. For example,

    ```
    Volume of hollow cylinder = 5089.38
    Weight of hollow cylinder = 22902.21
    ```

8. Only the characters A – Z, a – z, 0 – 9 and the underscore character (_) can be used for forming variable names. All other characters are illegal. Also, variable names should not match keywords.

9. A common error is to misspell variable names or keywords. If you misspell a variable or keyword, for example, **floot** instead of **float**, the compiler will give an error message indicating that the variable has not been defined.

10. Another common error is not distinguishing between uppercase and lowercase letters. In C, the variables **count** and **Count** are not the same.

11. The value assigned to a variable should be of a type that is appropriate to the type of the variable; otherwise, there can be a loss of precision. For example, if you assign a floating point number to an integer variable, the decimal portion of the number will be lost. Most — but not all — compilers will give a warning message if there is the

possibility of a loss of precision.

12. Variables must be assigned a value before they are used in any computations. A common source of errors in a program is using uninitialized variables. For example, the statement

```
z = x * y;
```

will yield an incorrect result for **z** if either **x** or **y** have not been assigned a value. Errors of this sort are difficult to detect since the compiler will not give an error message if an uninitialized variable is used. If a program gives incorrect computational results, you should check for variables that have not been initialized or have been initialized to an incorrect value.

13. You cannot place commas within large numbers. For example, you cannot write 58000 as 58,000. Also, you should not use the plus sign in front of positive numbers as in +580

The plus sign is used in C for representing addition.

14. You should note the difference between a character variable and a character string. A character variable can store only a single character, whereas a character string is an array of characters. In C, a character constant is enclosed in single quotes while character strings are enclosed in double quotes. Thus, **'a'** is a character constant, whereas **"a"** is a character string.

15. To assign a character constant to a variable of type **char**, you should enclose the character between single quotation marks. For example,

```
char ch;
ch = 'a';
```

and not

```
ch = a;    /* wrong! */
```

16. Except for escape sequences such as **'\t'** and **'\n'** only one symbol can be placed between the single quotes. The following is incorrect

```
char ch;
ch = 'ac';
```

17. Computations with floating point numbers involve inaccuracies. The error is usually small but can be magnified depending on the type and number of computations being performed.

18. You should be aware of the possibility of overflow or underflow whenever you are working with very small or very large numbers. Also, loss of precision can occur when adding or subtracting two numbers that

have very different orders of magnitude.

19. You may get an overflow or underflow error in a program that was working on one system when you run in on another system because of differences in hardware. You may be able to correct this by using a data type that has a larger range on the new system, such as **long double** instead of **double**.

EXERCISES

Review Questions

1. Write each of the following numbers in exponential form

    a. 123.456   b. 200000.55

    c. 0.0001568   d. 134.8×10^{10}

    e. 3000.44×10^{-7} f. 0.00000056

    g. 0.1234567   h. 0.00003367

    i. 2012.68×10^{-20} j. 10000.577

    k. 123.456   l. 15.567×10^{30}

2. Write each of the following numbers in fixed point format (that is, without an exponent):

    a. 1.0e-2   b. 0.01e2

    c. 0.0001e5   d. -5.675e4

    e. 1000e-4   f. 17.56e0

    g. 1.0e-4   h. 0.0001e-3

    i. -100.543e-1   j. 12.345e7

3. Some of the following are unacceptable as integer constants. Identify the errors.

    a. 123.4   b. -65.012

    c. -33500   d. -32300

    e. 13,456   f. 34200

    g. 100e5   h. -10e4

    i. 5000   j. 41500

4. Identify the data type for each of the following constants and give the **printf()** format specifier for printing these constants.

    a. 155   b. 4.5e-07

    c. 'c'   d. 24156L

    e. 0x7   f. 0x2

    g. 0x35   h. 12.8976

5. Some of the following numbers are unacceptable as floating point constants. Identify

them and state why they are unacceptable.

a.	520.5e-10	**b.**	86,541.1
c.	5.6e+42	**d.**	420.2e4
e.	355.68	**f.**	2.5e-3.2
g.	15.44e2.4	**h.**	0.0012345
i.	1.5688e-5	**j.**	-4.5e-10
k.	-0.005856	**l.**	5.6e+30

6. Distinguish between the notions of a constant and a variable in C.

7. What are the restrictions in naming variables?

8. How long can a variable name be on your system?

9. The following list contains both valid and invalid variable names. Explain why the invalid names are unacceptable.

a.	`mean_value`	**b.**	`sum_of.squares`
c.	`counter`	**d.**	`amount$`
e.	`x_next_step`	**f.**	`3y_max`
g.	`xount#`	**h.**	`max.grade`
i.	`max.Grade`	**j.**	`dollar$`
k.	`a_max_value`	**l.**	`flPoint`
m.	`_minvalue`	**n.**	`num-max`
o.	`tmpFc1`	**p.**	`altKey`

10. What is meant by the type of a variable?

11. Name the different integer data types available in C.

12. Name the different floating point data types available in C.

13. What are the advantages of data type **int** over data type **float**?

14. What are the minimum and maximum values for the integer types on your system? You can determine these by studying the file *limits.h*.

15. Using the information provided in the *float.h* header file provided with your compiler determine the following:

    a. Number of digits of precision for the types **float** and **double**

    b. Smallest machine precision for **float** and **double**

    c. Maximum value of **float** and **double**

    d. Minimum value for **float** and **double**

16. What data type would you use to represent the following items:

    a. Number of days between two dates

    b. The letter grade on an exam

    c. The average grade on an exam

    d.   The distance in miles from the earth to the moon

    e.   The number of students in a class

17. List the following characters in sequence according to their ASCII code:
      b, A, 0, 6, space

18. Write type declaration statements to declare

    a.   **count, score,** and **total** to be of type **int**

    b.   **pressure, temp,** and **volume** to be of type **float**

    c.   **big_num, epsilon** and **delta** to be of type **double**

    d.   **flag, first,** and **letter** to be of type **char**

    e.   **big_int,** and **large_num** to be of type **long int**

    f.   **abs_val,** and **max_value** to be of type **unsigned int.**

19. What is meant by round-off? What is the cause of round-off errors?

20. Briefly define the following terms

    a.   Overflow

    b.   Underflow

Programming Exercises

21. Write a program to convert a measurement in inches to centimeters and meters.

22. Write a program to read three data items a, b, and c and find and print the sum, product, and average.

23. Write a program to convert the weight of an object in pounds to kilograms. One pound is equal to 0.453592 kilograms.

24. Write a program that reads in a decimal value and outputs the equivalent value in hexadecimal and octal.

25. Write a program to calculate the weight, W of a thick-walled hollow sphere of outer diameter, D, wall thickness, t, and density, γ, using the following equations:

$$W = \gamma V$$

$$V = \frac{1}{3}\pi(R_0^3 - R_1^3)$$

$$R_0 = \frac{D}{2}$$

$$R_1 = \frac{D}{2} - t$$

5

ARITHMETIC OPERATIONS

One of the main functions of a computer is to perform arithmetic computations. In this chapter we present the C statements for performing arithmetic operations such as addition, subtraction, multiplication, and division. We describe the arithmetic assignment statement which is used to assign values to variables and present the operators that are used in arithmetic expressions such as the arithmetic operators, the assignment operators, and the increment and decrement operators. We also discuss the rules for using these operators and describe the order in which expressions are evaluated. One of the reasons why C is such a powerful and flexible language is that C has a large number of basic operators. There are over 40 operators in C.

In addition to the basic arithmetic operations, engineers also need to perform other routine operations, such as raising a number to a power, taking the square root or logarithm of a number and computing the sine or cosine of an angle. This chapter also presents the mathematical functions that are available in the C library for performing these types of operations.

5.1   OPERATORS

An *operator* is a symbol or word that represents some operation that is performed on one or more data values. The data values are called *operands* and can be either variables or constants. For example, the addition operator, which is represented by the plus (**+**) sign, adds two numbers. The numbers to be added are the operands.

Operators can be classified according to the type of operation that they perform. Operators that are used in arithmetic operations, such as addition and subtraction, are called *arithmetic operators*, while operators that are used for comparing two values such as the equal (**==**) and the greater than (**>**) operators are called *relational operators*. There are six types of operators in C. These are arithmetic, assignment, relational, logical, bitwise, and special operators. Operators can also be classified by the number of operands they require. Thus, a unary operator is one that requires one operand, a binary operator is one that requires two operands, and a ternary operator is one that requires three operands.

5.2   ASSIGNMENT STATEMENTS

The assignment statement is the primary means of assigning values to variables and for performing computations. The general form of the assignment statement is

> *variable = arithmetic expression;*

The way we read this statement is "assign the numerical value obtained from the expression on the right to the variable on the left."

The simplest form of assignment statement consists of the equal (**=**) symbol with a variable on the left and a constant on the right

> *variable = constant;*

For example, consider the statement

```
x = 5;
```

This statement could be read "*x* is assigned the value 5." The symbol = in the assignment statement is called the assignment operator and should be interpreted as "is assigned the value of" rather than as "equals". The use of the equal symbol for assignment sometimes creates confusion, since it implies that an equation is to be solved, which is really not the case. To avoid this confusion some computer languages use a different symbol than the equal sign. For example, in Pascal the symbol := is used for assignment.

It is important to recognize that the assignment operation represents a transfer of data from the expression on the right-hand side of the equal symbol to the variable on the left-hand side. The name of the variable receiving the value must always be on the left-hand side. It is also important to recognize that a variable can store only one value at a time. For example, suppose the following statements were executed one after another:

```
x = 20.3;
x = 30.5;
```

When the first statement is executed, the value 20.3 is stored in the memory location indicated by the variable **x**. When the second statement is executed, the new value 30.5 is stored in the memory location indicated by **x**, and the previous value is lost. Consider the statements

```
x = 50.0;
y = x;
```

In the first statement, **x** is assigned the value 50.0. When the second statement is executed, the value stored in the variable **x** is retrieved, and this value is assigned to the variable **y**. Thus **x** and **y** now have the same value 50.0. Note that the value of **x** is not lost when the second statement is executed since **x** is on the right-hand side of the assignment operator. The values stored in the memory locations represented by **x** and **y** after each statement has been executed are shown next. The question mark represents a variable that has not been assigned a value.

Statement	Contents of Variable	
	x	**y**
x = 50;	50.0	?
y = x;	50.0	50.0

The expression on the right-hand side of the assignment operator can be a constant, a variable, or an arithmetic expression. An arithmetic expression is some combination of constants, variables, and arithmetic operators. It describes the relationship between the constants and variables and also defines the order in which the operations will be performed.

Some examples of assignment statements are

```
rate = 10.5;
root = mid;
area = 3.141593 * r * r * h;
x = sqrt(y);
```

In the first statement, the variable `rate` is assigned the constant value 10.5. In the second statement the value stored in the memory location `mid` is retrieved, and this value is assigned to the variable `root`. In the third statement, the expression on the right is a combination of constants, variables, and mathematical operations. The numerical value of the expression on the right is evaluated using the values of the variables `r` and `h`, and the result is assigned to the variable `area`.

Expressions may contain functions such as the functions available in the C library. In the fourth statement, the value of `y` is retrieved, and the square root of this value is obtained by calling the C library function `sqrt()`. The result is assigned to the variable `y`.

In C we can write a statement of the form

```
sum = sum + term;
```

In this statement the variable `sum` appears on both sides of the assignment operator. In algebra this statement is meaningless, but in C it has a very important function. The statement instructs the computer to retrieve the value stored at the memory location `sum`, add to it the value stored at the memory location `term`, and then store the result back in the memory location `sum`. The previous value of `sum` is lost in the process; however. the value of `term` is unchanged. The values of the variables before and after execution of the foregoing statement are now shown assuming the initial values are `sum` = 100 and `term` = 10.

	sum	term
Before execution	100	10
After execution	110	10

Consider the statement

```
x = -x;
```

Again, in algebra this statement makes no sense, but it is a perfectly valid C statement. The statement has the effect of changing the sign of the number. The value stored at memory location `x` is retrieved, this value is then multiplied by -1, and the result is stored in the memory location `x`.

The assignment operator is a binary operator and thus has two operands. The operand on the left must be a variable or an expression that names a memory location. The expression on the right must be such that it will yield a value when evaluated. In C the values that can legally appear on the left-hand side of the assignment statement are called *lvalues*. Examples of lvalues are variable names and arrays. Values that can appear only on the right-hand side are called *rvalues*.

Examples of rvalues are constants and arithmetic expressions. The statements

```
5 = x;          /* illegal     */
a + b = 3;      /* also illegal */
```

are not valid in C since the left-hand side does not name a memory location. In the first statement, the expression on the left-hand side is a constant and unchangeable. It is not possible to assign a value to a constant. In the second statement, the left-hand side is an arithmetic expression and does not represent a memory location. Most C compilers will issue a compiler error message of the form "name is not an lvalue" when the expression on the left side of an assignment statement does not name a memory location.

Multiple assignments can occur in one statement. For example, in the statement

```
x = y = z = 10;
```

x, y, and z are all assigned the value 10. Assignments are made one at a time from right to left. First z is assigned the constant value of 10, then y is assigned the value of z, and then x is assigned the value of y.

5.3   ARITHMETIC OPERATORS

C provides operators for performing arithmetic operations such as addition, subtraction, multiplication, and division. Each operator is represented by a unique symbol. The arithmetic operations that can be performed and the corresponding symbols used for denoting the operation are shown in Table 5.1.

Table 5.1: Arithmetic operators

Operator	Operation	Sample Expression
+	addition	x + y
-	subtraction	x - y
*	multiplication	x * y
/	division	x /y
-	unary minus	-x
%	remainder	x % y

The operators +, -, *, /, and % are binary operators, that is, they take two operands. The operators +, - and / have the same meaning to those used in algebra. The asterisk (*) is used to denote multiplication. The minus (-) symbol serves a dual purpose in C. As a binary operator it is used for subtraction. As a unary operator the minus symbol is used to negate a value; that is, it multiplies its single operand by -1.

The modulus operator is denoted by the symbol %. The modulus operator yields the remainder of an integer division. The increment and decrement operators are unary operators. The increment operator (++) adds 1 to its operand, and the decrement operator (--) subtracts 1 from its operand. We will discuss these operators in detail in the sections that follow.

Examples of expressions containing these operators are

```
x * y                    (a* b) / (x + y)
pi * r * r               delta + beta * x
6.0 + 5.0                5.0 * y - 6.0 * y
b * b - 4. * a * c       a * x + b * y + c
x + y - z;               x * y / z;
a % b;                   x % y - c;
```

The arithmetic operators are frequently encountered in expressions that appear on the right-hand side of arithmetic assignment statements. Examples of assignment statements containing arithmetic operators are given below:

```
x = a + b;
z = 2.5 + 4.0 * x;
a = 15 + 2 * 2 + 5 * y;
alpha = (b * c)/(d - delta);
range = x_max - x_min;
func = a * x * x + b * x + c;
```

Example 5.1   Arithmetic Operators

The program shown in Figure 5.1 prints the results obtained for some of the common arithmetic operations. The program declares two variables **x** and **y** of type float. The statements

```
x = 20.5;
y = 6.5;
```

assign the value 20.5 to **x** and 6.5 to **y**. The program then prints the result of the operations **x+y**, **x-y**, **x*y**, and **x/y** using a series of **printf()** statements. For example, the **printf()** statement

```
printf("\n   x + y = %f", x + y);
```

prints the result of the operation **x + y**. As you can see from the preceding statement, we can use an arithmetic expression such as **x + y** as an argument to the **printf()** statement in place of a variable name. The output from the program is also shown in Figure 5.1.

```
/*****************************************************************/
/*   arithopr.c -- Arithmetic Operators                          */
/*                                                               */
/*   Illustrates the various arithmetic operators in C           */
/*****************************************************************/
#include <stdio.h>

main()
{
   float x,y;

   x = 20.5;
   y = 6.5;

   /*  print */
   printf("\n Arithmetic Operators");
   printf("\n x = %f    y = %f", x, y);
   printf("\n Addition: x + y = %f",x + y);
   printf("\n Subtraction: x - y = %f", x-y);
   printf("\n Multiplication: x * y = %f", x * y);
   printf("\n Division: x / y = %f", x/y);
}
```

Program output

```
Arithmetic Operators
x = 20.500000    y = 6.500000
Addition: x + y = 27.000000
Subtraction: x - y = 14.000000
Multiplication: x * y = 133.250000
Division: x / y = 3.153846
```

Figure 5.1   Arithemtic operators.

Division with floating point numbers results in a floating point number. However, when the division operator ($/$) is used with integer values, the result is an integer, and any fractional portion of the result is discarded. For example, the result of the expression 9/5 will be 1. If both the numerator and the denominator are integers, then the division is done using integer arithmetic. Floating point arithmetic is used if either operand is a floating point number.

Example 5.2   Integer and Floating Point Division

The program shown in Figure 5.2 illustrates the difference between integer division and floating point division. The statement

```
printf("\n  11/4 = %d", 11/4);
```

prints the result of the integer division 11/4. In the expression 11/4 both operands are integers, so the division is performed using integer arithmetic. It is important to note that in integer division, the result is truncated rather than rounded, which means that all digits after the decimal are discarded. The result of the division 11/4 is 2.75. However, since all digits after the decimal are discarded, the final result is 2 and not 3. Similarly, the result of the division 3/4 is 0.

The statement

```
printf("\n  11./4. = %f", 11./4.);
```

prints the result of the division **11./4.** Since both operands in the expression **11./4.** are of type **float** the division is performed using floating point arithmetic, and the result is 2.75. Similarly, the result of the division **3./4.** yields the result 0.75, since both operands are of type **float**. The output from the program is also shown in Figure 5.2.

```
/*************************************************************/
/*    division.c - Integer and floating point division      */
/*                                                           */
/*    This program illustrates the difference between        */
/*    integer and floating point division,                   */
/*************************************************************/
#include <stdio.h>

main()
{
    printf("\n  Integer division ");
    printf("\n  11/4 = %d", 11/4);
    printf("\n  3/4 = %d", 3/4);
    printf("\n  Floating point division");
    printf("\n  11./4. = %f", 11./4.);
    printf("\n  3./4. = %f", 3./4.);
}
```

Program output

```
Integer division
11/4 = 2
3/4 = 0
Floating point division
11./4. = 2.750000
3./4. = 0.750000
```

Figure 5.2   Integer and floating point division.

The Modulus Operator

The modulus operator, which is symbolized by the percent (%) sign, gives the remainder of an integer division. Examples of expressions containing the modulus operator are

```
7 % 2    = 1
8 % 2    = 0
11 % 4   = 3
-11 % 4  = 3
5 % 9    = 5
```

The modulus operator can only be used on data types **char** and **int**. It cannot be used with operands of type **float** or **double**. (To obtain the remainder of a division with floating point or double-precision numbers, you can use the library function **fmod()**).

The modulus operator has several applications in C programs. A common use of the modulus operator is to control the flow of a program. For example, if we wanted to print every third number in a list, we could set up a loop, use the expression

```
count % 3
```

where **count** is an integer that is incremented by one each time through the loop, and print only the result if the expression is zero.The result of the expression will be zero whenever the variable **count** is a multiple of 3.

5.4 ARITHMETIC ASSIGNMENT OPERATORS

In addition to the arithmetic and assignment operators, C has compound arithmetic assignment operators which are a combination of an arithmetic operator and the assignment operator. For example, the statement

```
x = x + delta;
```

in which the value of **delta** is added to the value of **x** and the result assigned to **x** can be rewritten as

```
x += delta;
```

Here the plus-equals (**+=**) arithmetic assignment operator, which is a combination of the addition operator (**+**) and the assignment operator (**=**) is used and produces the same result.

All the arithmetic operators can be combined with the assignment operator. The general format of an arithmetic assignment statement is

$$variable\ opr = operand;$$

where *opr* is an arithmetic operator such as **+**, **-**, *****, **/**, or **%**. The arithmetic assignment operator first performs the operation specified by the arithmetic operator and then assigns the result of the calculation to the variable as its new value. Table 5.2 lists all the arithmetic assignment operators. Examples of statements containing arithmetic assignment operators and the equivalent assignment statements are given in Table 5.3.

Table 5.2: Arithmetic assignment operators

Operator	Meaning
+=	add operand to variable and assign result to variable
-=	subtract operand from variable and assign result to variable
*=	multiply variable by operand and assign result to variable
/=	divide variable by operand and assign result to variable
%=	divide variable by operand and assign remainder to variable

Table 5.3: Examples of arithmetic assignment statements

Arithmetic Assignment Statement	Equivalent Assignment Statement
`delta += 0.5;`	`delta = delta + 0.5;`
`new_val -= step_size;`	`new_val = new_val - step_size;`
`next_step *= 10;`	`next_step = next_step * 10;`
`zeta /= 100;`	`zeta = zeta/100;`
`a %=2;`	`a = a % 2`

Example 5.3   Arithmetic Assignment Operators

PROBLEM STATEMENT: Give the value of the variable on the left side of the assignment operator (=) in each of the following. The statements are not executed sequentially. Assume that `i`, and `j` are of type **int** and `a` and `b` are of type **float**. The initial values are `i` = **5**, `j` = **3**, `a` = **2.5**, and `b` = **3.5**

a.	`j += i;`	**b.**	`b *= a;`
c.	`i -= j;`	**d.**	`j /= i;`
e.	`a *= b;`	**f.**	`b /=a;`
g.	`i %= j;`	**h.**	`a -= b;`

SOLUTON: The values assigned to the variable on the left side are

a.	`j = 3 + 5 = 8`	b.	`b = 3.5 * 2.5 = 8.75`
c.	`i = 5 - 3 = 2`	d.	`j = 3/5 = 0`
e.	`a = 2.5 * 3.5 = 8.75`	f.	`b = 3.5/2.5 = 1.4`
g.	`i = 5 % 3 = 2`	h.	`a = 2.5 - 3.5 = -1.0`

5.5   INCREMENT AND DECREMENT OPERATORS

A common programming task consists of increasing or decreasing the value of a variable by 1. C has two operators, not usually found in other programming languages, to perform these tasks. They are the increment and decrement operators, ++ and --. The increment operator ++ adds one to its operand. For example, the statement

```
x++;
```

adds 1 to the value of **x** and is equivalent to

```
x = x + 1;
```

The decrement operator -- subtracts one from its operand. For example, the statement

```
y-- ;
```

subtracts 1 from **y** and is equivalent to

```
y = y - 1;
```

We can put the increment and decrement operators either before the variable as in

```
++x;
--y;
```

or after the variable as in

```
x++;
y--;
```

When the operators are placed before the variable, they are termed *prefix* operators, and when placed after the variable, they are termed *postfix* operators. In either case, the variable is incremented or decremented. However, there is one important difference between the prefix and postfix operators, and it has to do with when the operation is performed. When the operator is placed in front of the variable, the incrementing or decrementing is performed *before* the variable is used. When the operator is placed after the variable, the incrementing or decrementing is not done until the next use of the variable. Consider the following sections of code:

```
/* Case 1 */              /* Case 2 */
int x, y;                 int x, y;
x = 5;                    x = 5;
y = ++x;                  y = x++;
```

In the first case, the prefix operator is used and **x** is incremented by 1 before the assignment takes place, so **y** is assigned a value of 6. In the second case, the postfix operator is used and **x** is incremented after the assignment takes place so **y** is set equal to 5. In both case, the final value of **x** is 6. The foregoing sections of code are equivalent to the following:

```
/* Case 1 */              /* Case 2 */
int x, y;                 int x, y;
x = 5;                    x = 5;
x = x + 1;                y = x;
y = x;                    x = x + 1;
```

The increment and decrement operators can be applied only to variables since they actually cause a change in the value of a variable stored in the computer memory. The statements

```
(x/y)++;
(a+b)++;
```

are illegal since the parenthesized expressions do not refer to memory locations.

Increment and decrement operators are used quite frequently in C programs. Most C compilers generate more efficient code for the increment and decrement operations than for the equivalent assignment statement.

Example 5.4   Increment and Decrement Operators

PROBLEM STATEMENT: Determine the value of **i** and **j** after we execute each of the following statements. Assume that the initial value of **i** is 5. The statements are not executed sequentially.

a.	j = ++i;	b.	j = i++;
c.	j = --i;	d.	j = i--;

SOLUTION:

a.   The value of **i** will be 6 and the value of **j** will be 6. The assignment takes place after **i** is incremented.

b.   The value of **i** will be 6 and the value of **j** will be 5. In this case **j** is assigned a value before i is decremented.

c.   Both i and j will be equal to 4. The assignment takes place after i has been incremented.

d.   The value of i will be 4, but the value of j will be 5, since j is assigned a value before i is decremented.

Example 5.5   Increment and Decrement Operators

PROBLEM STATEMENT: Determine the value of **x** and **y** after each of the following statements has been executed.

```
int x = 10, y = 20;
++x;
y = --x;
x = x-- + y;
y = x - ++x;
```

SOLUTION: The values of **x** and **y** at the end of each statement are as follows:

Statement	x	y
int x = 10, y = 20	10	20
++x;	11	20
y = --x;	10	10
x = x-- + y;	19	10
y = x - ++x;	20	0

You should be careful when using the increment and decrement operators in arithmetic expressions. If you place the **++** or the **--** operator before a variable, the compiler first increments or decrements the variable and then uses the new value of the variable to evaluate the expression. If you place the **++** or the **--** operator after the variable, the compiler uses the current value of the variable to evaluate the expression and then increments or decrements the variable.

Example 5.6 Increment and Decrement Operators in Expressions

PROBLEM STATEMENT: Determine the values of **x** and **z** after each of the following statements have been executed. Assume the value of **x** =10 and **y** = 20 prior to execution of each statement

    a.   z = ++x + y;
    b.   z = x++ + y
    c.   z = --x +y;
    d.   z = x-- + y;

SOLUTION: The expressions are evaluated as follows:

    a.   Since the **++** operator is placed before **x**, the variable **x** is incremented before the addition step is preformed. Thus **x** = 11, and **z** = 11 + 20 = 31.

    b.   The increment operator appears after the variable **x**, so the addition is done before **x** is incremented. Thus the final values are **z** = 10 + 20 = 30, and **x** = 11.

    c.   The **--** operator is placed before **x**, so **x** is decremented before the addition is done. Thus, the final values of **x** and **z** are **x** = 9, and **z** = 9 + 20 = 29.

    d.   The decrement operator appears after **x** and the addition is performed before the value of **x** is decremented. Thus the final values are **z** = 10 + 20 = 30, and **x** = 9.

5.6 PRECEDENCE OF OPERATORS

In an arithmetic expression containing several operators, the order in which the operations are performed is determined by a strict set of rules. These rules are formed by assigning each operator a precedence. We must understand and follow these rules of operator precedence, to ensure that an expression will be evaluated in the order that we desire. An arithmetic operation involving an operator of higher precedence is performed before one having an operator of lower precedence. When arithmetic operators have equal precedence (such as multiplication and division), they are generally evaluated from left to right.

Of the operators considered so far, the unary operators, that is, the negation (-), the increment (**++**), and the decrement (**--**) operators, have the highest precedence. Next in order of precedence are the multiplication (*****), division (**/**), and modulus (**%**) operators. These are followed by the addition (**+**) and subtraction (**-**)

operators. The assignment operator (=) and the arithmetic assignment operators
(+=, -+, *=, *=, %=) have the lowest precedence. Table 5.4 lists these operators in
order of precedence.

Table 5.4: Precedence of operators

Precedence	Operator	Use	Associativity
highest	()	Parentheses, function calls	left to right
	-	unary minus	left to right
	++ --	increment, decrement	right to left
	* / %	multiplication, division, modulus	left to right
	+ -	addition, subtraction	left to right
lowest	= += *= /= -= %=	assignment	right to left

The rules of operator precedence imply that the expression

`a + b * c`

will be evaluated as

`a + (b * c)`

where the parentheses indicate that the multiplication is performed before the
addition. Multiplication has higher precedence than addition, thus multiplication
will be performed first and then the addition. Similarly, the expression

`--x + y * z`

means

`(--x) + (y * z)`

The addition is performed last since both the decrement and the multiplication
operators have higher precedence than the addition operator.

Example 5.7 Operator Precedence

PROBLEM STATEMENT: Determine the value of the following C expressions

   a. `3.65 * 2.0 + 4.0 * 6.0`
   b. `3/7 + 6/7`
   c. `5/4 + 9/3`
   d. `5/4 * 6 + 3 * 4/8`

SOLUTION: The expressions are evaluated as follows:

a. Expression: = 3.65 * 2.0 + 4.0 * 6.0

    Step 1. Multiply (3.65 * 2.0) = 7.3 + 4.0 * 6.0

    Step 2. Multiply (4.0 * 6.0) = 7.3 + 24.0

    Step 3. Add (7.3 + 24.0)   = 31.3

    Final value   = 31.3

b. Expression: = 3/7 + 6/7

    Step 1. Divide (3/7) = 0 + 6/7

    Step 2. Divide (6/7) = 0 + 0

    Step 3. Add (0 + 0) = 0

    Final value   = 0

c. Expression: = 5/4 + 9/3

    Step 1. Divide (5/4) = 1 + 9/3

    Step 2. Divide (9/3) = 1 + 3

    Step 3. Add (1 + 3) = 4

    Final value   = 4

d. Expression: = 5/4 * 6 + 3 * 4/8

    Step 1. Divide (5/4)   = 1 * 6 + 3 * 4/8

    Step 2. Multiply (1 * 6) = 6 + 3 * 4/8

    Step 3. Multiply (3 * 4) = 6 + 12/8

    Step 4. Divide (12/8) = 6 + 1

    Step 5. Add (6 + 1)   = 7

    Final value   = 7

Associativity

Associativity refers to the order in which C evaluates operators having the same precedence. Operators can associate either left to right or right to left. Most of the arithmetic operators associate from left to right. Table 5.4 lists the arithmetic operators and their associativity. Consider the following expression

```
a = x * y / z;
```

The expression contain two operators (multiplication and division) having the same precedence. Since both multiplication and division associate from left-to-right the multiplication will be performed before the division.

Example 5.8   Hierarchy of Operations

PROBLEM STATEMENT: Determine the value of the following C expressions, if x, y, and z are of type **int** and have the values $x = 4$, $y = 2$, and $z = 8$.

a. `x / y * z`
b. `x * y / z`
c. `x / y / z`

The expressions are evaluated as follows:

a. Expression: `= 4 / 2 * 8`
    Step 1. Divide `(4/2)`   `= 2 * 8`
    Step 2. Multiply `(2 * 8)` `= 16`
    Final value   `= 16`

b. Expression: `= 4 * 2 / 8`
    Step 1. Multiply `(4 * 2)` `= 8/8`
    Step 2. Divide `(8/8)`   `= 1`
    Final value   `= 8`

c. Expression: `= 4 / 2 / 8`
    Step 1. Divide `(4 / 2)` `= 2 / 8`
    Step 2. Divide `(2 / 8)` `= 0`
    Final value   `= 0`

Use of Parentheses

The order of evaluation of arithmetic expressions as determined by the precedence of operators can be changed with the use of parentheses. If an arithmetic expression contains parentheses, the expression enclosed in parentheses is evaluated first. For example, in the statement

```
a = (x + y)/z;
```

the parentheses forces the addition operation to take place before the division even though the division operator has higher precedence that the addition operator. If there is more that one pair of parentheses, the operations contained within the innermost pair of parentheses are evaluated first, followed by the operations within the second innermost pair, and so on. Within a given pair of parentheses the normal precedence of operations applies. An example of a statement containing nested parentheses is shown below

```
y = ((a + b) * c) / d;
```

In this example, the addition is performed first, then the multiplication, and finally the division.

Parentheses are very useful in some situations. Consider the expression

```
a = x/y * z;
```

The result will depend on whether the division operation is performed first or whether the multiplication operation is performed first. Since both multiplication and division have the same precedence and both associate from left to right, the division operation will be performed first. Thus the expression is equivalent to

```
a = (x/y) * z;
```

To force the multiplication to be done first, we would have to write the expression as

```
a = x/(y * z);
```

In many situations the use of parentheses is absolutely necessary in order to arrive at the correct result. Consider the mathematical expression

$$\frac{x - 20}{y + 20}$$

This expression can be written as

```
x - 20 / y + 20;
```

or as

```
(x - 20)/(y + 20);
```

If the value of **x** is 50 and the value of **y** is 10, then the first expression gives a result of 68 while the second expression gives a result of 1. The correct result is 1. The first expression gives an incorrect result since the original mathematical expression contains "implied" parentheses. When we evaluate the expression using the rules of algebra, we first evaluate the numerato and then the denominator and then perform the division. To obtain the same result in C we have to include parentheses in our expressions.

When parentheses are used, it is important to remember that the parentheses must be matched; that is, the same number of left and right parentheses must be used. Unmatched parentheses will result in a syntax error. In fact, unmatched parentheses are the most common source of errors in arithmetic expressions. If there is any uncertainty about how the computer will evaluate an expression, use parentheses to make sure that it will be evaluated as desired. A few extra parentheses and spaces within arithmetic expressions help to make the program more readable.

It is important to understand and become familiar with the hierarchy rules in order to be able to translate algebraic expressions into C expressions. Some examples of the translation of algebraic expressions into C expressions, and vice versa, follow.

Example 5.9   Converting Algebraic Expressions to C

PROBLEM STATEMENT: Write the following algebraic expressions in C

a. $\dfrac{b(a^2 - b^2)}{a^2 + 2y^2}$

b. $\dfrac{x - y}{x + y}$

c. $\dfrac{a}{[a/(4.5 + b)] + 5.0}$

d. $\dfrac{a_2 c_2 - c_1 b_2}{a_2 b_1 - a_1 b_2}$

e. $\dfrac{a}{b} + \dfrac{c}{d}$

SOLUTION: The corresponding C expressions are as follows:

```
a.   b * (a * a - b * b)/(a * a + 2. * y * y)
b.   (x - y)/(x + y)
c.   a/(a/(4.5 + b) + 5.0)
d.   (a2 * c2 - c1 * b2)/(a2 * b1 - a1 * b2)
e.   a/b + c/d
```

Example 5.10   Converting C Expressions to Algebraic

PROBLEM STATEMENT: Convert the following C expressions into algebraic expressions

- **a.**   `c/d/e/f`
- **b.**   `(y1 * (x2 - x1) - (y2 - y1) * x1)/(x2 - x1)`
- **c.**   `(b * b - 4. * a * c)/(a * c - a * b)`
- **d.**   `y *(x - y)/(x * x - y * y)`

The algebraic expressions corresponding to these C statements are as follows:

- **a.** $\dfrac{c}{def}$

- **b.** $\dfrac{y1(x2-x1)-(y2-y1)x1}{x2-x1}$

- **c.** $\dfrac{b^2-4ac}{ac-ab}$

- **d.** $\dfrac{y(x-y)}{x^2-y^2}$

5.7   ARITHMETIC WITH MIXED TYPES

It is possible to mix data types in arithmetic expressions in C. For example, the following is perfectly legal in C:

```
int count;
double x_first, x_next, step;
x_next = x_first + count * step;
```

The expression

```
count * step
```

contains an integer operand `count` and a double-precision operand `step`.

When an expression contains operands of different types, a type conversion takes place. The exact nature of the conversion depends on the two operands. All data types in C are ranked according to the amount of memory storage they require. A data type that requires more storage is ranked higher than one that requires less storage. The ranking from lowest to highest is as follows

```
char < int < long < float < double
```

Type **char** is the narrowest data type and type **double** is the widest data type. When two operands have different types, the lower-ranking type is converted to the higher-ranking type. Thus, in the expression

```
count * step
```

the value of the integer variable **count** is converted to type **double** before the multiplication takes place and the multiplication is performed using double-precision arithmetic.

The basic rule is that in a operation involving two different data types, both values are converted to the higher ranking of the two types.

Example 5.11   Type Conversions

An interesting example of how C performs type conversions in arithmetic expressions is the program shown in Figure 5.3. The program *mixmode.c* evaluates two expressions and assigns the result to the floating point variables **result1** and **result2**.

In the statement

```
result1 = 2.56 + 3/2;
```

```
/***********************************************************/
/* mixmode.c - Mixed mode arithmetic                       */
/*                                                         */
/***********************************************************/
#include <stdio.h>

main()
{
        float result1, result2;
        result1 = 2.56 + 3/2;
        result2 = 2.56 + 3.0/2;
        printf("\n  Mixed mode arithmetic ");
        printf("\n  result1 = %f", result1);
        printf("\n  result2 = %f", result2);
}
```

Program output

```
Mixed mode arithmetic
result1 = 3.560000
result2 = 4.060000
```

Figure 5.3   Mixed mode arithmetic.

the expression **3/2** is evaluated using integer division since both 3 and 2 are integer constants. The result of the integer division is 1. This is added to the floating point constant 2.56 to give a final value of 3.56. This value is then assigned to the variable floating point variable **result1**. In the statement

```
result2 = 2.56 + 3.0/2;
```

the expression **3.0/2** is evaluated using floating point arithmetic since the numerator is a floating point constant (3.0). The division yields 1.5 as the result. This is then added to 2.56, and the final value of the expression on the right-hand side of the assignment statement is 4.06. This value is then assigned to the variable **result2**. In each of the two arithmetic assignment statements just shown, the expressions on the right side of the equal symbol contain a floating point constant; however, the presence of the floating point constant in the first expression does not affect the outcome since the division is performed before the addition. Any of the following expressions could have been used to prevent the integer division

```
3/2.0       3.0/2.0
```

The zero following the decimal is not significant. In terms of computational accuracy, the expression **3.0/2.0** is preferable since both operands are of the same type (**double**) and no type conversions are necessary. An expression is evaluated using floating point arithmetic if either operand in the expression is a floating point variable or constant.

Almost all C compilers perform the following conversions automatically when evaluating arithmetic expressions:

all **char** values are converted to **int**
all **float** values are converted to **double**

The conversion of **float** to **double** greatly reduces round-off errors that may otherwise occur. The final answer is converted back to a floating point value. Consider the following program segment

```
float a, b, c;
a = 10.5;
b = 15.8;
c = b/a;
```

In the last statement both **a** and **b** are converted to type **double**, and the division is performed using double-precision arithmetic. The double-precision result is then converted to a **float** and is assigned to **c**.

Type conversions are also performed during assignment. Regardless of the types on the right-hand side of an assignment statement, the final result of the expression is converted to the type on the left. If the variable on the left-hand side of the assignment statement has a higher or same rank as the expression on the right-hand side of the assignment operator, then there is no loss of precision. However, if the type on the left of the assignment symbol has a lower rank, then there can be a loss of accuracy. For instance, assigning a floating point result to an integer variable will result in the loss of the fractional part of the result. When the computer stores a floating point number in an integer variable it ignores the fractional portion and stores only the whole number portion of the number.

Precision is lost whenever a higher-ranking data type is assigned to a lower-ranking one. This is because the lower-ranking type may not be wide enough to hold the higher-ranking value. For example, an integer variable cannot hold the fractional part of a floating point number, and it cannot hold numbers that are smaller or larger than the range of integers, and a character variable can hold the integer 100 but not the integer 1000.

Example 5.12   Type Conversions

The program shown in Figure 5.4 demonstrates the type conversions that take place during assignment. The program assigns a value of type **char**, **int**, and **double** to variables of type **char**, **int**, **float**, and **double** and prints the result for each case. The program output is also shown in Figure 5.4.

The declaration statements

```
char c;
int i;
float f;
double d;
```

create four variables, **c** is of type **char**, **i** is of type **int**, **f** is of type **float**, and **d** is of type **double**. In the first set of assignment statements

```
c = 100;
i = 100;
f = 100;
d = 100;
```

the variables are assigned a value of l00, which is within the range of acceptable values for variables of type **char** (recall that characters are treated as integers). The value 100 corresponds to the ASCII code for the character "d." The output for this case is

```
c = 'd', i = 100, f = 100.000000, d = 100.000000
```

Since the data type on the right-hand side of the assignment (=) symbol in each of the assignment statements has a lower ranking than the variable on the left-hand

```
/***************************************************************/
/*    assign.c -- Type conversion during assignment            */
/*                                                             */
/*    Demonstrates how C performs type conversion when         */
/*    evaluating arithmetic assignment statments.              */
/***************************************************************/
#include <stdio.h>

main()
{
    char c;
    int i;
    float f;
    double d;

    printf("\n  Type conversion during assignment");
    /* assign character value to each type */
    c = 100;
    i = 100;
    f = 100;
    d = 100;
    printf("\n\n  Char value assigned to each type:\n");
    printf("   c = %c, i = %d, f = %f, d = %lf",c,i,f,d);

    /* assign integer value to each type */
    c = 600;
    i = 600;
    f = 600;
    d = 600;
    printf("\n\n  Int value assigned to each type:\n");
    printf("   c = %c, i = %d, f = %f, d = %15.10lf",c,i,f,d);

    /* assign float value to each type */
    c = 360.1234567891;
    i = 360.1234567891;
    f = 360.1234567891;
    d = 360.1234567891;
    printf("\n\n  Double value assigned to each type:\n");
    printf("   c = %c, i = %d, f = %f, d = %15.10lf",c,i,f,d);
}
```

Program output

```
  Type conversion during assignment

  Char value assigned to each type:
  c = d, i = 100, f = 100.000000, d = 100.000000

  Int value assigned to each type:
  c = X, i = 600, f = 600.000000, d =  600.0000000000

  Double value assigned to each type:
  c = h, i = 360, f = 360.123444, d =  360.1234567891
```

Figure 5.4   Type conversions during assignment.

side, there is no loss of precision.

In the next set of assignment statements

```
c = 600;
i = 600;
f = 600;
d = 600;
```

an integer value (600) is assigned to each of the variables on the left-hand side. The result is

```
c = 'X', i = 600, f = 600.000000, d =  600.0000000000
```

In the statement

```
c = 600;
```

the character variable **c** has a lower ranking than the integer constant on the right-hand side, and the result of the assignment is basically garbage as the C compiler places a 2-byte integer (on our system) in a 1- byte character variable.

In the third set of assignment statements

```
c = 360.1234567891;
i = 360.1234567891;
f = 360.1234567891;
d = 360.1234567891;
```

a constant of type **double** is assigned to each of the variables **c**, **i**, **f**, and **d**. The result is

```
c = 'h', i = 360, f = 360.123444, d =  360.1234567891
```

Except for **d**, all the other variables have a lower ranking than **double**, and so there is a loss of precision resulting from the assignment of a higher ranking value to a lower-ranking variable.

Example 5.13   Assignment with Mixed Types

PROBLEM STATEMENT: Give the value of the variable on the left side of the assignment operator = in each of the following assignment statements. The statements are not executed sequentially. Assume that **i**, **j**, and **k** are of type **int** and **a**, **b**, and **c** are of type **float**. The initial values are **i = 5**, **j = 3**, **a = 2.5**, and **b = 30.6**.

a. `k = i + a;`   b. `k = a + b;`

c. `c = i * a + j;`   d. `c = a/i + b/j;`

```
e.  k = i % j;          f.  k = j % i * 3;
g.  k = b;              h.  k = b/a;
i.  c = i/j + a;        j.  k = i/j + a;
```

SOLUTION: The values assigned to **k** and **c** are as follows:

```
a.  k = 5 + 2.5 = 7.5 = 7
b.  k = 2.5 + 30.6 = 33.1 = 33
c.  c = 5 * 2.5 + 3 = 15.5
d.  c = 2.5/5 + 30.6/3 = 0.5 + 10.2 = 10.7
e.  k = 5 % 3 = 2
f.  k = 5 * 3 * 3 = 15 * 3 = 45
g.  k = 30.6 = 30
h.  k = 30.6/2.5 = 12.24 = 12
i.  c = 5/3 + 2.5 = 1+ 2.5 = 3.5
j.  k = 5/3 + 2.5 = 1 + 2.5 = 3.5 = 3
```

Type Casting

Although C automatically performs type conversions when it encounters arithmetic expressions with mixed data types, it is sometimes convenient to explicitly specify the conversion we require. We can use the *cast* operator to force the compiler to convert a value to a specified type. The cast operator is written by enclosing the name of a C data type in parentheses before the expression

> *(type) expression;*

where *type* is one of the standard C data types such as **char, int, float,** and **double.** For example, if **i** is a variable of type **int** then the expression

```
(float) i;
```

explicitly requests that the value of **i** be converted to type **float** before it is used in any calculations. It is important to note that the value of **i** itself is not changed. The cast operator simply takes the value of its operand and converts it to a value of the type specified in parentheses.

Example 5.14   Type Casting

The program given in Figure 5.5 illustrates the use of the cast operator. The program declares two variable **i1** and **i2** of type **int**. In the first assignment statement

```
i1 = 2.6 + 3.8;
```

the expression 2.6 + 3.8 is evaluated using floating point arithmetic. The result is 6.4 which is then converted to an integer value and assigned to the variable **i1**, resulting in a final value of 6. In the second assignment statement

```
i2 = (int) 2.6 + (int) 3.8;
```

both 2.6 and 3.8 are converted to integers *before* the addition is performed. Thus the value 2.6 is converted to 2 and 3.8 is converted to 3. Also, since now both operands are integers, the addition is performed using integer arithmetic and so the result of the addition is 5. This result is then assigned to the variable **i2**. The cast operator explicitly converts a value to a specific type before any operations are performed on that value.

```
/***********************************************************/
/*  cast1.c - Type Casting                                 */
/*    Illustrates the use of the cast operator.            */
/***********************************************************/

#include <stdio.h>

main()
{
    int i1, i2;
    i1 = 2.6 + 3.8;
    i2 = (int) 2.6 + (int) 3.8;
    printf("\n Type casting ");
    printf("\n Value of i1 is: %d", i1);
    printf("\n Value of i2 is: %d", i2);
}
```

Progam output

```
Type casting
Value of i1 is: 6
Value of i2 is: 5
```

Figure 5.5   The cast operator.

Example 5.15 Using Type Casting to Convert an int to a float

An example of using type casting to convert integer data types to floating point values is shown in Figure 5.6. In the first assignment statement

        f1 = i1/i2;

the division is performed using integer arithmetic. The result from the integer division 3/2 is an integer value 1. This is then converted to float and assigned to the variable f1.

   In the second assignment statement

    f2 = (float) i1 / i2;   /* convert i1 to float */

the value of i1 is converted to type float because of the cast operator (float) and the division is performing using floating point arithmetic. The result is a floating point number that is then assigned to the variable f2.

```
/***********************************************************/
/*   cast2.c - Type Casting                                */
/*    Type casting to convert an int type to float.        */
/***********************************************************/
#include <stdio.h>

main()
{
    int i1=3, i2=2;
    float f1, f2;
    f1 = i1 / i2;
    f2 = (float) i1 / i2;              /* convert i1 to float */
    printf("\n  Type casting ");
    printf("\n  Value of f1 is: %f", f1);
    printf("\n  Value of f2 is: %f", f2);
}
```

Program output

```
Type casting
Value of f1 is: 1.000000
Value of f2 is: 1.500000
```

Figure 5.6   Type casting.

Type casting is also useful in passing information to functions. For example, consider a function named **square()** which has been defined as

```
double square(double);
```

The function expects a **double** value as an argument. This function may be called with an integer argument **i** by using a cast operator as in the statement

```
z = square( (double) i );
```

The cast operator **(double)** converts the integer value **i** to a **double**, and this **double** value is passed to the function.

5.8 MATHEMATICAL FUNCTIONS

Mathematical functions such as square roots, absolute values, logarithms, trigonometric and exponential functions appear routinely in a variety of engineering applications. Since these functions are commonly used, all C compilers provide a set of mathematical functions in their standard library. These functions can be referenced directly in an expression. For example, the statement

```
y = sqrt(x);
```

calls the library function **sqrt()** to compute the square root of the numerical value stored in the variable **x**. The value returned by the square root function is assigned to the variable **y**. In the assignment statement

```
y= fabs(-10.5) + 3.4;
```

the **fabs()** function is called. The **fabs()** function returns the absolute value of a floating point number. The value returned by **fabs()** is 10.5. This value is added to 3.5. The result of the addition, 13.9 is stored in the variable **y**.

It is also acceptable to use one function as the argument of another. For example, in the statement

```
y = sqrt(abs(x));
```

the square root of the absolute value of **x** is computed and the result is assigned to the variable **y**.

The names and descriptions of some commonly used functions are given in Table 5.5. To use these functions, you must provide the name of the function followed by one or more arguments enclosed in parentheses. For most of these functions the argument is a single number or variable such as **sqrt(x)** and **fabs(-10.5)**. A few functions require two arguments. Examples of these functions are the **pow()** function, which takes two arguments, x and y, and returns x^y, and the **atan2()** function, which also takes two arguments, x and y, and returns the arctangent of x/y.

Table 5.5: C library mathematical functions

Name	Description	Argument Type	Result Type
abs()	absolute value of an **int**	int	int
acos()	arccosine	double	double
asin()	arcsine	double	double
atan()	arctangent (between $-\pi/2$ and $\pi/2$)	double	double
atan2()	arctangent of x/y	double x, double y	double
ceil()	smallest **double** $\geq$ argument that can be represented as an **int**	double	double
cos()	cosine	double	double
cosh()	hyperbolic cosine	double	double
exp()	exponential, e^x	double	double
fabs()	absolute value of a floating point number	double	double
floor()	largest **double** $\leq$ argument that can be represented as an **int**	double	double
labs()	absolute value of a **long**	double	long
log()	logarithm to the base 10	double	double
log10()	natural logarithm	double	double
pow()	x to the y power, x^y	double x, double y	double
sin()	sine	double	double
sinh()	hyperbolic sine	double	double
sqrt()	square root	double	double
tan()	tangent	double	double
tanh()	hyperbolic tangent	double	double

The function declarations for the mathematical functions are included in the file *math.h*. You should include this header file in all programs that use any of the mathematical functions. You can use the following preprocessor directive

```
#include <math.h>
```

The function declarations for the **abs()** and **labs()** function are in the file *stdlib.h*, and so this file should be included when using either of these two functions.

Table 5.5 also lists the type of arguments expected by each function and the type of value returned by the function. When calling a library function you should be very careful that the type of argument being passed to the function matches the type that the function expects otherwise the value returned from the function may be incorrect. You can use the cast operator to cast the variable to the appropriate type before calling the function. For example, to compute the square root of an integer, we can use the following statements

```
double y;
int n;
...
y = sqrt( (double)  n);
```

Since the **sqrt()** function expects an argument of type **double**, the expressions

```
(double) n;
```

converts the integer value n to type **double** before passing it to the **sqrt()** function.

Two types of errors can occur when using the C library mathematical functions. A *domain error* occurs when the argument passed to a function is inappropriate for that function. Examples of a domain error are attempting to compute the square root of a negative number or calling the **asin()** or **acos()** function with an argument greater than 1 or less than −1. The second type of error is a *range error* which occurs when the value to be returned by the function is too large. The header file *math.h* defines several constants that are used to indicate the type of error that occurs during a mathematical operation. These constants include **EDOM**, which indicates a domain error, **ERANGE** which indicates a range error, and **HUGE_VAL**, which represents a value too large to be stored in a variable of type **double**.

When an error is encountered in a C libray function, the function sets a global variable of type **int** called **errno** to one of a list of predefined error codes to indicate the type of error. The constants representing the various error codes are defined in the header file *errno.h*.

Trigonometric and Inverse Trigonometric Functions

The functions **sin()**, **cos()** and **tan()** compute the sine, cosine and tangent of an angle x. The argument x for all the trigonometric functions is in radians. The secant, cosecant, and cotangent of an angle x can be obtained from

```
secx = 1.0/cos(x);
```

```
cosecx = 1.0/(sin(x);
cotx = 1/tan(x);
```

The inverse trigonometric functions are usually denoted by an "arc" prefix; for example, the inverse tangent function is arctangent x, which gives the angle whose tangent is x. Inverse functions are useful for determining angles when the sides of a triangle are known. The standard math library functions for computing the arcsine, arccosine, and arctangent functions are called **asin()**, **acos()**, and **atan()**, respectively. They all return an angle in radians. The **asin()** returns the arccosine of the argument x in the range $-\pi/2$ to $\pi/2$, and the **acos()** function returns a value in the range of 0 to π. For both the **asin()** and the **acos()** functions, the argument must be in the range of -1 to 1; otherwise, a range error occurs. The **atan()** function returns a value in the range of $-\pi/2$ to $\pi/2$. The math library also has a function **atan2()** which accepts two arguments **x** and **y** and returns the arctangent of x/y in the range $-\pi$ to π. The **atan2()** function uses the sign of both arguments to determine the quadrant of the return value.

Hyperbolic Functions

The hyperbolic functions are defined in terms of Euler's number e, as

$$\sinh x = \frac{e^x - e^{-x}}{2} \tag{5.1}$$

$$\cosh x = \frac{e^x + e^{-x}}{2} \tag{5.2}$$

$$\tanh x = \frac{e^x - e^{-x}}{e^x + e^{-x}} \tag{5.3}$$

The standard math library provides the functions **sinh()**, **cosh()**, and **tanh()** for computing the hyperbolic functions. The argument x for these functions is in radians.

Exponential and Logarithmic Functions

The exponential function **exp()** computes e^x, where e is Euler's number (2.718282...). The **log()** function computes the natural logarithm of the argument (base e), and the **log10()** function computes the logarithm of the argument to the base 10. For both the **log()** and **log10()** functions, a domain error occurs if the argument is negative, and a range error occurs if the argument is zero.

Miscellaneous Functions

The **fabs()** function returns the absolute value of a argument of type **double**. Most C implementations also provide an **abs()** function for determining the absolute value of integers and a **labs()** function for determining the absolute value of long integers. The function prototype for the **fabs()** function is in the header file *math.h*, while the function prototypes for the **abs()** and **labs()** functions are in the header file *stdlib.h*.

The **ceil()** function (for ceiling) returns the smallest integer that is larger than or equal to the argument. The **floor()** function returns the largest integer that is less than or equal to the argument. The value returned by both **ceil()** and **floor()** is of type **double**.

The **pow()** function takes two arguments x and y and returns x^y. A domain error occurs if x is 0 and y is negative, if both x and y are 0, and if x is negative and y is not an integer. An overflow results in a range error. The **sqrt()** function returns the square root of its argument. A domain error occurs if the argument is negative.

Example 5.16   C Library Math Functions

The program shown in Figure 5.7 uses the C library mathematical functions to compute the logarithm, absolute value, trigonometric and hyperbolic sine, cosine, and tangent, and the inverse sine, cosine, and tangent. The statements

```
double x = 10., y =-20. ;
double theta = PI/4. ;
int i = -120;
long l = -40000L;
```

declare and initialize several variables. The variables **x** and **y** and **theta** are of type **double**, the variable **i** is of type **int**, and the variable **l** is of type **long**. The statements

```
printf("\n Natural log: log(%f) = %f",x,log(x));
printf("\n Log to base 10: log10(%f) = %f",x,log10(x));
printf("\n Exponential function: exp(%f) = x,exp(x));"
```

call the **log()**, **log10()**, and **exp()** functions to compute and print $\log(x)$, $\log_{10}(x)$, and e^x. The statements

```
printf("\n Integer: abs(%d)= %d",i, abs(i));
printf("\n Long integer: labs(%ld)= %ld",labs(l));
printf("\n Float: fabs(%f)= %f",y,fabs(y));
```

call the **abs()**, **labs()**, and **fabs()** functions to compute and print the absolute value of a variable of type **int**, **long**, and **double** respectively. The file *stdlib.h* is included by the program since this file contains the function prototypes for the

```
/*****************************************************/
/*  mathfunc.c  -- C Library Mathematical Functions  */
/*                                                   */
/*  Illustrates the C library math functions.        */
/*****************************************************/

#include <stdio.h>
#include <math.h>
#include <stdlib.h>      /* for abs() and labs() */

#define PI 3.141592654

main()
{
   double x = 10., y =-20. ;
   double theta = PI/4. ;
   int i = -120;
   long l = -40000L;

   printf("\n C Library Mathematical Functions");
   /* logarithms and exponential functions */
   printf("\n\n Logarithmic and Exponential Functions");
   printf("\n Natural log: log(%f) = %f", x, log(x));
   printf("\n Log to base 10: log10(%f) = %f", x, log10(x));
   printf("\n Exponential function: exp(%f) = %f", x, exp(x));

   /* absolute values */
   printf("\n\n Absolute Value Functions ");
   printf("\n Integer: abs(%d)= %d", i, abs(i));
   printf("\n Long integer: labs(%ld)= %ld", l, labs(l));
   printf("\n Float: fabs(%f)= %f", y, fabs(y));

   /* trigonometric function */
   printf("\n\n Trigonometric Functions");
   printf("\n Sine: sin(%f) = %f", theta, sin(theta));
   printf("\n Cosine: cos(%f) = %f", theta, cos(theta));
   printf("\n Tangent: tan(%f) = %f", theta, tan(theta));

   /* inverse trigonometric functions */
   printf("\n\n Inverse Trigonometric Functions");
   printf("\n Arcsine: asin(1.0) = %f", asin(1.0));
   printf("\n Arccosine: acos(1.0) = %f", acos(1.0));
   printf("\n Arctangent: atan(1.0) = %f", atan(1.0));
   printf("\n Arctangent: atan2(-2./3.) = %f", atan2(-2.,3.));

   /* hyperbolic functions */
   printf("\n\n Hyperbolic Functions");
   printf("\n Hyperbolic sine: sinh(1.0) = %f", sinh(1.0));
   printf("\n Hyperbolic cosine: cosh(1.0) = %f", cosh(1.0));
   printf("\n Hyperbolic tangent: tanh(1.0) = %f", tanh(1.0));
}
```

Figure 5.7   C library mathematical functions.

`abs()` and `labs()` functions.

The trigonometric functions for the angle **theta** are computed in the statements

```
printf("\n Sine: sin(%f) = %f",theta, sin(theta));
printf("\n Cosine: cos(%f) = %f",theta,cos(theta));
printf("\n Tangent: tan(%f) = %f",theta,tan(theta));
```

The angle **theta** is in radians since **theta** was assigned the value PI/4. The inverse trigonometric functions are called in the statements

```
printf("\n Arcsine: asin(1.0) = %f", asin(1.0));
printf("\n Arccosine: acos(1.0) = %f", acos(1.0));
printf("\n Arctangent: atan(1.0) = %f", atan(1.0));
printf("\n Arctangent: atan2(-2./3.) = %f",atan2(-2.,3.));
```

The **atan2()** function uses the sign of its argument to determine the quadrant of the angle. The last three statements

```
printf("\n Hyperbolic sine: sinh(1.0) = %f", sinh(1.0));
printf("\n Hyperbolic cosine: cosh(1.0) = %f", cosh(1.0));
printf("\n Hyperbolic tangent: tanh(1.0) = %f", tanh(1.0));
```

compute the hyperbolic sine, cosine, and tangent of 1.0. The output from the program is shown in Figure 5.8.

```
C Library Mathematical Functions

Logarithmic and Exponential Functions
Natural log: log(10.000000) = 2.302585
Log to base 10: log10(10.000000) = 1.000000
Exponential function: exp(10.000000) = 22026.465795

Absolute Value Functions
Integer: abs(-120)= 120
Long integer: labs(-40000)= 40000
Float: fabs(-20.000000)= 20.000000

Trigonometric Functions
Sine: sin(0.785398) = 0.707107
Cosine: cos(0.785398) = 0.707107
Tangent: tan(0.785398) = 1.000000

Inverse Trigonometric Functions
Arcsine: asin(1.0) = 1.570796
Arccosine: acos(1.0) = 0.000000
Arctangent: atan(1.0) = 0.785398
Arctangent: atan2(-2./3.) = -0.588003

Hyperbolic Functions
Hyperbolic sine: sinh(1.0) = 1.175201
Hyperbolic cosine: cosh(1.0) = 1.543081
Hyperbolic tangent: tanh(1.0) = 0.761594
```

Figure 5.8   Output from program *mathfunc.c.*

5.9   PROGRAMMING PROJECT: RESULTANT OF TWO FORCES

Problem Statement

Write a program that computes the resultant of two planar forces F_1 and F_2 and the angle that this resultant makes with the x-axis.

Problem Analysis

The horizontal and vertical component of a force F that makes an angle θ with the x axis is given by

$$F_x = F\cos\theta \tag{5.4}$$

$$F_y = F\sin\theta \tag{5.5}$$

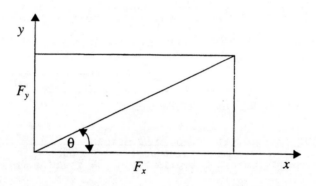

The resultant F_R of two forces F_1 and F_2 making and angle θ_1 and θ_2 with the x axis can be obtained by the following equations

$$F_{Rx} = F_{1x} + F_{2x} \tag{5.6}$$

$$F_{Ry} = F_{1y} + F_{2y} \tag{5.7}$$

$$F_R = \sqrt{F_{Rx}^2 + F_{Ry}^2} \tag{5.8}$$

$$\theta_R = \tan^{-1}\left(\frac{F_{Ry}}{F_{Rx}}\right) \tag{5.9}$$

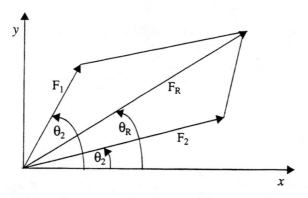

Input Variables
magnitude of forces F_1 and F_2 (**double f1, f2**)
angles θ_1 and θ_2 made by F_1 and F_2 with the x axis
    (**double theta1, theta2**)

Output Variables
magnitude of resultant force F_R (**double fr**)
angle θ_R made by F_R with the x-axis (**double theta_r**)

Intermediate Variables
We will also need two variables to store the x and y components, F_{Rx}
    and F_{Ry}, of the resultant (**double frx and fry**)

Algorithm

   1.   Read **f1, theta1**.
   2.   Read **f2, theta2**.
   3.   Compute **frx** from Equation (5.6).
   4.   Compute **fry** from Equation (5.7).
   5.   Compute **fr** from Equation (5.8).
   6.   Compute **theta_r** from Equation (5.9).
   7.   Print **f1, theta1, f2**, and **theta2**.
   8.   Print **fr** and **theta_r**.

Program

The program is shown in Figure 5.9. The preprocessor directives

```
#include <stdio.h>
#include <math.h>

#define PI 3.141592654
```

```
/*******************************************************/
/*   resultnt.c  -- Resultant of Two Torces          */
/*                                                   */
/*   Computes the resultant FR of two forces F1 and F2. */
/*******************************************************/

#include <stdio.h>
#include <math.h>

#define PI 3.141592654

main()
{
    double f1,f2;              /* magnitude of F1 and F2          */
    double theta1, theta2;    /* angles with the x-axis          */
    double fr,theta_r;        /* resultant and angle with x-axis */
    double frx,fry;           /* x and y components of resultant */

    /* input forces and angles */
    printf("\n Enter magnitude of force F1: ");
    scanf("%lf",&f1);
    printf(" Enter magnitude of force F2: ");
    scanf("%lf",&f2);
    printf(" Enter angle F1 makes with x-axis (degrees): ");
    scanf("%lf", &theta1);
    printf(" Enter angle F2 makes with x-axis (degrees): ");
    scanf("%lf", &theta2);

    /* convert angles to radians */
    theta1 = theta1 * PI/180. ;
    theta2 = theta2 * PI/180. ;

    /* compute x and y components of resultant */
    frx = f1 * cos(theta1) + f2 * cos(theta2);
    fry = f1 * sin(theta1) + f2 * sin(theta2);

    /* compute resultant and angle */
    fr = sqrt(frx * frx + fry * fry);
    theta_r = atan2(fry,frx);

    /* echo print input values and print results */
    printf("\n Magnitude of force F1 = %f",f1);
    printf("\n Magnitude of force F2 = %f",f2);
    printf("\n Angle F1 makes with x-axis = %f degrees",
           theta1 * 180./PI);
    printf("\n Angle F2 makes with x-axis = %f degrees",
           theta2 * 180./PI);
    printf("\n Magnitude of resultant force = %f",fr);
    printf("\n Angle resultant makes with x-axis = %f degrees",
           theta_r * 180.0/PI);
}
```

Figure 5.9   Program for computing the resultant to two forces.

include the *math.h* and *stdio.h* file and define the symbolic constant **PI**. The program declares the variables to be used with the statements:

```
double f1,f2;            /* magnitude of F1 and F2          */
double theta1, theta2; /* angles with the x-axis          */
double fr,theta_r;       /* resultant and angle with x-axis */
double frx,fry;          /* x and y components of resultant */
```

All variables are declared to be of type **double**.

The program then reads in **f1**, **theta1**, **f2**, and **theta2**. The angles are entered in degrees. Since the C library trigonometric functions expect all angles to be in radians the angles are converted to radians by the statements

```
theta1 = theta1 * PI/180. ;
theta2 = theta2 * PI/180. ;
```

The x and y components of the resultant force F_R are computed in

```
frx = f1 * cos(theta1) + f2 * cos(theta2);
fry = f1 * sin(theta1) + f2 * sin(theta2);
```

and the resultant and its angle with the x axis are computed in the statements

```
fr = sqrt(frx * frx + fry * fry);
theta_r = atan2(fry,frx);
```

The program then echo prints the input data and the resultant and its orientation with the x-axis.

Testing

For $F_1 = 20$ kips, $\theta_1 = 30°$, $F_2 = 40$ kips, $\theta_2 = 70°$, we get the following results:

$$F_{1x} = 20\cos 30 = 20(0.8660) = 17.32 \text{ kips}$$

$$F_{1y} = 20\sin 30 = 20(0.5) = 10.00 \text{ kips}$$

$$F_{2x} = 40\cos 70 = 40(0.3420) = 13.68 \text{ kips}$$

$$F_{2y} = 40\sin 70 = 40(0.9397) = 37.59 \text{ kips}$$

$$F_{Rx} = F_{1x} + F_{2x} = 17.32 + 13.86 = 31.00 \text{ kips}$$

$$F_{Ry} = F_{1y} + F_{2y} = 10.00 + 37.59 = 47.59 \text{ kips}$$

$$F_R = \sqrt{31.00^2 + 47.59^2} = 56.80 \text{ kips}$$

$$\theta_R = \tan^{-1}\left(\frac{47.59}{31.00}\right) = 56.92°$$

The program output for this input data is shown in Figure 5.10. You should run the program using other input values. For example, for $F_1 = 20$ kips, $\theta_1 = 0°$, $F_2 = 40$ kips, and $\theta_2 = 0°$, we should get $F_R = 60$ and $\theta_R = 0°$, since both forces are acting along the x axis. For $F_1 = 40$ kips, $\theta_1 = 90°$, $F_2 = 60$ kips, and $\theta_2 = 90°$, we should get $F_R = 100$kips and $\theta_R = 90°$, since both forces are now acting along the y axis.

```
RESULTANT OF TWO FORCES

Enter magnitude of force F1: 20.
Enter angle F1 makes with x-axis (degrees): 30.
Enter magnitude of force F2: 40.
Enter angle F2 makes with x-axis (degrees): 70.


INPUT DATA
Magnitude of force F1 = 20.00
Angle F1 makes with x-axis = 30.00 degrees
Magnitude of force F2 = 40.00
Angle F2 makes with x-axis = 70.00 degrees

RESULTS
Magnitude of resultant force = 56.79
Angle resultant makes with x-axis = 56.92 degrees
```

Figure 5.10   Output from program *resultnt.c.*

5.10 PROGRAMMING PROJECT: OPEN CHANNEL FLOW

Problem Statement

The flow of water in an open channel is given approximately by the Chezy–Manning equation

$$Q = \frac{1.486}{n} a r_H^{2/3} s^{1/2} \qquad\qquad (5.10)$$

where Q is the flow (cubic feet per second), n is the Manning roughness coefficient, a is the cross-sectional area of the channel (ft.^{2}), s is the slope of the channel (rise over run) and r_H is the hydraulic radius (area divided by the wetted perimeter).

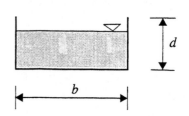

For a rectangular channel

$$a = bd \tag{5.11}$$

$$r_H = \frac{bd}{b + 2d} \tag{5.12}$$

where b is the width of the channel and d is the depth of water in the channel.

Problem Statement

Write a program to determine the flow Q in a channel for given values of b, d, n, and s.

Problem Analysis

Input Variables
width of channel, b (**double b**)
depth of water in channel, d (**double d**)
slope of channel bed, s (**double s**)
Manning's roughness coefficient, n (**double n**).

Output Variables
flow Q (**double q**)

Intermediate Variables
In addition to these variables we will need variables to store the following:
area a, (**double a**)
hydraulic radius, r_H (**double rh**)

Algorithm

1. Read **b**, **d**, **s**, and **n**.
2. Compute **a** from Equation (5.11)
3. Compute **rh** from Equation (5.12)
4. Compute **q** from Equation (5.10).
5. Print **b**, **d**, **s**, and **n**.
6. Print **q**.

Program

The program is shown in Figure 5.11. After declaring the various variables the program obtains input for **b**, **d**, **s**, and **n**. Since these variables are declared to be of type **double**, we use the **%lf** format specifier in the **scanf()** statements. For example, the statement

```
/*********************************************************/
/*   channel.c  -- Open Channel Flow                   */
/*                                                      */
/*   Computes the flow Q (in cfs) throught a trapezoidal */
/*   channel using the Chezy-Manning equation.         */
/*********************************************************/

#include <stdio.h>
#include <math.h>


main()
{
   double b;          /* channel width (ft)            */
   double d;          /* depth of water in channel (ft) */
   double s;          /* slope of channel             */
   double n;          /* Manning's coefficient        */
   double a;          /* area of x-section (ft)       */
   double rh;         /* hydraulic radius (ft)        */
   double q;          /* flow in cfs

   /* read input data */
   printf("\n FLOW THROUGH AN OPEN CHANNEL");
   printf("\n Enter channel width, b, (ft): ");
   scanf("%lf",&b);
   printf(" Enter depth of water in channel, d, (ft): ");
   scanf("%lf",&d);
   printf(" Enter slope of channel, s: ");
   scanf("%lf", &s);
   printf(" Enter Manning's coefficient, n: ");
   scanf("%lf",&n);

   /* compute area and hydraulic radius */
   a = b * d;
   rh = a /(b + 2. * d);

   /* compute flow */
   q = 1.486 * a * pow(rh,2./3.) * sqrt(s) / n;

   /* echo input data and print results */
   printf("\n Input Data");
   printf("\n Channel width, b, = %lf ft",b);
   printf("\n Depth of water in channel, d = %lf feet",d);
   printf("\n Slope of channel, s= %f",s);
   printf("\n Manning's coefficient, n= %lf",n);

   printf("\n\n Results");
   printf("\n Area of channel = %lf sq. ft",a);
   printf("\n Hydraulic radius = %lf feet \n",rh);
   printf("\n Calculated flow = %lf cfs",q);
}
```

Figure 5.11   A program to compute the flow in an open channel.

```
scanf("%lf",&b);
```

calls **scanf()** to read in the value of the channel width, **b**.

The area and hydraulic radius are computed in the statements

```
a = b * d;
rh = a /(b + 2. * d);
```

and the flow Q is computed in the statement

```
q = 1.486 * a * pow(rh,2./3.) * sqrt(s) / n;
```

The expression **pow(rh,2./3.)** calls the C library power function to compute $r_H^{2/3}$, and the expression **sqrt(s)** calls the C library square root function to determine the square root of s. The program then prints the input data, the area of the channel, the hydraulic radius, and the computed flow.

Testing

For $b = 10$ ft, $d = 5$ ft, $s = 0.002$, and $n = 0.015$, we get the following results:

$$a = bd = (10)(5) = 50 \text{ ft}^2$$

$$r_H = \frac{a}{b+2d} = \frac{50}{10+2(5)} = 2.5 \text{ ft}$$

$$Q = \frac{1.486}{0.015}(50)(2.5)^{2/3}(0.002)^{1/2} = 408.04 \text{ cfs}$$

The output from the program for this input data is shown in Figure 5.12. You should test the program using other input values.

```
FLOW THROUGH AN OPEN CHANNEL
Enter channel width, b, (ft): 10.
Enter depth of water in channel, d, (ft): 5.
Enter slope of channel, s: 0.002
Enter Manning's coefficient, n: 0.015

Input Data
Channel width, b, = 10.000000 ft
Depth of water in channel, d = 5.000000 feet
Slope of channel, s= 0.002000
Manning's coefficient, n= 0.015000

Results
Area of channel = 50.000000 sq. ft
Hydraulic radius = 2.500000 feet
Calculated flow = 408.042969 cfs
```

Figure 5.12   Output from program *channel.c*.

5.11 PROGRAMMING PROJECT: ALTERNATING CURRENT CIRCUIT

For an alternating current circuit containing resistance, capacitance, and inductance, the total impedance, current, phase angle, resonant frequency, and band width are given by

$$\text{total impedance} = Z = \sqrt{R^2 + [2\pi fL - 1/(2\pi fC)]^2} \ \ \text{ohms} \qquad \textbf{(5.13)}$$

$$\text{current} = I = \frac{V}{Z} \ \ \text{amperes} \qquad \textbf{(5.14)}$$

$$\text{phase angle} = \theta = \tan^{-1}\left[\frac{2\pi fL - 1/(2\pi fC)}{R}\right] \ \ \text{radians} \qquad \textbf{(5.15)}$$

$$\text{resonant frequency} = f_{res} = \frac{1}{\sqrt{4\pi^2 LC}} \ \ \text{hertz} \qquad \textbf{(5.16)}$$

$$\text{band width} = B = \frac{R}{2\pi L} \ \ \text{hertz} \qquad \textbf{(5.17)}$$

where R is the resistance (ohms), L is the inductance (henrys), C is the capacitance (farads), and f is the frequency (hertz).

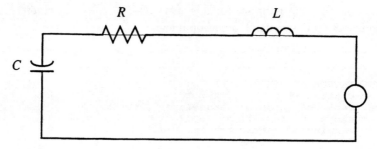

Problem Statement

Write a program that reads in R, L, C, V, and f and computes the impedance Z, the current I, the phase angle, θ, the resonant frequency f_{res}, and the band width B.

Problem Analysis

Input Variables

resistance, R (`double r`)

inductance, L (**double l**)
capacitance, C (**double c**)
voltage, V (**double v**)
frequency, f (**double f**)

Output Variables
total impedance, Z (**double z**)
current, I (**double i**)
phase angle, θ (**double theta**)
resonant frequency, f_{res} (**double f_res**)
band width, B (**double b**)

Algorithm

1.   Read **r**, **l**, **c**, **v**, and **f**.
2.   Compute **z** from Equation (5.13)
3.   Compute **i** from Equation. (5.14).
4.   Compute **theta** from Equation (5.15)
5.   Compute **f_res** from Equation (5.16).
6.   Compute **b** from Equation (5.17).
7.   Echo print **r**, **l**, **c**, **v**, and **f**
8.   Print **z**, **i**, **theta**, **f_res**, and **b**.

Program

The program is shown in Figure 5.13. The program consists of four distinct sections each of which is separated by a blank line and is preceded by a comment line. The first section declares the variables that will be used by the program. The second section reads the input data. The third section performs the computations. We use a temporary variable, **temp**, to simplify the expression for computing the impedance, Z, by breaking it up into two parts. In the last section of the program we echo print the input data and print the results.

Testing

The computations for R = 300 ohms, L = 0.05 henry, C = 0.001 farads, V = 110 volts and f = 60 hertz are as follows:

$$2\pi fL = 2(\pi)(60)(0.05) = 18.85$$

$$1/(2\pi fC) = 1/2(\pi)(60)(0.001) = 2.65$$

$$2\pi fL - 1/(2\pi fC) = 18.85 - 2.65 = 16.20$$

```c
/****************************************************************/
/*   circuit.c  -- Alternating Current Circuit              */
/*                                                          */
/*   Computes the total impedance, current, phase angle,   */
/*   resonant frequency, and band width for an ac circuit  */
/*   consisting of resistance, capacitance and inductance. */
/****************************************************************/
#include <stdio.h>
#include <math.h>
#define PI 3.141592654

main()
{
  double r, l, c;      /* resistance, inductance, capacitance */
  double v, f;         /* voltage, frequency                  */
  double z,i;          /* total impedance, current            */
  double theta;        /* phase angle                         */
  double f_res, b;     /* resonant frequency, band width      */
  double temp;         /* temporary storage                   */

  /* input */
  printf("\n ALTERNATING CURRENT CIRCUIT \n");
  printf(" Enter resistance R (ohms): ");
  scanf("%lf",&r);
  printf(" Enter inductance, L (henry): ");
  scanf("%lf",&l);
  printf(" Enter capacitance, C (farads): ");
  scanf("%lf",&c);
  printf(" Enter voltage, V (volts): ");
  scanf("%lf",&v);
  printf(" Enter frequency, f (hertz): ");
  scanf("%lf",&f);

  /* computations */
  temp = 2 * PI * f * l - 1./(2. * PI * f * c);
  z = sqrt(r*r + temp * temp);
  i = v/z;
  theta = atan(temp/r);
  f_res = 1./ sqrt(4. * PI * PI * l * c);
  b = r/(2. * PI * l);

  /* echo print input data */
  printf("\n Input Data ");
  printf("\n Resistance R = %.4f ohms ", r);
  printf("\n Inductance, L = %.4f henry ", l);
  printf("\n Capacitance, C = %.4f farads", c);
  printf("\n Voltage, V = %.4f volts",v);
  printf("\n Frequency f = %.4f hertz",f);

  printf("\n\n Results ");
  printf("\n Total impedance, Z = %.4f ohms",z);
  printf("\n Current, I = %.4f amperes",i);
  printf("\n Phase angle, theta = %.4f radians",theta);
  printf("\n Resonant frequence, fres = %.4f hertz",f_res);
  printf("\n Band width, b = %.4f hertz",b);
}
```

Figure 5.13   Program for the analysis of an alternating current circuit.

$$Z = \sqrt{300^2 + 16.2^2} = 300.44 \text{ ohms}$$

$$I = V/Z = 110/300.44 = 0.366 \text{ amps}$$

$$\theta = \tan^{-1}(16.20/300) = 0.054 \text{ radians}$$

$$f_{res} = \frac{1}{\sqrt{4\pi^2 LC}} = \frac{1}{\sqrt{4(\pi^2)(0.05)(0.001)}} = 22.51 \text{ hertz}$$

$$b = \frac{R}{2\pi L} = \frac{300}{(2)(0.05)(0.001)} = 954.93 \text{ hertz}$$

The program output for this input data is shown in Figure 5.14. The results obtained from the program agree with the computed values.

```
LTERNATING CURRENT CIRCUIT
Enter resistance R (ohms): 300.
Enter inductance, L (henry): .05
Enter capacitance, C (farads): 0.001
Enter voltage, V (volts): 110
Enter frequency, f (hertz): 60.

Input Data
Resistance R = 300.0000 ohms
Inductance, L = 0.0500 henry
Capacitance, C = 0.0010 farads
Voltage, V = 110.0000 volts
Frequency f = 60.0000 hertz

Results
Total impedance, Z = 300.4369 ohms
Current, I = 0.3661 amperes
Phase angle, theta = 0.0539 radians
Resonant frequence, fres = 22.5079 hertz
Band width, b = 954.9297 hertz
```

Figure 5.14   Output from program *circuit.c*.

5.12   SUMMARY

In this chapter we presented the statements for performing arithmetic operations such as addition, subtraction, multiplication, and division. We also presented the arithmetic assignment statement, which allows us to assign values to variables and the various operators that are used in arithmetic expressions.

An operator is a symbol or word that represents some operation that is performed on one or more data values. C has a large number of basic operators (over 40). The operators used in arithmetic assignment statements are called arithmetic operators. They include the +, -, * and / operators for addition, subtraction, multiplication, and division; the modulus (%) operator, which returns the remainder of an integer division, and the unary minus (-) operator, which changes the sign of its operand. The arithmetic operators are encountered in expressions that appear on the right-hand side of assignment statements.

In addition to the arithmetic operators, C has compound arithmetic assignment operators which are a combination of an arithmetic operator and the assignment operator. These arithmetic assignment operators first perform the operation specified by the arithmetic operator and then assign the result to the variable on the left-hand side of the assignment statement. The arithmetic assignment operators include the +=, -=, *=, /=, and %= operators.

Since increasing and decreasing the value of a variable by one is such a common operation, C provides the increment (++) and decrement (--) operators. The increment operator adds one to its operand, while the decrement operator subtracts one from its operand. These operators can be placed before the variable (prefix) or after the variable (postfix). If placed before the variable, the value of the variable is incremented or decremented before the variable is used in an arithmetic expression. If placed after the variable, the current value of the variable is used in the arithmetic expression and the variable is then incremented or decremented.

In this chapter we also presented the rules regarding operator precedence. The order in which operations are performed is determined by a strict set of rules, and it is important that we understand these rules to ensure that arithmetic expressions are evaluated correctly. We also discussed arithmetic with mixed types. When an arithmetic expression contains operands of different types, the C compiler performs a type conversion. The lower-ranking data type is converted to the higher-ranking type. We can also explicitly specify the conversion we require by using the cast operator. The cast operator forces the compiler to convert a value to the type specified in parentheses. Type casting is also useful when passing information to functions.

All C compilers provide a set of mathematical functions as part of the standard library. These include functions for evaluating square roots, absolute values, logarithms, and trigonometric and exponential functions. We need to include the header file *math.h* whenever we use these functions in our programs.

Key Terms Presented in This Chapter

associativity	cast operator
arithmetic expressions	decrement operator
arithmetic operators	increment operator
arithmetic assignment operators	integer arithmetic

PROGRAM STYLE, COMMON ERRORS, AND DEBUGGING GUIDE

1. To improve program readability you should insert a blank space before and after and the assignment operators and arithmetic operators.

2. You should break up long expressions into smaller subexpressions. For example, when evaluating a complex fraction, you should calculate the numerator and denominator in separate statements and then compute the final result.

3. When continuing a statement over more than one line, you should indent the continuation lines.

4. Extra parentheses and spaces within arithmetic expressions help to make the program more readable. If there is any uncertainty about how the computer will evaluate an expression, use parentheses to make sure that it will be evaluated as desired.

5. When printing numerical values, you should always print the physical units corresponding to the values being printed. This makes it easier to interpret the significance of the results.

6. Avoid using different data types within the same arithmetic expression whenever possible. You should use the cast operator to type cast the variable to the appropriate type. For example, if **i1** and **i2** are of type **int** and **x** is of type **float** the expression

   ```
   x =   (float) i1/i2;
   ```

   should be used instead of

   ```
   x = i1/i2;
   ```

7. In the second statement, since both **i1** and **i2** are integers, the division will be performed using integer arithmetic, and the fractional part of the result will be discarded.

8. Arithmetic operations cannot be implied. For example, the

mathematical expression

$$a = 5(b + 2c)$$

must be written as

```
a = 5 * (b + 2 * c)
```

and not as

```
a = 5(b + 2c)
```

An example of what can happen if we do not include the operator for an implied expression is given next. The program supposedly evaluates the expression **c** = **ab** for **a** = 5 and **b** = 10.

```
int a,b
a = 5;
b = 10
c = ab;
```

The operator * is missing in the arithmetic expression, so C interprets **ab** to be a variable name rather than the product of **a** and **b**. The compiler will generate an error message, since **ab** is not defined. If, however, in the rare case when there is a variable **ab** in the program, the error will not be detected.

9. There must be an equal number of left and right parentheses. This is a common error when writing arithmetic expressions. The following expressions are invalid:

```
c = ((a + b) + (x + y);
c = - (a + b) + (x + y)) + 15.0;
```

The compiler will generate an error message in each case.

10. The arithmetic expression must accurately represent the sequence of operations indicated by the original mathematical expression. This is by far the most common error. It is very easy to write an expression in C that appears to be correct but which does not result in calculations being performed in the same order as defined in the original mathematical expression. Such errors are difficult to detect since they do not result in syntax errors. The only way to avoid such errors is to become thoroughly familiar with the precedence and associativity rules for operators.

11. You should always check the placement of parentheses in an arithmetic expression. Since parentheses have precedence over other arithmetic operators, they can change the order of evaluation of an expression.

12. When using the C library mathematical functions, you should make

sure that the arguments passed to these functions are of the correct type. Use the cast operator to type cast a variable if necessary. For example, when computing the square root of an integer value, use the cast operator to convert the integer value to **double** before passing the value to the **sqrt()** function.

13. You should always include the header file *math.h* whenever you use any of the C library mathematical functions. This header file contains prototypes for the mathematical functions, and including it in your program ensures that the compiler has the necessary information it needs to correctly interpret a function call, such as the type and number of arguments used by the function and the type of value returned by the function.

14. Variables appearing on the right side of an arithmetic assignment statement must be assigned values prior to their use in the arithmetic expression. When an expression is evaluated, the current values of all variables appearing on the right side of the assignment statement are used. Since C does not automatically initialize variables, the value of a variable that has not been initialized will be whatever value happens to be lying around in memory at the time the expression is evaluated.

15. The variable on the left side of an arithmetic expression should have the same or higher ranking than the values on the right side. Precision is lost whenever a higher-ranking data type is assigned to a lower-ranking one. This is because the lower-ranking type is not wide enough to hold the higher-ranking value. For example, an integer variable cannot hold the fractional part of a floating point number and so the fractional part is lost.

16. You should be careful when using the increment and decrement operators in arithmetic expressions. If you place the increment or decrement operator before a variable, the compiler first increments or decrements the variable and then uses the variable to evaluate the expression. If you place the increment or decrement operator after the variable, the compiler first uses the value of the variable to evaluate the expression and then increments or decrements the variable.

17. The modulus operator can be used only with integer operands. You cannot write **x % y** where either **x** or **y** are of type **long**, **float**, or **double**. Both **x** and **y** must be of type **int**.

18. During division, if both operands are of type integer, the C compiler performs integer division. Thus the result of 12/5 is 2 and not 2.4.

EXERCISES

Review Questions

1. Write the following algebraic expressions as C expressions:

    a. $b^2 - 4ac$

    b. $\dfrac{a-b}{c-d}$

    c. $wlx^2 - \dfrac{wx^2}{2}$

    d. $x + y(x+z)$

    e. $\dfrac{y(x^2 - y^2)}{x^2 + 3xy}$

    f. $\dfrac{x}{5 + y/(4.5 + z)}$

    g. $\dfrac{y + z^{5.5}}{x}$

2. Convert the following C expressions into algebraic expressions:

    a. `a + b / c - d`

    b. `z / w * y;`

    c. `a/b*c/d`

    d. `(a*b)/(x-d)*5`

    e. `x*a/c*d-e`

    f. `(a+b)*(c+d)/(c-d)`

    g. `a/b/c/d`

    h. `y1*x1z1*w1*a1`

3. The following are some mathematical expressions and the corresponding C expressions. Each C expression contains at least one error. Indicate the errors and write the correct C expression.

    Mathematical Expression   **C Expression**

    a. $\dfrac{a+5}{b+8}$ `a + 5. /b + 8.`

b. $x\dfrac{y}{a+b}$ xy / (a +b)

c. $\dfrac{x}{y}+\dfrac{uv}{w}$ xy + uv / w

d. $(a+b)(c+d)$ a + b * c + d

4. Distinguish between the use of the equal sign (=) in C and in algebra.

5. Each of the following C assignment statements contains at least one error. Identify them.

   a.   x = 15.47y + cd;
   b.   func = w + 3.5 = x - 4.5;
   c.   8 = y + 4;
   d.   delta = x (y + (3x + (z + 15)));
   e.   x - 5 = y + 4;
   f.   -b = x + y - c;

6. Write C assignment statements for each of the following algebraic equations.

   a. $RT = \dfrac{1}{1/R_1 + 1/R_2}$

   b. $x = \dfrac{a+b}{a-b} \cdot \dfrac{ab}{cd}$

   c. $sum = \dfrac{n(n+1)(2n+1)}{6}$

   d. $f = x^3 - x^2 + 2x - 5$

   e. $y = \dfrac{165,004x + 10^6}{20,000,300b + 10^5}$

7. Write C statements for the equations shown below. Since the expressions are complicated, replace each equation with several simple equations.

   a. $x = \left[\dfrac{4ac}{x+y} - \dfrac{z^3}{6(z^2 + x - y)} \right]^{1/m}$

   b. $x_{max} = \dfrac{[7.897(c-d)^2 - (6.5x)/(c+d)]^4}{[(x^2 - y^2)^n + y^3]^{1/5}}$

8. Consider the following program:

```
#include <stdio.h>
main()
{
    float num;
    num = 30.4;
    num = 2.0 * num;
    printf("\n %f", num + 12.5);
}
```

Write down the value of the variable **num** after each line of the program has been executed.

9. Consider the following program:

```
#include <stdio.h>
main()
{
    int x,y;
    x = 10;
    y = 20;
    x = y;
    y = x;
    printf("\n x = %d, y = %d", x,y);
}
```

Write down the values of the variables **x** and **y** after each line of the program has been executed.

10. Rewrite the following statements using arithmetic assignment operators

a. `sum = sum + term;`

b. `princ = princ * 1.05;`

c. `stepsize = stepsize / 2.0;`

d. `count = count - 2;`

11. Determine the value that is assigned to the variable on the left-hand side for each of the assignment statements shown here. Assume that i is a variable of type **int**.

a. `i = (3 + 5) * 6;`

b. `i = 3/5 + 21.5;`

c. `i = 12.5 + 3/4;`

d. `i = (int) 4.6 + 3;`

e. `i = (3 + 4) * 5.5;`

f. `i = (10 + 4) / 2 * 3;`

12. What is the value assigned to the variable on the left of the assignment statement for each of the following. The statements are not executed sequentially, and the following is in effect for each case:

```
int i = 3, j = 2,k;
float a = 4.5, b = 6.0, c = 5.8, z;
```

a. `z = a/b * c;`

b.   `k = a/b * c;`

c.   `k = a/i + c;`

d.   `k = ++i - a;`

e.   `z = a * i + c * j;`

f.   `k *= j;`

g.   `k -= 2 * j`

h.   `k %= j;`

13. Compute the value that will be assigned to the variable on the left side of the each of the following assignment statements. The initial values for each case are as follows:

```
int i=3, j= 4, k, n;
double a = 2.1, b = 5.8, c, d;
```

a.   `c = a + b / a + b;`

b.   `n = j % i;`

c.   `k = a - b;`

d.   `k = a * b + j;`

e.   `n = a * i / j + b;`

f.   `n = ++i - j--;`

g.   `i = ++j - j--;`

h.   `d = j * a + b * i;`

i.   `d = j * a + i * a;`

j.   `a *= i++;`

14. The variables i, j, and k have the following values:

$i = 3$, $j = 2$, and $k = 4$

What is the value assigned to the variable on the left hand side of each of the following assignment statements? Assume that all variables are of type **int**.

a.   `l = i/j;`   1

b.   `m = k/j;`   2

c.   `a = k/i;`   1   9   4

d.   `x = 4 * k - 3 * i - 2 * j;`   = 1

e.   `m = k % i;`   1.333

f.   `n = i % j - i % k;`   0.75
     1.5 - 0.75 = 0.75

15. A segment of a C program follows. Indicate the values of the variables x, y, and z after each statement is executed.

```
float x = 4.0, y = 3.0, z;
z = x - y;          1.0
y = pow(x,y);       64
x = y/x;
y = y - 2. * x * z;   4.0
x = (y - 2. * x) + 2. * z;
```
      4.0 + 2.0   6.0

```
y = sqrt(2. * y) - z/2.;
```

16. The variables **a**, **b**, **c**, and **d** have the following values:

    ```
    a = 1.5, b = 2.5, c = 4.0, d = 5.0
    ```

    What is the value assigned to the variable on the left-hand side for each of the following assignment statements? Assume that all variables are of type **float**.

    a. `e = 4. * b + (b-a) * (b-a);`

    b. `f = b * (a-b) * (c + 5.);`

    c. `m = a * ((b+c) * (d * (b-a)));`

    d. `h = (b+c)/(a+b) * (c - a);`

    e. `i = ((b+c) /(a+b)) * (c-a);`

17. Give the value of **i** and **j** after each statement is executed. The statements are not executed sequentially. Assume that the following declarations are in effect prior to execution of each statement.

    ```
    int i,j,k;
    i = 4;
    j = 0;
    ```

    a. `j = ++i;`

    b. `j = --i;`

    c. `j = i ++;`

    d. `j = i--;`

    e. `i = k = j--;`

18. What is meant by truncation?

19. What is meant by mixed mode operations? What problems can arise with mixed mode operations?

20. Write C assignment statements for the following equations:

    a. $y = \log(x) + e^{(a+b)} + \cos\theta$

    b. $s = 8\cos^3 z \sin z - 4\cos z \sin z$

    c. $d = \log|x+y| + (\pi/2)\log|x|$

    d. $x = \dfrac{1 + \cos z}{1 - \cos z}$

21. Write C assignment statements for the following algebraic equations:

    a. $x = s\sin\theta + r\cos\theta$

    b. $z = \tan^{-1}(x/y) + e^{ax}(a/x)$

    c. $c = a^2 + b^2 - 2ab\cos\theta$

d. $f = \dfrac{1}{\sigma\sqrt{2\pi}}exp\left[-\dfrac{1}{2}\left(\dfrac{x-\mu}{\sigma}\right)^2\right]$

e. $g = \dfrac{1}{\sqrt{2\pi}\zeta x}exp\left[-\dfrac{1}{2}\left(\dfrac{lnx-\lambda}{\zeta}\right)^2\right]$

22. Write C statements for the following formulas:

   a.   Radius of a circle

$$r = [x^2 + y^2]^{1/2}$$

   b.   Cube root of a number x

$$y = x^{1/3}$$

   c.   The perimeter of an ellipse with semi-axis a, and b:

$$s = 2\pi[(a^2 + b^2)/2]^{1/2}$$

   d.   The area of a triangle, in terms of the lengths of its sides a, b, and c:

$$area = [s(s-a)(s-b)(s-c)]^{1/2}$$

   where $s = (a+b+c)/2$

   e.   The maximum buckling load on a long, slender column:

$$P = \dfrac{\pi^2 AE}{(l/r)^2}$$

   f.   The area moment of inertia of a rectangle

$$I = \dfrac{bh^3}{12}$$

   g.   The period of a pendulum

$$P = 2\pi\sqrt{\dfrac{L}{g}}\left(1 + \dfrac{1}{4}sin^2\left(\dfrac{\alpha}{2}\right)\right)$$

   h.   Reynolds number

$$N = \dfrac{DV\rho}{\mu g}$$

Programming Exercises

23. Write a C program to convert an angle exressed in degrees, minutes, and seconds to one expressed in decimal degrees. Use three **scanf()** statements to read in the degrees, minutes, and seconds. Each **scanf()** statement should be preceded by a call to a **printf()** statement which includes a prompt for the item.

24. The distance between two points (x_1, y_1) and (x_2, y_2) is given by

$$\text{dist} = \sqrt{(x_1 - x_2)^2 + (y_1 - y_2)^2}$$

Write a program that uses **scanf()** to read in the coordinates of four points (x_1, y_1), (x_2, y_2), (x_3, y_3) and (x_4, y_4). Calculate and print the distance between points 1 and 2, 1 and 3, 1 and 4, 2 and 3, 2 and 4, and 3 and 4. The output should be in the form of a table showning the coodinates of the two points and the distance between the points with appropriate headings.

25. Write a program to compute the value of a pocketful of change. Input to the program will consist of the number of coins of each denomination: pennies, nickels, dimes, quarters, and half-dollars. Print the total value in dollars and cents.

26. To check the accuracy of the C mathematical library trigonometric functions, we can compute the results given by the computer for the following trigonometric identities.

   a. $\sin^2\theta + \cos^2\theta = 1$

   b. $\sin 2\theta = 2\sin\theta\cos\theta$

   c. $\cos 2\theta = \cos^2\theta - \sin^2\theta$

   d. $\tan 2\theta = \dfrac{(2\tan\theta)}{(1 - \tan^2\theta)}$

   Write a program that reads the value of θ in radians and computes the left and right-hand sides of these trigonometric identities. Run your program for the following values of θ: 0, $\pi/6$, $\pi/4$, $\pi/3$, and $\pi/2$. Comment on your results.

27. The polar coordinates of a point in a plane are given by (r,θ) where r is the length of the line drawn from the origin to the point, and θ is the angle measured from the positive x axis to the line. Write a program that reads in the polar coordinates for a point and computes and prints its rectangular coordinates (x,y). You may use the following equations to obtain x and y:

   $x = r \cos \theta$

   $y = r \sin \theta$

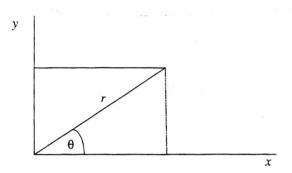

28. The equation of a straight line in the x-y plane is

$$y = mx + c$$

where m is the slope and c the intercept. Given a point P having coordinates (x_0, y_0), find the equations of lines through this new point that are, respectively, parallel and perpendicular to the original line.

The input to the program consists of m, c, x_0, and y_0. The program should print the equation of the original line, the coordinates of the point P, and the equations of the lines that are parallel and perpendicular to the original line.

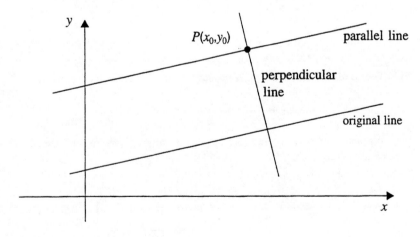

29. The area of a triangle is given by

$$area = \sqrt{s(s-a)(s-b)(s-c)}$$

where a, b, and c are the lengths of the sides, and s is the perimeter of the triangle ($s = (a+b+c)/2$). The radius of the inscribed circle r is given by the equation

$$r = (area)/s$$

and the radius of the enscribed circle is

$$R = (abc)/(4 \cdot \text{area})$$

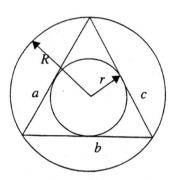

Write a program to read in the values of a, b, and c and compute and print the area, radius of the inscribed circle, and radius of the enscribed circle.

30. Write a program that reads a five digit integer and strips out and prints each digit of the number. For example, for $n = 31452$, the output would be

```
Number = 31452
First digit = 3
Second digit = 1
Third digit = 4
Fourth digit = 5
Fifth digit = 2
```

31. The combined resistance of N resistors arranged in parallel is equal to

$$R_T = \frac{1}{1/R_1 + 1/R_2 + ... + 1/R_N}$$

Write a C program to read four resistance values R_1, R_2, R_3, and R_4 and compute the combined resistance R_T.

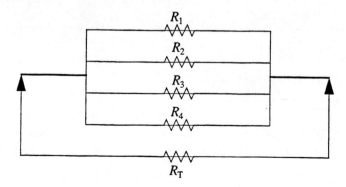

6

CONTROL STRUCTURES: SELECTION

Program statements within a C program are normally executed in sequence from the beginning to the end. However, there are many times when we will need to change this sequential order of execution. For us to develop computer solutions to many engineering problems, our programs must be capable of following different computational paths in response to user input or based on the results of previous computations. Also, since the solution to many engineering problems are of an iterative nature, our programs must be able to repeat the execution of a series of selected statements. In fact, it is the ability to follow different paths through a program that makes the computer such a powerful computational tool. As with all programming languages, C provides a number of statements that allow branching operations.

In Chapter 3 we introduced the three fundamental control structures from which all programs are developed:

1. Sequence structures
2. Selection structures
3. Loop structures

So far all our programs have used the sequence structure. The flow of control was from top to bottom and program statements were executed in sequence. In this chapter we present the C statements that alter the normal sequential flow of control and allow us to implement selection structures. We will present the C statements for implementing loop structures in Chapter 7. With the help of these statements, we can write programs that follow different computational paths and use numerical iterative techniques for the solution of engineering problems.

6.1   THE if STATEMENT

The if statement is a control statement that selects alternative statements for execution based on the result of a test. The simplest form of the if statement is

```
if ( condition )
        statement;
```

The if statement consists of the reserved word if followed by an expression in parentheses and a statement. Normally the expression in parentheses is a relational expression, that is, it compares the magnitude of two quantities. The expression in parentheses is known as the *test condition* or *test*. The statement following the expression can be any C statement.

When the if statement is executed, *condition* is evaluated. If *condition* is true (nonzero), then the *statement* following the test condition is executed. If the test condition evaluates to false (zero) then the *statement* is ignored and control passes to the next sequential statement.

The statement following the condition may be a single statement or a compound statement consisting of a number of single statements enclosed in braces.

```
if ( condition )
       {
       statement1;
       statement2;
       statement3;
       ...
       statementN;
       }
```

In this case of the statements in the block will be executed if the condition is true. Note that each statement within the block ends with a semicolon. The flowchart for the if statement is given in Figure 6.1.

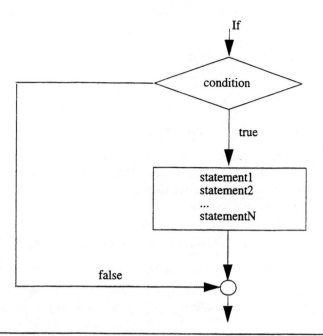

Figure 6.1   Flowchart for *if* statement.

An example of an **if** statement is

```
if (x < 0)
    x = -x;
```

When the foregoing statement is executed, the condition **x < 0** is evaluated. If the condition is true (that is, **x** is less than zero), then the statement

```
x = -x;
```

is executed. If the condition is false (that is, **x** is greater than or equal to zero) the program proceeds to the line following the **if** statement. Note that the effect of this **if** statement is to compute the absolute value of **x**, since whenever **x** is negative, it is converted to a positive value by the unary negation operator (-).

An example of an **if** statement containing a compound statement is the following:

```
if (count < max_items)
    {
    sum += count;
    ++ count;
    }
```

In this example, all the statements enclosed in braces will be executed if the condition is true, that is if **count** is less than **max_items**.

6.2   RELATIONAL OPERATORS

The decision regarding which statements are executed in an **if** statement is usually based on a comparison between two values. In addition to arithmetic operators, C provides *relational operators*, which allow us to compare two values. These relational operators are used in a *relational expression* which consists of the two quantities to be compared and a relational operator. Relational expressions are an essential part of control structures, such as the **if**, **while**, and **for** statements, and enable us to make conditional transfers.

A relational expression has the following form:

> (*value1*) *relational operator* (*value2*)

The quantities to be compared may be constants, variables, or arithmetic expressions. When a relational operator is evaluated, one of two possible values is obtained. If the comparison is true, an integer value of 1 is returned. If the comparison is false, then the integer value of 0 is returned. In C, true is any nonzero value, and false is zero. The relational operators are listed in Table 6.1.

Table 6.1: Relational operators

Relational Operator	Meaning
<	less than
>	greater than
>=	greater than or equal
<=	less than or equal
==	equal
!=	not equal

Some examples of relational expressions are the following:

```
x < 5                 a > b
x + y <= a + c        2. * y < 4. * x + 6.0
i == 5                y >= 2.5
```

You should note the difference between the relational equality operator and the assignment operator. In C, the equality operator is represented by the double equal sign (==), and the assignment operator is represented by a single equal sign (=). A common programming error is to use the assignment operator instead of the equality operator as in the expression

```
if (x = 5)      /* wrong! */
    y++;
```

The expression (x = 5) will always evaluate to true since the value of x is nonzero. The correct expression is

```
if (x == 5)
    y++;
```

Example 6.1   Maximum and Minimum of Three Numbers

The program given in Figure 6.2 computes the maximum and minimum of three numbers. The algorithm for this problem was presented in Chapter 3. Several if statements are employed to arrive at the maximum and minimum value. The program initially assigns the value of a to max and then compares the value of max

```
/**************************************************************/
/*  minmax3.c -- Mimimum and Maximum of Three Numbers         */
/*                                                            */
/*  Computes the minimum and maximum of three numbers         */
/**************************************************************/
#include <stdio.h>

main()
{
    float a,b,c,max,min;

    printf("\n Maximum and minium of three numbers");
    printf("\n Enter three numbers: ");
    scanf("%f%f%f",&a,&b,&c);

    max = a;
    min = a;
    if (b > max)
        max = b;
    if (c > max)
        max = c;

    if (b < min)
        min = b;
    if (c < min)
    min = c;

    printf("\n Maximum value = %f", max);
    printf("\n Minimum value = %f", min);
}
```

Figure 6.2   Maximum and minimum of three numbers.

to the variables **b** and **c**. In the statement

```
if (b > max)
    max = b;
```

if **b** is greater than the current value of **max**, then **max** is assigned the value of **b**. The value of **max** is then compared with **c**. In the statement

```
if (c > max)
    max = c;
```

If **c** is greater than **max** then **max** is assigned the value of **c**. A similar approach is used to compute the minimum value.

Table 6.2 shows a hand trace for this example for the case where **a** = 25, **b** = 15, and **c** = 30. The table shows the value of **max** and **min** as each statement in the program is executed.

Table 6.2: Trace table for Example 6.1.

Statement	a	b	c	max	min	Comments
`float a,b,c,max,min;`	?	?	?	?	?	declare variables
`scanf("%f%f%f", &a,&b,&c);`	25	15	30	?	?	read values
`max = a;`	25	15	30	25	?	max=25
`min = a;`	25	15	30	25	25	min=25
`if (b > max) max = b;`	25	15	30	25	25	15 > 25?, false
`if (c > max) max = c;`	25	15	30	30	25	30 > 25?, true max = 30
`if (b < min) min = b;`	25	15	30	30	15	15 < 25?, true min = 15
`if (c < min) min = c;`	25	15	30	30	15	30 < 15?, false

Example 6.2   True and False in C

The program shown in Figure 6.3 demonstrates what true and false mean in C. The program evaluates several relational expressions and assigns the result to the integer variables **result1** and **result2**. In the statement

```
result1 = (10 > 5);
```

```
/**********************************************************/
/*    trufalse.c  -- True and false in C                 */
/*                                                       */
/*    This program demonstrates what true and false mean in C  */
/**********************************************************/
#include <stdio.h>

main()
{
    int result1,result2;

    /* true expression */
    result1 = (10 > 5);
    /* false expression */
    result2 = (10 < 5);

    printf("\n Value of true in C is: %d", result1);
    printf("\n Value of false in C is: %d", result2);

    if (100)
        printf("\n 100 is also true in C");
    if (-100)
        printf("\n -100 is also true in C");

    printf("\n A non-zero value is true!!!");
}
```

Program output

```
True and false in C

Value of true in C is: 1
Value of false in C is: 0
100 is also true in C
-100 is also true in C
A non-zero value is true!!!
```

Figure 6.3   True and false in C.

the expression **(10 > 5)** is true, and so the variable **result1** is assigned the value of true. From the output from the program, it is seen that the value assigned to **result1** is 1. Thus in C, a true expression evaluates to 1.

In the statement

```
result2 = (10 < 5);
```

the result of the expression **(10 < 5)** is assigned to the variable **result2**. The program output indicates that the value assigned to **result2** is zero. Since the expression is false this means that a false expression evaluates to zero. The expressions **(100)** and **(-100)** are also true. Thus any nonzero value is true in C, and a zero value is false.

Table 6.3 shows some relational expressions and the result obtained when these expressions are evaluated

Table 6.3: Examples of relational expressions

Relational Expression	Result
25 < 6	0 (false)
5.5 > 4.0	1 (true)
10.8 <= 2.05	0 (false)
20 != 10	1 (true)
2 > 4	0 (false)

The relational operators have lower precedence that the arithmetic operators. Thus, when an expression containing both arithmetic and relational operators is evaluated, the arithmetic expressions on both sides of the relational operator are evaluated first and then the results are compared. Thus, the expression

```
15.6 + 2.8 > 10.5 + 4.6
```

is equivalent to

```
(15.6 + 2.8) > (10.5 + 4.6)
```

Example 6.3   Precedence of Operators

PROBLEM STATEMENT: Determine the value of each of the following expressions:

   a.   `25.4 + 32.3 <= 15.1 * 4.0`
   b.   `4.6 * 2.4 + 1.5 > 2.8 + 10.2`

SOLUTION: The expressions are evaluated as follows:

   a.   Expression   `= 25.4 + 32.3 != 15.1 * 4.0`
       Step 1. Multiply `(15.1 * 4.0)` `= 25.4 + 32.3 != 60.4`
       Step 2. Add `(25.4 + 32.3)`   `= 57.7 <= 60.4`
       Step 3. Evaluate `(<=)`   `= 1 (true)`
       Final value of expression   `= 1 (true)`

The arithmetic expressions on both sides of the relational operator <= are evaluated first, and then the comparison is performed. The final result is 1 (true) since 57.7 is not equal to 60.4.

b. Expression   `= 4.6 * 2.4 + 1.5 > 2.8 + 10.2`

     Step 1. Multiply `(4.6 * 2.40)` `= 11.04 + 1.5 > 2.8 + 10.2`

     Step 2. Add `(11.04 + 1.5)`   `= 12.54 > 2.8 + 10.2`

     Step 3. Add `(2.8 + 10.2)`   `= 12.54 > 13.`

     Step 4. Evaluate `(>)`   `= 0 (false)`

     Final value of expression   `= 0 (false)`

The multiplication is performed first, followed by addition. The comparison is made after both arithmetic expressions have been evaluated. The final value is 0 (false) since 12.54 is not greater than 13.

Although relational operators can be used with floating point numbers, you should avoid using the equality operator (`==`) to compare two floating point numbers. Floating point calculations are subject to round-off errors that can prevent two numbers from being equal even though they should be equal. For example, the result of the floating point expression

`1./6. * 6.0`

will not necessarily yield 1 since there is some round-off error in evaluating 1./6.

Example 6.4   Checking for Equality with Real Numbers

The program shown in Figure 6.4 illustrates why you should not use the equality operator when comparing two floating point numbers. The program stores the result of three relational expressions in the integer variables **result1**, **result2**, and **result3**. Although we would expect that all three expressions would evaluate to true, this is not the case. As we can be seen from the program output, all three expressions evaluate to false (0). This is due to the fact that computations with floating point numbers result in round-off errors.

When checking for equality between floating point numbers, you should always write the relational expression as

$$| (a - b) | < \varepsilon$$

```
/*********************************************************/
/*   equality.c -- Comparing Floating Point Numbers     */
/*                  Using the Equality (==) Operator     */
/*                                                       */
/*   This program illustrates why you should avoid       */
/*   using the equality operator to compare floating     */
/*   point numbers.                                      */
/*********************************************************/
#include <stdio.h>

main()
{
    int result1,result2,result3;

    result1 = (0.5 * 6.0 / 3.0 == 1.0);
    result2 = (0.1 + 0.2 + 0.3 + 0.4 == 1.0);
    result3 = (3.0 * 0.1 == 0.3);

    printf("\n result1 = %d",result1);
    printf("\n result2 = %d", result2);
    printf("\n result3 = %d",result3);
}
```

Program output

```
result1 = 0
result2 = 0
result3 = 0
```

Figure 6.4   Checking for equality with floating point numbers.

where ε is a small number (say, 1e-6). The value of ε will depend on the precision with which floating point values are stored in the machine.

6.3   LOGICAL OPERATORS

Logical operators allow us to combine two or more relational expressions to build compound test conditions. The individual relational expressions are linked by the logical operator as shown here

(*relational expression 1*) *logical operator* (*relational expression 2*)

The compound expression is called a *logical expression.* Table 6.4 lists the logical operators.

Table 6.4: Logical operators

Logical Operator	Meaning
&&	logical AND
||	logical OR
!	logical NOT

The logical operators && and || in C have a meaning similar to their meaning in English. The expression

(*expression1*) && (*expression2*)

evaluates to 1 (true) if both *expression1* and *expression2* are true; otherwise it evaluates to 0 (false). The expression

(*expression1*) || (*expression2*)

evaluates to 1 (true) if either one or both of the two individual expressions is true; that is, the entire expression is true if the expression on either side of the logical operator || is true.

The logical negation operator ! when placed before an expression negates the condition; that is, it tests for the complement of the condition. The expression

!(*expression*)

is true if *expression* is false and is false if *expression* is true.

Some examples of logical expressions are the following:

```
age < 65 && age >= 45
x > 5 || x < -5
(a + b) != (c - d)
x + y  < 20  && a + b > 10
ch > 'a' && ch < 'z'
a != b && c != d || x > y
!(x > 0)
```

Table 6.5 lists the results obtained when different relational expressions are combined with the logical operators.

Table 6.5: Combinations of relational and logical operators

Logical Expression	Result
(true) && (true)	true
(true) && (false)	false
(false) && (true)	false
(false) && (false)	false
(true) || (true)	true
(true) || (false)	true
(false) || (true)	true
(false) || (false)	false
(true)	false
(false)	true

Example 6.5   Logical Expressions

PROBLEM STATEMENT: Determine the value of each of the following logical expressions:

  a.   `6 > 4 && 4 > 34`
  b.   `6 > 4 || 4 > 3`
  c.   `!(8 < 6)`
  d.   `10.5 > 16.5 || 8.8 > 10.9`

SOLUTION: The final values of the expressions are as follows:

  a.   The expression `6 > 4` is true and the expression `4 > 34` is false, so the final value of the expression is `0` (false).

  b.   The final value is `1` (true) since the first expression `6 > 4` is true and the second expression `4 > 3` is true.

  c.   The expression `8 < 6` is false. The complement of this expression is true, so the final value is `1` (true).

  d.   The expressions on both sides of the logical `||` operator are false, so the final value is `0` (false).

Precedence of Relational and Logical Operators

The logical not (!) operator has the highest priority. It has a higher priority than multiplication and the same priority as the increment operators. The logical || operator has a lower priority than the && operator. Both the && and || operators have a lower priority than the relational operators and a higher priority than the arithmetic assignment operators. Table 6.6 shows the relative precedence of the relational and logical operators.

Table 6.6: Precedence of relational and logical operators

Precedence	Operator
highest	!
	== > >= < <=
	&&
lowest	||

The expression

    x < y && a == b

is equivalent to

    (x < y) && (a == b)

since the relational operators < and == have a higher precedence than the logical && operator. The expression

    x < y || a > b && c < d

is equivalent to

    (x < y) || ((a > b) && (c < d))

since the && takes precedence over the ||.

It is possible to write complex logical expressions in C. When writing logical expressions you should use parentheses to aid readability and to make sure that the expression is evaluated in the order that you intended. It is easier to be mistaken about the order of evaluation of logical expressions than it is for arithmetic expressions. Also, if possible, try not to make your expressions overly complex. You should break up your expressions into simpler expressions that are easier to read and debug.

6.4   THE `if-else` STATEMENT

Many algorithms involve a choice between two alternatives — one set of statements to be executed if the condition is true and another to be executed if the condition is false. The `if-else` statement lets us choose between two alternative statements. The general form of the `if-else` statement is

```
if ( condition )
    statement1;
else
    statement2;
```

When the `if-else` statement is executed, *condition* is evaluated. If *condition* is true, then *statement1* is executed. If *condition* is false, then *statement2* is executed. The flowchart for the `if-else` statement is shown in Figure 6.5.

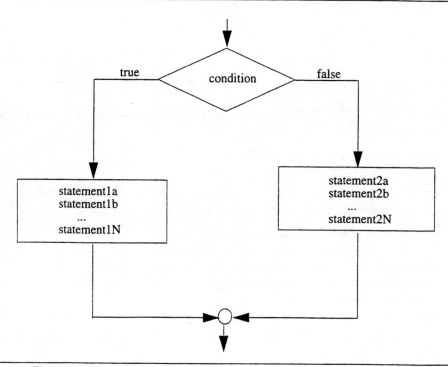

Figure 6.5   Flow chart for `if-else` statement

Some examples of **if-else** statements follow.

```
if (count <= 0)
    a = c + d;
else
    a = c - d;
```

In the foregoing statement, if **count** is less than or equal to zero, then the statement

```
a = c + d;
```

is executed. If **count** is greater than zero, then the statement

```
a = c - d;
```

is executed. The **if-else** statement given here computes the maximum of two numbers **a** and **b**.

```
if (a > b)
    max = a;
else
    max = b;
```

If **a** is greater than **b** then **max** is assigned the value of **a**. If **a** is less than or equal to **b**, then **max** is assigned the value of **b**.

```
if (ch >= 'A' && ch <= 'Z')
    printf("\n Uppercase letter ");
else
    printf("\Not an uppercase letter")
```

The **if-else** statement of the preceding example determines if the value of the variable **ch** represents an uppercase letter.

As with the **if** statement, the object of the **if** and **else** can be a single statement or a block of statements enclosed in braces. The general form of an **if-else** statement with compound statements as objects is

```
if ( expression )
    {
    statement1a;
    statement1b;
       . . .
    }
else
    {
    statement2a;
    statement2b;
       . . .
    }
```

An example of an **if-else** statement containing compound statements as objects of the **if** and **else** is the following

```
if (count <= max_num)
    {
    sum += count;
    ++count;
    }
else
    {
    average = sum/count;
    printf("\n Average is %f", average);
    }
```

If the value of **count** is less than or equal to **max_num**, then the statements

```
sum += count;
++count;
```

will be executed. If **count** is greater than **max_num**, then the statements

```
average = sum/count;
printf("\n Average is %f", average);
```

will be executed.

The statements that are the object of the **if** or **else** should be indented to clarify program structure and enhance readability. Also, for compound statements the opening brace is aligned vertically with the closing brace. This makes it easy to visualize which statements are executed as a result of a true or false condition. Since C is a free-form language it does not care if we indent statements or if the braces are aligned. However, our programs are easier to understand if we follow a logical style of writing code.

6.5   PROGRAMMING PROJECT: GROSS SALARY OF AN EMPLOYEE

Problem Statement

Write a program to compute the gross salary for an employee given the number of hours worked and the hourly rate. If the number of hours worked is greater than 40, the hourly rate shall be 1.5 times the normal hourly rate for all overtime hours. The program should print the number of overtime hours, the regular salary, the overtime salary, and the gross salary for the employee.

Problem Analysis

After reading in the number of hours worked and the hourly rate, we need to determine if the number of hours worked is greater than 40. If the number of hours worked is less than 40, the gross pay is obtained by simply multiplying the number of hours worked by the hourly rate. If the number of hours worked is greater than 40 we need to compute the overtime hours. The gross pay is then obtained from the following equation

Gross pay = 40 * hourly rate + overtime hours * 1.5 * hourly rate

The data requirements for the problem are as follows:

Input Variables
number of hours worked (`float hours`)
hourly rate (`float rate`)

Output Variables
number of overtime hours (`float overtime`)
regular salary (`float regular_pay`)
overtime salary (`float overtime_pay`)
gross salary (`float gross_pay`)

Algorithm

1. Read **hours, rate.**
2. Compute overtime hours, regular salary, and overtime salary as follows:

    If **hours** is less than 40, then do the following:

    > 2.1 Set **overtime equal to 0.**
    > 2.2 Calculate **regular_pay = hours * rate.**
    > 2.3 Set **ovetime_pay equal to 0.**

    else do the following:

    > 2.4 Calculate **overtime = hours - 40.**
    > 2.5 Calculate **regular_pay = 40 * rate.**
    > 2.6 Calculate **overtime_pay = overtime * 1.5 * rate.**

3. Calculate **gross_pay = regular_pay + overtime_pay**
4. Print **rate, hours**.
5. Print **overtime, overtime_rate, regualar_pay.**

Pseudocode
READ hours, rate
IF hours < 40
    regular_pay ← hours * rate

```
        overtime ← 0.
        overtime_pay ← 0.
ELSE
        regular_pay ← 40. * rate
        overtime ← hours - 40.
        overtime_pay ← overtime * 1.5 * rate
ENDIF
gross_pay ← regular_pay + overtime_pay
PRINT hours, rate
PRINT overtime, regular_pay, overtime_pay, gross_pay
```

Flowchart

The flowchart representation of the algorithm is shown in Figure 6.6.

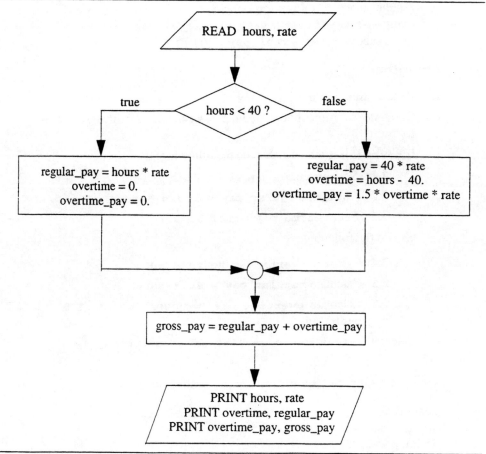

Figure 6.6   Flowchart for program *pay.c*.

Program

The program is shown in Figure 6.7. The program computes the regular salary and the overtime salary of the employee based on the number of hours worked and the hourly rate. The program uses an **if-else** statement to compute the pay for the two cases when: (1) the number of hours worked is less than or equal to 40 and (2) the number of hours worked greater than 40. The overtime rate is computed by multiplying the hourly rate by 1.5.

```
/********************************************************************/
/*    pay.c -- Gross Salary of an Employee                        */
/*                                                                 */
/*    Compute the gross slaary of an employee. If the number of   */
/*    of hours worked is greater than 40 an overtime rate of 1.5  */
/*    1.5 times the normal hourly rate is used.                   */
/********************************************************************/
#include <stdio.h>

main()
{
    float hours, rate;
    float regular_pay,overtime,overtime_pay;
    float gross_pay;

    printf("\n Enter number of hours worked: ");
    scanf("%f",&hours);
    printf(" Enter hourly rate: ");
    scanf("%f",&rate);

    if (hours <= 40)
        {
        regular_pay = hours * rate;
        overtime = 0.0;
        overtime_pay = 0.0;
        }
    else
        {
        regular_pay = 40.0 * rate;
        overtime = hours - 40.0.;
        overtime_pay = overtime * 1.5 * rate;
    gross_pay = regular_pay + overtime_pay;
        }
    printf("\n Number of hours worked:    %10.2f", hours);
    printf("\n Hourly rate:               %10.2f", rate);
    printf("\n Number of overtime hours: %10.2f", overtime);
    printf("\n Overtime rate:             %10.2f", 1.5 * rate);
    printf("\n Regular salary:            %10.2f",regular_pay);
    printf("\n Overtime salary:           %10.2f", overtime_pay);
    printf("\n Total salary:              %10.2f",gross_pay);
    }
```

Figure 6.7   A program to compute gross pay for an employee.

If the relational expression **(hours <= 40)** in the **if-else** statement is true, then the gross salary is computed using the normal hourly rate. If the relational expression is false, the program determines the number of hours worked in excess of 40 and multiplies this result by 1.5 times the normal hourly rate. The gross salary is computed by adding the regular salary and the overtime salary.

Testing

To test the program we use values of hours worked less than 40 and greater than 40. The program output for the two cases is shown in Figure 6.8. You should also run the program for the case when the number of hours worked is equal to 40.

```
Enter number of hours worked: 35.
Enter hourly rate: 25.

Number of hours worked:        35.00
Hourly rate:                   25.00
Number of overtime hours:       0.00
Overtime rate:                 37.50
Regular salary:               875.00
Overtime salary:                0.00
Total salary :                875.00



Enter number of hours worked: 50.
Enter hourly rate: 15.

Number of hours worked:        50.00
Hourly rate:                   15.00
Number of overtime hours:      10.00
Overtime rate:                 22.50
Regular salary:               600.00
Overtime salary:              225.00
Total Salary:                 825.00
```

Figure 6.8   Input and output for two sample runs.

6.6   PROGRAMMING PROJECT: BEAM ANALYSIS

A beam is an important member used in structures for carrying vertical loads. A common type of beam is a simply supported beam which is pinned at one end and has a roller support at the other end.

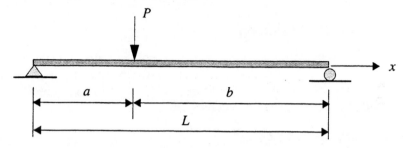

For a concentrated load P acting at a distance a from the left support, the reactions are obtained from

$$R_A = \frac{Pb}{L}$$ (6.1)

$$R_B = \frac{Pa}{L}$$ (6.2)

The shear force, bending moment, and deflection are given by the following equations:

For $x < a$

$$V(x) = \frac{Pb}{L}$$ (6.3)

$$M(x) = \frac{Pbx}{L}$$ (6.4)

$$y = -\frac{Pbx(L^2 - b^2 - x^2)}{(6EIL)}$$ (6.5)

For $x \geq a$

$$V(x) = -\frac{Pa}{L}$$ (6.6)

$$M(x) = P\left(\frac{bx}{L} - x + a\right) \qquad\qquad (6.7)$$

$$y(x) = -\frac{Pa(L-x)[2Lb - b^2 - (L-x)^2]}{(6EIL)} \qquad\qquad (6.8)$$

Problem Statement

Write a program to compute the support reactions and the shear force, bending moment, and deflection of a simply supported beam at a point located at a distance x from the left support. The beam is subjected to a concentrated load P acting at a distance a from the left support.

Problem Analysis

After reading in the input values we need to compute the left and right reactions using Equations (6.1) and (6.2). We then need to determine if x is less than a. If x is less than a, the shear, moment and deflection are computed using Equation (6.3) through Equation (6.5), otherwise, they are computed using Equation (6.6) through Equation (6.8).

The data requirements for the problem are the following:

Input Variables
span of beam, L (**double l**)
moment of inertia, I (**double i**)
modulus of elasticity, E (**double e**)
magnitude of concentrated load, P (**double p**)
distance of load from left support, a (**double a**)
distance x at which results are needed (**double x**)

Output Variables
left and right support reactions (**double ra, rb**)
shear force at distance x (**double v**)
bending moment at distance x (**double m**)
vertical deflection at distance x (**double y**)

Intermediate Variables
b distance from right support to load (**double b**)

Algorithm

1. Read **l**, **i** ,**e**, **p**, **a**, and **x**.
2. Compute **b = l - a**.

3.   Compute left reaction, **ra** from Equation(6.1) .

4.   Compute right reaction **rb** from Equation(6.2).

5.   Compute shear force, bending moment and deflection as follows:

   If $x \leq a$

   5.1 Compute shear force, **v**, from Equation (6.3).

   5.2 Compute bending moment, **m**, from Equation(6.4).

   5.3 Compute deflection, **y**, from Equation(6.5).

   else

   5.1 Compute shear force, **v**, from Equation(6.6).

   5.2 Compute bending moment, **m**, from Equation(6.7).

   5.3 Compute deflection, **y**, from Equation(6.8).

6.   Print **l, i, e, p, a, x**.

7.   Print **ra, rb**.

8.   Print **x, v, m, y**.

Pseudocode

```
READ l, i, e, p, a and x
b ← 1 - a
ra ← pb/l
rb ←   pa/l
    IF x < a
    v ← p*b/l
    m ← p*b*x/l
    y ← -p*b*x *(1*l-b*b-x*x)/(6.0*e*i*l)
ELSE
    v ← -p*a/l
    m ← p*(b*x/l - x + a)
    y ← (-p*a*(l-x)*(2.0*l*b-b*b-(l-x)*(l-x)))/(6.0*e*i*l)
ENDIF
PRINT l, i, e, p, a ,x
PRINT ra, rb
PRINT x, v, m, y
```

Program

   The program is shown in Figure 6.9. The program reads in the beam properties, the magnitude and location of the concentrated load, and the distance x at which results are to be evaluated. The left and right reations are then computed. An **if-else** statement is used to compute the shear, moment, and deflection.

```
/**********************************************************************/
/*  beam1.c  -- Shear, Moment and Deflection of a Simply           */
/*                Supported Beam Due to a Concentrated Load         */
/*                                                                  */
/* Compute and prints the shear, moment and deflection             */
/* and support reactions at a distance x from the left             */
/* support for a simply supported beam due to a                    */
/* concentrated load of magnitude P acting at a distance a.        */
/**********************************************************************/
#include <stdio.h>

main()
{
    double l;                    /* beam span                      */
    double i;                    /* moment of intertia of section  */
    double e;                    /* modulus of elasticity of material */
    double p,a,b;                /* load parameters                */
    double x,v;                  /* distance, shear                */
    double m,y;                  /* moment and deflection          */
    double ra,rb;                /* left and right reactions       */

    printf("\n SHEAR, MOMENT AND DEFLECTION OF A SIMPLY");
    printf("\n SUPPORTED BEAM DUE TO A CONCENTRATED LOAD");

    /* Input beam properties */
    printf("\n Enter beam span (in.): ");
    scanf("%lf",&l);
    printf(" Enter moment of inertia of section (in^4): ");
    scanf("%lf",&i);
    printf(" Enter modulus of elasticity of material (ksi): ");
    scanf("%lf",&e);

    /* Input magnitude and location of load */
    printf("\n Enter magnitude of concentrated load (kips): ");
    scanf("%lf",&p);
    printf(" Enter distance of load from left support (in.): ");
    scanf("%lf",&a);

    /* input point at which values are required */
    printf("\n Enter value of x (in.): ");
    scanf("%lf",&x);

    /* computations */
    b = l - a;

    /* compute reactions */
    ra = p*b/l;
    rb = p*a/l;

    /* compute shear, moment and deflection */
    if (x < a )
        {
        v = p*b/l;
        m = p*b*x/l;
        y = -p*b*x *(l*l-b*b-x*x)/(6.0*e*i*l);
        }
```

Figure 6.9   A program to compute shear, moment, and deflection for a simply
               supported beam due to a concentrated load.

```
    else
        {
        v = -p*a/1;
        m = p*(b*x/1 - x + a);
        y = -p*a*(1-x)*(2.0*1*b-b*b-(1-x)*(1-x));
        y = y/(6.0*e*i*1);
        }

    /*display results */
    printf("\n INPUT DATA");
    printf("\n Beam span = %-.2f inches",1);
    printf("\n Moment of inertia = %-.2f in^4",i);
    printf("\n Modulus of elasticity = %-.2f ksi",e);
    printf("\n Magnitude of concentrated load = %-.2f kips",p);
    printf("\n Distance of load from left support = %-.2f",a);

    printf("\n \n RESULTS");
    printf("\n Left reaction = %-.2f kips", ra);
    printf("\n Right reaction = %-.2f kips",rb);
    printf("\n\n At x = %-.2f in. from left support:",x);
    printf("\n Shear force = %-.2f kips",v);
    printf("\n Bending moment = %-.2f kip-in.", m);
    printf("\n Deflection = %-.4f in.", y);
}
```

FIGURE 6.9   (*continued*)

Control is transferred to two alternative sets of statements depending on the result of the test (**x < a**).

You should note that the program prints the physical units for each input value. The equations are unit dependent, and it is necessary to use a consistent set of units. The program as written uses kips for force and inches for length.

Testing

We need to test the program for two case, $x < a$ and $x \geq a$. For $L = 240$ in., $E = 29,000$ ksi, $I = 1000$ in^4, $P = 20$ kips, a $= 120$ in. and $x = 60$ in. we get the following results:

$$R_A = \frac{Pb}{L} = \frac{20(120)}{240} = 10 \ \text{kips}$$

$$R_B = \frac{Pa}{L} = \frac{20(120)}{240} = 10 \ \text{kips}$$

$$V = \frac{Pb}{L} = \frac{20(120)}{240} = 10 \ \text{kips}$$

$$M = \frac{Pbx}{L} = \frac{20(120)(60)}{240} = 600 \quad \text{kip-in}$$

$$y = \frac{-Pbx(L^2 - b^2 - x^2)}{6EIL} = -\frac{20(120)(60)(240^2 - 120^2 - 60^2)}{6(29000)(1000)(240)} = -0.1366 \text{ in.}$$

A sample run using the values just given is shown in Figure 6.10. The results from the program agree with those obtained by hand calculation.

To test the second case we can use the following values: $L = 240$ in., $E = 29,000$ ksi, $I = 1000$ in.^{4}, $P = 20$ kips, $a = 120$ in., and $x = 180$ in. The results for this case are $R_A = 10$ kips, $R_B = 10$ kips, $V = -10$ kips, $M = 600$ kip-in., and $y = -0.1366$. We can verify this by noting that the load P is acting at the center of the beam and so the moment and deflection at $x = 180$ in. will be the same as at $x = 60$ in. because of symmetry. The program output for this case is also shown in Figure 6.10.

```
INPUT DATA
Beam span = 240.00 inches
Moment of inertia = 1000.00 in^4
Modulus of elasticity = 29000.00 ksi
Magnitude of concentrated load = 20.00 kips
Distance of load from left support = 120.00

RESULTS
Left reaction = 10.00 kips
Right reaction = 10.00 kips

At x = 60.00 in. from left support:
Shear force = 10.00 kips
Bending moment = 600.00 kip-in.
Deflection = -0.1366 in.


INPUT DATA
Beam span = 240.00 inches
Moment of inertia = 1000.00 in^4
Modulus of elasticity = 29000.00 ksi
Magnitude of concentrated load = 20.00 kips
Distance of load from left support = 120.00

RESULTS
Left reaction = 10.00 kips
Right reaction = 10.00 kips

At x = 180.00 in. from left support:
Shear force = -10.00 kips
Bending moment = 600.00 kip-in.
Deflection = -0.1366 in.
```

Figure 6.10   Output from program *beam1.c*.

6.7 NESTED *if* STATEMENTS

The object of an **if** statement can be another **if** statement. A *nested* **if** statement is an **if** statement that is the object of either an **if** or an **else** as in

```
if ( condition1 )
    if ( condition2 )
        statement;
```

If both *condition1* and *condition2* are true, then *statement* will be executed. The above construct is equivalent to

```
if ( expression1 && expression2 )
    statement;
```

An example of a nested **if** statement is

```
if (x > 0)
    if (y != 0)
        z = x/y;
```

If **x** is greater than zero and **y** is not equal to zero, the statement

```
z = x/y;
```

is executed. If either of the expressions is false, then the statement is skipped.

An example of a nested **if-else** construct is

```
if ( expression1 )
    if ( expression2)
        statement1;
    else
        statement2;
else
    statement3;
```

In the preceding construct, if both *expression1* and *expression2* are true, then *statement1* is executed. If *expression1* is true and *expression2* is false, then *statement2* is executed. If *expression1* is false, then the inner **if** statement is skipped and *statement3* is executed. An example of this type of construction is

```
if (x > 0)
    if (y != 0)
        z = x/y;
    else
        z = x * y;
else
    z = y/x;
```

A nested **if** statement that causes some confusion is the one following:

```
if ( expression1 )
    if ( expression2 )
        statement1;
    else
        statement2;
```

The ambiguity comes from the fact that it is not obvious as to which `if` the `else` refers to. In C the `else` statement is always associated with the closest `if` statement that does not have an `else` statement. Thus, in the example just given, the `else` is linked to the second `if` statement and not the first. If we want the `else` to be associated with the first `if` statement, then we have to use braces

```
if ( expression1 )
    {
    if ( expression2 )
        statement1;
    }
else
    statement2;
```

Now the `else` is associated with the first `if` statement.

6.8 PROGRAMMING PROJECT: AXIAL LOAD FOR A STEEL COLUMN

The axial load capacity of a steel is given by the equation

$$P_a = F_a A \tag{6.9}$$

where F_a is the allowable stress and A is the cross-sectional area of the column. The allowable stress F_a as given by the Americal Institute for Steel Construction (AISC) Allowable Stress Design Specification is as follows:
When $KL/r < C_c$

$$F_a = \frac{\left\{ 1 - [(KL/r)^2 / (2C_c^2)] \right\}}{FS} \tag{6.10}$$

and when $KL/r \geq C_c$

$$F_a = \frac{12\pi^2 E}{23(KL/r)^2} \tag{6.11}$$

Here FS is the factor of safety given by

$$FS = \frac{5}{8} + \frac{3(KL/r)}{8C_c} - \frac{(KL/r)^3}{8C_c^3} \qquad (6.12)$$

In Equations (6.10) – (6.12), L is the length of the column, r is the radius of gyration, K is an effective length factor whose value depends on how the column is supported, KL/r is the slenderness ratio, $C_c = \sqrt{(2\pi^2 E)/F_y}$, E is the modulus of elasticity (29,000 ksi), and F_y is the yield stress of steel.

Equations (6.10) – (6.12) above apply to members which have slenderness ratios less than 200. Also, since a column can fail by buckling about either the strong x asis or the weak y axis, the value of KL/r to be used in these equations is the larger of $(KL/r)_x$ and $(KL/r)_y$, where the subscripts x and y refer to the strong and weak axes.

Problem Statement

Write a program to read in L_x, L_y, K_x, K_y, r_x, r_y, A, F_y and E for a steel column and compute the allowable load. The program should print an error message if KL/r is greater than 200.

Problem Analysis

After reading in the input data, we need to compute the slenderness ratio for the x and y axes and determine the larger of the two since the larger of $(KL/r)_x$ and $(KL/r)_y$ will determine the allowable stress for the column. We need to compare this value with the code-allowable value of 200. We also need to compute C_c to determine which equation (6.10 or 6.11) governs.

The data requirements for the problem are as follows:

Input Variables
distance between supports, L_x, L_y (**double lx, ly**)
effective length factors, K_x, K_y (**double kx, ky**)
radius of gyration, r_x, r_y (**double rx, ry**)
area of crosssection, A (**double A**)
yield stress of steel, F_y (**double Fy**)
modulus of elasticity, E (**double e**)
magnitude of concentrated load, P (**double p**)
distance of load from left support, a (**double a**)
distance x at which results are needed (**double x**)

Output Variables
allowable stress, F_a (**double fa**)
allowable axial load, P_a (**double pa**)

Program Variables
slenderness ratios, $(KL/r)_x$ and $(KL/r)_y$ for x and y axes
    (**double klrx, klry**)
maximum slenderness ratio, larger of $(KL/r)_x$ and $(KL/r)_y$
    (**double klr_max**)
C_c (**double cc**)

Algorithm

1. Read **lx, ly, kx, ky, rx, ry, a, fy**.
2. Set **e** = 29000 (ksi).
3. Compute **klrx** and **klry**.
4. If **klrx** > **klry** then
      4.1 klrmax = klrx.
  else
      4.1 klrmax = klry.
5. If **klrmax** ≤ 200
    5.1 Compute **cc**.
    5.2 If **klrmax** ≤ **cc**.
        5.2.1 Compute **fs** from Equation (6.12).
        5.2.2 Compute **fa** from Equation (6.10).
      else
        5.2.1 Compute **fa** from Equation (6.11).
    5.3 Compute **pa** from Equation (6.9).
    5.4 Print **fa, pa**.
  else
    5.5 Print error message.

Pseudocode

```
READ lx, ly, kx, ky, rx, ry, a, fy
e ← 29000
klrx ← kx * lx * 12/rx
klry ← ky * ly * 12/ ry
```

```
IF klrx < klry
    klrmax ← klrx
ELSE
    klrmax ← klry;
ENDIF
IF klrmax ≤ 200
    cc ← sqrt((2. * PI * PI * e)/fy)
    IF klrmax ≤ cc
        Compute fs from Eq. (6.12)
        Compute fa from Eq(6.10)
    ELSE
        Compute fa from Eq. (6.11)
    ENDIF
    pa ← fa * a
ELSE
    Print "KL/r is greater than 200"
ENDIF
```

Program

The program is shown in Figure 6.11. The program first reads in the input parameters. An **if-else** statement is used to determine the larger value of **klrx** and **klry**. The program employs pair of nested **if-else** statements to determine if **klrmax** is less than 200 and to compute the allowable stress if this condition is true. The statement begining with

```
if klrmax <= 200
```

determines if **klrmax** is greater than 200. If the condition is true, then **cc** is computed and the nested **if-else** statement beginning with

```
if klrmax <= cc
```

is executed. Depending on whether the condition just given is true of false, the appropriate equation is used to compute the allowable stress.

If **klrmax** is greater than 200, then the else part of the outer **if-else** statement is executed, and the computations for allowable stress are not performed. For this case the program prints the value of **klrmax** and displays a message indicating that the code equations do not apply.

Testing

To test the program we need to select data so that all three computational paths of the program are exercised, that is, $KL/r < C_c$, $KL/r > C_c$ and $KL/r > 200$.

```
/*************************************************************/
/*  steelcol.c -- Allowable Load for a Steel Column         */
/*                                                          */
/*  Computes the allowable load for a concentrically loaded */
/*  steel column.                                           */
/*************************************************************/
#define PI 3.141593
#include <stdio.h>
#include <math.h>

main()
{
   double lx; /* distance between supports - x axis buckling (ft.) */
   double ly; /* distance between supports - y axis buckling (ft.) */
   double kx; /* effective length factor - x axis                  */
   double ky; /* effective length factor - y axis                  */
   double rx; /* radius of gyration - x axis (in.)                 */
   double ry; /* radius of gyration - y axis (in.)                 */
   double area; /* area of column (sq. in.)                        */
   double fy;   /* yield stress of steel (ksi)                     */
   double e=29000.;   /* modulus of elasticity (ksi)               */
   double klr_x; /* slenderness parameter - x axis buckling        */
   double klr_y; /* slenderness parameter - y axis buckling        */
   double klr_max; /* maximum slenderness ratio                    */
   double fs;    /* factor of safety                               */
   double fa;    /* allowable stress (ksi)                         */
   double pa;    /* allowable axial load  (kips)                   */
   double cc;

   /* ------------------- read data ----------------------*/

   printf( "\n       ALLOWABLE CAPACITY OF A STEEL COLUMN\n");
   printf("\n Enter distance between supports - lx (ft) ");
   scanf("%lf",&lx);
   printf(" Enter distance between supports - ly (ft) ");
   scanf("%lf",&ly);
   printf(" Enter effective length factor, kx, for x-axis: ");
   scanf("%lf",&kx);
   printf(" Enter effective length factor, ky, for y-axis: ");
   scanf("%lf",&ky);
   printf(" Enter radius of gyration, rx, for x-axis: ");
   scanf("%lf",&rx);
   printf(" Enter radius of gyration, ry, for y-axis: ");
   scanf("%lf",&ry);
   printf(" Enter area of column (sq. in.): ");
   scanf("%lf",&area);
   printf(" Enter yield stress of steel (ksi): ");
   scanf("%lf",&fy);

   /* ------------------ computations ---------------------- */

   klr_x = kx*lx*12./rx;
   klr_y = ky*ly*12./ry;
```

Figure 6.11   A program to compute allowable axial load for a steel column.

```
/* compute maximum of klr_x and klr_y  */
if (klr_x > klr_y )
   klr_max = klr_x;
else
   klr_max = klr_y;


/* check for klr > 200  */
if (klr_max <= 200. )
   {
   /* klr < 200 so compute allowable stress */
   cc = sqrt((2.*PI*PI*e)/fy);

   if ((klr_max) <  cc )
      {
      /* klr < cc  */
      fs=5./3.+(3./8.)*klr_max/cc-(1./8.)*pow((klr_max/cc),3);
      fa = fy*(1. - .5*(klr_max/cc)*(klr_max/cc) )/fs;
      }
   else
      {
      /* klr >= cc  */
      fa = 12. * PI * PI * e/(23. * klr_max *klr_max);
      pa = fa * area;
      }
   pa = fa * area;
   }

/*------------------- print results ----------------------*/
printf( "\n\n Distance between supports, lx = %-.2f ft", lx);
printf( "\n Distance between supports, ly = %-.2f ft", ly);
printf( "\n Effective length factor, kx = %-.2f",kx);
printf( "\n Effective length factor, ky = %-.2f", ky);
printf( "\n Radius of gyration, rx = %-.2f in.",rx);
printf( "\n Radius of gyration, ry = %-.2f in.", ry);
printf( "\n Cross-sectional area, A = %-.2f sq. in.", area);
printf( "\n Yield stress, fy = %-.2f ksi",fy);

if (klr_max <= 200)
   {
   printf( "\n \n Allowable stress = %-.2f ksi", fa);
   printf( "\n Allowable axial load = %-.2f kips", pa);
   }
else
   {
   printf("\n \n The slenderness ratio of %-.2f exceeds",klr_max);
   printf ( "\n the code allowable value of 200.");
   }
}
```

FIGURE 6.11 *(continued)*

As an example, we will consider a column made from A36 steel having a W14×82 section with the following properties:

$L_x = L_y = 18$ ft, $K_x = K_y = 1.0$, $r_x = 6.05$ in., $r_y = 2.48$ in., $A = 24.1$ in.^{2}, and $F_y = 36$ ksi

For this case

$$\left(\frac{KL}{r}\right)_x = \frac{(1)(18)(12)}{6.05} = 35.70$$

and

$$\left(\frac{KL}{r}\right)_y = \frac{(1)(18)(12)}{2.48} = 87.10$$

Thus, $(KL/r)_{max} = 87.01$

$$C_c = \sqrt{\frac{2(\pi)^2(29000)}{36}} = 126.1$$

Since $(KL/r)_{max} < C_c$, equation (6.10) applies. The factor of safety *FS* is

$$FS = \frac{5}{3} + \frac{3(87.10)}{8(126.1)} - \frac{(87.1)^3}{8(126.1)^3} = 1.88$$

and the allowable stress is

$$F_a = \frac{\left[1 - \frac{87.1^2}{2(126.1)^2}\right](36)}{1.88} = 14.58 \text{ ksi}$$

Thus, the allowable load for the column is

$$P_a = (14.58)(24.1) = 351.4 \text{ kips}$$

The output from the program for this example for the case when *KL/r* is less than C_c is shown in Figure 6.12. The results agree with those obtained by hand calculation. We will leave it as an exercise for the reader to verify that the program does produce correct results for the other two cases.

```
        ALLOWABLE CAPACITY OF A STEEL COLUMN

Enter distance between supports - lx (ft) 18.
Enter distance between supports - ly (ft) 18.
Enter effective length factor, kx, for x-axis: 1.
Enter effective length factor, ky, for y-axis: 1.
Enter radius of gyration, rx, for x-axis: 6.05
Enter radius of gyration, ry, for y-axis: 2.48
Enter area of column (sq. in.): 24.1
Enter yield stress of steel (ksi): 36.


Distance between supports, lx = 18.00 ft
Distance between supports, ly = 18.00 ft
Effective length factor, kx = 1.00
Effective length factor, ky = 1.00
Radius of gyration, rx = 6.05 in.
Radius of gyration, ry = 2.48 in.
Cross-sectional area, A = 24.10 sq. in.
Yield stress, fy = 36.00 ksi

Allowable stress = 14.55 ksi
Allowable axial load = 350.57 kips
```

Figure 6.12 Output from program *steelcol.c.*

6.9 THE **else-if** CONSTRUCT

The statement following the **else** in an **if-else** statement can be another **if** statement. In fact, a series of **if** statements can be chained together, resulting in the following construction:

```
if ( expression1 )
    statement1;
else if ( expression2 )
    statement2;
else if ( expression3 )
    statement3;
    ...
    ...
else if ( expressionN)
    statementN;
else
    default statement;
next sequential statement;
```

The entire construction is a single **if** statement. When the statement is executed, the expressions are evaluated in order. If *expression1* is true, then *statement1* is executed. If *expression1* is false then *expression2* is evaluated. If it is true then *statement2* is executed. If both *expression1* and *expression2* are false, then *expression3* is evaluated and so on. If all expressions are false then *default statement* is executed. Note that in all cases, only one statement will be executed, and all others will be skipped. The default statement is optional. If it is omitted, and none of the expressions is true, then all statements are skipped and the next sequential statement is executed.

An example of the **else-if** construct is the following:

```
if (score <= 100 && score >= 90)
    grade = 'A';
else if (score <= 89 && score >= 80)
    grade = 'B';
else if (score <= 79 && score >= 70)
    grade = 'C';
else if (score <= 69 && score >= 60)
    grade = 'D';
else if (score < 60 )
    grade = 'F';
else
    grade = "*';
```

6.10 PROGRAMMING PROJECT: ROOTS OF A QUADRATIC EQUATION

The roots of a quadratic equation of the form

$$ax^2 + bx + c = 0 \qquad (6.13)$$

can be evaluated as follows. The nature of the roots is determined by the value of the discriminant, Δ:

$$\Delta = b^2 - 4ac \qquad (6.14)$$

If $\Delta \le 0$, then the roots are real and are given by

$$x_1 = \frac{-b + \sqrt{b^2 - 4ac}}{2a} \qquad (6.15)$$

$$x_2 = \frac{-b - \sqrt{b^2 - 4ac}}{2a} \qquad (6.16)$$

If $\Delta < 0$, then the roots are complex and are given by

$$x_1 = \frac{1}{2a}[-b + i(-\Delta)^{1/2}] \qquad\qquad (6.17)$$

$$x_2 = \frac{1}{2a}[-b - i(-\Delta)^{1/2}] \qquad\qquad (6.18)$$

where $i = (-1)^{1/2}$.

For the case when $a = 0$ the equation is no longer a quadratic equation but a linear equation and the root is given by

$$x = -\frac{c}{b} \qquad\qquad (6.19)$$

Problem Statement

Write a program to compute the roots of a quadratic equation. The program should determine whether the roots are real and equal, real and distinct, or imaginary and should print the roots for each case. The program should also consider the case where $a = 0$.

Problem Analysis

Since the nature of the roots depends on the value of the discriminant, we need to first evaluate the discriminant and based on its value select the appropriate equations for computing the roots. However, we also need to perform a check to see if a is equal to zero before computing the discriminant.

The data requirements for the problem are as follows:

Input Variables
coefficients a, b and c (**double a, b, c**)

Output Variables
roots of equation (**double root1, root2**)
real and imaginary parts of the roots if the roots are complex
   (**double real_part, imag_part**)

Intermediate Variables
discriminant, Δ (**double delta**)

Algorithm

1. Read **a**, **b**, and **c**.
2. Compute discriminant, `delta = b*b - 4. * a * c`.
3. If **a** = 0

      3.1 Compute `root1 = -c/b`.

      3.2 Print "Single root".

      3.3 Print `root1`.

   else if `disc` >= 0

      3.1 Compute `root1 = (-b + sqrt(delta))/(2.0 * a)`.

      3.2 Compute `root2 =(-b - sqrt(delta))/(2.0 * a)`.

      3.3 Print "Real Roots".

      3.4 Print `root1, root2` .

   else

      3.1 Compute `real_part = - b / (2.0 * a)`.

      3.2 Compute `imag_part = sqrt(-delta)/(2.0 * a)`.

      3.3 Print "Complex Roots".

      3.4 Print `real_part` "+" `imag_part` "i".

      3.5 Print `real_part` "-" `imag_part` "i".

Program

The program is shown in Figure 6.13.The output from the program is shown in Figure 6.14. To read in the values of **a**, **b**, and **c**, we call the `scanf()` function with the `%lf` format specifier and pass the address of each variable. The discriminant is computed in the statement

```
delta = b * b - 4. * a * c;        /* discriminant    */
```

An `else-if` construct is used to transfer control to different computational segments depending on the value of the discriminant. The statemement

```
if (a == 0.)
```

checks to see if *a* is equal to zero. If **a** is indeed equal to zero we have a single root. The condition in the `else if` statement checks to see if the discriminant greater than or equal to zero

```
else if (delta >=  0.)
```

If this condition is true we compute the two real roots of the equation. The `else`

```
/************************************************************/
/*    quadeqn.c  -- Roots of a Quadratic Equation.          */
/*                                                          */
/*    Computes roots of the equation                        */
/*              a*x*x + b*x + c = 0                          */
/************************************************************/

#include <stdio.h>
#include <math.h>


main()
   {
   double a,b,c,root1,root2,real_part,imag_part,delta;

   printf("\n\tROOTS OF A QUADRATIC EQUATION");
   printf("\n\nThis program computes the roots of the");
   printf("  quadratic equation");
   printf("\n\n\tA*x*x + B*x + C = 0");

   printf("\nEnter the value of A: ");
   scanf("%lf", &a);
   printf("Enter the value of B: ");
   scanf("%lf", &b);
   printf("Enter the value of C: ");
   scanf("%lf", &c);
   printf("\nThe roots of the equation are:");

   delta = b * b - 4. * a * c;        /* discriminant      */

   if (a == 0. )
      {
      root1 = -c/b;
      printf("\nSingle root");
      printf("\nRoot = %lf",root1);
      }
   else if (delta >= 0.)
      {
      root1 = ( -b + sqrt(delta) )/(2.0 * a);
      root2 = ( -b - sqrt(delta) )/(2.0 * a);
      printf("\nReal Roots");
      printf("\nRoot1 = %lf", root1);
      printf("\nRoot2 = %lf", root2);
      }
   else
      {
      real_part = - b / (2.0 * a);
      imag_part = sqrt(-delta)/(2.0 * a);
      printf("\nComplex Roots");
      printf("\nRoot1 = %lf   + %lf i", real_part, imag_part);
      printf("\nRoot2 = %lf   - %lf i", real_part, imag_part);
      }
   }
```

Figure 6.13   Program to determine the roots of a quadratic equation.

statement is executed if a is not equal to zero and the discriminant is negative. In this case the complex roots are computed. To compute square roots, the library function **sqrt()** is called. This function takes a **double** argument and returns the square root as a **double** value. The program includes the file *math.h*, which contains the function definitions for the **sqrt()** function

Testing

We should test the program for all four cases: (1) real and equal roots, (2) real and distinct roots, (3) imaginary roots, and (4) single root. For $a = 2$, $b = -10$, and $c = -5$ we have

$$\Delta = (-10)(-10) - 4(2)(-5) = 140.0$$

$$x_1 = \frac{10 + \sqrt{140}}{2(2)} = 5.458$$

```
        ROOTS OF A QUADRATIC EQUATION

This program computes the roots of the quadratic equation

        A*x*x + B*x + C = 0

Enter the value of A: 2
Enter the value of B: -10
Enter the value of C: -5

The roots of the equation are:
Real Roots
Root1 = 5.458040
Root2 = -0.458040


        ROOTS OF A QUADRATIC EQUATION

This program computes the roots of the quadratic equation

        A*x*x + B*x + C = 0

Enter the value of A: 10
Enter the value of B: 3
Enter the value of C: 20

The roots of the equation are:
Complex Roots
Root1 = -0.150000  + 1.406236 i
Root2 = -0.150000  - 1.406236 i
```

Figure 6.14   Output from program *quadeqn.c.*

$$x_2 = \frac{10 - \sqrt{140}}{2(2)} = -0.458$$

For $a = 10$, $b = 3$, and $c = 20$

$$\Delta = (3)(3) - 4(10)(20) = 791.0$$

$$x_1 = \frac{1}{2(10)}(-3 - \sqrt{791}\,i) = 0.15 + 1.406i$$

$$x_2 = \frac{1}{2(10)}(-3 - \sqrt{791}\,i) = -0.15 - 1.406i$$

The sample output for the two cases just given is shown in Figure 6.14. You should run the program for the cases when $a = 0$ and $\Delta = 0$ to verify that the program does indeed give the correct roots.

6.11   THE `switch` AND `break` STATEMENTS

The `switch` statement is a multiple branch decision statement in which one of several statements (or groups of statements) is executed depending on the value of an integer variable or expression. The need for this type of statement arises when the execution of one of many alternatives is to be selected. Although we can do this by using multiple `if-else` statements, it is usually more convenient to use the `switch` statement.

The general form of the `switch` statement is:

```
switch ( integer expression )
    {
    case constant1:
         statements;
         break;
    case constant2:
         statements;
         break;
    case constant3:
         statements;
         break;
    ...
    default:
         statements;
    }
next sequential statement
```

When the **switch** statement is executed, the value of *integer expression* is evaluated. Then the value of the expression is compared with the case constants *constant1*, *constant2*.... If the value of *integer expression* matches one of the case constants, the statements following that case are executed until the **break** statement is reached. The **break** statement signals the end of a particular case and causes execution of the **switch** statement to be terminated. If the value of *integer expression* does not match any of the case constants, the statements following the **default** case are executed.

The **default** is optional. If **default** is not present, no action takes place if none of the case constants match *integer expression*, and the next statement following the statement is executed.

In the construct just shown, a **break** statement ends each case constant block of statements. The **break** statement causes flow of control to be transferred out of the **switch**. The **break** statements are optional but are usually found in most **switch** statements. If the **break** statements are omitted then program execution will continue into the next case, and all statements from the matched case constant to the end of the **switch** will be executed.

Although the **switch** statement is a better construct than multiple **if-else** statements, it does have a few limitations. The expression in the **switch** statement must be of type **int** or **char**. Thus we cannot use a **switch** statement if our choice is based on a floating point variable. The **switch** statement can test only for equality, and the value following **case** can be only an integer constant and not a range of values. In an **if** statement we can evaluate a relational or logical expression. Thus we cannot use a **switch** statement if the selection is based on a range of values.

The **switch** statement is used quite frequently in menu-driven programs. These programs perform several tasks; the specific task to be performed is determined by user input.

Example 6.6   A Menu-Driven Program Segment

A segment of a menu-driven program for performing various matrix operations such as addition, subtraction, and multiplication appears in Figure 6.15. Only two functions, **main()** and **matrix_menu()**, are shown. The function **main()** calls **matrix_menu()**. The function **matrix_menu()** displays a list of options. It then calls the **scanf()** function to obtain user input. The option selected by the user is stored in the integer variable **choice**. The **switch** statement transfer control to the appropriate computational routine based on the value of **choice**. Note that the functions that perform the various matrix operations are not shown. (A detailed presentation of matrix operations appears in Chapter 14.)

```
/**********************************************************/
/*    matmenu.c -- Matrix Menu                            */
/*                                                        */
/*    Demonstrates the use of the switch statement for    */
/*    implementing a menu.               .                */
/**********************************************************/
#include <stdio.h>

main()
{
   matrix_menu();
}

matrix_menu()
{
   int choice = 0;
   /* display menu */
   printf("\n\t\t          MATRIX OPERATIONS\n");
   printf("\n\t 1 - Matrix addition        [C] = [A] + [B]");
   printf("\n\t 2 - Matrix subtraction     [C] = [A] - [B]");
   printf("\n\t 3 - Matrix multiplication  [C] = [A] * [B]");
   printf("\n\t 4 - Matrix transpose       [C] = [A] transpose");
   printf("\n\t 5 - Matrix inverse         [C] = [A] inverse");
   printf("\n\t 6 - Exit program");

   /* get user input */
   printf("\n\n\t Select operation you wish to perform: ");
   scanf("%d", &choice);

   switch (choice)
      {
      case 1:
         matrix_add ();
         break;
      case 2:
         matrix_subtract();
         break;
      case 3:
         matrix_multiply();
         break;
      case 4:
         matrix_transpose();
         break;
      case 5:
         matrix_inverse();
         break;
      case 6:
        return;
      default:
        printf("\n Invalid input");
        return;
      }
}
```

Figure 6.15   A segment of a menu-driven program.

6.12   THE CONDITIONAL OPERATOR

The conditional operator is somewhat unusual. It is the only ternary operator in C, that is, it requires three operands. The general format of the conditional operator is

> *condition ? expression1 : expression2*

Note that the final result of the conditional expression is a value. Two symbols are used to denote the conditional operator, the question mark (**?**) and the colon (**:**). *Condition* is a logical expression that evaluates to either true or false. *Expression1* and *expression2* are either values or expressions that evaluate to a value.

The conditional operator works as follows. First *condition* is evaluated. If *condition* is true, then *expression1* is evaluated, and its value becomes the value of the entire expression. If *condition* is false, then *expression2* is evaluated, and its value becomes the value of the entire expression. The conditional operator is used quite frequently in an assignment statement to assign one of two values to a variable. For example,

```
y = x > 0 ? 10 : 20;
```

In this statement, **y** is assigned the value 10 if the condition **x > 0** is true. If **x** is equal to zero or is negative, then **y** is assigned the value 20. Another example of a conditional expression is

```
c = a < b ? a : b;
```

The statement assigns to the variable **c** the smaller value of either **a** and **b**. When the statement is executed, the condition **a < b** is evaluated. If it is true, the entire conditional expression takes on the value of **a,** and this value is assigned to **c**. If the condition is false, the entire conditional expression evaluates to **b**, and this is then assigned to **c**. This assignment statement is equivalent to the following **if-else** statement

```
if (a < b)
    c = a;
else
    c = b;
```

Example 6.7   Absolute Value of a Floating Point Number

A program to compute the absolute value of a floating point number using the conditional operator is shown in Figure 6.16. The program reads in a floating point number and stores this in the variable **a**. It then makes use of the conditional operator to evaluate the absolute value of the number. The statement

```
b = a < 0 ? -a : a;
```

computes the absolute value of **a** and assigns the result to **b**. The program then prints both **a** and **b** with the following **printf()** statement.

```
printf("\n The absolute value of %f is %f",a,b);
```

```
/******************************************************************/
/*      abs.c -- Absolute value                                 */
/*                                                              */
/*      Computes the absolute value of a floating point number  */
/*      using the conditional operator.                         */
/******************************************************************/
#include <stdio.h>

main()
{
    float a,b;

    printf("\n Absolute value of a number");
    printf("\ Enter a floating point number:");
    scanf("%f", &a);
    b = a < 0 ? -a : a;
    printf("\n The absolute value of %f is %f",a,b);
}
```

Figure 6.16   Absolute value of a floating point number.

6.13   SUMMARY

In this chapter we presented the C statements that allow us to implement selection structures. With the help of these statements, we can write programs that follow different computational paths. The simplest control statement that selects alternative statements for execution is the **if** statement. In the **if** statement a condition is evaluated. If the condition is true, then the statements following the **if** test condition are evaluated. The condition consists of a relational or logical expression that evaluates to either true or false. Relational expressions are formed using relational operators. C provides the less than (`<`), greater than (`>`), greater than or equal (`>=`), less than or equal (`<=`), equal (`==`), and not equal (`!=`) relational operators. The relational operators have a lower precedence than the arithmetic operators.

We can use logical operators to combine two or more relational expressions to build compound conditions. The logical operators consist of the logical and (`&&`), the logical or (`||`), and the logical not (`!`) operators. The logical operators have a higher priority than the arithmetic operators but a lower priority than the relational operators.

The `if-else` statement lets us choose between alternative statements on the basis of a test condition. If the test condition is true, the statements following the `if` clause are executed; otherwise, the statements following the else clause are executed. In an `else-if` construct, a series of `if` statements are chained together. This makes it possible to test multiple conditions.

In this chapter we also presented the `switch` and `break` statements. The `switch` statement is a multiple branch decision statement in which one of several statements (or groups of statements) is executed depending on the value of an integer variable or expression. Although the `switch` statement is a better construct than a multiple `if-else` statement it can be used only with integer expressions, and the value following the `case` keyword can be only an integer constant. The `break` statement causes flow of control to be transferred outside of the current block. It is usually used in conjunction with the `switch` statement.

Key Terms Presented in This Chapter

break statement	logical operator
conditional operator	nested **if** statements
control structure	relational expression
if statement	relational operator
if-else statement	test condition
if-else if construct	selection structure
logical expression	**switch** statement

PROGRAM STYLE, COMMON ERRORS, AND DEBUGGING GUIDE

1. The statements that are the object of the `if` or `else` should be indented to clarify program structure and enhance readability. Also, for compound statements the opening brace should be aligned vertically

with the closing brace. This makes it easy to visualize which statements are executed as a result of a true or false condition. Since C is a free-form language, it does not care if we indent statements or if the braces are aligned. However, our programs are easier to understand if we follow a logical style of writing code.

2. You should place a blank space before and after the relational and logical operators. This makes your program more readable.

3. When writing logical expressions, you should use parentheses to aid readability and to make sure that the expression is evaluated in the order that you intended. It is easier to be mistaken about the order of evaluation of logical expressions than it is for arithmetic expressions. Also, if possible, try not to make your expressions overly complex. You should break up your expressions into simpler expressions that are easier to read and debug.

4. In an **if** statement the condition following the if must be enclosed in parentheses. The following statement will result in a syntax error:

```
if x > 5            /* error, no parentheses */
z = y + 10;
```

5. The **if** statement does not have the word then following the condition. Thus, the following statement will result in a syntax error:

```
if (x > 5) then    /* error, then is not a keyword */
   x = y + 10;
```

6. There is no semicolon following the condition in the **if** statement. Thus it is an error to write

```
if (x > 5);
```

Also, there is no semicolon following the keyword else. The following **if-else** statement is incorrect:

```
if (x > 5)
   x = y + 10;
else;
   x = y - 10;
```

The statement just given is equivalent to the following statements:

```
if (x > 5)
   x = y + 10;
else
   ;
x = y - 10;
```

As we can see, the target of the else is a null statement. Also, the statement

```
x = y - 10;
```

will always be executed regardless of the whether the condition is true or false.

7. A test for equality in an if statement may not give a correct answer if one of the expressions in the test condition is a floating point value. This is because of round-off errors that are always present when performing computations with floating point numbers. For example, if x is of type **float**, then the statement

```
if (x == 10.0)
    x = y + z;
```

should be replaced with

```
if ( fabs(x - 10.0) <= 1.e-5)
    x = y + z;
```

since it is quite possible that the value of x may be 10.000001 or 9.99999 as a result of computational error. In the second statement we are looking for a value close to 10 rather than exactly equal to 10.

8. In C, the **else** statement is always associated with the closest **if** statement that does not have an **else** statement. A nested **if** statement that causes some confusion is the one shown here:

```
if ( expression1 )
    if ( expression2 )
        statement1;
else
    statement2;
```

In this example, the **else** is linked to the second **if** statement and not the first. If we want the **else** to be associated with the first **if** statement, then we have to use braces

```
if ( expression1 )
    {
    if ( expression2 )
        statement1;
    }
else
    statement2;
```

Now the **else** is associated with the first **if** statement.

9. A common error and one that is difficult to detect is using the C assignment operator (=) in a test for equality instead of the C equality opera-

tor (==). For example, in the statement

```
if (x = y )
    c = a * b;
```

the expression **x** = **y** assigns the value of **y** to **x**. The correct statement is

```
if (x == y)
    c = a * b;
```

The expression **x** == **y** tests whether the variables **x** and **y** are equal.

10. The condition following the switch statement must be enclosed in parentheses. Thus the following will result in a syntax error:

```
switch j                    /* error,  no parentheses */
   {
    ...
```

11. The condition in the **switch** statement must be of type **int** or **char**. You cannot use a **switch** statement if your choice is based on a floating point variable.

12. The **switch** statement can test only for equality. Thus you cannot use the **switch** statement if the selection is based on a range of values.

13. The value that follows the keyword case in the **switch** statement must be an integer constant and not an integer variable.

14. A common error when using the **switch** statement is forgetting to put a **break** statement at the end of each case. Once the program finds a matching value, it continues to execute instructions until it encounters a **break** statement or reaches the end of the switch statement. If the **break** statements are omitted, then program execution will continue into the next case and all statements from the matched case constant to the end of the **switch** will be executed. This error is difficult to find since the compiler does not issue a warning if you do not include break statements at the end of each case.

15. The logical and operator is written as **&&** and not **&**. Also, the logical or operator is written as **||** and not as **|**.

16. If you find that a program containing selection structures is not working as expected, you should use **printf()** statements to trace the path of execution. For example, if you place a **printf()** statement within the **if** and **else** blocks of an **if** statement, you can quickly determine if the statements in these blocks were executed. You can also use **printf()** statements to print the result of the test condition in an if statement. Also it is quite possible that you did not set up the test condition correctly.

EXERCISES

Review Questions

1. Write C statements for each of the following English sentences:
   a. If A is negative, then add 1 to A; otherwise, set A to zero.
   b. If A is greater than zero, then let B be the logarithm of A.
   c. If the sum of A and B is greater than 15, then let C equal the product of A and B; otherwise, let C equal the difference of A and B.
   d. If both X and Y are nonnegative; compute the square root of the product of X and Y.
   e. If X is greater than Y and Y is greater than Z, then set $M = 0$; otherwise, set $M = 1$.
   f. If Y is greater than 6.0 but less than 12.0, print the value of X otherwise, print the value of Z.

2. What are the values of the following expressions?
   a. `2 + 3 >= 4`
   b. `2 + 3 <= 5`
   c. `2 > 1 && 3 > 5`
   d. `3 > 3 || 4 >5 || 5 > 6`
   e. `5 <= 5 && 6 <= 7`

3. What is the numerical value of each of the following expressions?
   a. `5 > 6`
   b. `3 + 4 > 2 && 3 < 5`
   c. `5 >= 3 || 6 < 3`
   d. `5 + (6 > 2)`
   e. `'Y' > 'S' ? 10 : 5`

4. Determine the value of the following logical expressions:
   a. true || false || !true
   b. true || false && true
   c. true && false || !true
   d. true || false && false && true
   e. true && false && !false
   f. true && false && true || false

5. If `x = 2.`, `y = 5.5`, and `z = 3.5`, determine if the following relational expressions are true or false. The variables `x`, `y`, and `z` are of type `float`.
   a. `x + z > y`.
   b. `(x + z) / y == 1.0`.
   c. `y - z < x`.

d.   `2. * y >= 2. * (x + z).`

e.   `y != x + x.`

f.   `x + z == y.`

g.   `x + z <= fabs(z - 1e-06).`

6.   Determine whether the following logical expressions are true or false. The statements are not executed sequentially, and the following is in effect for each case:

```
float a = 5.0,  b = 3.0, c = 2.0
```

a.   `b + c && c + a  >= 5.`

b.   `b + c || c + a >= 5.`

c.   `a - b >= c && b + c >= a.`

d.   `a + b + c >= 10. || c + a > 10. && b + c < 3.`

e.   `!(a > b).`

f.   `!(a-b) && (c>d).`

g.   `(a * b < 3. * b) && (c + a < 3. * b) && (b + c > 5.).`

7.   What is the value of **x** after the following code segment is executed?

```
float a = 4.5, b = 10.0, x;
    if (a >= b)
      x = a
    else
       if (2. * a >= b)
          x = b;
    else
       x = 0;
```

8.   What is the output from this program?

```
#include <stdio.h>
  main()
  {
  int i,j;
  i=j = 3;
  if (i == 0)
      if (j==3)
          printf("\n First printf() statement);
      else
          printf("\n Second printf() statement);
  printf("\n Third printf() statement);
```

9.   What is printed by the following program segment?

```
float a=4.5, b=9.5, c=3.4, d=4.2;
if (a >= )
    if (a >= c)
        if (a >= d)
            printf("\n a=%f", a);
        else
```

```
            printf("\n d=%f",d);
        else
            if (c >= d)
                printf("\n c = %f",c);
            else
                printf("\n c = %f",b);
```

Programming Exercises

10. Write a program to determine whether three lengths a, b, and c form a triangle. The three lengths a, b, and c can form a triangle if the following conditions are satisfied:

$$|a - b| < c$$

$$c < a + b$$

11. Modify the program of the previous exercise so that it also determines whether the triangle is isosceles or equilateral. The triangle is isosceles if any two of its sides are equal; that is,

$$a = b, a = c, \text{ or } b = c$$

The triangle is equilateral if all three sides are equal; that is

$$a = b, b = c, \text{ and } a = c.$$

12. Write a program to compute the change is quarters, dimes, nickels, and pennies to be returned from a one-dollar bill. Print the amount of purchase (which will be less than one dollar), the change, and the number of quarters, dimes, nickels, and pennies.

13. The bending moment in a simply supported beam of span L subjected to a concentrated load P at the midspan is given by

$$M(x) = \begin{cases} P\dfrac{x}{2} & 0 \le x < \dfrac{L}{2} \\ \dfrac{P}{2}(L - x) & \dfrac{L}{2} \le x \le L \end{cases}$$

where x is the distance from the left support.

length of beam
$$0 \le x \le L$$

$P \leftarrow N$

$x \leftarrow M$

$M \leftarrow Nm$

moment

do not permit a negative load

$P\dfrac{x}{2}$

$\dfrac{P}{2}(L-x)$

Write a program to read the load, P, the beam span, L, and the distance x and compute the bending moment.

14. A mathematical relationship is described by the following:

$$y = \begin{cases} Ax^2 + Bx + c & x > 5 \\ Ax^2 - Bx - C & x = 5 \\ Ax^2 + Bx & x < -5 \end{cases}$$

Write a program to read A, B, and C and three values of x, and compute y. Print a table of x and y.

15. The sales commission for each salesperson at Alpha Tech, Inc., is computed as follows: if the total sales is less than $5000, the sales commission is 6 percent of the total sales; if the total sales is between $5000 and $15,000, the sales commission is 10 percent of the total sales; if the total sales exceeds $15,000, the sales commission is 12 percent, and there is an additional bonus of $750. Write a program that reads in the total sales and computes the sales commission.

7

CONTROL
STRUCTURES: LOOPS

There are numerous engineering applications in which a series of calculations is repeated. For example, the design of engineering systems usually involves repetitive numerical computations with the substitution of different parameters into the design equations until the optimum design is obtained. Nowhere is the power of a computer more evident than its ability to perform repetitive tasks. In fact, the most common and useful structure in programming is the loop structure in which a sequence of statements is repeated.

There are two basic types of loops, *counting* loops and *conditional* loops. In a counting loop, a series of statements is repeated for a specified number of times, and the number of iterations is known beforehand. In a conditional loop, the number of repetitions is not known in advance but is determined by some condition existing at the time of program execution or by user input. Conditional loops are used in many numerical iterative solution techniques in which a sequence of computations is repeated until the difference in the results obtained for two consecutive computation cycles is within the desired degree of accuracy.

The construction of loops involves three essential steps:

1. Setting up and initializing a *loop control variable*. The loop control variable controls the number of repetitions of the loop.

2. Evaluating the value of a test condition either before or at the end of iterations. If the value of the condition is true, the *loop body* is executed, otherwise, the loop is terminated. The loop body constitutes the statements that are to be repeated. The test condition typically involves the loop control variable. If the test condition is evaluated at the beginning of each repetition, the loop is called a WHIILE loop or an *entry condition* loop. If the test condition is evaluated at the end of each repetition, the loop is called DOWHILE loop or an *exit condition* loop.

3. Incrementing the value of the loop control variable at the end of each repetition.

This chapter describes the three C statements for implementing loop structures — the **while, for**, and the **do-while** statements — and looks at related applications.

7.1   THE while LOOP

The **while** loop is probably the most frequently used loop construct. The **while** loop is a conditional loop in which execution of the loop body depends on the value of a condition that is evaluated prior to the execution of the loop body. The general form of a **while** loop is

> **while** (*condition*)
>
> *statement*;

When the **while** statement is executed, the condition in parentheses is evaluated. If the expression is true then the statements that form the loop body are executed. Control is then transferred back to the beginning of the **while** statement, and the expression is again evaluated. If the expression is still true, the loop body is executed again. This process continues until the expression finally evaluates to false, at which point the loop is terminated, and execution of the program continues with the next sequential statement. The statement that forms the body of the **while** loop can be a single statement or a compound statement. The flowchart for a **while** loop is shown in Figure 7.1.

An example of a **while** loop follows:

```
main()
{
  int n = 5;
  printf("\n Number    \tSquare  \tCube");
```

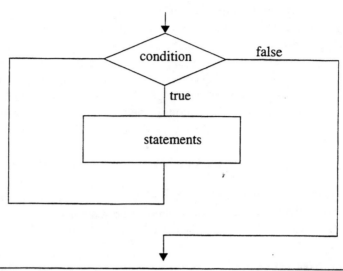

Figure 7.1   Flowchart for `while` loop.

```
while (n < 10)
    {
    printf("\n  %d    \t\t %d    \t\t %d", n,(n * n),(n*n*n));
    ++n;
    }
printf("The value of n at the end of the loop is %d",n);
    }
```

The example prints a table of the squares and cubes of integers from 5 to 10. The program initially sets the value of **n** to 5. The first **printf()** statement prints the heading. Execution of the **while** loop then begins. Since the initial value of **n** is 5, the expression **(n < 10)** is true and so the statements in the braces are executed. Control is then transferred back to the expression and the expression is again evaluated. Now the value of **n** is 6, so the condition is still true and the loop body is again executed. The loop is executed exactly five times. At the end of the fifth iteration, the value of **n** is 10, and so the expression now evaluates to false. The loop is terminated. The last **printf()** statement prints the value of **n** at the end of the loop. The output from this example is as follows:

Number	Square	Cube
5	25	125
6	36	216
7	49	343
8	64	512
9	81	729

The value of n at the end of the loop is 10

The **while** loop is an entry condition loop. The expression that controls the loop is evaluated before each iteration of the loop. If the expression is initially false, then the statements that form the loop body will not be executed.

It is important to remember that the statements being repeated must include something that changes the value of the logical expression so that it eventually becomes false; otherwise, the loop will never terminate. Consider the following:

```
int n = 1;
while (n <= 10)
        printf("\n An infinite loop");
```

The value of **n** does not change within the loop so the logical expression **n <= 10** is always true and the computer keeps executing the **printf()** statement.

To enhance program clarity the statement or statements forming the body of the **while** loop should be indented. This makes it easy to see exactly which statements are being repeated.

Although the **while** statement can have a compound statement as part of the loop body, the **while** statement is syntactically a single statement. Thus you should be careful not to place a semicolon after the logical expression in the **while** statement as in

```
while (count < max_num);    /* wrong! */
    {
    sum += count;
    ++count;
    }
```

In this above example, the semicolon after the logical expression marks the end of the **while** statement. The body of the **while** loop is a null statement, and so the loop does nothing. The foregoing statements are equivalent to

```
while (count < max_num)
    ;
    {
    sum += count;
    ++count;
    }
```

The compound statement is not part of the loop and is executed only after the **while** loop has terminated. If the logical expression is true when the **while** statement is executed, then the loop will not terminate since the value of **count** does not change and the condition **count < max_num** is always true.

Example 7.1   Computation of Factorial

The factorial of an integer n is defined by

$$n! = n(n-1)(n-2) \ldots (3)(2)(1)$$

as well as

$$0! = 1$$

$$n! = n(n-1)!$$

PROBLEM STATEMENT: Write a program to compute the factorial of an integer n.

SOLUTION: The program is shown in Figure 7.2. The program begins by assigning an initial value of 1 to the variable **factorial**. The computation of the factorial is performed in the following **while** loop.

```
/**********************************************************/
/*    factor11.c -- Factorials                          */
/*                                                      */
/*    Computes the factorial of an integer using a      */
/*    while loop.                                        */
/**********************************************************/
#include <stdio.h>

main()
   {
   int i,n;
   double factorial;

   /* get input */
   printf("\n Enter a positive integer: ");
   scanf("%d",&n);

   /* compute factorial */
   factorial = 1. ;
   i = 1;
   while (i <= n )
      {
      factorial *= i;
      ++i;
      }

   /* print result */
   printf("\n %d factorial is %.0lf", n, factorial);
   }
```

Figure 7.2   Computation of factorials.

```
while (i <= n )
    {
    factorial *= i;
    ++i;
    }
```

The statement

```
factorial *= i;
```

is executed as long as the condition (`i <= n`) is true. Note that this is a recursive expression since the next value is obtained from the previous value by multiplying the previous value by `i`. The statement

```
++i;
```

increments the value of `i` by 1 each time through the loop. Thus, the condition will eventually be false (when `i` is equal to `n + 1`) and the loop will terminate. A **double** value is used to store the result, since factorials can get quite large as the number increases. On our system we can compute the factorial of 170 without getting an overflow.

Example 7.2   Fibonacci Numbers

An interesting sequence of numbers is the Fibonacci sequence, in which each number is equal to the sum of the previous two numbers. Thus

$$F_i = F_{i-1} + F_{i-2} \tag{7.1}$$

where i refers to the ith Fibonacci number. The first two Fibonacci numbers are defined equal to one; that is, $F_1 = 1$, $F_2 = 1$.

PROBLEM STATEMENT: Write a program to generate N Fibonacci numbers and compute their sum.

SOLUTION: The program is shown in Figure 7.3. The variable **n** represents the number of terms. The variables **curr**, **prev1**, and **prev2** represent the terms corresponding to i, $i-1$ and $i-2$. The variable sum stores the sum of the terms. All these variables are declared to be of type **long** since the Fibonacci number can get quite large. The program begins by assigning an initial value of 1 to **prev1** and **prev2**. The variable **sum** and the loop control variable **count** are both assigned an initial value of 2. The relational expression in the **while** statement

```
    while (count <= n)
```

causes the statements in the body of the **while** loop to be executed as long as **count** is less than or equal to **n**. The statement

```
    curr = prev1 + prev2;
```

computes the current term as the sum of the previous two terms. The statement

```
    sum += curr;
```

adds the current term to **sum**. The program prints the value of **count**, **curr**, and **sum** for each iteration. The output from the program for $N = 10$ is shown in Figure 7.4.

```
/**********************************************************/
/*    fibonaci.c -- Fibonacci Numbers                     */
/*                                                        */
/*    Computes n Fibonacci numbers and their sum.         */
/**********************************************************/
#include <stdio.h>

 main()
 {
    int count,n;
    long curr,prev1,prev2,sum = 2;

    /* get input */
    printf("\n      FIBONACCI NUMBERS");
    printf("\n Enter number of terms: ");
    scanf("%d",&n);

    /* print heading and first two numbers */
    printf("\n\n    Index        Number        Sum ");
    printf("\n      1            1            1");
    printf("\n      2            1            2");

    /* compute remaining numbers */
    prev1 = 1;
    prev2 = 1;

    count = 2;                         /* initialize count   */
    while (count <= n )
       {
       curr = prev1 + prev2;          /* current term        */
       sum += curr;                   /* sum of terms        */
       printf("\n %5d %10ld %10ld", count, curr,sum);
       prev1 = prev2;                 /* update prev1        */
       prev2 = curr;                  /* update prev2        */
       ++count;                       /* increment counter  */
       }
 }
```

Figure 7.3   Program to compute Fibonacci numbers.

```
FIBONACCI NUMBERS
Enter number of terms: 10


     Index          Number          Sum
       1               1             1
       2               1             2
       2               2             4
       3               3             7
       4               5            12
       5               8            20
       6              13            33
       7              21            54
       8              34            88
       9              55           143
      10              89           232
```

Figure 7.4   Output from program *fibonaci.c* for *n* = 10.

7.2   PROGRAMMING PROJECT: SQUARE ROOTS BY ITERATION

Many problems involve equations that cannot be solved directly. In such cases it becomes necessary to resort to some type of numerical iterative technique. A well-known iterative method is Newton's method for calculating the square root of a number. According to this method the square root of a number N can be approximated by

$$r_1 = \frac{(r_0 + N/r_0)}{2} \tag{7.2}$$

where r_0 is the initial guess for the square root and r_1 is an improved estimate. This expression is a recursive relationship in which the new estimate is obtained from the previous estimate. Thus, this relationship can be written as

$$r_{i+1} = \frac{(r_i + N/r_i)}{2} \tag{7.3}$$

The subscripts i and $i + 1$ refer to the ith and the $(i + 1)$st approximation.

Problem Statement

Write a program to compute the square root of a number using Newton's method.

Problem Analysis

A simple starting point is to take r_0 equal to one-half the number N. To check the accuracy of our solution we can use one of the following criteria:

$$\left| r_{i+1}^2 - N \right| < \varepsilon \tag{7.4}$$

or

$$\left| r_{i+1} - r_i \right| < \varepsilon \tag{7.5}$$

where ε is a small number. The value of ε depends on the required accuracy and the number of significant digits retained by the computer.

A common difficulty with numerical iterative procedures is that the procedure does not always converge to the correct solution or converges too slowly. Thus it is important to include checks in all iterative programs. One method is to use a counter that counts the number of iterations and terminates the program if the number of iterations exceeds some predefined value. It is also a good idea to print the computed value of the root after each iteration to see how the calculation is progressing.

The data requirements for the problem are as follows:

Input Variables
number whose square root is to be computed (**double n**)
maximum number of iterations (**int max_iter**)
desired tolerance, ε (**double epsilon**)

Output Variables
square root of x (**double root**)
number of iterations (**int num_iter**)

Algorithm

1. Read **n, epsilon, max_iter**.
2. Compute initial estimate of root: **root = x /2**.
3. Set number of iterations equal to zero.
4. While (|**n - root * root** | < **epsilon**) and
        (**num_iter < max_iter**), do the following:

    4.1 Calculate new estimate of root from
            root = 0.5 * (n/root + root).

    4.2 Increment number of iterations, **num_iter**.

4.3 Print number of iterations, square root.

4.4 If number of iterations is equal to maximum iterations

4.4.1 Print "Did not converge after" **max_iter**, "iterations".

4.4.2 Print current estimate of square root.

else

4.4.1 Print "Square root is", **root**.

4.4.2 Print "Number of iterations = ", **num_iter**.

Pseudocode

```
READ n, epsilon, max_iter
root ← x/2
num_iter ← 0
WHILE (|n - root * root | < epsilon) and (num_iter < max_iter)
    root ← (x/root + root)/2
    num_iter ← num_iter + 1
    IF num_iter = max_iter
        PRINT "Did not converge after" num_iter, "iterations"
        PRINT "Current estimate of root ", root
    ELSE
        PRINT "Square root of ", n, "is", root
        PRINT "Number of iterations", num_iter
    ENDIF
END WHILE
```

Flowchart

The flowchart representation of the algorithm is shown in Figure 7.5.

Program

A program for computing square roots using Newton's method is shown in Figure 7.6. In the statements

```
root = x/2.0;           /* initial guess       */
num_iter = 0;           /* number of iterations */
```

the initial estimate of the root is taken as $x/2$ and the iteration counter **num_iter** is set equal to zero. The **while** statement

```
while ( (fabs(x - root * root) > epsilon)
    && (num_iter < max_iter) )
```

uses the logical **&&** operator to check for two conditions: if both conditions are true,

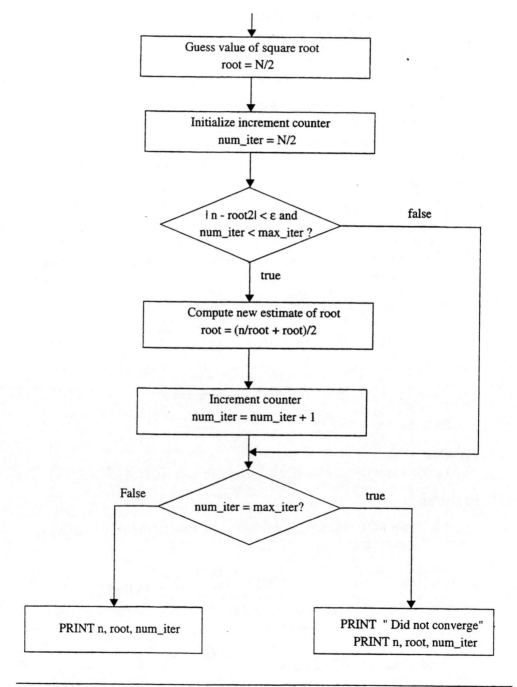

Figure 7.5   Flowchart for program *sqrroot.c*.

```
/***********************************************************/
/*   sqrroot.c  -- Square Roots Using Newton's Method      */
/*                                                         */
/* Computes the square root of a number using Newton's method */
/***********************************************************/
#include <stdio.h>
#include <math.h>

main()
{
  double n, root, epsilon;
  int num_iter, max_iter;

  printf("\n \t SQUARE ROOTS USING NEWTON'S METHOD");
  printf("\n \n This program computes the square root of a number");
  printf("\n using Newton's method");

  /* get input */
  n = -1. ;
  while (n < 0. )
     {
     printf("\n\nEnter number whose square root is desired: ");
     scanf("%lf", &n);
     }
  printf("\nEnter desired tolerance: ");
  scanf("%lf", &epsilon);
  printf("\nEnter maximum number of iterations: ");
  scanf("%d", &max_iter);

  /* initialize */
  root = n/2.0;                      /* initial guess          */
  num_iter = 0;                      /* number of iterations   */
  /* print heading */
  printf("\n Iteration       Square Root");

  /* computation loop */
  while ( (fabs(n - root * root) > epsilon) &&
          (num_iter < max_iter) )
     {
     root = 0.5 * (n/root + root);   /* new estimate of root */
     ++num_iter;
     printf("\n      %d          %.15lf",num_iter, root);
     }
  if (num_iter == max_iter)
     {
     printf("\n\nDid not converge after %d iterations",num_iter);
     printf("\n Current estimate of root of %lf is: " %.15lf",n);
     printf(" %.15lf", root);
     }
   else
     {
     printf("\n\nSquare root of %lf is %.15lf", n, root);
     printf("\nNumber of iterations = %d", num_iter);
     }
}
```

Figure 7.6   Square roots using Newton's method.

then the loop body is executed; if either of the conditions is false; that is, if the root has been computed to the desired accuracy or if the number of iterations **num_iter** is equal to the maximum number of iterations **max_iter** then the loop is terminated. The program uses the library function **fabs()** to compute the absolute value of a floating point number.

The statement

```
root = 0.5 * (x/root + root);   /* new estimate of root */
```

computes the new estimate of the root using the recursive relationship of Equation (7.3) and the statement

```
++num_iter;
```

adds one to the number of iterations.

Testing

We can test the program by entering several numbers and different values for the desired tolerance and maximum number of iterations. The output from the program for **x** = 10, **epsilon** = 1e-10, and **max_iter** = 10 is shown in Figure 7.7. As can be seen from the output, Newton's method converges very quickly. For our example it took only five iterations to compute the square root.

```
     SQUARE ROOTS USING NEWTON'S METHOD

  This program computes the square root of a number
  using Newton's method

Enter number whose square root is desired: 10

Enter desired tolerance: 1e-10

Enter maximum number of iterations: 10

  Iteration      Square Root
      1          3.500000000000000
      2          3.178571428571428
      3          3.162319422150883
      4          3.162277660444136
      5          3.162277660168380

Square root of 10.000000 is 3.162277660168380
Number of iterations = 5
```

Figure 7.7   Output from program *sqrroot.c*.

7.3   PROGRAMMING PROJECT: PROJECTILE TRAJECTORY

Consider a projectile thrown from a height y_0 above the ground. Its trajectory can be approximated by

$$x(t) = (v_0 \cos \theta)t \qquad (7.6)$$

$$y(t) = y_0 + (v_0 \sin \theta)t - \frac{gt^2}{2} \qquad (7.7)$$

where $x(t)$ is the horizontal displacement at time t, $y(t)$ is the vertical displacement at time t, v_0 is the initial velocity, θ is the angle of inclination, and g is the acceleration due to gravity.

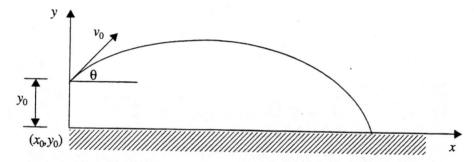

Problem Statement

Write a program that will accept v_0, θ, and y_0 as input parameters and print a table of x and y at specified time intervals until the projectile hits the ground. Your program should also print the horizontal distance traveled.

Problem Analysis

To be able to print the table we need to determine the time at which the projectile hits the ground. The time, t_f, required for the projectile to hit the ground can be determined by setting $y = 0$ and solving for t. This gives

$$t_f = \frac{v_0 \sin \theta + \sqrt{(v_0 \sin \theta)^2 + 2gy_0}}{g} \qquad (7.8)$$

We can compute the horizontal distance traveled by substituting t_f in Equation (7.6). The angle θ is entered in degrees. Since the C library trigonometric functions require that all angles be in radians, we will need to perform a conversion before passing the value of θ to the **sin()** and **cos()** functions.

The data requirements for the problem are as follows:

Input Variables
initial velocity, v_o (**double vo**)
initial height above ground, y_0 (**double y0**)
initial angle of inclination, θ (**double theta**)
time interval , Δt (**double delta_t**)

Output Variables
time, t, (**double t**)
horizontal displacement, x at time t (**double x**)
vertical displacement, y at time t (**double y**)
time to hit the ground, t_f (**double tf**)

Program Parameters
acceleration due to gravity, g (**G**)

Algorithm

1. Set **G** = 32.2 (ft/sec²), **PI** = 3.141593, and **t** = 0.
2. Read **y0, v0, theta, delta_t**.
3. Convert angle **theta** from degrees to radians.
4. Compute **tf** from Equation (7.8).
5. While (**t < tf**) do the following:
    5.1 Compute **x** from Equation (7.6).
    5.2 Compute **y** from Equation (7.7).
    5.3 Print **t, x**, and **y**.
    5.4 Compute new value of t from **t = t + delta_t**.
6. Compute horizontal distance traveled by substituting
    tf in Equation (7.6).
7. Print **tf** and horizontal distance traveled.

Pseudocode
```
G ← 32.2
PI ← 3.141593
READ y0, x0, theta, delta_t
theta ← theta * (PI/180.)
tf ←   (v0 * sin(theta) + sqrt(pow(v0*sin(theta),2)
      + 2. * G * y0))/G
```

```
WHILE (t < tf) do
    x ← v0 * cos(theta)*t
    y ← y0 + v0*sin(theta)*t - G*t*t/2
    PRINT x, y, t
    t ← t + delta_t
ENDWHILE
x ← v0 * cos(theta) * tf
PRINT "Time to hit the ground = " tf
PRINT " Horizontal distance traveled = " x
```

Program

The program is shown in Figure 7.8. The program first declares the variables **y0, theta, v0, t, x, y, delta_t**, and **tf**. These variables are all defined to be of type **double**. It assigns an initial value of 0 to **t**. It also declares an integer variable **i** and assigns it an initial value of 0. A series of calls to **printf()** and **scanf()** statements can then be used to display input prompts and obtain the required input. The statement

```
theta = theta * PI/180.;
```

converts the angle θ from degrees to radians and the statement

```
tf = (v0 * sin(theta) + sqrt(pow(v0*sin(theta),2)
        + 2. * G * y0))/G;
```

computes the time it take to hit the ground. This statement calls three C library functions; (1) the **sin()** function to compute the sin of the angle θ, (2) the **sqrt()** function to compute the square root, and (3) the **pow()** function to compute the square of the expression in parentheses.
The **while** loop beginning with

```
while (t < tf)
```

computes x and y, prints the current values of x, y, and t, and then increments t by Δt. The integer variable **i** serves as a counter. It is incremented in the statement

```
++i;                        /* increment counter      */
```

The new value of t is computed from

```
t = i * delta_t;        /* compute new value of t */
```

The reason for using a counter and computing **t** from the statement is to avoid roundoff errors that can accumulate if we perform repeated addition operations. The statements inside the body of the **while** loop are executed as long as **t** is less

```
/*********************************************************/
/*  projectl.c  -- Projectile Trajectory                 */
/*                                                        */
/*  Computes the trajectory of a projectile thrown from  */
/*  a height of y0 above the ground with an initial       */
/*  velocity of v0 and an angle of inclination of theta  */
/*  from the horizontal.                                  */
/*********************************************************/
#include <stdio.h>
#include <math.h>

#define G 32.2          /* acceleration due to gravity */
#define PI 3.141593

main()
{
   double y0;        /* initial height above ground (ft)      */
   double theta;     /* initial angle of inclination (degrees) */
   double v0;        /* initial velocity (ft/sec)             */
   double t = 0.;    /* time (sec)                            */
   double x;         /* horizontal position at time t         */
   double y;         /* vertical position at time t           */
   double delta_t;   /* step size (sec)                       */
   double tf;        /* time taken to hit the ground (sec)    */
   int i = 0;        /* counter                               */

   /* read input data */
   printf("\n PROJECTILE TRAJECTORY");
   printf("\n Enter initial velocity, v0 (ft/sec): ");
   scanf("%lf",&v0);
   printf(" Enter initial height above ground, y0 (ft): ");
   scanf("%lf",&y0);
   printf(" Enter initial angle of inclination (degrees): ");
   scanf("%lf", &theta);
   printf(" Enter step size (sec): ");
   scanf("%lf",&delta_t);
   /* echo print input data */
   printf("\n Initial velocity = %.4lf ft/sec",v0);
   printf("\n Initial height above ground = %.4lf ft", y0);
   printf("\n Initial angle of inclination = %.4lf degrees",
        theta);
   printf("\n Step size %.4lf sec",delta_t);


   /* print table heading */
   printf("\n -------------------------------------------");
   printf("\n Time        Horizontal        Vertical ");
   printf("\n             Displacement     Displacement ");
   printf("\n (sec)         (feet)           (feet) ");
   printf("\n -------------------------------------------");

   /* convert angle to radians */
   theta = theta * PI/180.;
```

Figure 7.8   A C program to compute the trajectory of a projectile.

```
/* compute time to hit the ground */
tf = (v0 * sin(theta) + sqrt(pow(v0*sin(theta),2)
      + 2. * G * y0))/G;
while (t < tf)
    {
    x = v0 * cos(theta)*t;
    y = y0 + v0*sin(theta)*t - G*t*t/2. ;

    /* print t, x, y */
    printf("\n %6.2lf        %10.4lf         %10.4lf",t,x,y);
    ++i;                      /* increment counter     */
    t = i * delta_t;         /* compute new value of t */
    }

printf("\n -------------------------------------------------");

/* compute horizontal distance traveled */
x = v0 * cos(theta) * tf;
printf("\n \n Time to hit the ground = %.4lf seconds",tf);
printf("\n Horizontal distance traveled = %.4lf feet ",x);
}
```

FIGURE 7.8 (*continued*)

than **tf**. The horizontal distance traveled is computed in the statement

    x = v0 * cos(theta) * tf;

The program then prints the time taken by the projectile to hit the ground and the horizontal distance traveled.

Testing

To test the program we compare the results obtained from the program with those from hand calculations. For $v_0 = 100$ ft/sec, $y_0 = 6$ ft. , $\theta = 70°$, and $\Delta t = 0.5$ sec, we get the following:

$$t_f = \frac{(100)\sin(70°) + \sqrt{[100\sin(70°)]^2 + 2(32.2)(6)}}{32.2} = 5.90 \text{ sec}$$

At $t = 2.0$ sec

$$x = (100)\cos(70°)(2) = 68.40 \text{ ft}$$

$$y = 6 + (100)\sin(70°)(2) - \frac{(32.2)(2)^2}{2} = 129.54 \text{ ft}$$

At $t = 4.0$ sec

$$x = (100)\cos(70°)(4) = 136.81 \text{ ft.}$$

$$y = 6 + (100)\sin(70°)(4) - \frac{(32.2)(4)^2}{2} = 124.28 \text{ ft.}$$

The output from the program for the preceeding values (see Figure 7.9) agrees with the results obtained by hand calculation.

```
PROJECTILE TRAJECTORY
Enter initial velocity, v0 (ft/sec): 100.
Enter initial height above ground, y0 (ft): 6.
Enter initial angle of inclination (degrees): 70
Enter step size (sec): 0.5

Initial velocity = 100.0000 ft/sec
Initial height above ground = 6.0000 ft
Initial angle of inclination = 70.0000 degrees
Step size 0.5000 sec
-----------------------------------------------
  Time        Horizontal          Vertical
             Displacement        Displacement
  (sec)        (feet)              (feet)
-----------------------------------------------
  0.00         0.0000              6.0000
  0.50        17.1010             48.9596
  1.00        34.2020             83.8693
  1.50        51.3030            110.7289
  2.00        68.4040            129.5385
  2.50        85.5050            140.2982
  3.00       102.6060            143.0078
  3.50       119.7070            137.6674
  4.00       136.8080            124.2771
  4.50       153.9090            102.8367
  5.00       171.0100             73.3463
  5.50       188.1110             35.8060
-----------------------------------------------

Time to hit the ground = 5.8998 seconds
Horizontal distance traveled = 201.7839 feet
```

Figure 7.9   Output from program *projectl.c*

7.4   THE for LOOP

The simplest type of loop is one in which a series of statements is repeated and the number of repetitions is known in advance. This is sometimes referred to as a counting loop. In C the **for** statement allows us to repeat a sequence of statements a specified number of times.

The general form of the **for** statement is

```
for ( initialization;  test condition;  increment )
      statement;
```

The three expressions in parentheses control the behavior of the **for** loop. The first expression performs the initialization. Initialization usually involves an assignment statement that is used to set the initial value of one or more loop control variables. The initialization is done once when the **for** statement first starts. The second expression is a test condition that is evaluated before each potential iteration of the loop. The test condition uses a relational or logical expression. If the test condition is true, then the statement forming the loop body is executed. If the test condition is false, the loop is terminated. The third expression is the increment expression. The increment expression is evaluated at the end of each iteration. The increment expression is usually used to define how the loop control variable changes each time the loop is repeated. The program statement that follows the parenthesized expressions constitutes the body of the **for** loop and can be a single statement or a compound statement.

The operation of the **for** loop is as follows:

1. The initialization expression is evaluated.
2. The test condition is evaluated.
3. If the test condition is false, the loop is terminated and control is transferred out of the **for** statement to the next sequential statement. If the test condition is true, then the loop body is executed.
4. The increment expression is evaluated and step 2 is repeated.

The flowchart for a **for** loop is shown in Figure 7.10.

The **for** loop repeats a group of statements as long as the test condition is true. It is generally used to specify a fixed number of repetitions. Like the **while** loop the **for** loop is an entry condition loop. The conditional test is evaluated at the beginning of the loop. This means that if the condition is initially false, the loop body may not be executed at all.

Some examples of **for** loops follow.

```
main()
{
    int count;
    for (count = 1; count <= 5 ++count)
        printf("\n %d", count);
}
```

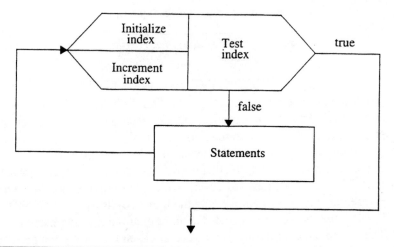

Figure 7.10   Flowchart for the `for` loop.

This example prints the numbers 1 through 5. The initialization expression is

```
count = 1;
```

Thus `count` is assigned an initial value of 1. The conditional test is

```
count <= 5
```

The increment expression is

```
++count
```

After each repetition of the loop, the value of `count` is incremented by 1. The `printf()` statement constitutes the body of the loop. This statement is executed five times. At the end of the fifth iteration, the value of `count` is incremented to 6, so the condition `count <= 5` evaluates to false and the loop is terminated. Another example of a `for` loop is

```
main()
{
    int x;
    for (x = 100; x >= 50; x -= 10)
        printf("%d", x);
}
```

This example counts backward from 100 to 50 in increments of 10. The variable `x` is initially assigned a value of 100. In the increment expression the value of `x` is decreased by 10 each time through the loop.

The body of a **for** loop can be a compound statement as in the example that follows:

```
for (count = 1; count <= num_items; ++ count)
   {
   sum += count;
   ++count;
   }
```

The two statements enclosed in braces are executed during each repetition of the loop.

Note that in all the preceding examples, the statements that form the loop body are indented. Also, for compound statements, the braces are indented and are vertically aligned. Although this is not a necessity, indenting the loop body helps to clarify the structure of the program and makes it easy to see which statements are repeated.

The **for** loop can be replaced by a **while** loop, since the **for** statement is exactly equivalent to the following two statements:

```
initialization;
while ( test condition )
   {
   statement;
   increment;
   }
```

Here the initialization is performed before entering the **while** loop. Also, the increment expression is included as part of the body of the **while** loop.

Example 7.3   Computation of Factorials

In Example 7.1 we computed the factorial of a number using the **while** loop. In this example we illustrate how we can accomplish the same task using a **for** loop. The program is shown in Figure 7.11. Note that the program is slightly smaller since in the **for** statement the initialization, increment, and conditional test is all on the same line.

---

for Statement Variations

The **for** statement in C offers much more flexibility than similar statements in BASIC and Pascal. Some of the variations in the **for** statement are described next.

1. The body of the loop may be a null statement. This is frequently used for time delay loops. An example of such a **for** statement is

```
/******************************************************************/
/*    factor12.c -- Factorials                                 */
/*                                                             */
/*    Computes the factorial of an integer using a for loop.   */
/******************************************************************/

#include <stdio.h>

main()
{
   int i,n;
   double factorial;

   /* get input */
   printf("\n Enter a positive integer: ");
   scanf("%d",&n);

   /* compute factorial */
   factorial = 1;
   for (i=2; i<=n; ++i)
      factorial *= i;

   /* print result */
   printf("\n %d factorial is %.0f", n, factorial);
}
```

Figure 7.11   Computation of factorial using `for` loop.

```
   /* kill some time */
      for (t = 1; t <=3000; ++t)
         ;
```

Since characters are treated internally as integers, the expression in the
`for` statement can consist of character variables. For example, the `for`
statement

```
   for (ch = 'a'; ch <= 'z'; ++ch)
      printf("%c ", ch);
```

prints the letters a through z.

2. Any or all of the loop control expressions can be omitted from the `for`
    statement. In the following example the increment expression is
    omitted.

```
   for (x = 0; num < 0;)
      {
      printf("\n Enter a positive number:");
      scanf("%d", &num);
      }
```

Here the loop is terminated when a negative number is entered. As another example, the **for** loop that starts

```
for (; i <= 100; ++i)
```

does not contain an initialization expression. The preceding statement could be used if **i** were initialized before the loop was executed.

3.   If all three expressions are omitted, then we have an infinite loop.

```
for (;;)
    {
    printf("\n Enter a positive number");
    printf("\n Enter a negative number to quit.");
    scanf("%lf", &x);
    if (x < 0)
        break;
        y = sqrt(x);
    }
```

Note that semicolons must be included even if the expressions are omitted. The example here computes the square root of a number. The **break** statement terminates the **for** loop when a negative value is entered. It is quite common for C programmers to use **for(;;)** to create infinite loops. Infinite loops can also be created using the following **while** statement

```
while (1)
    {
    . . .
    . . .
    }
```

4.   It is possible to change the value of the loop control variable within the body of the **for** loop. Consider the following code segments:

```
for (x = 0; x <= 50; ++x)
    {
    . . .
    if (x > 0 && x <= 100)
        x *= 2;
    if (x > 100 && x <= 200)
        x *= 1.2;
        . . .
    }
```

The value of the loop control variable **x** is changed within the body of the loop. If **x** is between 0 and 100 the value of **x** is doubled. If **x** is between 100 and 200 then the value of **x** is increased by 20 percent. Although it is possible to change the value of the **for** loop control variable within the body of the **for** loop, you should never do so since this makes it difficult to determine how many repetitions will be performed and can lead to unpredictable results.

5. The increment expression in the **for** statement does not have to change the value of the loop control variable. In fact, it can be any legal C expression. For example, all the following are perfectly legal **for** statements in C:

```
for (x = 1; x <= 20; y = a * b)
for (y = 1.5; y <= 200; step = 1.1 * step)
for (a = 100; b <= 200; c = a * b)
```

6. The test condition in the **for** statement can include logical operators to form complex conditions consisting of two or more relational expression. An example of this is

```
for (x = 1; x > 0 && x < 50; ++x)
```

Here the test condition includes the logical **&&** operator. The loop body is executed as long as **x** is greater than 0 and less than 50.

A common mistake in writing **for** loops is the following:

```
int count, n = 10, sum = 0;
for (count = 1; count <= n; ++count);     /* wrong! */
    sum += count * count;
```

The **for** loop supposedly computes the sum of the integers from 1 to 10. However, the effect of the semicolon at the end of the **for** statement is to create a **for** loop with a null statement as the body of the loop. These statements are equivalent to

```
int count, n = 10, sum = 0;
for (count = 1; count <= n; ++count)
    ;
sum += count * count;
```

The loop is executed 10 times. But since the statement that computes the sum is not part of the loop the value of **sum** does not change until *after* the loop has terminated.

The Comma Operator

It is possible to include more than one expression in the initialization or increment expression in a **for** statement by separating the expressions by the comma (**,**) operator. For example, we can initialize two or more variables by using the comma operator in the initialization expression as in this **for** statement:

```
for (a = 10, b = 20; a + b <= 100; ++a)
```

In this case both **a** and **b** control the loop, and both are initialized at the beginning of the loop. The statements **a = 10** and **b = 20** are separated by a comma, and both expressions are considered to be part of the initialization expression.

A **for** statement that uses the comma operator to update two variables is

```
for (a = 10, b = 20; a + b <= 100; ++a, b *= 2)
```

Here, both **a** and **b** are initialized at the start of the loop. After each iteration, the value of **a** is increased by 1, and the value of **b** is doubled. The example that follows computes the sum of the first 20 integers. Note that all the work is done in the **for** statement, and the body of the loop is a null statement.

```
for (i = 1, sum = 0; i <= 20; sum += i, ++i)
;
```

You should note that the statement

```
for (i = 1, sum = 0; i <= 20; ++i, sum += i)
;
```

will give an incorrect value for **sum**. The expression on the left of the comma operator is evaluated first, which means that the expression **++i** is evaluated before **sum += i** is evaluated.

7.5 PROGRAMMING PROJECT: TEST SCORES AND GRADES

Problem Statement

Write a program to compute the maximum, minimum, and average of N test scores. For each test score the program should also determine the grade according to the following scale:

Test Score	Grade
100 – 90	A
89 – 80	B
79 – 70	C
69 – 60	D
< 60	F

Problem Analysis

Our program will need to read in each test score and determine the corresponding grade. To compute the average we will also need to compute the sum of the test scores so that we can determine the average. To determine the minimum and maximum scores, we will use two variables and will update these each time we read in a test score.

The data requirements for the problem are as follows:

Input Variables
number of test scores, *N* (`int num`)
test score (`float score`)

Output Variables
grade (`char grade`)
maximum score (`float max`)
minimum score (`float min`)
average score (`float average`)

Program Variables
sum of scores (`float sum`)
loop counter (`int i`)

Algorithm

1. Set `max` = 0, `min` = 100 and `sum` = 0.

2. Read number of scores.

3. For each score do the following

    3.1 Read score.

    3.2 Add score to `sum`.

    3.3 If score is greater than current maximum score, then make this the current maximum store.

    3.4 If score is less than current minimum score, then make this the current minimum score.

    3.5 Determine grade corresponding to this score.

    3.6 Print score and grade.

4. Compute average score.

5. Print average, minimum, and maximum scores.

Pseudocode
```
max  ← 0
min  ← 100
sum  ← 0
READ num
```

```
FOR i  = 1 to num do
    READ score
    sum  ¨  sum + score
    IF max < score
        max ¨ score                    ·
    IF min > score
        min ← score
    IF  score <= 100 and score >= 90
        grade = 'A'
    ELSE IF score <= 89 and score >= 80
        grade = 'B'
    ELSE IF score <= 79 and score >= 70
        grade = 'C'
    ELSE IF score <= 69 and score >= 60  ·
        grade = 'D'
    ELSE
        grade = 'F'
    PRINT score, grade
END FOR
avg ← sum / n
PRINT min, max, avg
```

Program

A program to read test scores and compute the maximum, minimum, and average score is shown in Figure 7.12. The program reads in the number of students in the variable **n**. The variables **max** and **min** are initialized to 0 and 100. The **for** loop begins with

```
for (i = 1; i <= num; ++i)
```

The loop is executed as long as **i** is less than the number of students **num**.

Testing

Consider the following set of test scores:

98 85 62 45 77 90 83 94 89 74

The corresponding grades are

A B D F C A B A B C

The average score is 79.7, the maximum score is 98, and the minimum score is 45. The output from the program for the input data given is shown in Figure 7.13. It is seen that the output agrees with the foregoing results.

```
/*************************************************************/
/*   scores.c -- Average, Minimum and Maximum Test Scores   */
/*                                                           */
/*   Computes maximum, minimum and average of test scores   */
/*   Also compute the grade for each test score.            */
/*************************************************************/
#include <stdio.h>

main()
{
    int num,i;
    float score,min,max,average,sum;
    char grade;

    min = 100.;
    max = 0.;
    sum = 0.;

    printf("\n Enter number of students: ");
    scanf("%d", &num);

    for (i = 1; i <= num; ++i)
        {
        printf("\n Enter score for student #%d: ",i);
        scanf("%f",&score);
        sum += score;
        if (max < score)
            max = score;
        if (min > score)
            min = score;

        /* determine grade */
        if ( score <= 100 && score >= 90 )
            grade = 'A';
        else if ( score <= 89 && score >= 80 )
            grade = 'B';
        else if ( score <= 79 && score >= 70 )
            grade = 'C';
        else if ( score <= 69 && score >= 60 )
            grade = 'D';
        else
            grade = 'F';

        /* print score and grade */
        printf(" Score = %.2f Grade = %c \n", score, grade);
        }
    average = sum/num;
    printf("\n \n Average of %d test scores is
%.2f",num,average);
    printf("\n Lowest test score is %.2f",min);
    printf("\n Highest test score is %.2f",max);
}
```

Figure 7.12 Maximum, minimum, and average test scores and grades.

```
Enter number of students: 10

Enter score for student #1: 98
Score = 98.00 Grade = A

Enter score for student #2: 85
Score = 85.00 Grade = B

Enter score for student #3: 62
Score = 62.00 Grade = D

Enter score for student #4: 45
Score = 45.00 Grade = F

Enter score for student #5: 77
Score = 77.00 Grade = C

Enter score for student #6: 90
Score = 90.00 Grade = A

Enter score for student #7: 83
Score = 83.00 Grade = B

Enter score for student #8: 94
Score = 94.00 Grade = A

Enter score for student #9: 89
Score = 89.00 Grade = B

Enter score for student #10: 74
Score = 74.00 Grade = C


Average of 10 test scores is 79.70
Lowest test score is 45.00
Highest test score is 98.00
```

Figure 7.13   Output from program *scores.c.*

7.6   THE do-while LOOP

Both the **while** and the **for** loops are entry condition loops, that is, the expression that controls the loop is evaluated before each iteration of the loop. C also provides the **do-while** statement which enables us to implement an *exit condition* loop. In an exit condition loop the expression that controls the loop is evaluated at the end of each iteration instead of at the beginning.

The general form of the **do-while** loop is

```
do
      statement
while ( expression );
```

The statement between the **do** and the **while** is repeated until the expression is evaluated as false. The statement can be a single statement or a compound statement. Execution of the **do-while** statement proceeds as follows: the statement or statements between the **do** and the **while** are executed, and then the expression in parentheses following the keyword **while** is evaluated. If the expression is true, the loop body is executed again. This process is repeated as long as the expression is true. The loop is terminated when the expression becomes false, and control is transferred to the next sequential statement. The flowchart for the **do-while** loop is shown in Figure 7.14 . You should note that the flowchart for the **do-while** statement is identical to that for the DOWHILE structure presented in Chapter 3.

An example of a **do-while** loop is given next. The program segment reads a number between 0 and 100. If the number entered is not within this range, the loop is terminated.

```
do
    {
    printf("\Enter a number between 0 and 100");
    scanf("%f", &num);
    }
while (num > 0  && num < 100);
```

The main difference between the while loop and the **do-while** loop is that, in the **while** loop, the expression is evaluated at the beginning of the loop and, in the **do-while** loop, the expression is evaluated at the end of the loop. In both the **while** and the **do-while** loops the loop is executed when the expression is true and terminates when the expression is false. For situations   when the initial condition is true, the number of iterations is the same for both the **while** loop and

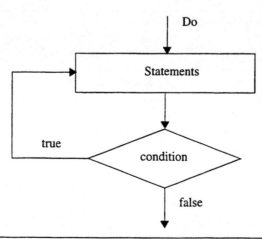

Figure 7.14   Flowchart for **do-while** loop.

the do-while loop. It is only when the condition is initially false that the number of iterations is different. In this case the do-while loop is executed once, since the expression in the do-while statement is evaluated at the end of the loop, and the while loop is not executed at all.

The do-while loop is useful for situations that require at least one iteration. However, only a small percentage of loops tend to be do-while loops. Since do-while loops are used so infrequently, it is considered good programming style to use braces in do-while loops even when they are not needed as shown in the example:

```
do
    {
      ++count;
    }
while (count < 100);
```

This makes the program easier to read and avoids the possibility of the reader confusing the do-while loop for a while statement followed by a null statement.

7.7   THE break STATEMENT

We introduced the break statement when describing the switch statement in Chapter 6. When used with switch, the break statement terminates execution of the switch statement and causes control to be transferred out of the switch to the next sequential statement.

The break statement can also be used with the while, do-while, and for loops where it performs a similar function. When a break statement is encountered within a loop the loop, is terminated and control is transferred to the next sequential statement following the loop.

The break statement is used in situations where a special condition can cause termination of the loop. For example, consider the following code segment:

```
while (1)
    {
    printf("\Enter a positive number");
    printf("\Enter a negative number to quit");
    scanf("%lf",x);
    if (x < 0 )
        {
        printf("\n Negative number entered, terminating
            program.");
        break;
        }
    y = sqrt(x);
    printf("\n %lf    %lf", x, y);
    }
```

The segment computes square roots of numbers entered by the user. The condition in the **while** statement is always true, so the loop will not terminate unless we use a **break** statement. The **if** statement tests for a negative number. If the value of **x** is less than zero, then the **break** statement is executed and control is transferred out of the **while** loop; otherwise, the square root of the number is computed.

When a **break** statement is executed from within a nested loop, only the innermost loop in which the **break** statement occurs is terminated. An example of this follows.

```
for (i = 1; i <=3; ++i)
   {
   for (j = 1; j <= 20; ++j)
      {
      printf("\n i = %d, j = %d", i, j);
      if ( j > 12 )
         break;
      }
   }
```

The **break** statement terminates the inner loop when **j** is greater than 12, but it does not terminate the outer loop. The outer loop is executed three times.

The **break** statement is used quite frequently in the **switch** statement where it is indeed necessary. However, the use of the **break** statement in loops is discouraged since it interrupts the normal sequential flow of execution and makes the program difficult to follow. It is usually possible to eliminate the need for a **break** statement in a loop by rewriting the conditional expression or by including a flag in the conditional expressions and testing for the value of this flag.

The **break** statement can be used only within a **switch, for, while**, or **do-while** statement.

Example 7.4   A Simple Calculator

A program to that emulates a simple calculator is given in Figure 7.15. The program is able to perform the following basic operations: (1) addition, (2) subtraction, (3) multiplication, and (4) division. The input to the program consists of the first operand, an operator (+,-, *, /), and the second operand. The program prints the result of the computation and allows the user to perform several calculations.

A brief description of the program follows. The preprocessor statements

```
#define TRUE 1
#define FALSE 0
```

define two symbolic constants **TRUE** and **FALSE**. The double precision variables **x**

```
/***************************************************************/
/*      calc.c  -- A Simple Calculator                       */
/*                                                            */
/*      Emulates a simple calculator. Uses a switch statement */
/*      to perform various operations such as +, -, *, and /. */
/***************************************************************/
#include <stdio.h>

#define TRUE 1
#define FALSE 0

void main(void);

void main(void)
    {
    double x,y,result;
    char opr,temp,temp1;
    int done = FALSE;

    printf("\n A Simple Calculator \n");

    do
        {
        printf("\n Enter first operand, operator, second operand ")
        printf("\n Valid operators are: ");
        printf("\n Addition             +");
        printf("\n Subtraction          -");
        printf("\n Multiplication       *");
        printf("\n Division             / \n ");
        scanf("%lf %c %lf" ,&x, &opr,&y);

        switch (opr)
            {
            case '+':
                result = x + y;
                printf("\n %g + %g = %g",x,y,result);
                break;

            case '-':
                result = x - y;
                printf("\n %g - %g = %g",x,y,result);
                break;

            case '*':
                result = x * y;
                printf("\n %g * %g = %g",x,y,result);
                break;

            case '/':
                if (y == 0.0)
                    {
                    printf("\n Error, cannot divide be zero");
                    break;
                    }
```

Figure 7.15   A simple calculator program.

```
                    else
                        {
                        result = x / y;
                        printf("\n %g / %g = %g",x,y,result);
                        }
                        break;

                default:
                    printf("\n You entered an invalid operator");
                    break;
            }   /* end switch */

            printf("\n\n Enter '1' to continue or '0' to quit ");
            scanf("%d", &temp);
            if (temp == 0)
                done = TRUE;
        }
    while (done == FALSE);
}
```

FIGURE 7.15 *(continued)*

and **y** represent the first and second operand. The result of the calculation is stored in the variable **result.** The character variable **opr** contains the operator. The program also defines an integer variable called **done** , which is initialized to false in the statement

int done = FALSE;

Program execution continues as long as **done** is false. In the **do-while** loop the expression

while (done == FALSE)

tests the value of **done.** The loop is terminated when **done** is true.

The computations are performed in the switch statement. The expression

switch(opr)

transfers control to the various cases based on the value of **opr.** If an invalid operator is entered, then control is transferred to the default case where an error message is printed. Notice that in the case of division, the program checks the value of the denominator and prints an error message if the denominator is zero.

7.8 THE continue STATEMENT

The **continue** statement causes termination of the *current* iteration of a loop and transfers control to the test condition in the loop. All statements that appear after the **continue** statement are skipped. The **continue** statement can be used only in loops. It cannot be used in the **switch** statement.

The **continue** statement is used to bypass a group of statements inside a loop. The difference between the **continue** statement and the **break** statement is that the **continue** statement terminates execution of the current iteration and transfers control to the loop control expression while the **break** statement terminates execution of the loop and transfers control out of the loop to the next sequential statement.

The use of the **continue** statement is discouraged since it interrupts normal sequential execution.

7.9   SUMMATION OF SERIES

Many engineering problems involve summations of series. Counter controlled loops are commonly used for this purpose. The steps involved in performing a summation consist of:

1. Initializing a counter variable which is used to count the number of terms of the series
2. Computing the current value of an individual term of the series. For most series, it is more efficient to compute the current term from the previous term by multiplying by the ratio of two successive terms.
3. Performing the summation. This involves an assignment statement of the form

    ```
    sum += term;
    ```

    where **sum** is the current value of the sum of the series.
4. Incrementing the counter.
5. Checking the counter. If the value of counter variable is less than or equal to the desired number of terms, steps 2 through 5 are repeated. For some series, a check on the absolute magnitude of the current term is also performed. If the current term is so small that its contribution to the sum is negligible, the loop is terminated.

Example 7.5   Sum of Squares of First n Numbers

Write a C program to compute the sum of the squares of the first n numbers:

$$sum = 1^2 + 2^2 + 3^2 + \dots + n^2$$

The program is given in Figure 7.16. The variable **term** contains the current term and the variable **sum** contains the sum of the series. Both variables are declared to be of type **double** to avoid the possibility of overflow. The sum of the above series is equal to $n(n + 1)(2n + 1)/6$.

```
/*****************************************************************/
/*   sum.c  -- Sum of First n Integers                         */
/*                                                             */
/*   This program computes the sum of the squares of the first */
/*   n integers.                                               */
/*****************************************************************/
#include <stdio.h>

main()
   {
   int n,count;
   double term, sum = 0.;

   printf("\n Enter number of terms: ");
   scanf("%d", &n);

   for (count = 1; count <= n; ++count)
      {
      term = count * count;
      sum += term;
      }
  printf("\n Sum of squares of first %d integers is: %.01f",n,sum);
   }
```

Figure 7.16   A program to evaluate the sum of the squares of the first *n* integers.

Example 7.6   Series Evaluation

Write a program to evaluate the sum of the following series

$$\text{sum} = \sum_{i = 1}^{n} \frac{1}{i^2}$$

The program is shown in Figure 7.17. The program is similar to the one shown in the previous example, except that now, a **while** loop is used instead of a **for** loop.

The above series converges to $\pi^2/6$, or 1.644934067. The result obtained from the computer program for different values of *n* is shown in Table 7.1. The accuracy of the result increases as more terms are included in the series.

```
/*******************************************************************/
/*    sum2.c  -- Summmation of a Series                        */
/*                                                             */
/*    This program computes the sum of the following series   */
/*         1/(1*1) + 1/(2*2) + 1/(3*3) + .... 1/(n*n)          */
/*******************************************************************/
#include <stdio.h>

main()
   {
   int n,i;
   double term, sum = 0.;

   printf("\n Enter number of terms: ");
   scanf("%d", &n);

   for (i = 1; i <= n; ++i)
      {
      term = 1. / ( (float ) i * (float) i) ;
      sum += term;
      }

   printf("\n Sum of the series for n = %d is %12.10lf",n,sum);
   printf("\n Last term of the series = %12.10f",term);
   }
```

Figure 7.17   A program to compute the sum of a series.

Table 7.1: Effect of adding more terms on the computed
sum of the series of Example 7.6

No. of Terms	Computed Sum	Last Term
100	1.6349839002	0.00010000
200	1.6399465460	0.00002500
500	1.6429360655	0.00000400
1000	1.6439345667	0.00000100
2000	1.6444341918	0.00000025

Infinite Series

Many mathematical functions can be represented by infinite series. Examples
of such series are

$$\sin(x) = x - \frac{x^2}{3!} + \frac{x^5}{5!} - \frac{x^7}{7!} + \cdots \qquad (7.9)$$

$$\cos(x) = 1 - \frac{x^2}{2!} + \frac{x^4}{4!} - \frac{x^6}{6!} + \cdots \qquad (7.10)$$

$$\log(1 + x) = x - \frac{x^2}{2} + \frac{x^3}{3} - \frac{x^4}{4} + \cdots \qquad (7.11)$$

$$e^x = 1 + x + \frac{x^2}{2!} + \frac{x^3}{3!} + \cdots \qquad (7.12)$$

Special techniques are required for evaluating the sum of infinite series. It is obviously not possible to add up an infinite number of terms. Thus, it becomes necessary to obtain an approximation to the exact value by adding a finite number of terms of the series. The number of terms needed to obtain an accurate result depends on how fast the series converges. A necessary condition for convergence of an infinite series is that the nth term approach 0 as n approaches infinity.

$$\lim_{n \to \infty} (a^n x^n) \to 0 \qquad (7.13)$$

There are, however, some circumstances in which the series may not converge even if the foregoing condition is true. A sufficient test for convergence is the *ratio test*. In this test, the ratio of successive terms in the series is evaluated. The ratio test requires that each term be smaller in absolute magnitude than the term that preceded it; that is,

$$\lim_{n \to \infty} \left| \frac{\text{term}_{n+1}}{\text{term}_n} \right| < 1 \qquad (7.14)$$

Consider, for example, the series

$$\log(1 + x) = x - \frac{x^2}{2} + \frac{x^3}{3} - \frac{x^4}{4} + \cdots$$

The ratio of successive terms of the series is

$$\text{ratio} = \frac{-n}{n+1} x \qquad (7.15)$$

As n approaches i, the absolute value of this ratio will approach x. Thus, the series will converge if $|x| < 1$. In the case of the sine series, the ratio of successive terms is

$$\text{ratio} = \frac{-x^2}{(2n+1)(2n)} \quad . \tag{7.16}$$

Again, this series will converge, but the number of terms required to achieve a desired degree of accuracy depends on the value of the argument x. For the same number of terms n, the result will be more accurate for small values of x than for large values of x.

In addition to convergence, there are several other factors that you need to be aware of when writing a program for evaluating the sum of a series. You should not attempt to sum a series by evaluating the individual terms in the series. Evaluating individual terms in not only inefficient, but can result in overflow errors and, in many cases, considerable loss of accuracy. As an example consider the series for e^x. An individual term of the series. is given by $x^n/n!$ To evaluate each individual term of the exponential series, we would have to evaluate x^n and $n!$ for all values of n. This can be very time consuming. For large positive values of x, x^n increases rapidly with n. Also, $n!$ can be quite large as n increases. Thus, computing the individual terms of the series can result in overflow errors.

A better and more efficient approach is to evaluate the next term of the series from the previous terms. For the logarithmic series, the relationship between successive terms is

$$\text{term}_{n+1} = \text{term}_n\left[-\frac{n}{(n+1)}x\right] \tag{7.17}$$

and for the exponential series the relationship is

$$\text{term}_{n+1} = term_n\left[-\frac{x}{(n+1)}\right] \tag{7.18}$$

For the sine series, the relationship between two successive terms is

$$\text{term}_{n+1} = \text{term}_n\left[\frac{x^2}{(2n)(2n+1)}\right] \tag{7.19}$$

Computing the next term of the series from the previous terms results in considerable computation efficiency. It also avoids some of the problems with overflow and loss of accuracy.

7.10 PROGRAMMING PROJECT: EVALUATION OF LOG(1+X) USING SERIES

Problem Statement

Write a program to evaluate $\log(1 + x)$ using the following series

$$\log(1 + x) = x - \frac{x^2}{2} + \frac{x^3}{3} - \frac{x^4}{4} + \cdots$$

You may assume that $|x| < 1$. The calculation should be terminated when the last term in the series has attained a value less than 1×10^{-12}.

Problem Analysis

The ratio of successive terms of the series is

$$\text{ratio} = \frac{-n}{n+1}x \tag{7.20}$$

As n approaches i, the absolute value of this ratio will approach x. Thus the series will converge if $|x| < 1$.

The data requirements for the problem are as follows:

Input Variables
x, should be between 1 and -1 (**double x**)

Output Variables
number of terms in the series, n (**int n**)
sum of series (**double sum**)

Program Variables
current term (**double term**)

Algorithm

1. Read **x** (should be between 1 and -1).
2. Set term equal to **x**.
3. Set sum of series equal to **x**.
4. Set number of terms, **n** equal to 1.
5. While I **term** I < 1e-12 do the following:

    5.1 Increment number of terms, **n** by 1.

    5.2 Compute new value of **term** from

        `term = - term * (x/n) * (n - 1)`.

    5.3 Add term to **sum**.

6. Print sum of series.

7. Print number of terms in the series.

Pseudocode

```
x ← 2
WHILE x > 1 and x < -1
    READ x
END WHILE
term ← x
sum ← x
n ← 1
WHILE | term | > 1e-12
    n ← n + 1
    term ← -term * (x/n) * (n-1)
    sum ← sum + term
END WHILE
PRINT " Sum of series is " sum
PRINT "Number of terms in series" n
```

Program

The program is shown in Figure 7.18. The variable **term** contains the current term of the series. The sum of the series is stored in the variable **sum**. Both variables are declared to be of type **double**. The variable **n** contains the number of terms in the series. The first **while** loop obtains user input and checks the value of **x** to make sure that it is between +1 and −1. The statements

```
term = x;
sum = x;
n = 1;
```

assign initial values to **term**, **sum**, and **n**. The summation is performed in the second while loop. The statements in the loop body are executed as long as the condition

```
( fabs(term) > 1e-12)
```

is true. The **fabs()** function is a standard C library function that computes the absolute value of a floating point number. You should include the header file

```
/******************************************************************/
/*     log.c  -- Summation of Logarithmic Series                  */
/*                                                                */
/*     This program evaluates log(x) using a series representation */
/*     for log(1+x). The calculation is terminated when the last   */
/*     term in the series is less than 1e-12.                      */
/******************************************************************/
#include <stdio.h>
#include <math.h>                        /* for fabs() function */

main()
{
    double sum, term, x = 2.;
    int n;

    while (x > 1. || x < -1. )
        {
        printf("\n Enter the value of x (between -1 and + 1): ");
        scanf("%lf",&x);
        }

    term = x;
    sum = x;
    n = 1;

    while ( fabs(term) > 1e-12)
        {
        ++n;
        term = -term * (x/n) * (n - 1);
        sum += term;
        }

    printf("\n The sum of the series is %12.10lf ",sum);
    printf("\n Number of terms in the series = %d", n);

}
```

Figure 7.18   A program to evaluate log(1 + x) using a series.

math.h whenever you use this or any of the other mathematical functions that are in the C library.

The statement

```
    term = -term * (x/n) * (n - 1);
```

computes the next term of the series by multiplying the pervious term by the ratio of successive terms. The program prints the sum of the series and the number of terms.

Testing

Table 7.2 shows the results obtained from the program for several values of *x*. It can be seen from the table that as *x* increases it considerably more terms to get the same degree of accuracy. .

Table 7.2: Effect of increasing x on the number of terms
required to evaluate the series for $\log(1 + x)$

x	log(1 + x)	Number of terms
0.1	0.0953101798	11
0.3	0.2623642645	21
0.5	0.4054651081	35
0.7	0.5306282511	66
0.9	0.6418538820	212

7.11 PROGRAMMING PROJECT: HEIGHT OF A CATENARY CABLE

The height of a catenary cable is given by

$$y(x) = \frac{T}{w}\cosh\left(\frac{wx}{T}\right) + y_0 - \frac{T}{w} \tag{7.21}$$

where T is the horizontal tensile force in the cable, w is the weight of the cable per unit length, and y_0 is the initial height (see Figure 7.19).

Problem Statement

Write a program to compute the height of a cable at equally spaced intervals. The input to the program shall be the weight of the cable, w, the horizontal tensile force, T at $x = 0$, the initial height, of the cable, y_0 at $x = 0$, the final value of x, x_{max}, and the number of intervals, n. Your program should print a table of the height y, versus the distance x.

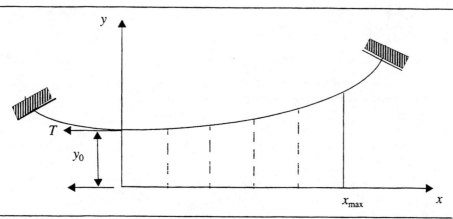

Figure 7.19   Height of a catenary cable.

Problem Analysis

The major tasks to be performed by the program are the following:

1. Read the input data.
2. Compute the value of x at each interval.
3. Compute the height of the cable for each value of x.
4. Print x and y for each value of x.

The data requirements for the problem are as follows:

Input Variables
w, weight of cable per unit length (**double w**)
T, horizontal tensile force at $x = 0$, (**double t**)
initial height of the cable, y_0 (**double y0**)
maximum value of x, x_{max} (**double xmax**)
number of intervals, n (**int n**)

Output Variables
value of x at each interval (**double x**)
height of cable y at x (**double y**)

Algorithm

1. Read w, T, y_0, x_{max} and n.
2. Print table heading.
3. For each interval do the following:

    3.1 Compute the value of **x** for this interval.

    3.2 Compute the value of **y** corresponding to this value of **x**.

    3.3 Print **x** and **y**.

Program

The program is shown in Figure 7.20.   The program first reads in the input parameters and then echo prints these values. It then prints the table heading and the value of y_0. All of computations are performed in the **for** loop

```
for (i = 1; i <= n; ++i)
    {
    x = xmax * (float) i/n;
    y = t/w * cosh(w*x/t) + y0 - t/w;
    printf("\n         %10.2f        %12.6f",x,y);
    }
```

First the value of x is computed. Notice that instead of adding the increment in x to

```
/******************************************************************/
/*    cable.c -- Height of a Catenary Cable                       */
/*                                                                */
/*    This program computes the height of a catenary cable at a   */
/*    user specified number of points.                            */
/******************************************************************/
#include <stdio.h>
#include <math.h>

main()
{
    double w,t,y0,xmax;
    int i,n;
    double x,y;

    /* get input */
    printf("\n Height of a Catenary Cable");
    printf("\n \n Enter weight per length: ");
    scanf("%lf",&w);
    printf(" Enter horizontal force at x=0: " );
    scanf("%lf",&t);
    printf(" Enter initial height, y0: ");
    scanf("%lf",&y0);
    printf(" Enter maximum value of x: ");
    scanf("%lf",&xmax);
    printf(" Enter number of intervals: ");
    scanf("%d",&n);

    /* print table heading and initial values */
    printf("\n\t---------------------------");
    printf("\n \t   Distance          Height");
    printf("\n\t---------------------------");
    printf("\n          %10.2f     %12.4f",0.,y0);

    /* compute x and y and print */
    for (i = 1; i <= n; ++i)
        {
        x = xmax * (float) i/n;
        y = t/w * cosh(w*x/t) + y0 - t/w;
        printf("\n          %10.2f     %12.6f",x,y);
        }
    printf("\n\t ---------------------------");
    }
```

Figure 7.20   A program to compute the height of a catenary cable.

---

obtain the value of x at each interval, the program computes x by multiplying xmax by i/n, where n is the number of intervals and i is a counter that goes from 1 to n in the statement

```
    x = xmax * (float) i/n;
```

This avoids the accumulation of roundoff errors that can occur when adding two numbers repeatedly. Since both i and n are integers, the cast operator is used to cast the result to a value of type float.

The height of the cable is computed in the statement

```
y = t/w * cosh(w*x/t) + y0 - t/w;
```

The statement calls the C library `cosh()` function to compute the hyperbolic cosine. The last statement in the body of the `for` loop prints the current values of `x` and `y`.

Testing

Since there are no `if` statements in the program, we can test the program by simply entering some values for the input data and checking the results given by the program with those obtained by hand calculation. The output from the program for the following input values

$$w = 2, T = 500, y_0 = 15, x_{max} = 50, n = 10$$

is shown in Figure 7.21.

```
Height of a Catenary Cable

Enter weight per length: 2.
Enter horizontal force at x=0: 500.
Enter initial height, y0: 15.
Enter maximum value of x: 50.
Enter number of intervals: 10


        Distance            Height
      ---------------------------------

           0.00            15.0000
           5.00            15.0500
          10.00            15.2000
          15.00            15.4501
          20.00            15.8004
          25.00            16.2510
          30.00            16.8022
          35.00            17.4540
          40.00            18.2068
          45.00            19.0609
          50.00            20.0167
      ---------------------------------
```

Figure 7.21   Output from program *cable.c*.

7.12 SUMMARY

There are many engineering applications that involve repetitive numerical computations. Computers are used extensively for such applications because of their ability to perform repetitive tasks. The loop structure, in which a sequence of statements is repeated, is the most common and useful structure in programming.

In this chapter we described the two basic types of loops, counting loops, in which a series of statements is repeated for a predetermined number of times, and conditional loops, in which the number of iterations is determined by a test condition. We also outlined the steps for construction loops.

The **while** and **do-while** statements allow you to implement conditional loops. The while loop is an entry condition loop in which the condition is tested before the statements that form the body of the loop are executed. The **do-while** loop is an exit condition loop in which the loop body is executed before the condition controlling the number of iterations is tested. The for statement lets us implement a counting loop. We also introduced the **break** statement, which is useful for terminating a loop, and the **continue** statement, which causes termination of the current iteration of a loop.

Many engineering applications use series representations and an important problem in the determination of the sum of a series. In fact many of the mathematical functions such as the trigonometric and inverse trigonometric functions, the logarithmic function, and the exponential function can be represented as a sum of a series. The steps required in evaluating the sum of a series were described, and several programming examples for computing the sum of a series were presented.

Key Terms Presented in This Chapter

conditional loop	loop body
continue statement	loop counter
counting loop	loop control variable
do-while statement	loop structure
entry condition loop	nested loops
exit condition loop	series summation
for statement	**while** statement
increment value	

PROGRAM STYLE, COMMON ERRORS, AND DEBUGGING GUIDE

   1.   You should indent all the statements that form the body of a loop. Indenting the loop body helps to clarify the structure of the program and makes it easy to see which statements are repeated. Also, for compound statements, we align the braces vertically.

2.   Since **do-while** loops are used so infrequently, it is a good idea to use braces in **do-while** loops even when they are not needed as shown in this example:

```
do
    {
    ++count;
    }
while (count < 100);
```

This makes the program easier to read and avoids the possibility of the reader confusing the **do-while** loop for a **while** statement followed by a null statement.

3.   The **break** statement is used quite frequently in the **switch** statement, where it is indeed necessary. However, the use of the **break** statement in loops is discouraged, since it interrupts the normal sequential flow of execution and makes the program difficult to follow. You can usually eliminate the need for a **break** statement in a loop by rewriting the conditional expression or by including a flag in the conditional expressions and testing for the value of this flag.

4.   A common difficulty with numerical iterative procedures is that the procedure may not always converge to the correct solution or that it may converge too slowly. You should include checks in all iterative programs. One method is to use a counter which counts the number of iterations and terminates the program if the number of iterations exceeds some predefined value. It is also a good idea to print the computed values at the end of each iteration to see how the calculation is progressing.

5.   The use of the **continue** statement is discouraged since it interrupts normal sequential execution.

6.   It is important to remember that in the **while** loop and the **do-while** loop the statements being repeated must include something that changes the value of the logical expression so that it eventually becomes false; otherwise the loop will never terminate. Consider the following:

```
int n = 1;
while (n <= 10)
printf("\n An infinite loop");
```

The value of **n** does not change within the loop, so the logical expression **n <= 10** is always true, and the computer keeps executing the **printf()** statement.

7.   You should not use a check for equality or inequality as the basis for termination of a **while** loop when the loop control variable is a float-

ing point value. Consider the following:

```
float x = 0.0;
while  (x != 1.5)
   printf("\n x = %f", x);
x += 0.3;
```

These statements may result in an infinite loop. The variable **x** is initialized to 0 and incremented by 0.3 during each repetition of the loop. After five iterations it should have the value 1.5 and the loop should terminate. However, the logical expression **x != 1.5** may remain true because of the error in representing floating point numbers.

8. Although the **while** statement can have a compound statement as part of the loop body, the **while** statement is syntactically a single statement. Thus you should be careful not to place a semicolon after the logical expression in the **while** statement as in

```
while (count < max_num);    /* wrong! */
   {
   sum += count;
   ++count;
   }
```

In this example, the semicolon after the logical expression marks the end of the **while** statement. The body of the **while** loop is a null statement, and so the loop does nothing. These statements are equivalent to

```
while (count < max_num)
   ;
   {
   sum += count;
   ++count;
   }
```

The compound statement is not part of the loop and is executed only after the **while** loop has terminated. If the logical expression is true when the **while** statement is executed, then the loop will not terminate since the value of **count** does not change and the condition **count < max_num** is always true.

9. Incorrectly set up loops are one of the more common causes of program errors. You can insert **printf()** statements within the loop body to print the values of the loop control variables. You should also check the conditions that must be satisfied (1) for the loop to be entered, (2) for the loop to be continued, and (3) for an exit from the loop to occur.

10. A common error when using loops is that the there is one more or one less repetition of the loop. This is usually a result of not setting up the

loop condition correctly. For example, the statement

```
for (i = 1; i < 10; ++i)
```

will result in 9 repetitions. If we wanted the loop to execute 10 times then we would need to set up the condition as

```
for (i = 1; i <= 10; ++i)
```

11. A common mistake in writing **for** loops is the following:

```
int count, n = 10, sum = 0;
for (count = 1; count <= n; ++count);    /* wrong! */
    sum += count * count;
```

The **for** loop supposedly computes the sum of the integers from 1 to 10. However, the effect of the semicolon at the end of the **for** statement is to create a **for** loop with a null statement as the body of the loop. These statements are equivalent to

```
int count, n = 10, sum = 0;
for (count = 1; count <= n; ++count)
    ;
sum += count * count;
```

The loop is executed 10 times. But since the statement that computes the sum is not part of the loop, the value of **sum** does not change until *after* the loop has terminated.

12. Although it is possible to change the value of the control variable in a **for** loop, you should never do so, since this makes it difficult to determine how many repetitions will be performed and can lead to unpredictable results.

13. The main difference between the **while** loop and the **do-while** loop is that, in the **while** loop, the test condition is evaluated at the beginning of the loop, and in the **do-while** loop, the expression is evaluated at the end of the loop. In both the **while** and the **do-while** loops, the statements that form the body of the loop are executed when the expression is true and terminates when the expression is false.

14. For situations when the initial condition is true, the number of iterations is the same for both the **while** loop and the **do-while** loop. When the condition is initially false, the loop body in a **do-while** loop is executed once since the expression in the **do-while** statement is evaluated at the end of the loop. In a **while** loop, since the condition is tested at the beginning of the loop, the loop body is not executed.

15. The **break** statement can be used only within a **switch, for, while,** or **do-while** statement.

16. The **continue** statement can be used only in loops. It cannot be used in the **switch** statement.

17. When a **break** statement is executed from within a nested loop, only the innermost loop in which the **break** statement occurs is terminated. An example of this is

```
for (i = 1; i <=3; ++i)
    {
    for (j = 1; j <= 20; ++j)
        {
        printf("\n i = %d, j = %d", i, j);
        if ( j > 12 )
            break;
        }
    }
```

The **break** statement terminates the inner loop when **j** is greater than 12, but does not terminate the outer loop. The outer loop is executed three times.

18. The **continue** statement causes termination of the *current* iteration of a loop and transfers control to the test condition in the loop. All statements that appear after the **continue** statement are skipped.

19. The difference between the **continue** statement and the **break** statement is that the **continue** statement terminates execution of the *current* iteration and transfers control to the loop control expression while the **break** statement terminates execution of the loop and transfers control out of the loop to the next sequential statement.

EXERCISES

Review Questions

1. What is the output from the following code segments?

    a.

    ```
    int i=0;
      do
    {
    printf("\n %d", i);
    i -= 2;
    } while (i <= 6);
    ```

    b.

    ```
    int i = 0;
    do
        {
        i -= 2;
        printf("\n %d",i);
    ```

```
    } while (i <= 6);
```

c.

```
int i = 0;
do
    {
    printf("\n %d", i);
    } while (i < 0);
```

2. What is printed by the following code segments?

a.

```
int i = 0;
while (i <= 6)
      i += 2;
printf("\n %d",i);
```

b.

```
int i = 0;
while (i <= 6)
    {
    printf("\n %d",i);
    i += 2;
    }
```

c.

```
int i=0;
while (i <= 6)
    {
    i +=  2;
    printf("\n %d", i);
    }
```

3. Explain the effect of the following code:

```
int j;
...
...
while (j = 1)
    {
    printf("\n Value of j is %d", j);
    j = 0;
    }
```

4. Write small C program segments for each of the following:

a. Read in a series of numbers and compute their sum. Stop reading data when a negative value is entered.

b. Read in three values, *a*, *b*, and *c* and compute their sum. Stop reading data when either of the three values is negative.

c. Read in two positive integers n_1 and n_2 (n_2 is larger than n_1) and print the square roots of all integers between n_1 and n_2.

d. Read in a series of floating point numbers and determine the largest and smallest. Stop reading data when a negative value is entered.

5. What will the following program print?

[handwritten: This is case 0]
[handwritten: " 1]
[handwritten: " 2]
[handwritten: — this is default case]
[handwritten: this is case 1]
[handwritten: " 2]
[handwritten: — this default case]
[handwritten: this is case 2]
[handwritten: this default case —]

[handwritten: pg 235]

```
#include <stdio.h>
main()
{
    int i = 0;
    while (i < 3)
        {
        switch (i++)
            {
            case 0:
                printf("\n This is case 0");
            case 1:
                printf("\n This is case 1");
            case 2:
                printf("\n This is case 2");
            default:
                printf("\n This is the default case");
            } /* end switch */
        } /* end while */
}
```

6. What is the value of count after each of the following loops has been executed?

a.

```
for (i = 1; count = 0; i < 5; ++I)
    ++count;
```

[handwritten table: i / count; 1 0; 2 1; 3 2]

b.

```
for (j = 9, count = 5; j <= 11 && j >= 9; j--)
    --count;
```

[handwritten: 3; 5 4]

c.

```
for (i = 10; count = 4; i + count < 25; i *= 2)
    count *= 2;
```

d.

```
int i = 0;
int count = 0;
do
    {
    ++ count;
    i *= 10;
    } while (i < 20);
```

7. Compute the number of times the statements in the body of the following for loops will be executed.

a.

```
int i, sum;
for (i =3; i <= 5; ++i)
    sum += i;
```

b.

```
int i, sum;
for (i = 1; i <= 5; i += 2)
    sum += i;
```

c.

```
int i, sum;
for (i = 10; i >= 1; i--)
    sum += i;
```

d.

```
for (i = 10; i >= 1; i -= 3)
    sum += i;
```

8.   Give the value of **count** after each of the following loops is executed:

a.

```
int count = 0, i,j;
for (i=1, i <= 10; ++i)
    for (j = 1; j <= 5, ++j)
        count += 1;
```

b.

```
int i,j,count = 0;
for (i = 4; i >= -3; --i)
    for (j = 5; j <= 8; ++j)
        count += 2;
```

c.

```
int i,j,count = 0;
for (i = 1; i >= -3; --i)
    for (j = 4; j >= 1; --j)
        count += 1;
```

d.

```
int i,j,count = 0
for (i = 1; i <= count; ++i)
    for (j = 4; j >= 1; --j)
        ++count;
```

Programs

9.   Write a program to read in *N* values and count the number of positive values, the

number of negative values, and the number of zero values.

10. The sum of the first n integers is given by

$$S = 1^2 + 2^2 + \cdots + n^2 = \frac{n(n+1)(2n+1)}{6}$$

Write a program that will find S for $n = 10, 20, 40, 40, \ldots , 100$ and print a table of n versus S.

11. The oscillating frequency of a spring mass system is given by

$$f = \left(\frac{1}{2\pi}\right)\sqrt{\frac{k}{m}}$$

where f = frequency in cycles per second, k = spring constant, and m = mass. Write a program to print a table of k versus f. Input to the program will be the mass and the starting and ending values of k. Upon completion the program should ask whether another table is desired.

12. Write a program to tabulate values of the function

$$y = \frac{x^3 - 2x^2 + 3x + 4}{x^2 - 4}$$

for values of x of

a. 10, 12, 14, ..., 40
b. 3, 6, 9, ..., 30
c. 0.1, 0.2, 0.3, ..., 1.0

Use a **for** loop to generate the values of x.

13. Repeat the previous problem using a **while** loop.

14. Write a program to tabulate the values of the function

$$z = \frac{x^3 - 4xy^3 - 3y^2 - x}{x^2 - 2xy + y^2}$$

for all pairs of x and y values in the range $x = 5, 6,..., 10$; $y = 3, 4, 5,..., 8$. Use a pair of nested **for** loops to generate the x and y values.

15. The reciprocal of a number N can be obtained without division from the following recursive relationship:

$$x_{i+1} = x_i(2 - Nx_i)$$

where x_i is the ith estimate of $1/N$.

Write a program to compute $1/N$ using this approach. Test for convergence by determining if

$$\left|1.0 - Nx_{i+1}\right| < 10^{-6}$$

Note that the procedure will not work if the initial estimate of x is negative. Print the number N and the reciprocal after each iteration.

16. The cube root of a number N can be calculated using the recursive relationship

$$x_{i+1} = \frac{1}{3}\left(\frac{N + 2x_i^3}{x_i^2}\right)$$

Write a program to read a number N and calculate the cube root. To test for convergence use the following criterion

$$\left|\frac{x_{i+1} - x_i}{x_i}\right| < \varepsilon$$

where ε is a small number. Print the number and the cube root for each iteration.

17. The normal probability distribution is the most common distribution in probability and statistics. Many populations have distributions which can be fit very closely be a normal distribution. The normal probability density function is given by

$$f(x) = \frac{1}{\sqrt{2\pi}\sigma}\exp\left[-\frac{1}{2}\left(\frac{x-\mu}{\sigma}\right)^2\right], \qquad -\infty < x < \infty$$

where μ is the mean value and σ is the standard deviation. The standard normal density function has a mean value of 0 and a standard deviation of 1 and can be written as

$$f(x) = \frac{1}{\sqrt{2\pi}}\exp\left(\frac{-x^2}{2}\right)$$

Write a program to generate a table of values for the standard normal probability density function for values of x from -5 to 5 in increments of 0.5.

18. Write a program that computes and prints a table showing the conversion from degrees Celsius to degrees Fahrenheit for temperatures ranging from $0°\,$C to $100°\,$C in increments of 10 degrees.

19. Write a program that computes and prints the sum S of the series

$$S = \frac{1}{(1)(2)} + \frac{1}{(2)(3)} + \frac{1}{(3)(4)} + \cdots + \frac{1}{(n)(n+1)}$$

for the first n terms.

20. The infinite series for arcsine x valid for |x| < 1 is given by

$$\arcsin x = x + \sum_{n=1}^{\infty} \frac{(2n-1)(2n-3)...(1)x^{2n+1}}{2^n n! \; 2n+1}$$

Write a C program to evaluate arcsine x using the first 10 terms of the series shown. Test your result for the case where $x = 0.25, 0.5$, and 0.75.

21. The value of π can be estimated by the series

$$\frac{\pi}{4} = 1 - \frac{1}{3} + \frac{1}{5} - \frac{1}{7} + \frac{1}{9} - \cdots$$

Write a C program to compute the value of π using the given series. You should terminate computation when an individual term in the series becomes less than 1×10^{-5}

22. Write a program which will read in an integer number N and determine if the number is prime. To do this, divide the number N by each of the numbers 2 through $N/2$. If any remainder is zero, the number is not prime; otherwise the number is prime.

23. The efficiency of the program of the previous problem can be improved by dividing the number N by 2 and then using only odd-valued test divisors up to the integer value closest to, but below, the square root of N. Write a program to implement this approach.

24. The exponential function e^x can be represented by the infinite series

$$e^x = 1 + x + \frac{x^2}{2!} + \frac{x^3}{3!} + \cdots + \frac{x^n}{n!}$$

Note that the nth term in the series can be obtained by multiplying the $(n-1)$th term by (x/n); that is,

$$\text{term}_n = (\text{term}_{n-1}) \left(\frac{x}{n} \right)$$

Write a program to calculate e^x using the given series. Your program should read the value of x and print the value of the sum and the increment to the sum for each term. Terminate computation when the absolute value of the last term is less than 1×10^{-6}. Run your program for several values of x and compare the results with the C library function exp(). Note that for large values of x this series will result in significant errors because of rounding. The situation is even worse for large negative values of x. Can you think of some ways of improving the accuracy of your program?

25. The equation of motion of a falling body, without air resistance, are

$$y = y_0 + v_0 t - \frac{1}{2} g t^2$$

where y is the vertical position (feet), y_0 is the initial position (feet), v_0 is the initial velocity (ft/sec), t is the time in seconds, and g is the acceleration due to gravity (32.2 ft/sec^2).

Write a program to print a table of the position y of an object dropped from a height of y_0 for every second after the time of release until the body reaches the ground. The input to the program will be the height from which the object is released. Note that v_0 is equal to zero for this case. The time it takes for the body to hit the ground can be obtained from $t = \sqrt{(2y_0)/g}$.

8

===========

FUNCTIONS

In Chapter 3 we described the technique of top-down design for developing algorithms. One of the consequences of top-down design is that the program is developed as a series of smaller subprograms or modules. Most of the problems that we have looked at thus far have been relatively small and simple, and so our programs have consisted of only one module or main program. Many programs for engineering applications tend to be quite large. When dealing with complex problems, the task of developing the program is considerably simplified if we use modular design.

The C language equivalent of a module is the function. Every C program is made up of one or more functions. In this chapter we describe some of the attributes of functions and discuss the advantages of writing programs as a series of functions. We present the C statements for creating our own functions and for using functions in our programs. We also present several applications that take advantage of functions.

8.1 MODULAR DESIGN

A valuable strategy when writing complex programs is to break down the program into several smaller modules. A module (or function at it is called in C) is a small self-contained section of an algorithm. In modular design, each major program step is implemented as an independent program module or subprogram. These modules are then combined to form a complete program. It is much easier to develop and test separate smaller modules than it is to test the entire program at once. In fact, most professional programmers agree that modular design is the best strategy to use to write a complex program.

There are a number of advantages to modular design. These include the following:

1. A modular program is much easier to develop. Each module can be written and tested separately. Focusing on solving a series of simpler well-defined tasks makes it much easier to solve the overall complex problem.

2. Modular design makes it easier to debug your programs since you are working on smaller sections of the program. Each module can be tested and debugged independently. After the module has been tested, it can be incorporated into the program.

3. Programs can be developed by several programmers since different people can work on different modules. This is important when developing large programs.

4. Modules can be used in several places in the same program and in other programs. In many programs there are certain tasks that are performed repeatedly. If the same sequence of operations is to be performed in different places within a program, the operations can be included in a module and the module invoked when needed rather than rewriting these statements,

5. Modular design results in program that have a simpler design and are easier to read and understand.

6. Modular design also results in increased program reliability. Once a module has been developed and tested, it can be incorporated in different programs. By using previously tested modules in a program, we reduce the possibility of errors.

The following is a list of desirable attributes of modules:

1. A module should be relatively small. Although there are differing opinions on exactly what the size of a module should be, a good heuristic is to limit the size of a module to no more than one or two pages. If the module exceeds this limit, it should be broken up into smaller modules.

2. Whenever possible, a module should have only one entry point and one exit point. This makes it possible to access the module as a single unit and also to modify it or replace it without having to replace other segments of the program.

3. A module should be independent and self-contained so that it can be

developed and tested separately.

4. A module should perform a single, well-defined task. Simply breaking up a program into modules does not itself guarantee that the program will be modular. The key factor in achieving modularity is that each module should perform a specific task.

5. A module should have a well-defined interface. The interface defines what input is required by the module and what result will be returned by the module. In a well-defined interface, these values are clearly specified in the module.

Many experienced programmers develop a number of general-purpose modules which they can incorporate in several different programs. This reduces program development time and enhances program reliability. The most significant advantage of modular design is that it limits complexity and simplifies the design of the program. The logic of the program is thus easy to follow and to understand. As mentioned in Chapter 3, modular design is a natural consequence of the top-down approach to algorithm design since the overall problem is broken into a series of smaller subtasks which can be implemented as modules.

8.2 FUNCTIONS

The C programming language fully supports modular design through the concept of functions. A C function is a self-contained and independent block of statements. Every C program consists of one or more functions. All C functions have equal importance, which means that any C function can call any of the other functions in a program including itself and be called by any other function. The function **main()** is somewhat special in that program execution begins with the first statement in **main()**. All C programs must have a function called **main()**.

Functions can appear in any order in a C program. Also, **main()** does not have to be the first function in a program. Since execution begins with **main()**, it is traditional for **main()** to be the first function in a C program. Unlike some other programming languages such as Pascal, C functions cannot be nested, that is, a function cannot appear within the body of another function. Figure 8.1 shows a C program containing three functions, **main()**, **area()**, and **volume()**. Function **main()** can call both **area()** and **volume()**. Also **area()** can call **volume()**, and vice versa.

8.3 THE STRUCTURE OF A C FUNCTION

A C function consists of two parts: a function *header* and a *body* (see Figure 8.2). A C function begins with a header statement. The function header specifies the name of the function, the type of value that the function returns, a list of parameters, and the data type of each parameter.

```
main()
{
...
...
}
```
function

main()

```
double volume(double radius)
{
...
...
}
```
function

volume()

```
float area(float width, float height)
{
...
...
}
```
function

area()

Figure 8.1   Functions in a C program.

```
float area(float width, float height)
```
function

header

```
{
   double result;

   result = width * height;
   return (result);
}
```
function

body

Figure 8.2   Structure of a C function.

The general syntax of the function header is

---

type function_name(*type1 parm1, type2 parm2, type3 parm3, ..., typeN parmN*)

---

function_name is the name given to the function, *type* is the data type of the value
returned by the function, *type1* is the data type of the first parameter, *parm1*, *type2*
is the data type of the second parameter, *parm2*, and so on. The parameter list is
enclosed in parentheses, and each parameter is separated by a comma. There is no
semicolon at the end of the function header.

Figure 8.3 shows a function called **max3()**. This function determines the
maximum of three integer values, **a**, **b** and **c** and returns the result to the calling
function. The function header for integers, **a**, **b**, and **c**. The header for function
max3() is

```
int max3(int a, int b, int c)
```

This function header defines a function called **max3()**. The function has three
parameters **a**, **b**, and **c** all of type **int**. The function returns a value of type **int**.

```
int max3(int a, int b, int c) ◄─────────────── function header
{ ◄─────────────── opening brace
    int max_value;

    max_value = a;
    if (b > max_value)
        max_value = b;                            function
    if (c > max_value)                            body
        max_value = c;

    return (max_value); ◄──────── return statement
} ◄────────────────────────── closing brace
```

Figure 8.3   A C function for computing the maximum of three integers.

All C functions must have names. The rules for forming function names are
the same as for variable names. The function parameters receive values from the
calling function when the function is invoked. Thus the function parameters
provide the mechanism for transferring information from the calling function. It is
important to note that the right parenthesis is *not* followed by a semicolon.

The parameter list may consists of variable names and the data type for each
variable in the list. There can be zero or more parameters in the parameter list. The
parameters are separated by commas. Parentheses are required after the function
name even if there are no parameters. When the function is called, the parameters
receive values from the calling function.

The type of value returned by the function can be any valid C data type. It is specified in the function header and precedes the function name. The default data type is **int**, which means that the C compiler assumes that the function returns a value of type **int** if a return type is not specified in the function header. For functions that do not return a value, we use the special type **void**. The keyword **void** informs the compiler that the function does not return a value. Figure 8.4 illustrates the various elements of the function header for function **max3()**.

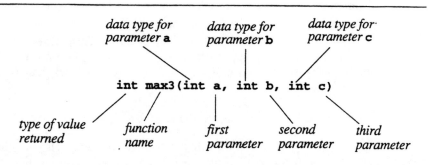

Figure 8.4   Function header for function **max3()**.

The function body consists of a group of statements enclosed in braces. The left brace marks the beginning of the body and the right brace marks the end of the body. The function body contains the actual C statements that are executed when the function is invoked. For functions that return a value, at least one of the statements in the function is a **return** statement. For example, in the function **max3()** the **return** statement is

```
return (max_value);
```

When the function is invoked the value of the variable **max_value** is returned to the calling function. We will present detailed descriptions of how information is passed to a function and how a function returns a value to the calling function in the sections that follow.

Some examples of function headers are the following:

```
int cube_number(int n)
```

This function header defines a function **cube_number()** that returns an **int** result. The function has one parameter, **n**, which is defined to be of type **int**.

```
float square(float a)
```

This function header defines a function named **square()**. The function returns a result of type **float** and has one parameter **a** of type **float**.

        double area(double width,double height)

This function header defines a function **area()** which has two parameters, **width** and **height** of type **double**. The function returns a **double** value.

        void draw_circle (float x, float y, float radius)

This function header defines a function called **draw_circle()**. The data type **void** in the type specifier indicates that the function does not return a value. The function has three parameters, **x** and **y** and **radius** all of type **float**.

        double power(double x, int n)

This function header defines a function called **power()** which returns a value of type **double**. The function has two parameters, **x** is of type **double** and **n** is of type **int**.

        void print_line(void)

This function header defines a function called **print_line()**. The function has no arguments. This is indicated by the keyword **void** in the parameter list. It does not return a value since the return type of the function is **void**.

8.4   INVOKING A FUNCTION

A function can be invoked in two different ways. If the function does not return a value then the function is invoked by simply using its name followed by a list of *arguments*.

> *function_name(arg1, arg2, arg3, ..., argN)*

The arguments are separated by commas and are enclosed in parentheses. The arguments in the function call correspond to the parameters in the function definition. If a function does not have any arguments, the argument list is empty. Parentheses are still required to let the compiler know that it is a function and not a variable. Examples of function calls for functions that do not return a value are

```
print_line();
printf("Calling printf() function");
draw_circle(10.0,5.0,r);
```

The first example calls a function **print_line()**. No arguments are passed to the function. Also, the function does not return a value. The second example calls the `printf()` library function and passes it the character string `"Calling printf()` `function"` as an argument. The third example calls the function `draw_circle()` and passes it three arguments. The first two arguments are constants, and the third argument is variable. Notice that there is a semicolon at the end of each of the preceding examples.

Function arguments can be constants, variables, or expressions. For example,

```
draw_circle(10., 5., 15.);
```

The function is invoked with three constants as arguments. In the statement

```
draw_circle(x,y,r);
```

all three arguments are variables, and in the statement

```
draw_circle(x/2., 2. * y, r/3.) ;
```

all three arguments are expressions. The expressions in the argument list are first evaluated before the function is invoked.

If a function returns a value, the function may be invoked in the following way

$$result = function\_name(arg1, \ arg2, \ arg3, ..., \ argN)$$

Here the function name appears on the right-hand side of the assignment statement. Consider the following statement:

```
a = square(3);
```

This example shows how a function is called within an assignment statement. In this case the function `square()` is called with an argument of 3. The value returned from the function is assigned to the variable **a**. In the statement

```
total_area = area(x,y) + area1;
```

the function `area()` is called with the arguments **x** and **y**. The value returned from the function is added to the variable **area1**, and the result is assigned to the variable **total_area**. Thus for functions that return a value, the function invocation can be used in place of a C variable. Other examples of function calls are the following

```
largest = max3(i,j,k);
total = max3(i,j,k) + max3(10,15,20);
```

In the first example the function **max3()** is called with the arguments **i**, **j**, and **k**. The value returned by **max3()** is assigned to the variable **largest**. In the second example, the function **max3()** is called two times. In the first call it is passed the arguments **i**, **j**, and **k**. In the second call it is passed the arguments 10, 15, and 20. The sum of the values returned by the two calls is assigned to the variable **total**. From this example, you can see that if a function returns a value, the function name can be used anywhere a single variable can appear.

When a function is called or invoked, the program branches to the function. The statements in the function body are executed until a **return** statement or until the closing brace that marks the end of the function body is reached. Control is then transferred to the statement that called the function. Figure 8.5 illustrates the flow of control when a function is invoked. The statement

```
largest = max3(x,y,z);
```

in **main()** invokes the function **max3()**. Control is transferred to function **max3()** and statements in the function body are executed until a **return** statement or the closing brace that marks the end of the function is reached. Control is then transferred back to **main()**, and execution continues from the statement following the function call.

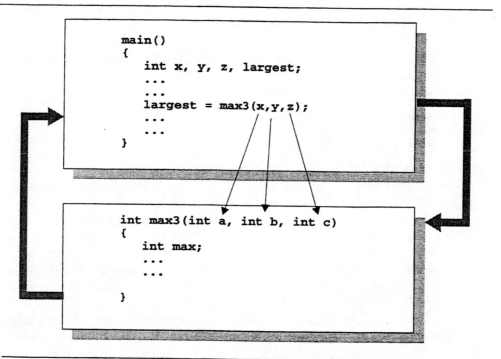

Figure 8.5   Control flow between calling and called function.

Arguments and Parameters

Functions can be written that do not need to communicate with the calling function. Some functions do not receive information from the calling function, and some functions do not return values to the calling function. However, these types of functions are limited in their flexibility and usefulness. Most functions need to communicate with the calling function. Normally a C function receives information from the calling function and returns a value to the calling function. For example, a function for computing the square root of a number receives the number whose square root is to be computed and returns the square root.

Information is passed from the calling function to the called function through arguments. The called function returns a value through the **return** statement, which is described in the next section.

The arguments given when the function is called correspond to the formal parameters in the function definition. When a function is invoked, the functions arguments are evaluated and the values of these arguments are assigned to the corresponding formal parameters in the function definition. In C any expression can be an argument. The following example illustrates this.

Example 8.1   Calling a Function

A function called **cube()** which computes the cube of an integer is shown in Figure 8.6. The function has one formal parameter **n**. The function is called by **main()** several times, and each time a different argument is used.

```
cube(5);
cube(a);
cube (5 * a + 3);
```

In the first call, the argument is a constant value 5. This value is assigned to the formal parameter **n**; that is, **n** takes on the value of 5. The function **cube()** then computes the cube of 5 and prints the result. In the second call the argument is a variable **a**. The value of **a** is 3. This value is assigned to the formal parameter **n**, so now **n** takes on the value 3. In the third call the argument is an expression. The expression is evaluated, and the resulting value of 18 is assigned to the formal parameter **n**. Figure 8.7 illustrates the relationship between the argument in the function call and the corresponding parameter in the function being called for this example.

There is a one-to-one correspondence between arguments in the calling function and formal parameters in the function definition. This means that the first argument is assigned to the first formal parameter, the second argument is assigned to the second formal parameter and so on.

```
/****************************************************/
/*  cube.c  -- Computes the cube of an integer   */
/*                                               */
/****************************************************/
#include <stdio.h>

void cube(int);

main()
{
   int a=3;
   cube(5);
   cube(a);
   cube(5 * a + 3);
}

void cube(int n)
{
   int n_cubed;
   n_cubed = n * n * n;
   printf("\n %d cubed is %d",n, n_cubed);
}
```

Program output

```
5 cubed is 125
3 cubed is 27
18 cubed is 5832
```

Figure 8.6   Calling a function.

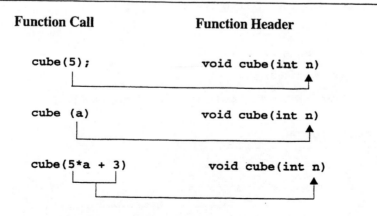

Figure 8.7   Arguments and parameters.

Example 8.2   Arguments and Formal Parameters

The program shown in Figure 8.8 illustrates the correspondence between function
arguments and formal parameters. The program consists of two functions **main()**
and **max3()**. The function **max3()** has three formal parameters, **a**, **b**, and **c**, all of
type **int**. The function determines the maximum value of **a**, **b**, and **c** and prints this
value. In **main()** three variables **x**, **y**, and **z** of type **int** are created and assigned
initial values. The function **main()** invokes **max3()** three times. Each time
max3() is called it is passed three arguments **x**, **y**, and **z**. However the order in

```
/************************************************************/
/*   max3.c -- Maximum of Three Numbers                    */
/*                                                         */
/************************************************************/
#include <stdio.h>
void max3(int,int,int);    /* function prototype */

main()
{
   int x,y,z;
   x = 10;
   y = 30;
   z = 15;
   max3(x,y,z);         /* call function */
   max3(y,x,z);         /* call function */
   max3(z,y,x);         /* call function */
}


void max3(int a,int b,int c)
{
   int max;
   max = a;
   if (max < b)
      max = b;
   if (max < c)
      max = c;
   printf("\n The largest of %d %d %d is %d",a,b,c,max);
}
```

Program output

```
The largest of 10 30 15 is 30
The largest of 30 10 15 is 30
The largest of 15 30 10 is 30
```

Figure 8.8   Arguments and formal parameters.

which these arguments are passed is different for each case.

In the first call to `max3()` the function is called as

```
max3(x,y,z);
```

Thus the first argument **x** is assigned to the first parameter **a**, the second argument **y** is assigned to the second formal parameter **b**, and the third argument **z** is assigned to the third formal parameter **c** (see Figure 8.9). In the second call to `max3()`, the function is called with the following statement

```
max3(y,x,z);
```

This time the first argument **y** is assigned to the first parameter **a**, the second argument **x** is assigned to the second parameter **b**, and the third argument **z** is assigned to the third parameter **c**. In the third call to `max3()` the function is called as

```
max3(z,y,x);
```

Now parameter **a** receives the value of argument **z**, parameter **b** receives the value

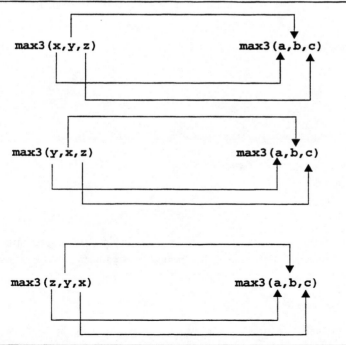

Figure 8.9   Relationship between arguments and formal parameters.

of argument **y**, and parameter **c** receives the value of argument **x**. It can be seen from the earlier example that the arguments in the call statement are assigned to parameters in the function definition according to the location of the parameter in the function definition.

Arguments and formal parameters need not have the same names, but function arguments should match function parameters in both number and data type. (Note: It is possible in C to have functions that have a variable number of arguments. An example of a function with variable number of arguments is the **printf()** library function). For example, if a function is defined as having two parameters, the first one of type **int** and the second one of type **double**, then the function should be invoked with two arguments, the first one being of type **int** and the second one of type **double**. It is very important to make sure that the data type of each argument matches the data type of each formal parameter.

8.5   FUNCTIONS THAT RETURN A VALUE

Almost all functions return a value. The only exception to this is a function of type **void**. The type of value returned by a function is specified in the function header. For example, the function **square** defined here returns a value of type **float**.

```
float square(float x)
{
   ...
   ...

}
```

and the function **sqr_root()** defined here returns a value of type **double**

```
double sqr_root(double x)
{
   ...
   ...
}
```

A function that returns a value can be used in a program almost like a variable. The value returned by the function can be assigned to a variable or used in other functions or calculations. For example, the statement

```
y = square(x);
```

assigns the value returned by the function **square()** to the variable **y** and the statement

```
z = 2.0 * sqr_root(x);
```

uses the value returned by the function **sqr_root()** in an expression.

The return Statement

The **return** statement provides the mechanism for returning a value to the calling function. The syntax of the **return** statement is

```
return ( expression );
```

where *expression* is any valid C expression.

The **return** statement serves two purposes in a function. First, it terminates execution of the function and returns control to the calling function. Second, it evaluates the expression in parentheses and returns the value of the expression to the calling function. Some examples of **return** statements are

```
return(a);
return(x * y);
return (--x);
return(10);
return;
return a+b;
```

The **return** statement may or may not include an expression. Nor is it necessary to enclose the expression in parentheses. However, it is considered good programming practice always to enclose the expression in a **return** statement in parentheses. This makes the program easier to understand and clearly indicates what value is being returned to the calling function.

A function can have more than one **return** statement. Execution of the function is terminated when the first **return** statement is encountered. For example, the function **abs_value()** shown here contains two return statements:

```
double abs_value(double x)
{
   if (x <= 0.0)
      return(x);
   else
      return (-x);
}
```

It is not a good idea to use more than one **return** statement in a function, since this makes it difficult to follow the control flow through the function. The function **abs_value()** can be rewritten as

```
double abs_value(double x)
{
    if (x >= 0.0)
        x = -x;
    return (x);
}
```

Now there is only one **return** statement.

Some functions do not contain a **return** statement. In this case, contrc passes back to the calling function when the closing brace of the function body i encountered.

We do not have to make use of the value returned by a function. An exampl of this is the **printf()** function. The **printf()** function returns the number c characters printed. However, we generally do not require this information, and s all our examples have not used the value returned by **printf()**.

An important limitation of the **return** statement is that it can return only on value. Some other programming languages such as Pascal and FORTRAN make distinction between functions and subroutines (procedures). In these languages, subroutine or procedure can return more than one value through its argument: while a function returns only one argument. In C there are only functions, and function can only return a single value. For a function to return more than on value, we have to use a somewhat different mechanism and pass the addresses c variables using pointers. This is described in Chapter 10.

8.6 FUNCTION PROTOTYPES

So that the C compiler can correctly interpret function calls it is necessary t declare each C function before it is used in a program. The C language provides statement for declaring function called a *function prototype*. A function prototyp informs the compiler about the type of value returned by the function and the tyr and number of arguments that the function expects. For example, the functic prototype for the function **max3()** is

```
int max3(int, int, int);
```

This declaration indicates that the function **max3()** expects three arguments type **int** and that it returns a value of type **int**. The function prototype for **max3** (could also have been written as

```
int max3(int a, int b, int c);
```

In this declaration, the parameter names are also included. Parameter names a optional in function prototype, but it is useful to include them since this helps documenting the function and also provides all the necessary information regardir the function in one place. The function prototype is similar to a function head except that the function prototype has a semicolon at the end and the function header does not.

Some examples of function prototypes are

```
int square(int);
double abs_value(double);
void draw_circle(float, float, float);
void print_line(void);
```

The first statement declares that the function `square()` returns a value of type `int` and that it expects one argument of type `int`. The second statement declares that the function `abs_value()` returns a value of type `double` and receives an argument of type `double`. The third declaration indicates that the function `draw_circ()` does not return a value, but it expects to receive three arguments all of type `int`. The last declaration states that the function `print_line()` does not return a value and does not have any arguments. The function prototypes could also have been written with optional argument names as follows:

```
int square (int number);
double abs_value(double x);
void draw_circ(float x_center,float y_center,float rad);
void print_line(void);
```

A function declared to be of type **void** explicitly informs the compiler that the function does not return a value. Any attempt to use a function declared as having a return type **void** in an expression or assignment statement will result in a compiler error message. Examples of function prototypes that use the keyword **void** are

```
void kill_time(void);
void print_value(float x);
```

The following statement will result in a error message since it is attempting to use the return value from a function declared as having a return type **void**.

```
result = print_value(200.23);
```

Function prototypes must appear before the function is actually called. Function prototypes are usually placed either near the beginning of the function definition of the calling function or near the beginning of the program. If the function prototype is placed near the beginning of the program, it makes the prototype available to all functions in the program.

C allows you to omit the argument list in function prototypes. For example, we can write the function prototype for the function **max3()** as

```
int max3();
```

We strongly urge you not to use this form. This declaration indicates that the function **max3()** returns a value of type **int** but does not say anything about the type and number of arguments it expects. By including the arguments in the function prototype, we are providing the compiler with the information it needs to convert each argument in the statements that call the function to the correct type.

Consider a function called **abs_value()** that computes the absolute value of a number. Suppose that the function is used in the following code segment:

```
double abs_value(double);
main()
{
...
...
double result;
int n = -10;
...
...
result = abs_value(n);
```

In the statement

```
result = abs_value(n);
```

the argument, **n**, passed to the function **abs_value()** is of type **int**. However, the function **abs_value()** expects an argument of type **double**. The compiler automatically converts the integer value **n** to a **double** value before passing it to the function **abs_value()**. If the argument list in the function prototype had been omitted, the integer value **n** would not have been converted to **double**, and this would have produced an incorrect result. The exact nature of the error is implementation dependent. If the function prototype is omitted, then the compiler assumes that the **abs_value()** function returns a value of type **int** instead of **double**, which is even worse.

There are several important advantages to using function prototypes. Function prototypes allow the compiler to check function calls to determine if the number of arguments and the type of arguments in the function call match the parameters in the function definition. With the information given to the compiler in the function prototype, the compiler can ensure that functions are being called properly. If there are too few or two many arguments, then the compiler will give an error message. Also, if there is a mismatch in the data types of the argument and the corresponding parameter, the compiler will issue a warning and perform a type cast to convert the argument to the same type as the parameter. Function prototypes also help to document a program and make it more readable since all the information need to use the function is available in one place in the function prototype.

All functions should be declared before they are used. The importance of including function prototypes in all your programs cannot be overemphasized. In addition to ensuring proper transfer of information between the calling function and the called function, function prototypes improve program readability. It is very easy to see from the declaration what the name of the function is and the type of value that it returns.

Function Prototypes for Library Functions

When using the standard C library functions it is important that we provide the compiler with the appropriate prototypes for these functions. The function prototypes for each function in the C library are contained in header files that are provided with the compiler. The library functions are arranged in groups with each group having its own header file. For example, the function prototypes for the standard input output functions are contained in the header file *stdio.h*, which is why we placed the preprocessor statement

```
#include <stdio.h>
```

near the beginning of our programs to include this file in all programs that have used the C library input/output functions such as the **printf()** and **scanf()** functions. The function prototypes for the mathematical functions are contained in the header file *math.h*. Thus, when using the standard math functions, we must include this file in our programs. When using any of the C library functions, it is important that you include the appropriate header file in your programs so that the prototypes for the functions in the library are read into your programs. This saves you the effort of typing function prototypes for library functions and also ensures that they are entered correctly. In fact, you should never type in the function prototypes for library functions. You should always use the header files. We also recommend that you create include files containing function prototypes for any functions that you develop as part of your own library and include these in any programs that make use of these functions.

8.7   CALL BY VALUE

A C function is typically passed information from the calling function. The called function uses this information to perform its task and then returns a result to the calling function. Although a function can use the values of the arguments provided by the calling function, it cannot change the value of these arguments. This is because when a function is called, the compiler evaluates each argument and makes a copy of the argument. It is this copy that is passed to the function instead of the actual argument itself. This mechanism of passing information to a function is known as *call by value*. Since the function operates on copies of the arguments, the original arguments in the calling function are not affected by anything that happens within the function.

Example 8.3 Call by Value

The program shown in Figure 8.10 illustrates call by value. The program consists of two functions, **main()** and **change_it()**. The function **change_it()** is called by **main()** and receives one argument.

The variable **i** is initially assigned a value of 10 in **main()**. It is then passed as an argument to function **change_it()** and replaces the formal parameter **j** in the function. The function **change_it()** changes the value of the argument. The **printf()** statements print the initial and final values of the argument in both **main()** and in **change_it()**. It is seen from the program output that the value of **i** in **main()** is not affected by the changes made to it in **change_it()**.

```
/**************************************************************/
/*  calbyval.c -- Illustrates call by value                 */
/*                                                          */
/**************************************************************/
#include <stdio.h>
void change_it(int);

main()
{
   int i = 10;
   printf("\n Value of i before function is called %d", i);
   change_it(i);
   printf("\n Value of i after function is called %d", i);
}

void change_it(int j)
{
   printf("\n Initial value of j in function %d", j);
   j = 2 * j + 5;   /* change value of parameter */
   printf("\n Final value of j in function %d", j);
}
```

Program output

```
Value of i before function is called 10
Initial value of j in function 10
Final value of j in function 25
Value of i after function is called 10
```

Figure 8.10   Call by value.

There are several advantages of call by value. Since the function works on copies of the argument rather than the actual argument, the function is prevented from changing the actual argument. This eliminates any harmful side effects that may result from a function changing the value of a variable that is used in other functions and localizes program errors. We do not have to search through the entire program to find an error in a function since the effects are limited to a single function. Call by value makes our programs truly modular since functions act as independent units and do not affect the operation of other functions or variables in the program.

C also provides another mechanism for passing arguments to a function which allows the function to change the value of its argument. The mechanism involves passing the actual addresses or storage locations of the arguments. We will delay the discussion of passing addresses as arguments to functions until we have presented pointers since the mechanism for passing addresses involves the use of pointers.

Example 8.4   A Function to Evaluate x^n

PROBLEM STATEMENT: Write a function to evaluate x^n where x is a real number and n is an integer.

SOLUTION: The program is shown in Figure 8.11. The function to evaluate x^n is called **power()**. It returns a value of type **double**. The function **main()** function reads in the values of x and n, calls function **power()** and prints the result.

The function header for **power()** is written as

```
double power(double x, int n)
```

The function has two parameters: **x**, which is of type **double**, and **n**, which is of type **int**. The value of x^n is determined by multiplying x by itself n times in the following **for** loop

```
for (i = 1; i <= abs(n); ++i)
    result *= x;
```

Since the exponent n can be positive or negative, the C library **abs()** function is used to obtain the absolute value of the variable **n**. Notice that there are three **return** statements in the function **power()**. If n is zero, the function returns 1.0. If n is positive, the function returns **result**. For negative values of n, the function returns (**1.0/result**) since negative powers are the same as positive powers in the denominator, that is,

$$x^{-n} = 1/x^n \qquad\qquad (8.1)$$

```
/*******************************************************************/
/*    power.c -- Raise x to the power n.                         */
/*                                                               */
/*  This program determines the value of x raised to the power  */
/*  n where x is of type double and n is of type integer. The   */
/*  computation is performed by the function power().           */
/*******************************************************************/
#include <stdio.h>
#include <stdlib.h>
double power(double x,int n);

main()
{
   double x, result;
   int n;

   /* obtain input */
   printf("\n Enter a floating point number: ");
   scanf("%lf", &x);
   printf("\n Enter an integer exponent: ");
   scanf("%d", &n);

   /* call power function */
   result = power(x,n);
   /* print result */
   printf("\n %lf raised to the power %d is %lf", x,n,result);
}

/*---------------------------------------------------------------*/
/*   Function: Power                                             */
/*                                                               */
/*   Computes x raised to the power n.                           */
/*                                                               */
/*   Input Parameters:                                           */
/*     x - number                                                */
/*     n - integer exponent                                      */
/*                                                               */
/*   Output Parameters:                                          */
/*     none                                                      */
/*                                                               */
/*   Returns:                                                    */
/*     x raised to the power n (double value)                    */
/* --------------------------------------------------------------*/
double power(double x, int n)
{
   int i;
   double result = 1.0;

   if (n == 0)
      return(result);
   for (i = 1; i <=abs(n); ++i)
      result *= x;
   if (n > 0)
      return (result);
   else
      return (1.0 / result);
}
```

Figure 8.11   Program to compute x^n.

The function prototype for the function is written as

```
double power(double x, int n);
int abs(int);
```

This declaration appears near the beginning of the program. It informs the compiler that the function `power()` expects two arguments, the first of type `double` and the second of type `int`. It also states that the function returns a value of type `double`. The program also includes the header file *stdlib.h* since this file contains the prototype for the `abs()` function.

Example 8.5   Evaluation of $(x + a)^n$ Using a Series Expansion

The function $(x + a)^n$ can be written as

$$(x+a)^n = \binom{n}{0}x^n a^0 + \binom{n}{1}x^{n-1}a^1 + \cdots + \binom{n}{n}x^0 a^n = \sum_{r=0}^{n} x^{n-r}a^r \qquad (8.2)$$

Note that n is an integer. The quantity $\binom{n}{r}$ is the binomial coefficient and is given by

$$\binom{n}{r} = \frac{r!(n-r)!}{n!}, \qquad r = 0, 1, 2, \ldots, n \qquad (8.3)$$

Using factorials directly to evaluate the binomial coefficients is inefficient and can result in overflow problems since factorials can be quite large. A better method for evaluating binomial coefficients is to use successive multiplication. The first term is equal to 1, and each succeeding term can be determined by multiplying the previous term by

$$\frac{n-i+1}{i}, \qquad i = 1, 2, \ldots, n \qquad (8.4)$$

PROBLEM STATEMENT: Write a function to compute the value of $(x + a)^n$. The function should have three formal parameters, **x**, **a**, and **n**. The parameters **x** and **a** are of type **double**, and **n** is of type **int**. The function should return a **double** value. You will also need to write a second function called **binom()** to evaluate the binomial coefficients. You may use the **power()** function given in the previous example to evaluate x^{n-r} and a^r.

SOLUTION: The program is shown in Figure 8.12. In addition to `main()`, the program contains three functions: `x_plus_a()`, which evaluates the series, `binom()` which evaluates the binomial coefficients, and `power()`, which computes the value of *x* raised to an integer power. The function prototypes for these functions are given as

```
double x_plus_a(double x, double a, int n);
double binom(int n, int r);
double power(double x, int n);
```

In the function `x_plus_a()`, the series is evaluated within the `for` loop

```
for (r = 0; r <= n; r++)
    sum += binom(n,r) * power(x,n-r) * power(a,r);
```

In this statement, the `binom()` function is called with arguments `n` and `r` to obtain the binomial coefficient. Also, the `power()` function is called twice, once to obtain x^{n-r} and then to obtain a^r. The `return` statement

```
return(sum):
```

returns the sum of the series to the calling function (which in this case is `main()`)

In function `binom()` the binomial coefficients are computed in the following `for` loop

```
for (i = 1; i <= r; ++i)
    result *= (n - i + 1) / (double) i ;
```

Note the use of the cast operator. Since both `n` and `i` are variables of type `int` the result of the division would be an integer value. To avoid round-off errors which would occur as a result of this, the variable `i` is cast as a `double`.

The structure chart for the program follows.

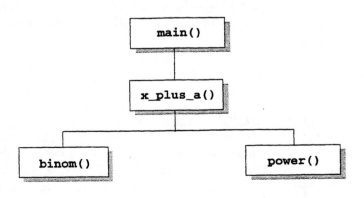

```
/****************************************************************/
/*    binom.c -- Evaluate (x + a) raised to the power n        */
/*                                                             */
/*    This program evaluates (x + a) raised to the power n using */
/*    a series expansion. Both x and a are of type double and n */
/*    is of type int.                                          */
/****************************************************************/
#include <stdio.h>
#include <stdlib.h>
/* function prototypes */
double x_plus_a(double x, double a, int n);
double binom(int n, int r);
double power(double x, int n);

main()
{
    double x,a,result;
    int n;
    /* obtain input */
    printf("\n Enter the value of x: ");
    scanf("%lf", &x);
    printf("\n Enter the value of a: ");
    scanf("%lf", &a);
    printf("\n Enter the value of n: ");
    scanf("%d",&n);

    /* call x_plus_a function */
    result = x_plus_a(x,a,n);
    /* print result */
    printf("\n (%lf + %lf) raised to the power %d is %lf",
        x,a,n,result);
}

/*-------------------------------------------------------------*/
/*    Function: x_plus_a                                       */
/*    Evaluates (x+a) raised to the power n using a series     */
/*                                                             */
/*    Input Parameters:                                        */
/*       x - number (double)                                   */
/*       a - number  (double)                                  */
/*       n - integer exponent (int)                           */
/*                                                             */
/*    Output Parameters:                                       */
/*       none                                                  */
/*                                                             */
/*    Returns:                                                 */
/*       (x+a) raised to the power n as a double value         */
/* -----------------------------------------------------------*/
double x_plus_a(double x, double a, int n)
{
    int r;
    double sum = 0.0;

    for (r = 0; r <= n; r++)
        sum += binom(n,r) * power(x,n-r) * power(a,r);
    return(sum);
}
```

Figure 8.12   A program to evaluate $(x + a)^n$ using a series.

```
/*------------------------------------------------------------*/
/*  Function: binom                                           */
/*                                                            */
/*  Computes the binomial coefficient.                        */
/*                                                            */
/*  Input Parameters:                                         */
/*    n                                                       */
/*    r                                                       */
/*                                                            */
/*  Output Parameters:                                        */
/*    none                                                    */
/*                                                            */
/*  Returns:                                                  */
/*    The binomial coefficient B(n,r) as a double value       */
/*------------------------------------------------------------*/
double binom(int n, int r)
{
   int i;
   double result = 1.0;

   for (i = 1; i <= r; ++i)
      result *= (n - i + 1) / (double) i ;
   return (result);
}


/*------------------------------------------------------------*/
/*  Function: power                                           */
/*                                                            */
/*  Computes x raised to the power n.                         */
/*                                                            */
/*  Input Parameters:                                         */
/*    x - number                                              */
/*    n - integer exponent                                    */
/*                                                            */
/*  Output Parameters:                                        */
/*    none                                                    */
/*                                                            */
/*  Returns:                                                  */
/*    x raised to the power n (double value)                  */
/*------------------------------------------------------------*/
double power(double x, int n)
{
   int i;
   double result = 1.0;

   if (n == 0)
      return(result);

   for (i = 1; i <=abs(n); ++i)
      result *= x;

   if (n > 0)
      return (result);
   else
      return (1.0 / result);
}
```

FIGURE 8.12   (continued)

8.8   PROGRAMMING PROJECT: TRIANGLE SOLUTION

Consider a triangle have sides a, b, and c and angles A, B, and C as shown here. A common problem consists of determining the remaining sides and angles knowing some of the sides and angles of the triangle. More specifically, we are interested in solving for the remaining quantities given the following:

1.   Two angles and one side (A, B and a)
2.   Two sides and included angle (a, b and C)
3.   Three sides (a, b, and c)
4.   Two sides and adjacent angle (a, b, and A).

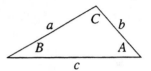

Problem Statement

Write a program to that allows the user to choose one of the four options given, then reads in the input data, and finally displays the lengths of the three sides of the triangle and the angles between them. The program should also compute the area of the triangle. You should write a separate function for each of the four cases. The program should also include separate functions for selecting one of the four cases and for printing the results.

Problem Analysis

We can use the following equations to obtain a solution for the four cases.

$$A + B + C = 180° \tag{8.5}$$

$$\frac{a}{\sin A} = \frac{b}{\sin B} = \frac{c}{\sin C} \tag{8.6}$$

$$a^2 = b^2 + c^2 - 2bc \cos A \tag{8.7}$$

$$b^2 = a^2 + c^2 - 2ac \cos B \tag{8.8}$$

$$c^2 = a^2 + b^2 - 2ab \cos C \tag{8.9}$$

The area of the triangle is given by

$$\text{area} = \sqrt{s(s-a)(s-b)(s-c)} \tag{8.10}$$

where s is the semi-perimeter and is equal to $(a + b + c)/2$.
The major tasks to be performed by the program are the following:

1.   Determine the type of triangle to be solved.
2.   Obtain necessary input.

3. Compute remaining angles and/or sides.
4. Print sides and angles.
5. Compute and print the area of the triangle.

The data requirements for the problem are as follows:

Program Variables
lengths of sides *a*, *b*, and *c* (**double a, b, c**)
angles *A*, *B*, *C* (**double A, B, C**)
user's choice of the four options (**int choice**)
(Depending on the type of problem being solved, some variables
will be input variables while others will be output variables.)

Algorithm

The program is divided into the following functions:

1. **main()** — calls function **get_selection()** to obtain the user's
   choice of one of the four cases and calls the appropriate computational
   function.
2. **get_selection()** — prints the list of options, obtains user's choice,
   and returns this value as an integer to **main()**.
3. **triangle_ABa()** — solves the triangle for the case when two angles
   and one side are given (A, B, a).
4. **triangle_abC()** — solves the triangle for the case when two sides
   and included angle are given (*a*, *b*, and *C*).
5. **triangle_abc()** — solves the triangle for the case when three sides
   are given (*a*, *b*, and *c*).
6. **triangle_abA()** — solves the triangle for the case when two sides
   and an adjacent angle are given (*a*, *b*, and *A*).
7. **print_results()** — prints the lengths of the three sides and the
   included angles. Also computes and prints the area of the triangle.

The structure chart of the program is given in Figure 8.13.

Algorithm for main()
1. Call **get_selection()** to obtain user's choice.
2. Call the corresponding triangle computation function based on the
   value of **choice**.

Algorithm for get_selection()
1. Print list of options.
2. Read in user's choice.
3. Return **choice**.

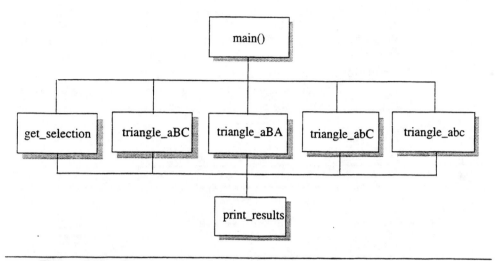

Figure 8.13 Structure chart for program *triangle.c*.

Algorithm for `triangle_aBC()`

1. Read *a*, *B*, and *C*.
2. Convert angles *A* and *B* to radians.
3. Compute side *b* from

    ```
    b = a* sin(B)/sin(A);
    ```
4. Compute angle *C* from

    ```
    C = PI - (A + B);
    ```
5. Compute side *c* from

    ```
    c = sqrt(a*a + b*b - 2.*a*b*cos(C));
    ```
6. Call `print_results()` to print results.

The other triangle computation functions are similar, and so their algorithms are not presented.

Algorithm for print_results()

1. Print lengths of sides *a*, *b*, and *c*.
2. Print angles *A*, *B*, and *C* in degrees.
3. Compute *s* from

    ```
    s = (a + b + c)/2.;
    ```
4. Compute area of triangle from

    ```
    area = sqrt(s* (s-a) * (s-b) * (s-c));
    ```
5. Print area of triangle.

Program

The program is show in Figure 8.14. The program includes the *math.h* header file since it uses the C library trigonometric functions and the square root function. It also defines the symbolic constant **PI**. It is important to note that in all the triangle computational routines, the angles are first converted to radians, since of the trigonometric library functions expect the angle to be in radians. For example, in function **triange_aAB()**, the angle A is converted to radians in the statement

```
A *= PI/180.;
```

```
/****************************************************************/
/& triangle.c -- Triangle Solutions                          */
/*                                                            */
/* Determines the remaining angles and/or sides of a triangle */
/* given the other sides and angles. Also computes the area   */
/* of the triangle.                                           */
/****************************************************************/
#include <stdio.h>
#include <math.h>
#define PI 3.141593

/* function prototypes */
int get_selection(void);
void triangle_aAB(void);
void triangle_abA(void);
void triangle_abC(void);
void triangle_abc(void);
void print_results(double A,double B,double C,
     double a,double b, double c);
main()
{
   int choice;

   choice = get_selection();
   switch(choice)
       {
        case 1:
           triangle_aAB();
           break;
        case 2:
           triangle_abA();
           break;
        case 3:
           triangle_abC();
           break;
        case 4:
           triangle_abc();
        default:
           break;
       }
}
```

Figure 8.14   Triangle solution.

```
/*------------------------------------------------------------*/
/*   Function: get_selection                                  */
/*   Obtains user's choice from a list of options.            */
/*                                                            */
/*   Returns:                                                 */
/*      Interger value representing choice                    */
/*------------------------------------------------------------*/
int get_selection(void)
{
    int choice = 0;
    printf("\n TRIANGLE COMPUTATION ");
    printf("\n Select one of the following:");
    printf("\n 1 - Side a, angle A and angle B");
    printf("\n 2 - Side a, side b, and angle A");
    printf("\n 3 - Side a, side b and angle C");
    printf("\n 4 - Side a, side b, side b");
    printf("\n Your choice (1-4): ");
    scanf("%d",&choice);
    return(choice);
}


/*------------------------------------------------------------*/
/*   Function: triangle_aAB                                   */
/*   Obtains inpuut and computes and prints remaining lengths */
/*   of sides and angles of the triangle for the case when the*/
/*   side a and angles A and B are given.                     */
/*------------------------------------------------------------*/
void triangle_aAB(void)
{
    double A,B,C;      /* angles */
    double a,b,c;      /* sides  */

    /* get input */
    printf("\n Enter length of side a: ");
    scanf("%lf", &a);
    printf(" Enter angle A (degrees): ");
    scanf("%lf", &A);
    printf(" Enter angle B (degrees): ");
    scanf("%lf", &B);

    /* compute */
    A *= PI/180.;      /* convert to radians */
    B *= PI/180.;
    b = a*sin(B)/sin(A);
    C = PI - (A + B);
    c = sqrt(a*a + b*b - 2.*a*b*cos(C));

    /* print results */
    print_results(A,B,C,a,b,c);

}
/*------------------------------------------------------------*/
/*   Function: triangle_abA                                   */
/*   Obtains inpuut and computes and prints remaining lengths */
/*   of sides and angles of the triangle for the case when    */
/*   the sides a and b and the angle A are   given.           */
/*------------------------------------------------------------*/
```

FIGURE 8.14 *(continued)*

```
 ── void triangle_abA(void)
    {
        double.A,B,C;      /* angles */
        double a,b,c;      /* sides  */

        /* get input */
        printf("\n Enter length of side a: ");
        scanf("%lf", &a);
        printf(" Enter length of side b: ");
        scanf("%lf", &b);
         printf(" Enter angle A (degrees): ");
        scanf("%lf", &A);

        A *= PI/180. ;           /* convert to radians */
        B = asin(b*sin(A)/a);
        C = PI - (A + B);
        c = sqrt(a*a + b*b - 2.*a*b*cos(C));

        /* print results */
        print_results(A,B,C,a,b,c);
    }

    /*------------------------------------------------------------*/
    /*  Function: triangle_abC                                    */
    /*  Obtains inpuut and computes and prints remaining lengths  */
    /*  of sides and angles of the triangle for the case when     */
    /*  the sides a and b and the angle C are given.              */
    /*------------------------------------------------------------*/
 ── void triangle_abC(void)
    {
        double A,B,C;
        double a,b,c;

        /* get input */
        printf("\n Enter length of side a: ");
        scanf("%lf", &a);
        printf(" Enter length of side b: ");
        scanf("%lf", &b);
        printf(" Enter angle C (degrees): ");
        scanf("%lf", &C);
        /* compute */
        C *= PI/180.;        /* convert to radians */
        c = sqrt(a*a + b*b - 2. *a*b*cos(C));
        A = acos((b*b + c*c - a*a)/(2.*b*c));;
        B = PI - (A + C);

        /* print results */
        print_results(A,B,C,a,b,c);
    }

    /*------------------------------------------------------------*/
    /*  Function: triangle_abc                                    */
    /*  Obtains inpuut and computes and prints remaining lengths  */
    /*  of sides and angles of the triangle for the case when     */
    /*  the sides a, b and c are given.                           */
    /*------------------------------------------------------------*/
```

FIGURE 8.14   (*continued*)

```
void triangle_abc(void)
{
    double A,B,C;    /* angles */
    double a,b,c;    /* sides */

    /* get input */
    printf("\n Enter length of side a: ");
    scanf("%lf", &a);

    printf(" Enter length of side b: ");
    scanf("%lf", &b);
    printf(" Enter length of side c: ");
    scanf("%lf", &c);

    /* compute */
    A = acos((b*b + c*c - a*a)/(2.*b*c));
    B = asin(b*sin(A)/a);
    C = PI - (A + B);

    /* print results */
    print_results(A,B,C,a,b,c);
}

/*-----------------------------------------------------------*/
/*  Function: print_results                                  */
/*                                                           */
/*  Prints the lengths of the sides of the triangle and the  */
/*  angles. Also computes and prints the area of the triangle.*/
/*                                                           */
/*  Input Parameters:                                        */
/*     a, b, c - lengths of sides of the triangle            */
/*     A, B, C - angles                                      */
/*  ---------------------------------------------------------*/
void print_results(double A,double B,double C,double a,
        double b,double c)
{
    double s, area;
    printf("\n\n Side a = %f",a);
    printf("\n Side b = %f", b);
    printf("\n Side c = %f", c);
    printf("\n Angle A = %.2f degrees",A * 180. / PI);
    printf("\n Angle B = %.2f degrees", B * 180. / PI);
    printf("\n Angle C = %.2f degrees", C * 180. / PI);

    /* compute area */
    s = (a + b + c)/2.;
    area = sqrt(s* (s-a) * (s-b) * (s-c));
    printf("\n Area of triangle = %f", area);
}
```

FIGURE 8.14 (*continued*)

Also, in the **print_results()** function, these angles are converted back to degrees before they are printed. For example, in the **printf()** statement that prints the angle *A*

```
printf("\n Angle A = %.2f degrees",A * 180. / PI);
```

the angle is converted to degrees by the expression **A * 180. /PI**.

Testing

To test the program we can use a righttriangle with $a = 5$, $b = 3$, and $c = 4$. The corresponding values of the angles are $A = 90°$, $B = 36.87°$ and $C = 53.13°$. The area of the triangle is 6. We leave it as an exercise for the user to verify that the output from the program for the four cases does indeed agree with the values given.

8.9   PROGRAMMING PROJECT: COLOR CODING OF RESISTORS

The resistance of nonmetallic resistors is represented by means of four color bands on the resistor body. The first two colors represent the first two significant digits of the resistance value. The third color band represents the multiplier factor. Table 8.1 shows the values that correspond to the first three color bands. The fourth color band denotes the resistance tolerance. A gold band indicates a 5 percent tolerance, a silver band indicates a 10 percent tolerance, and the absence of the fourth band indicates a tolerance of 20 percent.

Table 8.1: Relationship between color of band and its value

First and Second Bands		Third Band	
Color	Value	Color	Value
black	0	black	0
brown	1	brown	10
red	2	red	100
orange	3	orange	1,000
yellow	4	yellow	10,000
green	5	green	100,000
blue	6	blue	1,000,000
violet	7	silver	0.1
gray	8	gold	0.01
white	9		

Figure 8.15 shows a resistor with the color bands. The first band is green, and so the first digit is 5. The second band is blue, which has the value 6. The third band is orange, so the multiplier is 1000. Thus the resistance value for the resistor is

$$(5 \times 10 + 6) \times 1000 = 56,000 \text{ ohms}$$

The fourth band is silver, which indicates that the resistor has a tolerance of 10 percent.

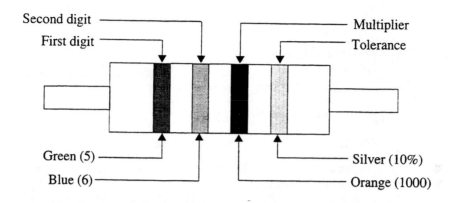

Figure 8.15   Resistor with color bands and decoding schemes.

Problem Statement

Write a program to decode the color markings on a resistor into a resistance value. The program should consist of a main program that computes and prints the result and three functions that obtain the color for bands 1 and 2, band 3, and band 4 and determine the value corresponding to the color. These functions should display a list of colors for each color band, prompt the user to select the color of the band from this list, and determine the corresponding value for that color band.

Problem Analysis

Our program will need to read in the color for each band and compute the resistance value. One method for doing this is to display a list of colors for each band and allow the user to make a selection from this list. Since the colors for the first two bands are the same, we can use one function to display the list of colors for the first two bands. With some minor modifications, the same function can also be used to display the list of colors for the third band, since most of the colors for the third band are the same as those for the first two bands. We will also need separate functions to decode the values for each of the four color bands.

The data requirements for the problem are as follows:

Input Variables
values for band 1 and band 2 (`int band1, band2`)
multiplier for band 3 (`double multiplier`)
tolerance (`double tolerance`)

Output Variables

resistance value (**double resistance**)

Program Variables

number corresponding to the selected color (**int choice**). This variable
is used in the functions that obtain user input.

Algorithm and Structure Chart

The functions in the program are as follows:

1. **main()** — Calls other functions to obtain input. Computes resistance
   value and prints results.
2. **display_codes()** — displays color codes for the first three bands.
3. **get_band_value()** — gets user's selection for the first two bands.
4. **get_multiplier()** — gets user's selection for the third band,
   decodes it, and returns the correponding multiplier value.
5. **get_tolerance()** — gets user's selection for the fourth band,
   decodes it, and returns the corresponding tolerance value.

The structure chart for the program follows.

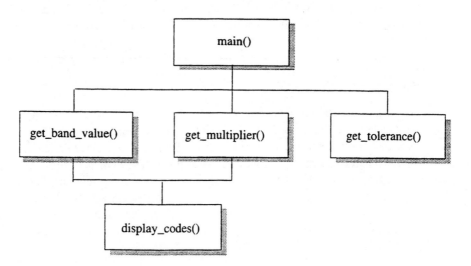

Algorithm for main()

1. Call function **get_band_value()** with an argument of 1 to get the value
   for band 1.
2. Call function **get_band_value()** with an argument of 2 to get the
   value for band 2.

3. Call function **get_multiplier()** to get value for **multiplier**.
4. Call function **get_tolerance()** to get value for **tolerance**.
5. Compute resistance from
    resistance = (band1 * 10 + band2) * multiplier;
6. Print **resistance, tolerance**.

Algorithm for get_band_value()

1. Set **choice** equal to −1.
2. Call function **display_codes()** with an argument of 1 or 2 to display the color codes for the corresponding band.
3. While (**choice** < 0 or **choice** > 9) do the following:
    3.1 Read **choice**.
4. Return **choice** to caller.

Algorithm for get_multiplier()

1. Set **choice** equal to −1.
2. Call function **display_codes()** with an argument of 3 to display color codes for the third band.
3. While (**choice** < 0 or **choice** > 8) do the following
    3.1 Read **choice**.
4. If **choice** <= 6
    4.1 Return 10^{choice} to caller.
    Else if **choice** = 7
    4.2 Return 0.1 to caller.
    Else
    4.3 Return 0.01 to caller.

Algorithm for get_tolerance()

1. Set **choice** equal to 0.
2. Print color codes corresponding to fourth band.
3. While (**choice** < 1 or **choice** > 3) do the following:
    3.1 Read **choice**.
4. If **choice** =1 or **choice** = 2
    4.1 Return (**choice** * 5) to caller.
    Else
    4.2 Return 20 to caller.

Program

The program is shown in Figure 8.16. The function **main()** is fairly small since most of the work is done by the other functions. After declaring variables, **main()** calls **get_band_value()** two times to obtain the value corresponding to the color for the first and second bands. In the first call

```
band1 = get_band_value(1);
```

the function **get_band_value()** is passed an argument of 1, indicating that value for the first color band is needed. In the second call to **get_band_value()**

```
band2 = get_band_value(2);
```

the argument is 2, which indicates that the color value for the second band is needed. **main()** then calls **get_multiplier()** and **get_tolerance()** to obtain the multiplier value and the tolerance value

```
multiplier = get_multiplier();
tolerance = get_tolerance();
```

The resistance is computed in the statement

```
resistance = (band1 * 10 + band2) * multiplier;
```

The function then print the resistance value and the tolerance value.

The function **get_band_value()** returns an integer result representing the value corresponding to the color of the first or second band. This function has one argument of type **int** which can have a value of 1 or 2 and represents the color band — band 1 or band 2. The function passes this value on to the function **dislay_codes()**, which it calls. The function **display_code()** displays a list of color codes for the first, second, or third bands depending on the value of the argument passed to it. It is called by both the **get_band_value()** and the **get_multiplier()** functions. The **get_band_value()** function calls **display_codes()** with an argument of either 1 or 2 in the following call statement

```
display_codes(band_number);
```

where **band_number** is a the value passed to **get_band_value()** by **main()**. The **get_tolerance()** function calls **display_codes()** with the following call statement

```
display_codes(3);
```

to display the list of colors for the third band.

```
/*******************************************************/
/*   resistor.c -- Nonmetallic Resistors               */
/*                                                      */
/*   Computes the resistance value for nonmetallic      */
/*   resistors from the colors of the four bands on the */
/*   resistor.                                          */
/*******************************************************/
#include <stdio.h>
#include <math.h>

/* function prototypes */
void display_codes(int band_number);
int get_band_value(int band_number);
double get_multiplier(void);
double get_tolerance(void);

main()
{
  int band1,band2;      /* values for first and second band  */
  double multiplier;    /* value for third band (multiplier) */
  double tolerance;     /* value for fourth band (tolerance) */
  double resistance;    /* resistance value                  */

  printf("\n RESISTANCE VALUE FOR NONMETALLIC RESISTORS");

  /* get values for each band */
  band1 = get_band_value(1);
  band2 = get_band_value(2);
  multiplier = get_multiplier();
  tolerance = get_tolerance();

  /* compute resistance */
  resistance = (band1 * 10 + band2 ) * multiplier;

  /* print resistance and tolerance  */
  printf("\n Resistance = %lf ohms",resistance);
  printf("\n Tolerance  = %lf percent", tolerance);
}

/*-----------------------------------------------------*/
/*   Reads in color for first or second band and       */
/*   determines corresponding value                    */
/*                                                      */
/*   Input Parameters                                   */
/*    band_number - 1 = first band, 2 = second band     */
/*                                                      */
/*   Output Parameters                                  */
/*     None                                             */
/*                                                      */
/*   Returns                                            */
/*     tolerance - tolerance value (percent)            */
/*                                                      */
/*   Calls:                                             */
/*     display_codes() to display list of colors        */
/*-----------------------------------------------------*/
```

Figure 8.16   Resistance value for nonmetallic resistors.

```
int get_band_value(int band_number)
{
   int choice=-1;

   display_codes(band_number);
   while (choice < 0 || choice > 9)
      {
      printf("\n Enter color of band %d (0-9): ",band_number);
      scanf("%d",&choice);
      }
   return(choice);
}

/*-----------------------------------------------------*/
/*   Reads in color of third band and determines       */
/*   corresponding value of multiplier                 */
/*                                                     */
/*   Input Parameters                                  */
/*     None                                            */
/*                                                     */
/*   Output Parameters                                 */
/*     None                                            */
/*                                                     */
/*   Returns                                           */
/*     multiplier                                      */
/*-----------------------------------------------------*/
double get_multiplier(void)
{
   int choice = -1;

   display_codes(3);
   while (choice < 0 || choice > 8)
     {
     printf("\n Enter color of band 3: ");
     scanf("%d",&choice);
     }
   if (choice <=6)
      return (pow(10,choice));

   else if (choice == 7)
       return (0.1);        /* silver */
   else
       return(0.01);        /* gold   */
}

/*-----------------------------------------------------*/
/*   Displays color codes for the first three bands    */
/*                                                     */
/*   Input Parameters                                  */
/*     band_number - 1 = first band, 2 = second band   */
/*                   3 = third band                    */
/*                                                     */
/*   Output Parameters                                 */
/*     None                                            */
/*-----------------------------------------------------*/
```

FIGURE 8.16 (continued)

```
void display_codes(int band_number)
{
   printf("\n COLOR CODES FOR BAND %d",band_number);
   printf("\n 0 - Black");
   printf("\n 1 - Brown");
   printf("\n 2 - Red");

   printf("\n 3 - Orange");
   printf("\n 4 - Yellow");
   printf("\n 5 - Green");
   printf("\n 6 - Blue");

   if (band_number == 1 || band_number == 2)
      {
      printf("\n 7 - Voilet");
      printf("\n 8 - Gray");
      printf("\n 9 - White");
      }
   else
      {
      printf("\n 7 - Silver");
      printf("\n 8 - Gold");
      }
}


/*---------------------------------------------------*/
/*   Obtains tolerance value for fourth band         */
/*                                                   */
/*   Input Parameters                                */
/*      None                                         */
/*                                                   */
/*   Output Parameters                               */
/*      None                                         */
/*                                                   */
/*   Returns                                         */
/*      tolerance - tolerance value (percent)        */
/*---------------------------------------------------*/
double get_tolerance(void)
{
   int choice=0;
   printf("\n COLOR CODES FOR FOURTH BAND (TOLERANCE)");
   printf("\n 1 - Gold");
   printf("\n 2 - Silver");
   printf("\n 3 - None");
   while (choice < 1 || choice > 3)
      {
      printf("\n Enter color of fourth band (1-3): ");
      scanf("%d",&choice);
      }
   if (choice == 1 || choice == 2)
      return(choice * 5.);
   else
      return (20.0);
}
```

FIGURE 8.16 (*continued*)

Testing

A sample run and the output from the program is shown in Figure 8.17. The results from the program agree with those obtained by hand calculation. You should also test the results for the resistors shown in Table 8.2.

```
RESISTANCE VALUE FOR NON-METALLIC RESISTOR

COLOR CODES FOR BAND 1
0 - Black
1 - Brown
2 - Red
3 - Orange
4 - Yellow
5 - Green
6 - Blue
7 - Voilet
8 - Gray
9 - White
Enter color of band 1 (0-9): 5

COLOR CODES FOR BAND 2
0 - Black
1 - Brown
2 - Red
3 - Orange
4 - Yellow
5 - Green
6 - Blue
7 - Voilet
8 - Gray
9 - White
Enter color of band 2 (0-9): 6

COLOR CODES FOR BAND 3
0 - Black
1 - Brown
2 - Red
3 - Orange
4 - Yellow
5 - Green
6 - Blue
7 - Silver
8 - Gold
Enter color of band 3: 3

COLOR CODES FOR FOURTH BAND (TOLERANCE)
1 - Gold
2 - Silver
3 - None
Enter color of fourth band (1-3): 2

Resistance = 56000.000 ohms
Tolerance  = 10.000 percent
```

Figure 8.17   Sample run and output from program *resistor.c*.

Table 8.2: Resistance values of three resistors

Resistor	Band 1	Band 2	Band 3	Band	Resistance	Tolerance
1	green	blue	brown	gold	560	5
2	violet	green	orange	silver	75,000	10
3	white	yellow	red	none	9,400	20

8.10 STORAGE CLASSES

There are two attributes associated with every C variable: *data type* and *storage class*. The storage class of a variable tells the compiler how the variable is to be stored and how long the variable remains in existence. The storage class also determines the variable's visibility or scope, that is, where in the program the variable can be accessed. There are four storage classes in C: *automatic*, *external*, *static*, and *register*, with the corresponding keywords **auto**, **extern**, **static**, and **register**.

Local Variables

Variables that are declared within the body of a function such as temporary variables for storing intermediate results of calculations are *local variables*. Local variables are visible only to the function in which they are defined and are invisible to all other functions. Thus local variables can be accessed only from within the function. They cannot be accessed by any other function. Local variables are also called *automatic* variables since they are automatically created each time the function is called and are destroyed after the function has completed execution. For example, the variable **i** in the function **kill_time()** is a local variable and is known only to the function **kill_time()**, but not to any other function.

```
void kill_time(void)
{
int i;
for (i = 1; i <= 30000; ++i)
    ;
}
```

We can also use the keyword **auto** to declare an automatic local variable as in

```
auto int i;
```

However, since any variable defined inside a function is by default assumed by the compiler to be an automatic local variable, the keyword **auto** is rarely used.

Example 8.6   Local Variables

The program shown in Figure 8.18 contains three functions, **main()**,
function1(), and **function2()**. Inside each function there is a variable named
i. The variable **i** is local to each function, and each function assigns a different
value to **i**. The value of **i** is printed in **main()** before **function1()** and
function2() are called from **main()**. Each function prints the value of **i**, and
main() prints the value of **i** after the functions have been called. Since each
variable is local to the function in which it is defined, its value is not affected by
changes made to **i** in any other function.

```
/*************************************************************/
/*   locals.c  -- Automatic local variables                 */
/*   Illustrates automatic local variables in functions.    */
/*************************************************************/
#include <stdio.h>
/* function prototypes */
void function1(void);
void function2(void);

main()
{
   int i=1;      /* visible only to main() */
   printf("\n Initial value of i in main() is %d", i);
   function1();
   function2();
   printf("\n Final value of i in main() is %d", i);
}

void function1(void)
{
   int i;       /* visible only to function1() */
   i = 10;
   printf("\n Value of i in function1() is %d", i);
}

void function2(void)
{
   int i;       /* visible only to function2() */
   i = 20;
   printf("\n Value of i in function2() is %d", i);
}
```

Program output

```
Initial value of i in main() is 1
Value of i in function1() is 10
Value of i in function2() is 20
Final value of i in main() is 1
```

Figure 8.18   Local variables.

Global Variables

External or global variables, as they are commonly called, are variables that are defined outside a function. Global variables are visible to all functions that follow the definition. The example tHAT follows creates two global variables, **seed** and **new_seed**.

```
int random(void);    /* function prototype */
int reseed(void);    /* function prototype */
int seed;            /* global variable */

main()
{
  ...
  ...
}

int new_seed;        /* global variable */

int random(void)
{
  ...
  ...
}

int reseed(void);
{
  ...
  ...
}
```

The variable **seed** is visible to the functions **main()**, **random()**. The variable **new_seed** is visible to **random()** and **reseed()** but not visible to **main()**, since it was defined after **main()**.

Global variables are assigned permanent storage and exist for the entire duration of the program.

Example 8.7   Visibility of Global Variables

The program shown in Figure 8.19 illustrates that global variables are available to all functions and can be modified within a function. The program creates a global variable **beta** and assigns it an initial value of 3. The function **main()** calls **funct1()**, which changes the value of **beta**. The initial and final value of **beta** in both **main()** and **funct1()** are printed.

```
/********************************************************/
/*    global1.c  -- Visibility of global variables      */
/*                                                      */
/********************************************************/
#include <stdio.h>
void funct1(void);      /* function prototype */
double beta = 3.0;      /* beta is global */

main()
{
   printf("\n Initial value of beta in main() = %f", beta);
   funct1();
   printf("\n Final value of beta in main() = %f", beta);
}

void funct1(void)
{
  printf("\n Initial value of beta in funct1() = %f", beta);
  beta = 4.0;
  printf("\n Final value of beta in funct1() = %f", beta);
}
```

Program output

```
Initial value of beta in main() = 3.000000
Initial value of beta in funct1() = 3.000000
Final value of beta in funct1() = 4.000000
Final value of beta in main() = 4.000000
```

Figure 8.19   Visibility of global variables.

If a global variable and a local variable have the same name, then all references to the variable inside the function that contains the local variable apply to the local variable and not to the global variable. This is illustrated in Example 8.8.

Example 8.8   Global and Local Variables with Same Name

The program in Figure 8.20 creates two variables named **a**. The definition outside **main()** creates a global variable

```
int a = 12;
```

and assigns it an initial value of 12. The definition inside function **funct1()** creates a local variable **a.** Since both the local and global variables have the same

```
/***************************************************************/
/* global2.c -- Global and local variables with same name     */
/*                                                             */
/***************************************************************/
#include <stdio.h>
void funct1(void);       /* function prototype */

int a = 12;              /* a is global */

main()
{
    printf("\n Initial value of a in main() = %d", a);
    funct1();
    printf("\n Final value of a in main() = %d", a);
}

void funct1(void)
{
    int a;               /* a is local to funct1() */
    a = 200;
    printf("\n Value of a in funct1() = %d", a);
}
```

Program output

```
Initial value of a in main() = 12
Value of a in funct1() = 200
Final value of a in main() = 12
```

Figure 8.20   Global and local variables with the same name.

name, the global variable is hidden from **funct1()**, and any references to **a** in **funct1()** apply to the local variable and not the global variable. In **funct1()**, **a** is assigned a value of 200. However, since this assignment is made to the local variable, the value of global variable **a** remains unchanged.

External variables are initialized only once — when storage is allocated. If an external variable is defined but not explicitly initialized, the compiler initializes it to zero.

Global variables defined in one file are not automatically made available to other source files unless they are also declared in the other files. We use the keyword **extern** to declare global variables. The specifier **extern** informs the compiler that the variables that follow have already been defined elsewhere. The following example is written in two files: *file1.c* and *file2.c*.

file1.c   file2.c

```
double alpha, beta;                   extern double alpha, beta;
int gamma;                            int delta;


main()                                funct2()
{                                     {
   ...                                   ...
   ...                                   ...
}                                     }


funct1()                              funct3()
{                                     {
   ...                                   ...
   ...                                   ...
   beta = 3.0;                        }
   alpha = 5.0;
   ...
   ...
}
```

In *file1.c*, two global variables of type **double**, **alpha** and **beta**, are defined. A global variable of type **int** named **gamma** is also defined. These global variables are available to all functions in *file1.c*. In *file2.c* the declaration

extern double alpha, beta;

indicates that the variables **alpha** and **beta** have been defined elsewhere (in our case, in *file1.c*). This makes the variables **alpha** and **beta** available to all functions in *file2.c*. Since there is no **extern** declaration for the global variable **gamma** defined in *file1.c*, the variable **gamma** is not visible to any of the functions in *file2.c*. Also, the global variable **delta** defined in file 2 is not visible to any of the functions in *file1.c*. If we wanted to make **delta** visible to **main()** and **funct1()**, then we would have to include the following declaration *file1.c* before the definition of **main()**:

extern int delta;

Table 8.3 shows which variables are visible to the functions in the two files.

Table 8.3: Visibility of global variables

Variable	Visible to			
alpha	main(),	funct1(),	funct2(),	funct3()
beta	main(),	funct1(),	funct2(),	funct3()
gamma	main(),	funct1()		
delta	funct2(),	funct3()		

The advantage of using the storage class specifier **extern** lies in the fact that it allows us to link separately compiled modules of a large program. We can break up a large program into several smaller files and compile each file separately. This reduces program development time considerably since only those files that have been changed need to be compiled again. The execution of a program obtained by combining separately compiled files is no different from a program obtained by compiling a single file.

Since global variables are visible to many functions, they provide a way to transfer information across functions. However, we should limit the number of global variables in our programs whenever possible. There are a number of disadvantages to using global variables. These include

1. Programs containing global variables are prone to errors. In a program with many global variables, it becomes difficult to keep track of what each variable does.

2. Since many functions have access to global variables, unwanted side effects can occur. A function can unknowingly change the value of a global variable resulting in problems when this variable is used elsewhere. Such errors are difficult to trace.

3. Using global variables instead of local variables makes a function less general. Functions that make use of global variables must also rely on these variables being defined elsewhere in the program. It is more difficult to include such functions in libraries since the functions are no longer independent.

4. Global variables are assigned permanent storage and take up memory the entire time the program is executing. Local variables, on the other hand, are created as needed and are destroyed when no longer needed.

One of the key concepts of structured programming is that a program is developed as a series of independent modules. In C, this is achieved through the use of functions and local variables. Thus the preferred method for passing information to a function is through the use of parameters, not through global variables.

Static Variables

Static variables are permanent variables, which means that they remain in existence for the entire execution of the program. Static variables can be defined either inside or outside a function. A static variable defined inside a function is local to the function and is visible only within the function. A static variable defined outside a function is visible to all functions in the file that follow the definition. The essential difference between static variables and external variables is that static variables are known only to the block in which they are defined. Since the static storage class has a different effect on local and global variables, we will consider each separately.

Static Local Variables

We can define a static local variable by beginning the definition with the keyword **static** as in

```
int counter(void)
{
   static int count;
   ...
   ...
}
```

Here the static variable **count** is local to the function **counter()**. Static local variables are different from automatic variables in that they are assigned permanent storage and remain in existence for the duration of the program. Local static variables retain their values between function calls. Thus, if a program executes the same function again, the static variables will have the same values they had the last time the function was executed.

Example 8.9   Static Local Variables

The difference between static local and automatic local variables is demonstrated by the program shown in Figure 8.21. The variable **a** in function **square_it()** is a static local variable, while the variable **b** is an automatic local variable. In both programs **main()** calls **square_it()** three times. The automatic variable **b** is created and initialized to 2 each time the function **square_it()** is called and is destroyed when the function is terminated. Thus, no matter how many times we call the function **square_it()**, the variable **b** always has the final value of 4.

The variable **a** is a static local variable and retains its value upon each entry

```
/*******************************************************/
/*   static.c -- Automatic and Static Variables        */
/*                                                      */
/*   Illustrates the difference between local           */
/*   auotmatic and local static variables               */
/*******************************************************/
#include <stdio.h>
void square_it(void);

main()
{
    square_it();
    square_it();
    square_it();
}

void square_it(void)
{
    static int a = 2;     /* static local      */
    int b = 2;            /* automatic local   */

    a *= a;
    b *= b;
    printf("\n Final value of a = %d", a);
    printf("\n Final value of b = %d", b);
}
```

Program output:

```
Final value of a = 4
Final value of b = 4
Final value of a = 16
Final value of b = 4
Final value of a = 256
Final value of b = 4
```

Figure 8.21 A program to illustrate the difference between automatic and static variables.

into the function. After the first call to `square_it()`, `a` has the value 4. This value persists until the next call to `square_it()`. At the end of the second call to `square_it()`, `a` has the value 16. The third time `square_it()` is called, `a` has the value of 16. This value is squared to yield the final value of 256.

Another important difference between automatic and static local variables has to do with how they are initialized. When we specify an initial value for an automatic variable, that value is assigned each time the function in which the variable appears is executed. On the other hand, the initial value in assigned to a static variable only once — at the time the program is compiled. Thus, in Figure 8.21, the automatic local variable `b` is created and initialized three times, while the static variable `a` is initialized only once.

Static variables that are not explicitly initialized are initialized to zero by the compiler. Automatic variables are not initialized and can be assumed to contain garbage.

Static local variables are extremely useful for functions that need to preserve the value of some program variables between calls. This feature make is possible for us to write generalized functions. If static variables were not available, then we would need to use global variables. Static variables are preferable to global variables since they are local to the function and do not result in side effects as do globals. Functions containing static variables are easier to include in libraries than functions requiring global variables.

Static Global Variables

Static variables can be defined outside a function. This makes them global. The example that follows defines a static global variable.

```
funct1()
{
    ...                     /* delta not visible here */
    ...
}

static int delta;   /* static global variable */

funct2()
{
    ...                     /* delta visible here      */
    ...
}

funct3()
{
    ...                     /* delta visible here      */
    ...
}
```

Since the static variable **delta** is defined outside **funct11()**, it is visible to **funct1()** and **funct2()**. However, it is not visible to **main()**. Static global variables are visible to all functions in the remainder of the source file in which they are defined. The difference between external variables and static global variables is that external variables can be used by functions in any file, but static global variables are private to the file containing them and can be used only by functions in the same file in which they are defined. Thus static global variables are not available to functions in other files or functions defined earlier in the same file.

The following example illustrates the difference between external and static global variables.

file1.c   *file2.c*

```
double delta;


main()
{
   ...
   ...
}



funct1()
{
   ...
   ...
   beta = 3.0;
   alpha = 5.0;
   ...
   ...
}
```

```
extern double delta;
static double beta;


funct2()
{
   ...
   ...
}


funct3()
{
   ...
   ...
}
```

In *file1.c* an external variable **delta** of type **double** is defined. In *file2.c* the declaration

    extern double delta;

makes **delta** available to all functions in *file2.c*. Thus the variable **delta** is visible to **main()**, **funct1()**, **funct2()**, and **funct3()**. The static global variable **beta** is defined in *file2.c* as

    static double beta;

This variable is known only to the functions **funct2()** and **funct3()** in *file2.c*. It is not visible to any of the functions in *file1.c*.

Static global variables make it possible to share variables between a few functions that need them without having to use external variables. Since static global variables are visible only in the file that contains them, we can create a file containing only the functions that need the static global variable and compile the file separately. This avoids the possibility of side effects that can occur with external variables. Static variables are very useful for developing large and complex programs since they make it possible to hide sections of a program from other functions and provide a privacy mechanism that is essential for developing modular programs.

8.11   RECURSIVE FUNCTIONS

In this section we present an interesting programming technique called *recursion*. Recursion is a powerful way to solve a large class of problems. The basic approach consists of decomposing the original problem into a series of simpler subproblems that are similar to the original problem. The process of decomposition is continued until it yields subproblems that can be solved easily. The solution to the original problem is obtained by combining the solutions to the subproblems.

A recursive function is a function that calls itself. Any C function can call itself. When a C function is called, the computer substitutes the actual parameters for the formal parameters and begins executing the code in the body of the function. When a function calls itself, the system temporarily suspends execution of the current function, saves all the information it needs to continue execution, and proceeds to evaluate the recursive call. When the recursive call is evaluated, a new set of variables is created. These variables do not affect the variables created by a previous call to the function. When the recursive call is completed, the result is passed to the previous call, which then completes the computation.

An example of recursion is the problem of computing factorials. The factorial of a number n is given by

$$n! = n \cdot (n-1) \cdot (n-2) \cdots 3 \cdot 2 \cdot 1 \qquad \textbf{(8.11)}$$

Also, by definition $0! = 1$. The factorial of a number n can be expressed by the following recursive relationship

$$n! = n \cdot (n-1)! \qquad \textbf{(8.12)}$$

Notice that in Equation (8.12), the original problem of computing n! has now been decomposed into the simpler problem of computing $(n-1)!$ The problem of computing $(n-1)!$ can be further simplified as

$$(n-1)! = (n-1) \cdot (n-2)! \qquad \textbf{(8.13)}$$

We can continue this process until we finally arrive at the simple problem of computing 1!. We can thus write a recursive function for computing factorials using Equations (8.11) and (8.12). Such a function would call itself with a different argument each time. This is shown in Example 8.10.

Example 8.10 A Recursive Function for Computing Factorials

PROBLEM STATEMENT: Write a recursive function for computing n!. Write a main program that obtains input, calls the factorial function, and prints the result.

SOLUTION: A program for computing factorials using recursion is shown in Figure 8.22. The program consists of two functions: **main()** and **factorial()**. The function **main()** is a driver function that obtains input, calls **factorial()**, and then prints the result returned from **factorial()**.The function **factorial()** is a recursive function. The first part of the **if** statement

```
if (n==0)
    return(1);
```

```
/*****************************************************/
/*     fact.c -- Computes the factorial of an integer    */
/*               using a recursive function              */
/*****************************************************/
#include <stdio.h>
void main(void);
float factorial(int n);

void main()
{

float result;
int num = - 1;

while (num < 0)
    {
    printf("\n Enter a positive integer");
    scanf("%d", &num);
    }

result = factorial(num);

printf("\n The factorial of %d is %f", num,result);
}


float factorial(int n)
{
    if (n == 0 )
        return (1.0);
    else
        return(n * factorial(n-1));
}
```

Figure 8.22 A recursive function for computing factorials.

contains a test to see if a recursive call is necessary. If **n** = 0, there is no need to make a recursive call and the function returns 1. In the **else** clause

```
else
    return(n * factorial(n-1));
```

the **return** statement contains the recursive call to **factorial()**. When the recursive call is made, execution of the current function is suspended and a second version of **factorial()** is executed with a new set of variables. The first version of the function does not terminate. It waits for the subsequent version to return a value before continuing. Thus at a given time, there may be several versions of the recursive function in operation. For example, if the program were to compute 4!, there would be five calls to the factorial function, each with a different argument. This is shown in Figure 8.23.

The function **main()** calls **factorial()** with an argument of 4. The level 1 **factorial()** function calls the level 2 **factorial()** function with an argument of 3; which in turn calls the level 2 **factorial()** function with an argument of 2, and so on, until the fifth level, when the **factorial()** function is called with an argument of 0. Since 0! is 1, the level 5 **factorial()** function does not make a recursive call and returns a value of 1. This value is returned to the level 4 **factorial()** function, which uses this value to complete its computation. It returns a value of 1 to the level 3 **factorial()** function, and so on, until control is transferred back to the level 1 **factorial()** function. This function completes its computation and returns a value of 120 to **main()**.

When using recursion you should keep the following points in mind:

1. Each level of the recursive function has its own set of variables. Thus **n** in the level 1 **factorial()** function is different from **n** in the level 2 **factorial()** function.

2. Although each level of recursion has its own set of variables, the code is the same, since the same function is being called.

3. There must be some situations in which the recursive function does not call itself. This is called the *base case*. In our example, the **factorial()** function does not call itself when *n* = 0 but instead returns a value of 1. Every recursive function should contain a statement to test for this base case.

4. The recursive function should contain a statement in which it calls itself. Also, when the function calls itself, the values used in testing for the base case must change. For our example, in the call to **factorial()**

```
return(n * factorial(n-1) ;
```

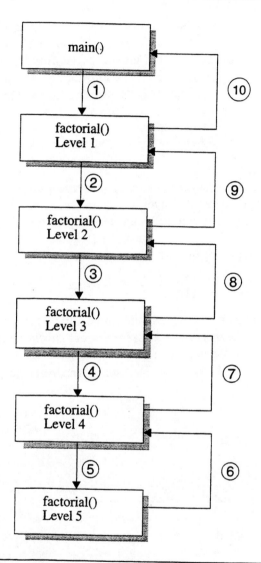

Figure 8.23 Flow of control for program *fact.c*

the argument passed to the function **(n-1)** changes with each call
made. If instead we had written

```
return(n * factorial(n) ;
```

then the value of *n* would not change and we would have infinite
recursion.

5.   When a function is invoked, the invoked function always returns

control back to the function that called it. Thus, at the end of the last recursion level, control is passed back to the previous recursion level. In the example given, the level 6 `factorial()` function returns control to the level 4 `factorial()` function, which in turn returns control back to the level 3 `factorial()` function.

6. Statements in a recursive function that precede the recursive call are executed in the same order in which the functions are called. However, statements in a recursive function that follow the recursive call are executed in the opposite order from which the functions are called.

An important point to remember when writing a recursive function is that a recursive function must test for the base case before it calls itself. Forgetting to do so will result in infinite recursion. The function should be written so that it will ultimately terminate by executing code that does not depend on recursion. The statement in the function `factorial()`

```
if (n==0)
   return(1.0);
```

does not make a recursive call. Another important point is that the function should call itself with a different argument from the one it received.

As a second example of a recursive solution, consider the problem of computing x^n, where x is a real number and n is an integer power. We can write x^n as

$$x^n = x \cdot x^{n-1} \tag{8.14}$$

Also, for negative values of n, we can write

$$x^{-n} = 1/x^n \tag{8.15}$$

Using Equations (8.14) and (8.15), we can set up a recursive solution for x^n as follows:

$$x^n = x \cdot x^{n-1}, \quad \text{when } n > 0$$

$$x^n = 1, \quad \text{when } n = 0$$

$$x^n = 1/x^{-n}, \quad \text{when } n < 0$$

A program that computes x^n using the foregoing recursive solution is given in Example 8.11.

Example 8.11   Recursive Function for Computing x^n

PROBLEM STATEMENT: Write a recursive function for computing x^n where x is a real number and n is an integer exponent. Write a main program to read in x and n, call the recursive function to compute x^n, and print the result.

SOLUTION: A C program for computing x^n using a recursive relationship is shown in Figure 8.24. The function **main()** obtains the values of x and n, calls the **power()** function, and prints the result. The recursive function **power()** has two formal parameters, **x**, which is of type **float** and **n**, which is of type **int**. It returns a value of type **float**.

The first part of the **if** statement

```
if (n==0)
   return (1.0);
```

tests for the base case. If **n** is equal to 0, then the function does not call itself and simply returns a value of 1. In the **else if** clause

```
else if (n > 0)
   return (x * power(x,n-1);
```

if $n > 0$, then the function calls itself but now it passes an argument of **n-1** instead of **n**. The **else** clause

```
else
   return(1.0/power(x,-n);
```

also contains a recursive call to the **power()** function. This time the function is called with an argument of **-n** instead of **n**.

It is not absolutely necessary for us to write recursive functions. In fact, for most types of problems it is possible to replace a recursive function with a nonrecursive function. The nonrecursive function is typically an iterative function that uses a loop instead of recursion. The iterative version of the factorial function is

```
float factorial1(int n)
{
   float factorial = 1.0;
   int i;

   for (i = 2; i <= n; ++i)
        factorial *= i;

   return(factorial);
}
```

The iterative version of the power function was given in Figure 8.11. Notice that in both cases, the recursive call has been replaced by a **for** loop.

```
/*********************************************************/
/*    power.c -- Computes x raised to an integer power n */
/*              using a recursive function.            */
/*********************************************************/
#include <stdio.h>
void main(void);
float power(float x, int n);

void main()
{

  float x, result;
  int n;

  printf("\n Enter x: ");
  scanf("%f", &x);
  printf("\n Enter n (should be integer): ");
  scanf("%d",&n);

  result = power(x,n);

  printf("\n %f raised to the power %d is %f", x,n,result);
  }


float power(float x, int n)
{
  if (n == 0 )
       return (1.0);
  else if (n > 0 )
         return ( x * power(x, n-1));
  else
         return (1.0 / power(x,-n));
}
```

Figure 8.24   A recursive function for computing x^n

Although recursive functions tend to be more elegant and compact and are easier to read, they are not necessarily more efficient. In fact, on most computer systems, recursive functions run slower and require more storage than the corresponding iterative function. This is due to the overhead associated with function calls. For each call to a recursive function, the system creates a new set of variables. Also, since the previous version of the function is temporarily suspended, the system has to save the variables associated with the previous version of the function so that it can continue the computation after the current version has completed execution. If the number of recursive calls is large, then a large amount of storage is needed to keep track of all the recursive calls.

As a final example of recursion we will consider the problem of generating Fibonacci numbers. Recall from Chapter 7 that the Fibonacci numbers are obtained by adding the two previous Fibonacci numbers. Thus,

$$F_i = F_{i-1} + F_{i-2}$$

Also, the first two Fibonacci numbers are defined to be equal to 1; that is,

$$F_1 = F_2 = 1$$

Example 8.12 Fibonacci Numbers

PROBLEM STATEMENT: Write a recursive function to compute the nth Fibonacci number, F_n

SOLUTION: The function is shown in Figure 8.25. The computation is performed by the recursive function **fibonacci()**. This function expects one argument of type **int**. It returns a value of type **float** representing the required Fibonacci number.

In the first part of the **if** statement the function checks the value of **n** to see if it needs to make a recursive call. If **n** is less than or equal to 2, it returns the value 1 (since F_1 and F_2 are both equal to 1). If **n** is greater than 2, the **else** clause

```
else
    return (fibonacci(n-1) + fibonacci(n-2));
```

is executed and the function calls itself twice, once with an argument of **n-1** and then with an argument of **n-2**.

This function is quite inefficient since it makes two recursive calls each time it is invoked. Even for small values of n the number of calls become quite large. Table 8.3 lists the number of times the function is invoked for various values of n. It can be seen from Table 8.3 that even for small values of n the number of calls can get quite large.

Table 8.4: Number of recursive calls required to compute F_n

n	5	10	15	20	25	30
number of calls	9	109	1219	13,529	150,049	166,407

There are advantages as well as disadvantages to using recursion. The major advantage is that recursion is the most natural way to solve some types of problems. Recursive functions are also smaller and much easier to understand. The disadvantages of recursion is that it is less efficient and requires more storage than the equivalent iterative function. The difference in efficiency depends on the number of recursive calls.

```
/***********************************************************/
/*     fibonacci.c -- Fibonacci numbers                    */
/*                                                         */
/*     Computes Fibonacci numbers using a recursive        */
/*     function                                            */
/***********************************************************/
#include <stdio.h>
void main(void);
float fibonacci(int n);

void main()
{
  float result;
  int n=0;

  while ( n <= 0)
    {
    printf("\n Enter n: ");
    scanf("%d",&n);
    }

  result = fibonacci(n);
  printf("\n F(%d) = %.0f",n,result);
  }

float fibonacci(int n)
{
   if (n <= 2)
      return (1.0);
   else
        return (fibonacci(n-1) + fibonacci(n-2));
}
```

Figure 8.25   A recursive function for computing Fibonacci numbers.

8.12 SUMMARY

In this chapter we presented the C language statements for creating and using functions in our programs. These statements make it possible to write programs as a series of independent selfcontained modules or subprograms. Subprograms are easier to develop and debug. They are also easier to read and maintain. The desirable attributes of modules are that they should be small and independent, perform a single task, and have a well-defined interface.

A C function is an independent block of statements. Every C program consists of one or more functions. One of these functions is called **main()**. Program execution begins with **main()**. A C function consists of two parts. The function header specifies the name of the function, the type of value the function returns and the data type of each parameter. The function body contains the actual C statements that are executed when the function is invoked.

A C function that does not return a value is invoked by simply using its name followed by a list of arguments. A C function that returns a value is invoked by using the function name on the right-hand side of an assignment statement or as part of an expression in a C statement. When a function is invoked, control is transferred to the function, and the statements in the function body are executed until a **return** statement or the closing brace that marks the end of the function is reached. Control is then transferred back to the calling function. When a function is invoked the arguments in the function call are evaluated, a copy of the arguments is made, and the values of these arguments are assigned to the corresponding parameters in the function definition. There is a one-to-one correspondence between the arguments in the function call and the parameters in the function definition.

Functions in C can only return one value. The **return** statement provides the mechanism for returning a value to the caller. Also, the function cannot change the values of the arguments since it receives a copy of the arguments and does not have access to the original arguments.

C provides a statement for declaring a function called a function prototype. A function prototype informs the compiler about the type of value returned by the function and the type and number of arguments that the function expects. Function prototypes should be used in all your programs since they ensure proper transfer of information between the calling and called function and avoid many of the common errors that occur when using functions.

In this chapter we also discussed storage classes. The storage class of a variable tells the compiler how the variable is to be stored and how long the variable remains in existence. The storage class also determines the scope of the variable. Local or automatic variables are only visible to the function in which they are defined. They are created when the function is called and are destroyed when the function has completed execution. Extern or global variables are variables that are defined outside of a function. They are visible to all functions that follow the definition and exist for the entire duration of the program. Static variables are also permanent variables and remain in existence for the entire execution of the program. When defined inside a function, static variables are visible only to the function. When defined outside a function, they are visible to all functions that follow. This chapter also described a programming technique called recursion. A recursive function is a function that calls itself. Recursive functions tend to be more elegant and compact but are less efficient.

Key Terms Presented in This Chapter

automatic variables	functions
call by value	function arguments
extern keyword	function body

function call	modular design
function declaration	parameters
function definition	recursive functions
function header	**return** statement
function prototypes	**static** variables
global variables	storage classes
local variables	visibility (of variables)

PROGRAM STYLE, COMMON ERRORS, AND DEBUGGING GUIDE

1. When developing computer programs for solving complex problems, you should write your program as a series of modules or subprograms. Using the top-down approach, you can divide the problem into simpler subproblems and continue this process until the subproblems are simple enough that they can be written as functions.

2. Writing your programs as a collection of small functions makes it easier to debug your programs.

3. Each function should be written so that it performs a single well-defined task.

4. You should try to limit your functions to at most about one page in length. If the function is too long, it becomes difficult to read and to debug. You should consider breaking long functions into several smaller functions.

5. You should choose meaningful function names since this makes your program more readable. The function name should provide some indication of what the function does. Examples are **get_input()**, **compute_roots()**, and **integrate()**.

6. All functions should have several comment lines near the beginning describing the function, the task it performs, any input and output variables and the value that it returns. You may also want to list any other functions that this function calls and describe the local variables used by the function.

7. You should insert one or more blank lines between function definitions to separate functions. This enhances program readability.

8. You should provide a function prototype for every function that is used in your program. The function prototype should appear before any statements in which the function is called.

9. It is a good idea to place function prototypes for all the functions in your program in a separate header file and to include this header file in

your program with a **#include** statement such as

```
#include "myprotos.h"
```

10. You should avoid using global variables for passing information to functions. If you use global variables, your functions are no longer independent, and there is the possibility of unwanted side effects that are difficult to trace.

11. Although it is not required by the C compiler, we encourage you to enclose the returned value in the **return** statement in parentheses. This makes it easier to see what value is being returned. The following two statements are both correct but we prefer the second format.

```
return 3*x;
return (3*x);
```

12. Every C program must have a function called **main()**. The function **main()** can be physically located anywhere in the file (although it is usually the first function in the file). Program execution begins with **main()** and ends with the termination of **main()**.

13. You cannot have two functions in the same program that have the same name.

14. There should not be a semicolon at the end of a function header. For example, the following is an error

```
float square_root(float num); /*extra semicolon */
{
  ...
  ...
}
```

15. There should be a semicolon at the end of a function prototype. For example, the following statement is incorrect

```
float square_root(float) /* missing semicolon */
```

16. A function can return at most one value using the **return** statement. The following return statement is incorrect since the function attempts to return two values, **x1** and **x2**.

```
return(x1, x2);
```

17. When calling a function, you should make sure that the number of arguments in the function call is equal to the number of parameters in the function; definition otherwise, you will get an error. An exception to this is a function that has been defined and declared as having a

variable number of arguments.

18. You should remember always to include the parentheses for the argument list when declaring or defining a function, even if the function has no arguments. For example, it is an error to declare the function `square_root()` as

```
float square_root    /* parentheses missing */
```

Without the parentheses following the function name, the compiler treats `square_root()` as a variable rather than a function.

19. When defining a function, you should specify the data type of each variable in the argument list. In the function definition

```
float compute_root(float a,b,c)
```

the data type for the variables **b** and **c** are not declared.

20. When passing arguments to a function you should not make any assumptions regarding the order in which the arguments are evaluated. Consider the following function header:

```
void evaluate(int n1, int n2)
```

If the function is called as follows

```
n = 10;
evaluate (++n, --n);
```

the values of the arguments passed to the function could be 11 and 10 or 10 and 9 depending on which argument is evaluated first.

21. A function declared as **void** cannot return a value. For example, consider the following function:

```
void solve(float x1, float x2)
{
    float result;
    ...
    ...
    return (result);
}
```

This function attempts to return a value but has been defined to return type **void**. The compiler will generate a syntax error when this function is compiled.

22. C functions cannot be nested, that is, you cannot define a function inside another function. For example, the following code segment will generate an error:

```
float outside(float x, float y)
{
  . . .
  . . .
  float inside(float a) /* nested function */
  {
    . . .
    . . .
  }
}
```

23. The return type of a function should be stated explicitly. Also, the type of each parameter in the parameter list should be explicitly stated.

24. You should always remember to return a value from a function that is supposed to return a value.

25. You cannot use the same variable name for both a function parameter and a local variable. For example, in the following code:

```
float area (float length, float width)
{
  float length;    /* WRONG */
```

the variable **length** is used both as a function parameter as well as a local variable.

26. If a function prototype is placed outside a function definition, then it becomes available to all functions that appear after the prototype. A function prototype placed inside the body of a function is available only to calls made from the function

```
float area(float l,float b);
. . .
. . .
float funct1(float x, float y)
{
float sqare_root(float);
. . .
. . .
z = square_root(25.5);
. . .
. . .
}
```

In the example, the function prototype for **area()** is available to all functions following it in the file. The function prototype for **square_root()** is available only to **funct1()**.

27. Since functions are independent they should be tested separately. One technique is to write a short driver program that calls the function, passes information to it, and prints the value returned by the function.

28. You can test functions using most of the same techniques discussed in previous chapters. Print statements can be used to check control paths. You should pay close attention to the transfer of information between the calling function and the function being called. Use `printf()` statements to print the values of the function arguments prior to the call and the values of the function parameters within the function to verify that the correct information is being passed to the function. You should also print the return value just prior to the return statement and after control has been transferred to the calling function.

EXERCISES

Review Questions

1. What is the difference between an actual argument and a formal parameter?

2. Find the syntax errors in the following function prototypes:

    a. `void some(int a, b);`

    b. `void all (int, float, double)`

    c. `double most(int a, double b, c char);`

    d. `float none (double a, b, c int d);`

3. Answer true or false to the following:

    a. All C functions are equal.

    b. C functions can be only called from `main()`.

    c. To return from a C function you must use the keyword `return`.

    d. Every function returns a value to its invoker.

    e. C functions can be nested.

    f. Every C program must have a function called `main()`.

    g. A function argument and the corresponding parameter must have the same name.

    h. A function may contain more than one `return` statement.

    i. A function argument can be a constant, a variable, an expression or a function call.

    j. A C function can invoke itself.

4. What is meant by "call by value"?

5. What is a structure chart? Why is a structure chart so critical in the development of a program?

6. What is the difference between automatic, local, static, and global variables?

7. In the following C program identify the following:

    a.   Local variables

    b.   Global variables

    c.   Function arguments

    d.   Function parameters

```
double y = 15.0;
int n = 10;
main()
{
    double result;
    result = product(y,n);
    printf("\n %lf multiplied by itself %d times = %ld",
      result);
}

double product(double x, int n)
{
  int i;

    for (i = 1; i <= n; ++i)
        x *= x;

    return(x);
}
```

8.   For each variable in the program here list all the functions that can access the variable.

```
/* file 1 */            /* file 2 */
int a;                   extern a;
main()                   static int c;
{
    int b;               double f2(void);
}                        {
                            double temp;
                             temp = a * c;
void f1(int c)              return(temp);
{                        }
  int d = 10;
  c = d;
}
```

Programs

9.   Write a recursive function to compute the sum of the series

$$S(n) = 2 + 4 + 6 + \cdots + 2n$$

The relationship between $S(n)$ and $S(n-1)$ is

$$S(n) = S(n-1) + 2n$$

10.   Write a function **printf_n_chars()** that prints the same character *n* times. The function header is

```
void print_n_chars(char c, int n);
```

where **c** is the character to be printed and **n** is the number of times the character is printed.

11. Write a function called **grades()** that takes a numerical test score and returns a letter grade. The function header is

    ```
    char grades(int score);
    ```

    The function has one argument of type **int** and returns a value of type **char**. Letter grades are assigned as follow

Score	Grade
90 – 100	A
80 – 89	B
70 – 79	C
60 – 69	D
< 60	F

12. Write C functions for the following mathematical functions
    a. Hyperbolic secant sech(x)
    b. Hyperbolic cosecant cosech(x)
    c. Byperbolic cotangent coth(x).

13. Write a function to compute the logarithm of a number to base b. Use the following relationship

    $$\log_b(x) = \frac{\ln(x)}{\ln(b)}$$

    where ln is the natural logarithm. You may use the C library **log()** function to compute the natural logarithm. The function header for the function is

    ```
    double logb(double x, int b);
    ```

14. Write a C function that has as arguments the coordinates of two points $P_1(x_1, y_1)$ and $P_2(x_2, y_2)$ and returns the distance between the two points. The distance between the two points is given by

    $$dist = \sqrt{(x_1 - x_2)^2 + (y_1 - y_2)^2}$$

    The function header is

    ```
    double distance (double x1, double y1, double x2, double y2)
    ```

15. The trigonometric sine of an angle x expressed in radians can be represented by the following series

$$\sin(x) = x - \frac{x^3}{3!} + \frac{x^5}{5!} - \frac{x^7}{7!} + \cdots$$

Write a function to compute $\sin(x)$ using the series just given. The function should accept a single argument of type `double` and should return a value of type `double`. The function header is

```
double sine(double x);
```

To obtain an accurate result and at the same time maintain computational efficiency, you will need to reduce the argument so that x is small. You can use the following relationships

$$\sin(2n\pi + x) = \sin(x)$$

$$\sin(-x) = -\sin(x)$$

9

ONE-DIMENSIONAL ARRAYS

In many of our applications we will be working with groups of related quantities arranged in the form of a list or table. The individual elements in the group will usually be related to one another. Examples of lists of related data include student names and grades; employee payroll information, such as names and addresses, social security numbers, and salary; and weather information, such as temperature, snow, wind, and rainfall data.

In mathematics, it is common practice to use subscripts when working with groups of related items. For example, if we have several different items that are similar in nature, such as student grades, we might call them x_1, x_2, x_3, ..., x_n rather than assigning them unique names such as grade1, grade2, grade3, ... gradeN. The variable x represents the entire list of grades and an individual element in the list is indicated by the subscript after the name as shown here:

Student Grades

x_1	x_2	x_3	x_4	x_5	x_6	x_7	x_8

Thus, x_1 refers to the first item in the list, x_2 refers to the second item in the list, and

x_8 refers to the last item in the list. The complete set of quantities is called an *array*, and the individual quantities are called *elements*.

An array is a collection of variables of the same data type that are referenced by the same name. Arrays provide us with a systematic, compact, and flexible way to handle groups of related data. They allow us to store information in an organized manner so that it can be easily accessed. For example, a list of names and addresses can be logically organized using five arrays, one each for the name, address, city, state, and zip code. If single variables were used, it would be necessary to assign a separate name for each item on the list as shown here

```
name1    address1    city1    state1    zip1
name2    address2    city2    state2    zip2
name3    address3    city3    state3    zip3
name4    address4    city4    state4    zip4
```

If the number of items on the list is large, it becomes quite cumbersome to define new variables for each item in the list. With arrays we can use one variable name for all the names, another for all the addresses, and so on.

The C programming language provides many features for creating and manipulating arrays. In this chapter we present the C statements for using one-dimensional arrays. We discuss how the elements of an array can be manipulated and how we can use them in functions. A number of applications involving arrays are also presented.

9.1   ARRAYS IN C

One of the more useful features of C is the ability to create arrays for storing a collection of related data items. An array in C is a collection of data items of the same type, associated with a single name. Any valid variable name can be used as the name of the array. The individual elements of an array are referenced by appending a subscript to the array name. For example, we can create an array **x[]** consisting of six elements. The individual elements of the array are **x[0]**, **x[1]**, **x[2]**, **x[3]**, **x[4]**, and **x[5]**. The array subscript (also called the array index), which is the number enclosed in square brackets after the array name, defines the position of the individual element in the array. In C, all array subscripts begin with 0, which means that the first element of the array is **x[0]**, the second element of the array is **x[1]**, and the last element is **x[5]**. To prevent the possibility of confusion between ordinary variable names and array names, we will be using empty square brackets after the array name as in **x[]** to represent arrays throughout this text. Figure 9.1 shows an integer array **x[]** representing student grades. The array consists of eight elements. The values assigned to the elements of the array are 85, 93, 70, 65, 91, 83, 68, and 79.

Arrays that have a single subscript are called *one-dimensional* arrays. In C, we

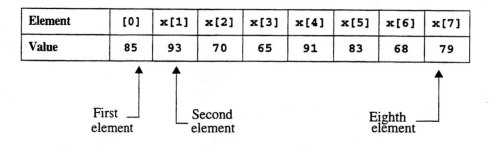

Element	[0]	x[1]	x[2]	x[3]	x[4]	x[5]	x[6]	x[7]
Value	85	93	70	65	91	83	68	79

Figure 9.1   The elements of array **x[ ]**.

can create arrays with more than one subscript. For example, an array having two subscripts is called a *two-dimensional* array. Two-dimensional arrays can be used for storing information that is in the form of a table or a matrix. Two-dimensional arrays are discussed in Chapter 14. Arrays containing two or more dimensions are called *multidimensional* arrays.

9.2   ARRAY DECLARATION

Before we can use an array in a C program we must first declare an array. An array declaration specifies the type of the array and the number of elements in the array. All arrays in C must be explicitly declared so that the compiler can allocate the necessary memory for the array. The general form of the declaration for a one-dimensional array is

> *type_specifier array_name[size]*

in which *type-specifier* is the data type of each element in the array, *array_name* is the name of the array and the *size* in square brackets is the number of elements in the array. Array names use the same naming convention as variable names.

Figure 9.2 shows the syntax of an array declaration for a one-dimensional array. The statement declares an array called **wind_speed[]** of type **double**. The array has 31 elements.

Examples of array declarations are

```
int x[8];
float alpha[50];
double beta[10];
char buffer[80];
```

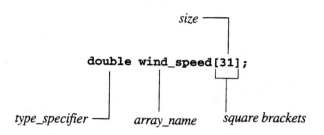

Figure 9.2   Array declaration for a one-dimensional array.

The first statement creates an array of type **int**, called **x[]**, having 8 elements. The second statement creates an array named **alpha[]** of type **float.** The array has 50 elements. The third statement creates an array named **beta[]** consisting of 10 elements each of type **double.** The last statement creates an array of type **char** having 80 elements. The name of the array is **buffer[]**.

We must use an integer constant or constant expression to declare the size of an array. We cannot use a variable or an expression containing a variable to declare the size of an array. Thus the following declarations are illegal:

```
int delta [i];           /* illegal */
float gamma[3 * i + 6];   /* illegal */
```

The first declaration uses an integer variable **i** to declare the size of the array **delta[]**. The second declaration uses an expression containing a variable. We can, however, use a constant expression to declare the size of an array as in

```
#define MAX_SIZE 20
...
...
float x[MAX_SIZE];
float y[2 * MAX_SIZE];
```

Here a symbolic constant **MAX_SIZE** is used in the declaration. It is a good programming practice to use symbolic constants to declare the size of arrays since this makes it easy to change the size of the array. All we have to do is change the value of the symbolic constant in the **#define** statement.

The total number of bytes of storage allocated to an array will depend on the size of the array and the type of data being stored. The total number of bytes can be determined from the following expression:

*total_bytes = sizeof (type_specifier) * size*

Thus, on a system that uses 2 bytes for an integer, the declaration

```
int x[3];
```

results in a total of 6 bytes being allocated for the array. The elements of an array are stored in consecutive memory locations. If, for example, the starting address of the first element of the array `x[]` is 1001, then on a system that uses 2 bytes for an integer, the elements of the array will be stored as:

Array element	x[0]		x[1]		x[2]		x[3]	
Memory location	1001	1002	1003	1004	1005	1006	1007	1008

9.3   ARRAY INITIALIZATION

Most C compilers allow the initialization of arrays having the **extern** or **static** storage class. Under the ANSI C standard it is also possible to initialize automatic arrays. On compilers conforming to the older Kernighan and Ritchie standard, initialization of automatic arrays is not permitted.

The general form of array initialization for a one-dimensional array is

type_specifier array_name[size] = { list_of_values }

in which *list_of_values* is a comma separated list of constants having the same data type as the array. When the array is initialized, the first constant in the list is assigned to the first element of the array, the second constant is assigned to the second element, and so on. For example, the statement

```
static float x[5] = { 5.0, 10.0, 15.0, 20.0, 25.0 };
```

assigns the following values to the elements of the array `x[]`:

Element	x[0]	x[1]	x[2]	x[3]	x[4]
Value	5.0	10.0	15.0	20.0	25.0

If the number of items in the list of initializers is less than the number of elements in the array, then the remaining elements of the array are initialized to zero. Consider the following statement:

```
static double y[5] = { 1.0, 6.0, 3.0 };
```

In this statement, the initialization list contains only three elements, but the array consists of five elements, so the last two elements of the array are initialized to zero as shown here:

Element	x[0]	x[1]	x[2]	x[3]	x[4]
Value	1.0	6.0	3.0	0.0	0.0

If the size of the array is not specified during initialization, the compiler will automatically count the number of items in the list of initializers and create an array that has the same size as the number of items in the list. Thus the statement

```
static double z[] = { 1.0, 2.0, 3.0, 4.0, 5.0 };
```

creates an array of type **double** having five elements.

Element	z[0]	z[1]	z[2]	z[3]	z[4]
Value	1.0	2.0	3.0	4.0	5.0

As with external and static variables, if an external or static array is not initialized, the compiler automatically initializes all the elements of the array to zero. The elements of an automatic array are not initialized and therefore contain garbage.

In ANSI C it is possible to initialize an automatic array. An automatic array is an array that is defined inside a function. The syntax for initializing an automatic array is identical to that just described for external and static arrays. Thus the statement

```
main()
   {
   int squares[5] = { 1, 2, 4, 8, 16};
```

initializes the automatic array **squares[]**. The first element **squares[0]** is assigned the value 1, the second element **squares[1]** is assigned the value 2, and so on. For compilers that do not support the ANSI C standard, it is not possible to initialize automatic arrays, and the only way to give values to the elements of an automatic array is to assign values to the elements individually using assignment statements.

9.4 ARRAY SUBSCRIPTS

Array subscripts identify individual elements of an array. In C, all arrays start with the subscript 0. Suppose that an array **x[]** has been declared as

```
int x[10];
```

then **x[0]** refers to the first element of the array, **x[4]** refers to the fifth element of the array and **x[9]** refers to the tenth and last element of the array. You should note that the last element of the array is `x[9]` and *not* `x[10]`, since we begin counting from 0 and not from 1. An array subscript can be an integer constant or variable, or an arithmetic expression that evaluates to an integer. Examples of valid array subscripts are

```
x[3]           /* integer constant   */
y[i]           /* integer variable   */
z[3 * i + 4];  /* integer expression */
```

In these examples, `i` is a variable of type `int`.

Example 9.1   Array Subscripts

PROBLEM STATEMENT: Consider the integer array `x[]` consisting of eight elements. If `i = 2` and `j = 3`, identify the elements `x[i]`, `x[j]`, `x[i+j]`, `x[2*i-j]`, and `x[j+4]`.

x[0]	x[1]	x[2]	x[3]	x[4]	x[5]	x[6]	x[7]
85	93	70	65	91	83	68	79

```
   x[2 * i-j]      x[i]    x[j]            x[i+j]           x[j+4]
```

SOLUTION: The elements of the array are referenced as follows:

`x[i]` refers to `x[2]`, which is the third element of the array `x[]`.

`x[j]` refers to `x[3]`, which is the fourth element of the array `x[]`.

`x[i+j]` refers to `x[5]`, which is the sixth element of the array `x[]`.

`x[2 * i-j]` refers to `x[1]`, which is the second element of the array.

`x[j+4]` refers to `x[7]`, which is the eighth element of the array .

The array subscript is used to identify a particular element of an array. The array subscript points to the memory cell which contains the actual value of the element.

Unlike some other programming languages such as Pascal, FORTRAN, and BASIC, *C does not perform any array bounds checking.* This means that your program is not prevented from using subscripts that exceed the bounds of an array.

The compiler does not give an error message if you use an out of bounds subscript. Thus is possible that your program may accidentally overwrite other program variables or even sections of the program code itself resulting in a system crash. It is the responsibility of the programmer to ensure that subscripts remain within the bounds of an array.

9.5   ARRAY PROCESSING

The individual elements of an array can be used anywhere that a variable can be. Thus, an array element with a legal subscript is no different from an ordinary variable and can be used in assignment statements, arithmetic expressions, and as an argument to a function. We can assign the value of an array element to another variable, as for example,

```
a = x[5];
b = x[i];
c = x[i + j];
```

In the first statement, the value contained in `x[5]` is assigned to the variable `a`. In the second statement, the value of `x[i]` is assigned to `b`. In the last statement, the value of `x[i + j]` is assigned to the variable `c`.

We can also assign a value to the individual elements of an array by placing the element on the left side of an assignment statement. For example,

```
x[3] = 20;
y[i] = a;
z[i+j] = 2 * a + b;
```

In the first statement, the constant value 20 is assigned to the element `x[3]` of the array. In the second statement, the value of the variable `a` is assigned to the element `y[i]` of the array `y[]`. In the third statement, the result of the arithmetic expression in the right side of the equal (`=`) operator is assigned to the element `z[i+j]` of the array `z[]`. Arrays elements can also appear in arithmetic expressions. Some examples are

```
a = x[i] - x[j];
b = x[i] * x[j] / x[k];
c = 2 * y[i] * z[i - j] + d;
```

All operations on arrays in C are performed on an element by element basis. This means that we can change only one element of an array at a time in any statement. Thus we cannot assign an entire array to another array, but we can assign individual elements of an array to individual elements of another array. Since array elements are accessed individually, the most efficient way of manipulating array elements is to use **for** or **while** loops. The loop control variable is used as the array subscript. This lets us reference each element of the array as the value of the loop-control variable changes when the loop is executed.

Example 9.2   Average of Test Scores

PROBLEM STATEMENT: Write a program to read test scores in an array and compute the average test score.

SOLUTION: The program is shown in Figure 9.3. The program first reads in the number of test scores. It then reads in the individual test scores. The scores are stored in an array **scores[]**, which is defined as

```
float scores[MAX_SCORES];
```

The symbolic constant **MAX_SCORES** contains the size of the array and is defined to be equal to 100 in the preprocessor statement

```
#define MAX_SCORES   100
```

```
/**************************************************************/
/*    avg_score.c -- Average of Test Scores                 */
/*                                                          */
/*    This program computes the average score on a test.    */
/**************************************************************/
#include <stdio.h>
#define MAX_SCORES 100

main()
{
   float scores[MAX_SCORES];
   float average, sum = 0.0 ;
   int n,i=0;

   printf("\n Enter number of students in class: ");
   scanf("%d", &n);

   /* read scores and compute sum of scores */
   while (i < n)
      {
      printf("\n Enter score # %d :", i+1);
      scanf("%f", &scores[i]);
      sum += scores[i];
      }

   /* compute and print average */
   average = sum/n;
   printf("\n The average score is: %.2f",average);
}
```

Figure 9.3   A program to compute the average test score.

In the **while** statement

```
while (i < n)
```

the loop control variable **i** goes from 0 to **n-1**, where **n** is the number of students in the class. The **scanf()** statement

```
scanf("%f", &scores[i]);
```

in the body of the **while** loop reads in the score of each student and stores these in the corresponding element of the array. The statement

```
sum += scores[i];
```

computes the sum of the scores. The average is computed by dividing **sum** by **n**.

Example 9.3 Maximum and Minimum Value in an Array

Many engineering applications require that we compute the maximum and minimum values of a list of items. For example, if we were investigating thermal stresses, we would be interested in the maximum and minimum temperature in a given period of time. If we were designing a steel or concrete beam, we would be interested in the maximum bending moments or the maximum stress along the length of the beam.

PROBLEM STATEMENT: Write a program that determines the maximum and minimum values in an array and their location in the array.

SOLUTION: Let us first consider the problem of determining the maximum value in an array **x[]**. The basic algorithm consists of the following steps:

1. The value stored in the first element **x[0]** is defined as the current maximum and is stored in the variable **xmax**. The corresponding index is stored in the variable **imax**.
2. The next item in the list is checked. If its value is larger than the current maximum, it becomes the current maximum. The earlier value is discarded and **xmax** and **imax** are updated. If the value of the next item is less than the current maximum, the current values of **xmax** and **imax** are retained.
3. Step 2 is repeated until all elements of the array **x[]** have been processed.

The algorithm for computing the minimum is similar to the one just described except that now we are searching for the minimum value and the corresponding index.

A program to evaluate the minimum and maximum values and their location in an array is shown in Figure 9.4. The program first declares the variables **xmin** and **xmax** and creates an array having a size of **MAX_SIZE** in the statement

```
double xmin, xmax, x[MAX_SIZE};
```

The symbolic constant **MAX_SIZE** represents the size of the array **x[]** and is defined to be equal to 50 in the preprocessor directive

```
#define MAX_SIZE 50
```

The program reads in the number of items in the list and the value of each item. The **scanf()** statement

```
scanf("%lf",&x[i]);
```

stores the value read in the element **x[i]**.

The variables **xmin** and **xmax** are set equal to the first element of the array **x[0]** in the statements

```
xmin = x[0];
xmax = x[0];
```

and the corresponding indices are set equal to zero (so they point to the first element of the array **x[]**). The maximum and minimum values are computed in the **while** loop. The **if** statement

```
if (x[i] < xmin)
   {
   xmin = x[i];
   imin = i;
   }
```

compares the value of **x[i]** with the current minimum value stored in **xmin**. If **x[i]** is less than **xmin**, then **xmin** is assigned the value of **x[i]** and the corresponding index **imin** is set equal to **i**. The **if** statement

```
if (x[i] > xmax)
   {
   xmax=x[i];
   imax = i;
   }
```

uses a similar approach to determine the maximum value in the array.

```
/***************************************************************/
/*    minmax.c - Maximum and Minimum In An Array               */
/*                                                             */
/*    This program computes the minimum and maximum            */
/*    values in an array and their location.                   */
/***************************************************************/
#define MAX_SIZE 50

main()
{
    double xmin,xmax,x[MAX_SIZE];
    int imin,imax,n,i;

    printf("Enter number of items in list: ");
    scanf("%d",&n);
    for (i = 0; i < n; i++)
        {
        printf("Enter value for x[%d]: ", i);
        scanf("%lf",&x[i]);
        }

    xmin = x[0];
    xmax = x[0];
    imin = 0;
    imax = 0;
    while (i < n)
        {
        if (x[i] < xmin)
            {
            xmin = x[i];
            imin = i;
            }
        if (x[i] > xmax)
            {
            xmax = x[i];
            imax = i;
            }
        }

    printf("\nMinimum value = %lf", xmin);
    printf("\nElement %d contains minimum value", imin+1);
    printf("\n\nMaximum value = %lf", xmax);
    printf("\nElement %d contains maximum value", imax+1);
}
```

Figure 9.4   Minimum and maximum of an array and their location.

9.6   ARRAYS AND FUNCTIONS

Arrays can be used within the body of a function or as function arguments. Passing a single element of an array to a function is no different from passing an ordinary variable or value to a function. To pass a single element to a function, the array name along with the subscript is specified as an argument to the function. For example, if we wanted to compute the absolute value of the element `x[i]` of an array `x[]` of type `int`, we could use the library function `abs()` and pass the element `x[i]` as an argument of the function as in the statement

```
absval = abs(x[i]);
```

The value of `x[i]` is copied into the formal parameter of the function `abs()`, when the function is called. As with ordinary variables, a copy of the value of the element is passed to the function and not the original element.

Arrays as Function Arguments

An entire array can be passed to a function as an argument. To pass an array to a function, we simply state the array's name without the subscript in the function call. For example, to pass an array defined as

```
static int scores[10] = {95,86,99,78,84,74,51,88,94,72};
```

to a function called `sort_list()` that sorts the elements of the array we could use the following call

```
sort_list(scores);
```

The name of the array is specified without the subscript, which essentially tells the compiler to send the entire array to the function.

For a function to receive an array, the array has to be specified in the formal parameter list. The parameter list for a one-dimensional array includes the type of the array followed by empty square brackets. For example, the function header for the function `sort_list()` would be

```
void sort_list (int [])
```

or

```
void sort_list (int a[])
```

if we include the name of the array in the parameter list. This function header indicates that the function `sort_list()` is to receive an array of type `int` as an argument. The square brackets after the array name tell the compiler that the parameter is an array and not an ordinary variable. You should note that it is not necessary to include the size of a one-dimensional array in the parameter list. The function does not need to know the size of the array to access the elements of a one-dimensional array.

Example 9.4   Functions with Array Arguments

PROBLEM STATEMENT: Write a program to compute the maximum, minimum, and average value of a list of numbers. The program should consist of the following functions:

1. `main()` — reads in the array, calls other functions, and prints results.
2. `max_array()` — computes the maximum value in the array.
3. `min_array()` — computes the minimum value in the array.
4. `mean_array()` — computes the average of the list of numbers.

SOLUTION: The program is given in Figure 9.5. The function `main()` reads in the number of items in the list and the value of each item. It then calls the other three functions and prints the results. The function `max_array()` determines the maximum value in the array. The function header for `max_array()` is

```
double max_array(double a[], int n).
```

The function has two arguments, an array of type **double** and an integer variable representing the number of items in the list. The function `min_array()` determines the minimum value in the list and the function `mean_array()` determines the average of the values in the list. The formal parameter declarations for these functions are identical to that of `max_array()`. Passing the number of items in the list as an argument to these functions makes them more general, since we can now use these functions to determine the maximum, minimum, and mean value of arrays of different sizes. The functions are called in `main()` in the following call statements:

```
xmax = max_array(x,n);     /* compute maximum value */
xmin = min_array(x,n);     /* compute minimum value */
xmean = mean_array(x,n);   /* compute mean value    */
```

Note that in each of these function calls, only the name of the function (without the parentheses) is specified as the argument. The value returned by the function is assigned to the variable on the left-hand side of the assignment statement.

There are several important differences between passing arrays as arguments and passing ordinary variables. When an array is passed as a function argument, the compiler does *not* make a copy of the array but passes the original array to the function. This is done for reasons of efficiency. Since arrays can be quite large and can occupy considerable storage space it is not efficient to copy an entire array.

When we pass an array's name to a function, we are actually passing the

```
/****************************************************************/
/*    minmax2.c -- Maximum, Minimum and Mean Value in a Array   */
/*                                                              */
/*    This program reads in a one-dimensional array and         */
/*    determines the maximum, minimum and mean value.           */
/****************************************************************/
#include <stdio.h>

#define SIZE 100                 /* maximum number of elements */

/* function prototypes */
double max_array(double a[], int n);
double min_array(double a[], int n);
double mean_array(double a[], int n);

main()
{
    double x[SIZE];
    double xmax, xmin, xmean;
    int i, n;
    printf("Number of points: ");
    scanf("%d",&n);
    for (i = 0;  i < n;  i++)
        {
        printf("Enter value of x[%d]: ", i);
        scanf("%lf",&x[i]);
        }

    xmax = max_array(x,n);      /* compute maximum value */
    xmin = min_array(x,n);      /* compute minimum value */
    xmean = mean_array(x,n);    /* compute mean value    */

    printf("\n Number of items in list = %d", n);
    printf("\n Maximum value = %lf", xmax);
    printf("\n Minimum value = %lf", xmin);
    printf("\n Mean value = %lf", xmean);
}

/*--------------------------------------------------------------*/
/*    Function:  max_array                                      */
/*                                                              */
/*    Determines the maximum value in an array.                 */
/*                                                              */
/*    Input parameters:                                         */
/*       a[]  - array containing list of numbers                */
/*       n    - number of elements in the array                 */
/*                                                              */
/*    Returns:                                                  */
/*       value of type double representing the largest value    */
/*--------------------------------------------------------------*/
double max_array(double a[], int n)
{
    double a_max = a[0];   /* maximum value */
    int i;

    for (i = 1;  i < n;  ++i)
```

Figure 9.5   Maximum, minimum and mean value in an array.

```
                  if ( a_max <  a[i] )
                     a_max = a[i];

          return (a_max);
      }



      /*-------------------------------------------------------------*/
      /*    Function:  min_array                                     */
      /*                                                             */
      /*    Determines the minimum value in an array.                */
      /*                                                             */
      /*    Input parameters:                                        */
      /*       a[]  - array containing list of numbers               */
      /*       n    - number of elements in the array                */
      /*                                                             */
      /*    Returns:                                                 */
      /*       value of type double representing the smallest value  */
      /*-------------------------------------------------------------*/
      double min_array(double a[], int n)
      {
          double a_min = a[0];    /* minimum value */
          int i;

          for (i = 1; i < n; ++i)
             if ( a_min >  a[i] )
                 a_min = a[i];

          return (a_min);
      }



      /*-------------------------------------------------------------*/
      /*    Function:  mean_array                                    */
      /*                                                             */
      /*    Determines the average value of the elements in an array.*/
      /*                                                             */
      /*                                                             */
      /*    Input parameters:                                        */
      /*       a[]  - array containing list of numbers               */
      /*       n    - number of elements in the array                */
      /*                                                             */
      /*    Returns:                                                 */
      /*       value of type double representing the average value   */
      /*-------------------------------------------------------------*/
      double mean_array(double a[], int n)
      {
          double a_mean = 0.0 ;   /* mean value */
          int i;

          for (i = 0; i < n; ++i)
             a_mean += a[i] ;
          a_mean /= n;

          return (a_mean);
      }
```

FIGURE 9.5   (continued)

address of the array, that is, its location in memory, to the function (see Figure 9.6). The name of the array without subscripts represents the memory address of the first element of the array. For an array called **scores[]**, the expression.

```
scores           /* address of first element of scores[] */
```

is equivalent to

```
&scores[0]    /* address of first element of scores[] */
```

Thus, when we pass an array to a function, the function is given the actual location of the array in memory. This mechanism of passing an argument by its address is known as *call by reference*. An important consequence of call by reference is that, since the function has the address of the array, it can change the value of any of the elements of the array. In fact, any changes made to an array argument inside the function are made to the original array and not to a copy of the array.

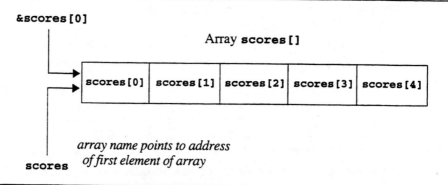

Figure 9.6   Relationship between array name and the address of the first element of the array.

Example 9.5   Polynomial Evaluation

PROBLEM STATEMENT: A real polynomial $f(x)$ of degree n is given by

$$f(x) = a_0 + a_1 x + a_2 x^2 + a_3 x^3 + \cdots + a_n x^n$$

with the coefficients a_0, a_1, ..., a_n representing real numbers. Write a function that returns the value of the polynomial $f(x)$ evaluated at x. The function prototype for the function is

```
double polynomial(double a[], double x, int n);
```

Write a main program to read in n and the coefficients a_i and the value of x at which the polynomial is to be evaluated. The function **main()** should store the coefficients in an array **a[]**, call **polynomial()** to evaluate $f(x)$, and print the value returned by **polynomial()**.

SOLUTION: The program is shown in Figure 9.7. The **#define** statement

```
#define MAXN 20
```

defines a symbolic constant **MAXN** and assigns it a value of 20. This represents the maximum value of n in the polynomial. The statement

```
double a[MAXN]
```

creates an array **a[]** of type **double** to store the coefficients of the polynomial. The **while** loop

```
while (n < 0 || n > MAXN)
    {
    printf("\n Enter value of n (between 0 and 20)");
    scanf("%d", &n);
    }
```

reads in the value of n. The **for** loop

```
for (i = 0; i <= n; ++i)
    {
    printf("\n Enter a[%d]:, i);
    scanf("%lf", &a[i]);
    }
```

reads the values of the coefficients a_i and stores these in the corresponding elements **a[i]** of array **a[]**.
The statement

```
result = polynominal(a,x,n);
```

calls the function **polynomial()**. The value returned by **polynomial()** is assigned to the variable **result** and is subsequently printed.

The function **polynomial()** computes the value of $f(x)$ for a given value of x. The function header for the function is

```
double polynomial(double a[], double x, int n)
```

The function expects three arguments. The first argument, **a[]**, is an array of type **double** representing the coefficients of the polynomial, the second argument, **x**, is a value of type **double** representing the value of x at which the polynomial is to be evaluated, and the third argument, **n**, is a value of type **int** representing the number of terms in the polynomial. The variable **fx** in function **polynomial()** contains the value of the function $f(x)$ evaluated at x. This variable is initially assigned the

```
/****************************************************************/
/*    poly.c -- Evaluate a Real Polynomial                      */
/*                                                              */
/*    Computes the value of a real polynomial evaluated at x.   */
/****************************************************************/
#include <stdio.h>
#define MAXN 20
double polynomial(double a[],double x,int n);

main()
{
    double a[MAXN],x,result;
    int i,n=-1;

    while (n < 0 || n > MAXN)
        {
        printf("\n Enter value of n: ");
        scanf("%d", &n);
        }
    for (i=0; i <= n; ++i)
        {
        printf("\n Enter a[%d]: ",i);
        scanf("%lf", &a[i]);
        }
    printf("\n Enter x: ");
    scanf("%lf", &x);

    result = polynomial(a,x,n);
    printf("\n The value of f(x) evaluated at %lf is %lf",x,result);
}

/*--------------------------------------------------------------*/
/*    Function:  polynomial                                     */
/*                                                              */
/*    Evaluates a polynomial for a given value of x.            */
/*                                                              */
/*    Input parameters:                                         */
/*        a[] - array containing coefficients of the polynomial */
/*        x   - value at which polynomial is to be evaluated    */
/*        n   - degree of the polynomial                        */
/*                                                              */
/*    Returns:                                                  */
/*        value of type double representing f(x) evaluated at x.*/
/*--------------------------------------------------------------*/
double polynomial(double a[],double x,int n)
    {
    int i;
    double fx,powx;

    fx = a[0];
    powx = 1.0;
    for (i = 1; i <=n; ++i)
        {
        powx *= x;
        fx += a[i] * powx;
        }
    return(fx);
}
```

Figure 9.7   A program to evaluate a real polynomial *f(x)*.

value `a[0]`. The variable `powx` contains the value of x raised to the ith power, where i varies from 0 to n. The variable `powx` is initialized to 1 near the beginning of the function and with each iteration of the `for` loop it is multiplied by `x`. Within the `for` loop the statement

```
fx =+= a[i] * powx;
```

adds the contribution of the current term to `fx`. The value of `fx` is returned to the calling function in the statement

```
return (fx);
```

9.7 PROGRAMMING PROJECT: TEMPERATURE DISTRIBUTION ALONG A BAR

Consider a solid insulated metal bar that is maintained at a constant (but different) temperature at each end. Heat will flow from the end of the bar that has the higher temperature to the end that has the lower temperature. We are interested in determining the temperature distribution along the bar.

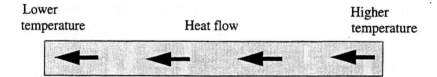

Lower temperature   Heat flow   Higher temperature

Problem Statement

Write a program to compute the temperature distribution along a solid insulated metal bar that is maintained at constant temperature at each end.

Problem Analysis

To compute the temperature distribution, we can divide the bar into a number of segments. Then we need to compute the temperature at the boundary of each segment which we will call a *node*. The figure below shows a bar that is divided into 10 segments.

Nodes 0   1   2   3   4   5   6   7   8   9   10

To determine the temperatures at the intermediate nodes when the bar reaches a state of equilibrium, we will need to use an iterative procedure. We can determine the temperature at the intermediate nodes by taking the average of the temperature at that node and the two adjacent nodes. Since we know only the temperature of the two end nodes, we will need to make an initial guess of the temperature at the intermediate nodes. For our initial guess we will assume that the temperature at the intermediate nodes is equal to the average of the temperatures at the two end nodes, that is,

$$T_i^1 = \left(\frac{T_0 + T_{10}}{2}\right) \qquad\qquad (9.1)$$

The superscript indicates the iteration number.

The second estimate of the temperature at each node is given by

$$T_i^2 = \left(\frac{T_{i-1}^1 + T_i^1 + T_{i+1}^1}{3}\right) \qquad\qquad (9.2)$$

where T_i^2 is the second estimate of the temperature at node i, and T_{i-1}^1, T_i^1, and T_{i+1}^1 are the first estimates of the temperature at nodes $i - 1$, i and $i + 1$, respectively. We repeat this process of computing new estimates of the temperature at each node until the difference between the new temperature and the old temperature at each node is less than some small value, ε, that is

$$\left| T_i^{new} - T_i^{old} \right| < \varepsilon \qquad\qquad (9.3)$$

For any given iteration, we can write Equation (9.2) as

$$T_i^{new} = \left(\frac{T_{i-1}^{old} + T_i^{old} + T_{i+1}^{old}}{3}\right) \qquad\qquad (9.4)$$

Notice that in Equation (9.4) the new temperature at a node is computed from the old temperatures at all three nodes. We can make the procedure more efficient if we modify Equation (9.4) as follows:

$$T_i^{new} = \left(\frac{T_{i-1}^{new} + T_i^{old} + T_{i+1}^{old}}{3}\right) \qquad\qquad (9.5)$$

Since we have already computed the new temperature at the previous node, we use this value in computing the new temperature for the current node.

The data requirements for the problem are as follows:

Program Variables
number of nodes (**int n**)
array to store the temperatures at the nodes (**double t[]**)
temperature at left end (stored in **t[0]**)
temperature at right end (stored in **t[n-1]**)
desired accuracy (**double tolerance**)
flag to indicate if desired accuracy has been achieved (**int done**)
temporary storage to save the old temperature at a node (**double t_old**)
iteration counter (int **count**)

Algorithm

1. Read in the number of nodes.
2. Read in temperatures at the two ends.
3. Read in the value of the desired tolerance.
4. Initialize the temperature at the intermediate nodes using Equation 9.1.
5. For each node compute temperatures of the intermediate nodes using Equation 9.5.
6. Repeat Step 5 until the desired accuracy has been achieved.
7. Print the temperatures at each node.

Program

The program is show in Figure 9.8. The symbolic constant **MAXNODES** defines the maximum number of nodes. Its value is set equal to 101, but it can easily be changed. The program also defines two other symbolic constants, **TRUE** and **FALSE**. The value of **TRUE** is set to 1, and the value of **FALSE** is set to 0. These values correspond to true and false in C. After the input data has been read, the temperatures at the intermediate nodes are set equal to the average of the temperatures at the ends of the bar in the **for** loop

```
for (i=1; i < n-1; ++i)
    t[i] = (t[0] + t[n-1])/2.;
```

The iterations are performed in a **while** loop beginning with

```
while (done == FALSE)
```

The variable **done** is initialized to **FALSE**, so the **while** loop is executed at least

```
/*******************************************************/
/*  temp.c -- Temperature Distribution Along a Bar     */
/*                                                     */
/*  This program computes the temperature distribution */
/*  along a bar that is maintained at a constant       */
/*  temperature at each end.                           */
/*******************************************************/
#include <stdio.h>
#include <math.h>

#define MAXNODES 101
#define TRUE 1
#define FALSE 0

main()
{
  double t[MAXNODES];   /* temperature at each node */
  double tol;           /* desired tolerance        */
  double t_old;         /* old temperature          */
  int n;                /* number of nodes          */
  int i;                /* loop counters            */
  int done=FALSE;       /* flag                     */
  int count=0;          /* number of iterations     */

  printf("\n Temperature Distribution Along a Bar");
  printf("\n Number of nodes? ");
  scanf("%d",&n);
  printf(" Temperature at left end? ");
  scanf("%lf",&t[0]);
  printf(" Temperature at right end? ");
  scanf("%lf",&t[n-1]);
  printf(" Tolerance? ");
  scanf("%lf",&tol);

  /* initialization */
  for (i=1; i < n-1; ++i)
      t[i] = (t[0] + t[n-1])/2.;

  while (done == FALSE)
    {

    done = TRUE;
    ++count;

    for (i=1; i < n-1; ++i)
        {
        /* save previous value of t[i] */
        t_old = t[i];

        /* compute new value of t[i] */
        t[i] = (t[i-1] + t[i] + t[i+1])/3.;
```

Figure 9.8   Temperature distribution along a bar.

```
          /* set flag to false if difference between old
             and new values is greater than desired tolerance  */
          if ( fabs(t[i] - t_old) > tol)
               done = FALSE;
       }
   }

   /* print results */
   printf("\n \n -----------------------------");
   printf("\n    Node        Temperature ");
   printf("\n  -----------------------------");
   for (i = 0; i < n; ++i)
      printf("\n  %3d          %10.2f",i,t[i]);

   printf("\n  -----------------------------");
   printf("\n Number of iterations = %d",count);
   }
```

FIGURE 9.8   (continued)

---

once. Within the **while** loop the statement

> **done = TRUE;**

resets the flag **done** to **TRUE**. The new temperatures are computed in the **for** loop beginning with the statement

> **for (i=1; i < n-1; ++i)**

The loop counter **i** goes from 1 to $n - 2$ so the first and last elements of the array **t[]** are not modified. The old value of T_i is saved in the variable **t_old** prior to the computation of the new value. The **if** statement

> **if (fabs(t[i] - t_old) > tol)**
>   **done = FLASE;**

sets the flag **done** to **FALSE** if the difference between the new and the old value of T_i is greater than the desired tolerance. Since this statement is within the **for** loop the flag **done** will be set to **FALSE** if the temperatures at any of the intermediate points does not meet this condition.

Testing

We can easily test the program by noticing that the distribution of temperature should be linear. The output from the program for the case when the number of nodes is equal to 11 and the temperatures at the two ends are 10° and 120° is shown in Figure 9.9.

```
TEMPERATURE DISTRIBUTION ALONG A BAR

Number of nodes? 11
Temperature at left end? 10.
Temperature at right end? 110.
Tolerance? 0.0001


------------------------------------------
  Node          Temperature
------------------------------------------
    0              10.00
    1              20.00
    2              30.00
    3              40.00
    4              50.00
    5              60.00
    6              70.00
    7              80.00
    8              90.00
    9             100.00
   10             110.00
------------------------------------------
Number of iterations = 164
```

Figure 9.9   Output from program *temp.c*.

9.8   PROGRAMMING PROJECT: VECTOR OPERATIONS

Many science and engineering applications make use of vectors. An *n*-dimensional vector is represented as

$$\mathbf{a} = (a_1, a_2, a_3, ..., a_n) \tag{9.6}$$

The sequence of numbers a_1, a_2, ..., a_n represent the components of the vector. A vector is said to be of dimension *n* if it consists of *n* components.

The magnitude (or length or norm) of **a** is given by

$$|\mathbf{a}| = \sqrt{a_1^2 + a_2^2 + ... + a_n^2} \tag{9.7}$$

A unit vector is a vector in the same direction as **a** and is defined as

$$\frac{\mathbf{a}}{|\mathbf{a}|} = \frac{a_1}{|\mathbf{a}|}, \frac{a_2}{|\mathbf{a}|}, ..., \frac{a_n}{|\mathbf{a}|} \tag{9.8}$$

For two n-dimensional vectors, **a** and **b**, the sum and difference of **a** and **b** are defined by

$$\mathbf{a} + \mathbf{b} = (a_1 + b_1, a_2 + b_2, ..., a_n + b_n)$$

                          (9.9)

$$\mathbf{a} - \mathbf{b} = (a_1 - b_1, a_2 - b_2, ..., a_n - b_n)$$

                          (9.10)

Two vectors **a** and **b** with the same number of components can be multiplied together to form the dot product of **a** and **b** which is defined by

$$\mathbf{a} \cdot \mathbf{b} = \sum_{i=1}^{n} (a_1 b_1 + a_2 b_2 + ... + a_n b_n)$$

                          (9.11)

The dot product is a scalar quantity.

The angle θ between two vectors **a** and **b** can be found from the following formula

$$\cos(\theta) = \frac{\mathbf{a} \cdot \mathbf{b}}{|\mathbf{a}||\mathbf{b}|}$$

                          (9.12)

where $\mathbf{a} \cdot \mathbf{b}$ is the dot product of the two vectors and |a| and |b| are the magnitudes of **a** and **b**.

  Vectors can easily be represented by means of one-dimensional arrays. For example, a vector **a** having n-components can be represented by a one-dimensional array **a[]** of size **n**. The first element of the array **a[0]** represents the component a_1, the second element of the array **a[1]** represents the second component a_2, and so on.

  Vectors are commonly used in physics and mechanics to represent forces. A force F in a three-dimensional space can be broken up into three components, F_x, F_y, and F_z parallel to the x, y, and z directions. The force can then be written as a vector as

$$F = (F_x, F_y, F_z)$$

We can now use vectors to perform various operations on forces. For example, the magnitude of the force F can be determined from

$$|F| = \sqrt{F_x^2 + F_y^2 + F_z^2}$$

                          (9.13)

Two forces F_1 and F_2 can be represented as

$$F_1 = (F_{1x}, F_{1y}, F_{1z})$$

$$F_2 = (F_{2x}, F_{2y}, F_{2z})$$

The resultant, F_R of these forces can be determined by adding the components of these forces. Thus

$$F_R = (F_{1x} + F_{2x}, F_{1y} + F_{2y}, F_{1z} + F_{2z}) \qquad \text{(9.14)}$$

Note that the resultant is also a vector and has the same number of elements as the two vectors. The angle θ between the forces F_1 and F_2 can be obtained from

$$\cos \theta = \frac{F_1 \cdot F_2}{|F_1||F_2|} \qquad \text{(9.15)}$$

Problem Statement

Write a program that reads in two vectors F_1 and F_2 representing two forces and computes the magnitude of each force, the resultant of the two forces, and the angle between the two forces. Your program should also compute the dot product of F_1 and F_2.

Problem Analysis

A force F can be represented by a one-dimensional array **f[]** having three elements, with the first element **f[0]** representing the x component F_x, the second element **f[1]** representing the y component, F_y, and the third element **f[2]** representing the z component, F_z, of the force. Thus, we can use three one-dimensional arrays to represent the forces F_1, F_2, and F_R.

The major tasks to be performed by the program are the following:

1.   Read in two vectors F_1 and F_2.
2.   Compute the magnitude of each vector, $|F_1|$, $|F_2|$.
3.   Compute the resultant of F_1 and F_2.
4.   Compute the angle between F_1 and F_2.
5.   Compute the dot product of F_1 and F_2.
6.   Print the results.

The data requirements for the problem are as follows:

Program Variables
vectors F_1, F_2 (**double f1[3],f2[3]**)
vector F_R representing the sum of F_1 and F_2 (**double fr[3]**)
dot product of F_1 and F_2 (**double dot**)
angle between F_1 and F_2 (**double angle**)

Algorithm

The program is divided into the following functions:

1. **main()** — calls functions to read in the vectors F_1 and F_2 and compute the resultant, the angle between F_1 and F_2, and the dot product. Prints the two vectors and the results.
2. **vector_input()** — reads in the x, y, and z components of the force and saves these in an array.
3. **vector_sum()** - computes the resultant of F_1 and F_2 and returns the result in the array **fr[]**.
4. **dot_product** - computes the dot product of F_1 and F_2 and returns the result as a value of type **double**.
5. **vector_angle()** - computes the angle between F_1 and F_2 and returns the result as a value of type **double**.

Program

The program is show in Figure 9.10. The program includes the *math.h* header file since it uses the C library **acos()** and **sqr()** functions. It also defines the symbolic constant **PI**. The functions in the program are fairly small and contain only a few lines of code each. The program could have been written as one function, but it is more readable when written as several smaller functions.

In function **main()** three one-dimensional arrays **f1[]**, **f2[]**, and **fr[]** are created by the statements

```
double f1[3], f2[3];    /* vectors F1 and F2    */
double fr[3];           /* sum of F1 and F2     */
```

Each array has three elements to store the three components of the forces. The function makes two calls to **vector_input()** to read in the values of F_1 and F_2. For example, to read in the first force the function is called as

```
vector_input(f1);
```

The function **vector_input()** reads in the three components of the force and stores these values in the three elements of the array. The function **main()** then calls **vector_sum()** which computes the resultant of the two forces.

The function header for **vector_sum()** is

```
void vector_sum(double f1[],double f2[],double fr[])
```

The arguments to the function are the three arrays **f1[]**, **f2[]**, and **fr[]**. The resultant is returned in the array **fr[]**.

Function **main()** also calls **dot_product()** to compute the dot product of F_1 and F_2 and **vector_angle()** to compute the angle between F_1 and F_2 and prints the results of the various vector operations.

```
/***************************************************************/
/*   vectors.c  -- Vector Operations                          */
/*                                         .                  */
/*   Computes the sum of two vectors, the angle between them  */
/*   and the dot product.                                     */
/***************************************************************/
#include <stdio.h>
#include <math.h>

#define PI 3.141593

/* function prototypes */
void vector_input(double f[]);
void vector_sum(double f1[],double f2[],double fr[]);
double dot_product(double f1[],double f2[]);
double vector_angle(double f1[],double f2[]);

main()
{
    double f1[3], f2[3];     /* vectors F1 and F2         */
    double fr[3];            /* sum of F1 and F2          */
    double dot;              /* dot product of F1 and F2  */
    double angle;            /* angle between F1 and F2   */

    /* get input */
    printf("\n VECTOR OPERATIONS");
    printf("\n Enter force F1 ");
    vector_input(f1);
    printf("\n Enter force F2");
    vector_input(f2);

    /* compute resultant of F1 and F1 */
    vector_sum(f1,f2,fr);

    /* compute dot product */
    dot = dot_product(f1,f2);

    /* compute angle between F1 and F2 */
    angle =  vector_angle(f1,f2);

    /* display results */
    printf("\n\n First vector: (%f,%f,%f)",f1[0],f1[1],f1[2]);
    printf("\n Second vector: (%f,%f,%f)",f2[0],f2[1],f2[2]);
    printf("\n Sum of vectors: (%f,%f,%f)",fr[0],fr[1],fr[2]);
    printf("\n Dot product: %f",dot);
    printf("\n Angle between vectors: %f degrees",angle);
}

/*-------------------------------------------------------------*/
/*    Function: vector_input                                   */
/*                                                             */
/*    Purpose:                                                 */
/*        Reads in the x, y and z components of a force        */
/*                                                             */
```

Figure 9.10   Vector operations.

```
/*    Input Parameters:                                           */
/*         none                                                   */
/*    Output Parameters:                                          */
/*        f[]  - array containing three elements                 */
/*                the x, y and z components are returned in f[]   */
/*--------------------------------------------------------------*/
void vector_input(double f[])
{
   printf("\n Enter x component of vector: ");
   scanf("%lf", &f[0]);
   printf(" Enter y component of vector: ");
   scanf("%lf", &f[1]);
   printf(" Enter z component of vector: ");
   scanf("%lf", &f[2]);
}


/*--------------------------------------------------------------*/
/*    Function: dot_product                                      */
/*                                                               */
/*    Purpose:                                                   */
/*        Computes the dot product of two vectors               */
/*                                                               */
/*    Input Parameters:                                          */
/*        f1[] - array containing first vector, F1              */
/*        f2[] - array containing second vector, F2             */
/*                                                               */
/*    Output Parameters:                                         */
/*        f3[] - array containing the dot product of F1 and F2  */
/*--------------------------------------------------------------*/
double dot_product(double f1[],double f2[])
{
   double result = 0.;
   int i;

   for (i = 0; i < 3; ++i)
       result += f1[i] * f2[i];

   return(result);
}


/*--------------------------------------------------------------*/
/*    Function: vector_angle                                     */
/*                                                               */
/*    Purpose:                                                   */
/*        Computes the angle between two vectors                */
/*                                                               */
/*    Input Parameters:                                          */
/*        f1[] - array containing first vector, F1              */
/*        f2[] - array containing second vector, F2             */
/*                                                               */
/*    Returns:                                                   */
/*        angle - angle between F1 and F2 (in degrees)          */
/*--------------------------------------------------------------*/
double vector_angle(double f1[],double f2[])
{
```

FIGURE 9.10 (*continued*)

```
double dot;       /* dot product of F1 and F2          */
double angle ;    /* angle between F1 and F2           */
double m1,m2;     /* magnitude (length) of F1 and F2 */

/* compute |F1| and |F2| */
m1 = sqrt(f1[0]*f1[0] + f1[1]*f1[1] + f1[2]*f1[2]);
m2 = sqrt(f2[0]*f2[0] + f2[1]*f2[1] + f2[2]*f2[2]);

/* compute dot product of F1 and F2 */
dot = dot_product(f1,f2);

angle = acos(dot/(m1 * m2));
angle *= 180. / PI;              /* convert to degrees */

return(angle);
}

/*--------------------------------------------------------------------*/
/*    Function: vector_sum                                            */
/*                                                                    */
/*    Purpose:                                                        */
/*       Computes the sum of two vectors                              */
/*                                                                    */
/*    Input Parameters:                                               */
/*       f1[] - array containing first vector, F1                     */
/*       f2[] - array containing second vector, F2                    */
/*                                                                    */
/*    Output Parameters:                                              */
/*       fr[] - array containing the sum of F1 and F2                 */
/*--------------------------------------------------------------------*/
void vector_sum(double f1[],double f2[],double fr[])
{
   int i;

   for (i = 0; i < 3; ++i)
      fr[i] = f1[i] + f2[i];

}
```

FIGURE 9.10   *(continued)*

Testing

Consider two forces F_1 and F_2 where

$$F_1 = (3.5, 2.0, 6.6)$$

and

$$F_2 = (4.0, -3.0, 8.0)$$

The resultant of the two forces is

$$F_R = (3.5 + 4.0, 2.0 - 3.0, 6.6 + 8.0) = (7.5, -1.0, 14.6)$$

The dot product of F_1 and F_2 is

$$F_1 \cdot F_2 = (3.5)(4.0) + (2.0)(-3.0) + (6.6)(8.0) = 60.8$$

The magnitude of F_1 is

$$|F_1| = \sqrt{3.5^2 + 2.0^2 + 6.6^2} = 7.734$$

and the magnitude of F_2 is

$$|F_2| = \sqrt{4.0^2 + (-3.0)^2 + 8.0^2} = 9.434$$

Thus the angle between F_1 and F_2 is

$$\theta = \mathrm{acos}\left(\frac{60.8}{(7.734)(9.434)}\right) = \mathrm{acos}(0.8333) = 33.56°$$

The output from the program is shown in Figure 9.11. It can be seen that the results agree with those obtained by hand computation.

```
VECTOR OPERATIONS
Enter force F1
Enter x component of vector: 3.5
Enter y compnent of vector: 2.0
Enter z component of vector: 6.6

Enter force F2
Enter x component of vector: 4.0
Enter y compnent of vector: -3.0
Enter z component of vector: 8.0


First vector: (3.500000,2.000000,6.600000)
Second vector: (4.000000,-3.000000,8.000000)
Sum of vectors: (7.500000,-1.000000,14.600000)
Dot product: 60.800000
Angle between vectors: 33.556725 degrees
```

Figure 9.11   Output from program *vectors.c*.

9.9   PROGRAMMING PROJECT: BEAM ANALYSIS

The first step in the design of beams is the computation of the shear force and bending moment at various points along the beam. Deflection calculations are also required to ensure against the possibility of excessive deflections. Two of the more common types of loads that are applied to a beam are uniformly distributed loads and concentrated loads. Figure 9.12 shows the variation of the shear force $V(x)$ and bending moment $M(x)$ for a beam that is simply supported at both ends and subjected to a uniformly distributed load, w. The reactions at the left and right supports are given by

$$R_L = \frac{wL}{2} \tag{9.16}$$

$$R_R = \frac{wL}{2} \tag{9.17}$$

where R_L is the reaction at the left support, and R_R is the reaction at the right support, and L is the distance between the supports. The shear force, bending moment, and deflection at a distance x from the left support are given by

$$V(x) = w\left(\frac{L}{2} - x\right) \tag{9.18}$$

$$M(x) = \frac{wx}{2}(L - x) \tag{9.19}$$

$$y(x) = \frac{wx}{24EI}(L^3 - 2Lx^2 + x^3) \tag{9.20}$$

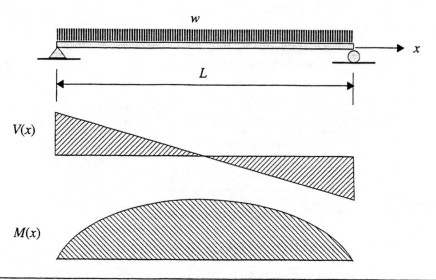

Figure 9.12   Shear, moment, and deflection diagrams for a simply
supported beam subjected to a uniformly distributed load.

where $V(x)$ is the shear force, $M(x)$ the bending moment, $y(x)$ the deflection at a distance x from the left support, I is the moment of inertia, and E is the modulus of elasticity.

The shear force and bending moment, for a simply supported beam subjected to a concentrated load P are shown in Figure 9.13. The support reactions are given by

$$R_L = \frac{Pb}{L} \qquad (9.21)$$

$$R_R = \frac{Pa}{L} \qquad (9.22)$$

The shear force, bending moment, and deflection at any point along the beam can be obtained as follows:

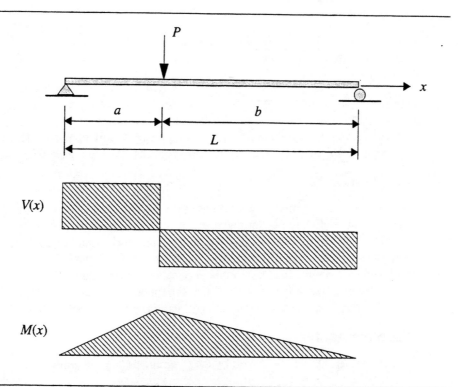

Figure 9.13 Shear, moment and deflection diagrams for a simply supported beam subjected to a concentrated load.

For $0 < x < a$

$$V(x) = \frac{Pb}{L} \qquad (9.23)$$

$$M(x) = \frac{Pbx}{L} \qquad (9.24)$$

$$y(x) = \frac{Pbx}{6EIL}(L^2 - b^2 - x^2) \qquad (9.25)$$

For $a < x < L$

$$V(x) = -\frac{Pa}{L} \qquad (9.26)$$

$$M(x) = P\left(\frac{bx}{L} - x + a\right) \qquad (9.27)$$

$$y(x) = \frac{Pa(L-x)}{6EL}[2Lb - b^2 - (L-x)^2] \qquad (9.28)$$

Since most beams are subjected to more than one load, we are interested in computing the response of the beam when several uniformly distributed loads and concentrated loads are applied. We can obtain the response of the beam to more than one load by simply adding the responses of each individual load. This is called the principle of superposition and is valid as long as we have linear elastic behavior.

Problem Statement

Write a program for computing support reactions, shear force, bending moment, and deflection at various points along a simply supported beam subjected to several uniformly distributed and concentrated loads. Input to the program will consist of the span length, moment of inertia, modulus of elasticity, the number of uniformly distributed loads, the number of concentrated loads, and load parameters for each load. The program should print the support reactions and a table of shear force, bending moment, and deflection at various points along the beam.

Problem Analysis

The major tasks to be performed by the program are the following:

1. Read in the beam parameters such as the span length, moment of inertia, and modulus of elasticity.

2. Initialize all arrays containing the total response to zero.
3. Read in the number of uniformly distributed loads and the intensity of each load
4. Read in the number of concentrated loads and the load parameters for each concentrated load
5. For each uniformly distributed load, compute support reactions, shear force, bending moment, and deflection at the specified number of points along the beam and add these values to the corresponding totals.
6. For each concentrated load, compute support reactions, shear force, bending moment, and deflection at the specified number of points along the beam and add these values to the totals.
7. Print reactions and a table of shear, moment, and deflection values.

The data requirements for the problem are as follows:

Program Variables
span of beam, L (**double L**)
moment of inertia of beam cross section (**double I**)
modulus of elasticity of beam material, E (**double E**)
reaction at left support, R_L (**double rl**)
reaction at right support, R_R (**double rr**)
number of points at which results are required (**int num_points**)
number of concentrated loads (**int num_conc**)
number of uniformly distributed loads (**int num_uniform**)
intensity of uniformly distributed load (**double w**)
magnitude of concentrated load (**double p**)
distance of concentrated load from left support (**double a**)
left support reaction for combined loads (**double rl_tot**)
right support reaction for combined load (**double rr_tot**)

In addition to these variables we will need the following arrays

x[], v[], m[], y[]

to store the distance x from the left support, the shear force, bending moment, and deflection at each point along the beam for a given load, and

v_tot[], m_tot[], y_tot[]

to store the shear force, bending moment, and deflection due to the combined loads.

Program Structure

The program is divided into the following functions:

1. **main()** — obtains all input and calls the appropriate computational functions and the function to print results.

2. **conc_load** — computes the reactions, shear force, bending moment, and deflection for a concentrated load. This function is called once for each concentrated load applied to the beam.
3. **uniform_load()** — computes reactions, shear force, bending moment, and deflection for a uniformly distributed load. This function is called once for each uniformly distributed load applied to the beam.
4. **combine** — this function adds the results obtained for each load to the total to obtain results for the combined load.
5. **print_results()** — this function prints the reactions and a table of the distance x from the left support for each point and the shear force, bending moment, and deflection for this value of x.

The structure chart of the program is as follows:

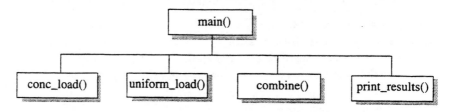

Algorithm for main()

1. Read beam properties **l, i, e**.
2. Read number of points for which results are required.
3. Compute the value of x for each point.
4. Initialize arrays.
5. Read number of concentrated loads.
6. For each concentrated load

    6.1 Read load parameters.
    6.2 Compute support reactions.
    6.3 Call **conc_load()** to compute shear, moment, and deflections.
    6.4 Call **combine()** to update totals.
7. Read number of uniform loads.
8. For each uniform load

    8.1 Read magnitude of load.
    8.2 Compute support reactions.
    8.3 Call **uniform_load()** to compute shear, moment, and deflections.
    8.4 Call **combine()** to update totals .

9. Call `display_results()` to display results.

Algorithm for `uniform_load()`

1. For `k` = 0 to `num_points`

    1.1 Compute `v[k]` from Equation (9.18).

    1.2 Compute `m[k]` from Equation (9.19).

    1.3 Compute `y[k]` from Equation (9.20).

Algorithm for `conc_load()`

1. For `k` =0 to `num_points`

2. If `x[k]` is less than `a`

    2.1 Compute `v[k]` from Equation (9.23).

    2.2 Compute `m[k]` from Equation (9.24).

    2.3 Compute `y[k]` from Equation (9.25).

3. Else

    3.1 Compute `v[k]` from Equation (9.26).

    3.2 Compute `m[k]` from Equation (9.27).

    3.3 Compute `y[k]` from Equation (9.28).

Program

The program is show in Figure 9.14.

Testing

To test the program we will compute the results for the beam shown in Figure 9.15. The beam has three loads: a uniformly distributed load of 0.25 kips/in. and two equal concentrated live loads of magnitude 20 kips at one-third points. Since the loading is symmetric we should expect a symmetric response.

The computed values of the support reactions, shear force, bending moment, and deflection at various points along the beam are shown in Tables 9.1 through 9.4. The output from the program for the test problem is shown in Figure 9.15. It is seen that the results obtained from the program agree with those obtained by hand calculation.

Table 9.1: Support reactions (kips)

Location	P_1	P_2	w	Total
Left support	13.3	6.7	36.0	56.0
Right support	6.7	13.3	36.0	56.0

```
/*-------------------------------------------------------------*/
/* beam.c  -- Shear, Moment and Deflection of a Simply         */
/*              Supported Beam                                 */
/*                                                             */
/* Compute and prints the shear, moment and deflection         */
/* and support reactions at several points for a simply        */
/* supported beam subjected to a combination of concentrated,  */
/* and uniformly distributed loads.                            */
/*-------------------------------------------------------------*/
#include <stdio.h>
#define MAXPTS 101
/* function prototypes */
void uniform_load(double w,double l,double e, double i,
      int num_points,double x[],double v[],double m[],double y[]);
void conc_load(double p,double a,double l,double e, double i,
      int num_points,double x[],double v[],double m[],double y[]);
void combine(int num_points,double v[],double m[],double y[],
      double v_tot[],double m_tot[],double y_tot[]);
void display_results(double l,double e,double i,int num_points,
      double rl_tot,double rr_tot,double x[],double v_tot[],
      double m_tot[],double y_tot[]);
main()
{
  double l;                    /*beam span                       */
  double i;                    /* moment of inertia of section   */
  double e;                    /* modulus of elasticity of material */
  int num_points;              /* number of points               */
  int num_conc;                /* number of concentrated loads    */
  int num_uniform;             /* number of uniformly dist. loads */
  double x[MAXPTS],v[MAXPTS];  /* distance, shear                */
  double m[MAXPTS],y[MAXPTS];  /* moment and deflection          */
  double v_tot[MAXPTS],m_tot[MAXPTS]; /*  shear and moment for   */
                                      /*  combined loads         */
  double y_tot[MAXPTS];        /* deflection for combined loads  */
  double rl_tot, rr_tot;       /* reactions for combined loads   */
  int k;                       /* loop counter */
  double w,p,a;                /* load parameters */

  printf("\n SHEAR, MOMENT AND DEFLECTION ANALYSIS");
  printf("\n FOR A SIMPLY SUPPORTED BEAM");

  /* Input beam properties */
  printf("\nEnter beam span (in.): ");
  scanf("%lf",&l);
  printf("Enter moment of inertia of section (in^4): ");
  scanf("%lf",&i);
  printf("Enter modulus of elasticity of material(ksi): ");
  scanf("%lf",&e);
  printf("Enter number of points - (maximum is 101): ");
  scanf("%d",&num_points);
  /* initialization */
  for (k= 0; k < num_points; ++k)
    {
    x[k] = k*l/(num_points-1.0);
```

Figure 9.14   Shear, moment, and deflection analysis of a simply
supported beam.

```
       v_tot[k] = 0.0;
         }
  y_tot[k] = 0.0;
  m_tot[k] = 0.0;

  rl_tot = 0.0;
  rr_tot = 0.0;

/* input loads */
/* concentrated loads */
printf("\n Number of concentrated loads: ");
scanf("%d", &num_conc);

if (num_conc > 0)
    {
    printf("\n  CONCENTRATED LOADS");
    for (k = 1; k <= num_conc; ++k)
        {
        /* input magnitude and location of conc. load */
        printf("\nConcentrated load %d ",k);
        printf("\nEnter magnitude of concentrated load (kips): ");
        scanf("%lf",&p);
        printf("Enter distance of load from left support (in.): ");
        scanf("%lf",&a);

        /* compute reactions */
        rl_tot += p * (l-a) / l;
        rr_tot += p * a / l;
        /* compute shear, moment and deflection */
        conc_load(p,a,l,e,i,num_points,x,v,m,y);

        /* combine results */
        combine(num_points,v,m,y,v_tot,m_tot,y_tot);
        }
    }

/* uniformly distributed loads */
printf("Number of uniformly distributed loads: ");
scanf("%d", &num_uniform);
if (num_uniform  > 0)
    {
    printf("\n  UNIFORM LOADS");
    for (k=1; k <= num_uniform; ++k)
        {
        /* input magnitude of uniform load */
        printf("\nUniform Load %d",k);
        printf("\nEnter magnitude of uniform load (kips/in): ");
        scanf("%lf",&w);

        /* compute reactions */
        rl_tot += w * l / 2.0;
        rr_tot += w * l / 2.0;

        /* compute shear, moment and deflection */
        uniform_load(w,l,e,i,num_points,x,v,m,y);
        /* combine results */
```

FIGURE 9.14   (*continued*)

```
            combine(num_points,v,m,y,v_tot,m_tot,y_tot);
         }
      }
   /*display results */
   display_results(l,e,i,num_points,rl_tot,rr_tot,x,
               v_tot,m_tot,y_tot);
}

/*-------------------------------------------------------------------*/
/* This function displays results of the analysis on the screen     */
/*                                                                   */
/*   Input Parameters                                                */
/*      None                                                         */
/*                                                                   */
/*   Output Parameters                                               */
/*      None                                                         */
/*-------------------------------------------------------------------*/
void display_results(double l,double e,double i,int num_points,
      double rl_tot,double rr_tot,double x[],double v_tot[],double
      m_tot[],double y_tot[])
{
 int k;          /* loop counter */

 /* echo print input data */
 printf("\n SHEAR, MOMENT AND DEFLECTION ANALYSIS FOR A SIMPLY");
 printf("\n SUPPORTED BEAM");
 printf("\n Beam Span .....................%8.2f inches",l);
 printf("\n Moment of Inertia .............%10.4f in^4",i);
 printf("\n Modulus of Elasticity ........%10.4f ksi\n",e);

 /* print reactions */
 printf("\n Reaction at left support:  %10.2f kips",rl_tot);
 printf("\n Reaction at right support: %10.2f kips\n", rr_tot);

/* print table of shear, moment and deflections */
 printf("\n -----------------------------------------------------------");
 printf("\n     Distance        Shear         Moment      Deflection");
 printf("\n     (inches)        (kips)        (kip-in)    (inches)");
 printf("\n -----------------------------------------------------------");
 for (k = 0; k < num_points; ++k)
     printf("\n    %8.2f    %12.2f   %12.2f    %12.6f",
        x[k],v_tot[k],m_tot[k],y_tot[k]);
 printf("\n -----------------------------------------------------------");
}


/*-------------------------------------------------------------------*/
/*   This function uses the principle of superposition to compute    */
/*   support reactions, shear, moment and deflections for a combin-  */
/*   ation of loads.                                                 */
/*                                                                   */
/*   Input Parameters                                                */
/*      num_points - number of points                                */
/*      v[]  - array containing shear values                         */
/*      m[]  - array containing moment values                        */
/*      y[]  - array containing deflection values                    */
/*                                                                   */
/*   Output Parameters                                               */
```

FIGURE 9.14 (*continued*)

```
/*     v_tot[] - shear values for combined loads                */
/*     m_tot[] - moment values for combined loads               */
/*     y_tot[] - deflection values for combined loads           */
/*-------------------------------------------------------------*/
void combine(int num_points,double v[],double m[],double y[],
        double v_tot[],double m_tot[],double y_tot[])
{
    int k;

    for (k=0; k < num_points; ++k)
        {
        v_tot[k] += v[k];
        m_tot[k] += m[k];
        y_tot[k] += y[k];
        }
}


/*-------------------------------------------------------------*/
/*  This function computes the shear, moment and deflection    */
/* at intervals along a simply supported beam for a uniformly  */
/* distributed load of magnitude w.                            */
/*                                                             */
/* Note: Load is positive when acting down.                    */
/*                                                             */
/*   Input Parameters                                          */
/*     w           - magnitude of uniformly distributed load   */
/*     l           - beam span                                 */
/*     e           - modulus of elasticity                     */
/*     i           - moment of inertia                         */
/*     num_points - number of points                          */
/*     x[]         - array containing location of each section */
/*                                                             */
/*   Output Parameters                                         */
/*     v[]  - array containing shear and moment values         */
/*     m[]  - array containing moment values                   */
/*     y[]  - array containing deflection values               */
/*-------------------------------------------------------------*/
void uniform_load(double w,double l,double e, double i,
     int num_points,double x[],double v[],double m[],double y[])
{
  int k;                        /* loop counter     */
  double x2,x3;                 /* x squared, x cubed */

  for (k=0; k < num_points; ++k)
     {
     x2 = x[k] * x[k];
     x3 = x2*x[k];
     v[k] = w*(l/2.0 -  x[k]);
     m[k] = 0.5*w*x[k]*(l - x[k]);
     y[k] = -w*x[k]*(l*l*l-2.0*l*x2+x3)/(24.0*e*i);
     }
}
```

FIGURE 9.14 *(continued)*

```
/*-------------------------------------------------------------*/
/*  This function computes the shear, moment and deflection    */
/*  at intervals along a simply supported beam for a           */
/*  concentrated load of magnitude P acting at a distance a    */
/*  from the left support.                                     */
/*                                                             */
/* Note: Load is positive when acting down.                    */
/*                                                             */
/*  Input Parameters                                           */
/*      p              - magnitude of concentrated load        */
/*      a              - distance of load from left support    */
/*      l              - beam span                             */
/*      e              - modulus of elasticity                 */
/*      i              - moment of inertia                     */
/*      num_points - number of points                          */
/*      x[]            - array containing location of each point */
/*                                                             */
/*   Output Parameters                                         */
/*      v[] - array containing shear and moment values         */
/*      m[] - array containing moment values                   */
/*      y[] - array containing deflection values               */
/*                                                             */
/*-------------------------------------------------------------*/
void conc_load(double p,double a,double l,double e, double i,
    int num_points,double x[],double v[],double m[],double y[])
{
    int k;     /* loop counter */
    double b; /* l - a        */

    b = l - a;

    for (k = 0; k < num_points; ++k)
        {
        if (x[k] < a )
            {
            v[k] = p*b/l;
            m[k] = p*b*x[k]/l;
            y[k] = -p*b*x[k]*(l*l-b*b-x[k]*x[k])/(6.0*e*i*l);
            }
        else
            {
            v[k] = -p*a/l;
            m[k] = p*(b*x[k]/l - x[k] + a);
            y[k] = -p*a*(l-x[k])*(2.0*l*b-b*b-(l-x[k])*(l-x[k]));
            y[k] = y[k]/(6.0*e*i*l);
            }
        }
}
```

FIGURE 9.14 (*continued*)

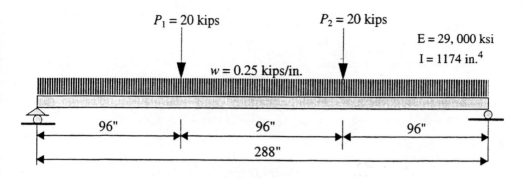

Figure 9.15 Test beam with applied loads.

Table 9.2: Shear force (kips)

Location	P_1	P_2	w	Total
$x = 0$ in.	13.3	6.7	36.0	56.0
$x = 72$ in.	13.3	6.7	18.0	38.0
$x = 144$ in.	−6.7	6.7	0.0	0.0
$x = 216$ in.	−6.7	−13.3	−18	−38.0
$x = 288$ in.	−6.7	−13.3	−36.0	−56.0

Table 9.3: Bending moment (kip-in)

Location	P_1	P_2	w	Total
$x = 0$ in.	0.0	0.0	0.0	0.0
$x = 72$ in.	960.0	480.0	1944.0	3384.0
$x = 144$ in.	960.0	960.0	2592.0	4512.0
$x = 216$ in.	480.0	960.0	1944.0	3384.0
$x = 288$ in.	0.0	0.0	0.0	0.0

Table 9.4: Deflection (in.)

Location	P1	P2	w	Total
$x = 0$ in.	0.0	0.0	0.0	0.0
$x = 72$ in.	−0.192	−0.161	−0.572	−0.822
$x = 144$ in.	−0.249	−0.249	−0.658	−1.156
$x = 216$ in.	−0.161	−0.192	−0.572	−0.822
$x = 288$ in.	0.0	0.0	0.0	0.0

```
SHEAR, MOMENT AND DEFLECTION ANALYSIS
 FOR A SIMPLY SUPPORTED BEAM
Enter beam span (in.): 288.
Enter moment of inertia of section (in^4): 1174.
Enter modulus of elasticity of material(ksi): 29000.
Enter number of points - (maximum is 101): 5

 Number of concentrated loads: 2

   CONCENTRATED LOADS
Concentrated load 1
Enter magnitude of concentrated load (kips): 20.
Enter distance of load from left support (in.): 96.

Concentrated load 2
Enter magnitude of concentrated load (kips): 20.
Enter distance of load from left support (in.): 192.
Number of uniformly distributed loads: 1

   UNIFORM LOADS
Uniform Load 1
Enter magnitude of uniform load (kips/in): 0.25

   SHEAR, MOMENT AND DEFLECTION ANALYSIS FOR A SIMPLY
   SUPPORTED BEAM
   Beam Span ..................... 288.00 inches
   Moment of Inertia ............. 1174.0000 in^4
   Modulus of Elasticity ........29000.0000 ksi

Reaction at left support:      56.00 kips
Reaction at right support:     56.00 kips

---------------------------------------------------------
  Distance        Shear        Moment       Deflection
  (inches)        (kips)      (kip-in)       (inches)
---------------------------------------------------------
     0.00         56.00          0.00        0.000000
    72.00         38.00       3384.00       -0.821924
   144.00          0.00       4512.00       -1.155857
   216.00        -38.00       3384.00       -0.821924
   288.00        -56.00          0.00        0.000000
---------------------------------------------------------
```

Figure 9.16   Sample input and output from program *beam.c* for test problem.

9.10 SORTING

Sorting is the process of arranging data according to some specified order. Examples of sorting include arranging a list of numbers in numerical order and arranging a list of names in alphabetical order. Computers are extremely useful for performing such operations. Sorting is an extremely important task and has therefore received considerable attention by software developers. Many sorting procedures have been developed, and many books have been written on the subject. Since the procedures can be extremely time consuming, even when performed on a computer, the objective of most sorting algorithms is to make the task as efficient as possible. In the sections that follow we present several procedures for sorting numerical data in ascending order. These procedures can be easily be modified for sorting numerical data in descending order or for sorting alphabetic data. The data to be sorted will be stored in an array.

9.11 SELECTION SORT

One of the simplest algorithms for sorting a list of elements is the *selection sort*. The selection sort algorithm is similar to the commonsense approach that you would use to sort a list. It consists of the following steps:

1. Find the smallest element in the list of n elements.
2. Place this element at the top of the list.
3. Find the smallest element in the remaining list of n - 1 elements.
4. Place this element in the second position in the list.
5. Repeat until the remaining list contains only one element.

The selection sort begins by examining the unsorted list to find the smallest element in the list. This element is then moved to the top of the list, and the element that is currently at the top of the list is moved to the place occupied by the smallest element. The unsorted list now consists of the remaining $n - 1$ elements. The search is repeated, and the smallest element in the unsorted list is found. This element is swapped with the element currently at the top of the list, that is, the element at the second position from the top. Now the first two elements are in their correct positions.

This process is repeated until there is only one element left in the unsorted list. With each pass, one more element is placed in its correct position in the list, and the unsorted list shrinks by one. After $n - 1$ passes, the list must be sorted. The first $n - 1$ elements are now in their correct positions. There is only one element left in the list, and it too, must be in the correct position.

As an example of the selection sort procedure, consider the array **x[]** containing six elements that has the following initial configuration:

x_1	x_2	x_3	x_4	x_5	x_6
8	5	9	3	1	7

Figure 9.17 shows the exchanges that take place during each pass of the selection sort. The dotted line shows the number of elements remaining in the unsorted list at the end of each pass through the list. Since there are six elements in the list, it takes five passes to sort the list.

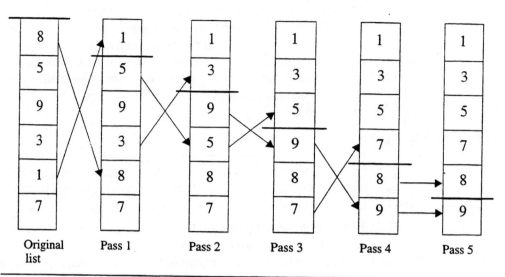

Original list   Pass 1   Pass 2   Pass 3   Pass 4   Pass 5

Figure 9.17 Selection sort

Example 9.6 A C Program for the Selection Sort

A C program for sorting a list of real numbers in ascending order is shown in Figure 9.18. The program *selsort.c* uses the selection-sort algorithm to sort the list. The elements in the list are stored in the array **x[]**, which is declared to be of type **double**. The function **main()** reads in the number of elements in the list and stores this in the integer variable **num_items**. The **for** loop in **main()** reads in the values for each element and stores these in **x[]**. Function **main()** then calls **selection()** to sort the list and prints the sorted list.

The function **selection()** uses the selection-sort algorithm to sort the list. The function arguments are the array to be sorted and the number of elements in the array. The function has two nested loops. The outer loop goes from **0** (the first element in the list) to **n-2** (the next to last element in the list). It uses the variable **pass** as the loop counter. The inner loop counts from **pass+1** to **n-1**. The subscript **pass+1** represents the element that is at the top of the currently unsorted list. The subscript **n-1** represents the last element in the unsorted list (which is also the last element in the list). You should note that the function returns the sorted array in **x[]**. This is typical of all sorting routines and is more efficient in terms of storage space since it does not require the creation of a second array to store the sorted data which would be quite inefficient for large lists.

```
/*******************************************************************/
/*  selsort.c  -- Selection Sort                                  */
/*                                                                */
/* This program sorts a list of n elements in ascending order     */
/* using the selection sort algorithm.                            */
/*******************************************************************/
#include <stdio.h>

#define MAX_ITEMS 100

void main(void);
void selection(double x[], int n);

void main(void)
{
    double x[MAX_ITEMS];   /* array to be sorted      */
    int num_items;         /* number of items in list */
    int i;                 /* loop counter            */

    /* read in array to be sorted */
    printf("\n Selection Sort");
    printf("\n Number of elements in array ");
    scanf("%d",&num_items);

  for (i = 0; i < num_items; ++i)
      {
      printf("Enter x(%d): ", i);
      scanf("%lf", &x[i]);
      }

    /* call selection sort function */
    selection(x,num_items);

    /* print sorted list */
    printf("\n The sorted list is : ");
    for (i = 0; i < num_items; ++i)
       printf(" %lf ", x[i]);
}


/*---------------------------------------------------------------*/
/*  Function: Selection Sort                                     */
/*                                                               */
/* Purpose: Sorts an array in ascending order                    */
/*                                                               */
/*  Input Parameters:                                            */
/*  x[] - array to be sorted                                     */
/*   n   - number of elements in the array                       */
/*                                                               */
/*  Output Parameters:                                           */
/*    x[] - sorted array                                         */
/*---------------------------------------------------------------*/
```

Figure 9.18   A C program for selection sort.

```
void selection(double x[],int n)
{
    int pass;       /* pass number also represents position of  */
                    /* first element in unsorted list           */

    int i;          /* loop counter                    */
    int imin;       /*  position of smallest element */
    double min;     /* minimum value                   */
    double temp;    /* temporary storage               */

    for (pass = 0; pass < n-1; ++pass)
       {
       min = x[pass];
       imin=i;

       /* find the smallest element in the unsorted list */
       for (i = pass+1; i < n; ++i)

          {
          if (x[i] < min)
             {
             min = x[i];
             imin=i;
             }
          }
       /* interchange element on top of list with smallest  */
       /* element in the unsorted list                      */
       temp = x[pass];
       x[pass] = min;
       x[nmin] = temp;
       }

}
```

FIGURE 9.18 (*continued*)

9.12   THE BUBBLE SORT

The *bubble sort* is the simplest sorting algorithm. The procedure consists of comparing adjacent pairs of elements in the array to be sorted. The first two numbers are compared, and if the second is smaller than the first, the numbers are exchanged. Then the values of the next adjacent pair of elements are compared and exchanged if necessary. This sequence of comparisons is continued until the last two elements of the array have ben compared. For an array having n elements the procedure starts with comparing elements 1 and 2, then 2 and 3, and so on, until the elements n - 1 and n are compared. This sequence of comparisons is called a *pass*.

A single pass through the array does not guarantee that the array will be sorted, so this sequence of comparisons is repeated starting with the second pair of elements. A maximum of n - 1 passes is needed to sort the array. As an example of the bubble-sort procedure, consider the array x[] containing six elements which has the following initial configuration:

x_1	x_2	x_3	x_4	x_5	x_6
8	5	9	3	1	7

Pass 1. Figure 9.19 shows all the comparisons and exchanges that take place during the first pass. The following steps are performed

1. The first two numbers are compared and exchanged since x_2 is smaller than x_1.
2. The second and third numbers are compared. No exchange is made since the third is larger than the second.
3. x_3 and x_4 are compared and interchanged since x_4 is smaller than x_3.
4. x_4 and x_5 are compared and swapped.
5. Finally, the last two elements x_5 and x_6 are compared and exchanged. Note that the largest number has now "sunk" to the bottom of the list, while the smallest numbers have moved toward the top of the list. This property of "bubbling" to the top of the list is the reason the procedure is called a bubble sort.

Pass 2. Figure 9.20 shows all the exchanges made during the second pass. At the end of the second pass, the second largest number in the array is moved in x_5.

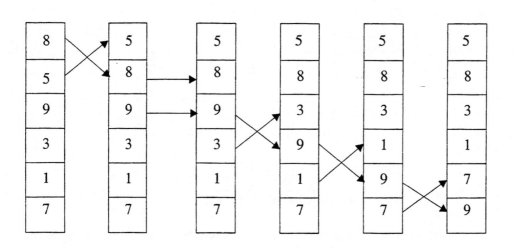

Figure 9.19 Bubble sort, pass 1. t

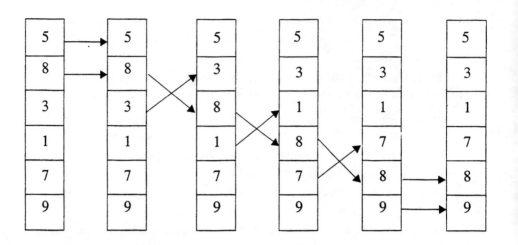

Figure 9.20   Bubble sort, pass 2.

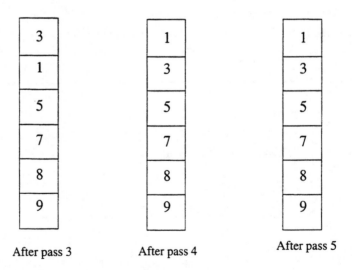

After pass 3   After pass 4   After pass 5

Figure 9.21   Bubble sort, passes 3, 4, and 5.

Passes 3, 4, and 5. Figure 9.21 shows the contents of the array at the end of passes 3, 4, and 5. At the end of the third pass the third largest number is in the third element from the bottom (that is, x_4). The array is sorted at the end of pass 4, and no exchanges are made during pass 5.

Example 9.7   A Bubble-Sort Program

A program to sort a list of numbers in ascending order using the bubble-sort technique appears in Figure 9.22. The list to be sorted is stored in the array **x[]**. The total number of elements is **num_items**. The function **main()** reads in the array using a series of **scanf()** statements. The bubble sort function (**bubble_sort()**) is passed two arguments, **x[]** is the array to be sorted and **n** is the number of elements. The sorted array is returned in **x[]**. Two **for** loops are used. The inner loop makes the comparison and exchanges. The index of this loop varies from 0 to **n-2**. This represents a complete pass through the array. If a pair of elements is out of order, they are exchanged. This exchange is performed in the following statements

```
temp = x[i];
x[i] = x[i+1];
x[i+1] = temp;
```

The variable **temp** is used to save the value of **x[i]**, since the statement

```
x[i] = x[i+1];
```

destroys the value that was contained in **x[i]**. The outer loop is executed $n - 1$ times. This results in $n - 1$ passes being made.

```
/************************************************************/
/*    bubble1.c -- Bubble Sort                              */
/*                                                          */
/*    This program sorts and array using a bubble sort.     */
/*    Source file: bubble.c                                 */
/* ************************************************************/
#include <stdio.h>

#define MAX_SIZE 50

void main(void);
void bubble_sort1(double x[], int n);

void main(void)
{
    double x[MAX_SIZE];    /* array to be sorted        */
    int num_items;         /* number of elements in array */
    int i;                 /* loop counter               */
```

Figure 9.22   Bubble-sort program.

```
   /* read in array */
   printf("\n Bubble sort");
   printf("\n Enter number of items in list: ");      .
   scanf("%d",&num_items);

   for (i = 0; i < num_items; ++i)
      {
      printf("Enter x(%d): ", i);
      scanf("%lf",&x[i]);
      }

   /* call bubble sort function */
   bubble_sort1(x,num_items);

   /* print sorted array */
   printf("\n\nSorted array");

   for (i = 0; i < num_items; ++i)
      printf(" %lf ", x[i]);


/*------------------------------------------------------------*/
/*    Function: bubble_sort1                                  */
/*                                                            */
/*    Purpose:                                                */
/*       This function sorts an array in ascending order      */
/*                                                            */
/*    Input Parameters:                                       */
/*       x[]  - array to be sorted                            */
/*       n    - number of items in the array                 */
/*                                                            */
/*------------------------------------------------------------*/
void bubble_sort1(double x[], int n)
{
   double temp;        /* temporary storage */
   int pass;           /* pass number       */
   int i;              /* counter for inner loop */

   for (pass = 0; pass < n-1; ++pass)
      {
      for (i = 0; i < n-1 ; ++i)
         {
         if (x[i] > x[i+1])
            {
            temp = x[i];
            x[i] = x[i+1];
            x[i+1] = temp;
            }
         }
      }
}
```

FIGURE 9.22   (*continued*)

Modifications to the Bubble-Sort Function

The bubble-sort function present in the previous section has several limitations. For one, the function does not check to see if the array is already sorted. In the example presented, the array was sorted after the fourth pass, and it was not necessary to perform the fifth pass. Thus the routine presented will perform poorly if the array is almost in order. We can improve our program by adding a test to determine whether the array has been sorted. If no exchange is made during a pass, it is obvious that the array must already be sorted.

We can modify the bubble sort routine presented earlier to take this into account. We use an integer variable called **is_sorted** to indicate whether or not the list has been sorted. At the beginning of a pass, this variable is set to **TRUE**. During a pass, the variable is set to **FALSE** (to indicate that the list has not been sorted) each time an interchange takes place. The contents of **is_sorted** is examined at the beginning of the next pass. If no exchange took place in the previous pass, the value of **is_sorted** is **TRUE** and sorting is terminated by jumping out of the loop.

Another problem with the bubble-sort algorithm presented earlier is that after the first pass, the largest number in the list always ends up at the bottom of the list. We do not need to compare the last two elements in the list after the first pass. Also, at the end of the second pass, the second largest number ends up in the second from last position. Thus, after the second pass, we do not have to compare the last three numbers. At the end of each pass we have one less comparison to make. We include this in our program by modifying the inner **for** loop so that it reads

```
for(i =0; i < n-pass)
```

rather than

```
for(i=0; i < n-1)
```

A listing of the modified bubble-sort function is given in Figure 9.23. This version of the bubble-sort function is more efficient.

9.13 THE SHELL SORT

The bubble sort is easy to understand and code, but it is probably the most inefficient procedure for sorting an array, because it always compares and exchanges (when necessary) adjacent elements of an array. A large number of comparisons and exchanges have to be made even for arrays having a few elements. Many of these comparisons are unnecessary. In the bubble sort, elements are moved one position at a time. It is usually more efficient to move an element several positions in one long jump than it is to move it one position at a time in a series of little jumps.

```
/*----------------------------------------------------------------*/
/*    Function: bubble_sort2                                    */
/*                                                              */
/*    Purpose:    Sorts sorts an array in ascending order       */
/*                                                              */
/*    Input Parameters:                                         */
/*       x[]   - array to be sorted                             */
/*       n     - number of items in the array                  */
/*----------------------------------------------------------------*/
void bubble_sort2(double x[], int n)
{
    double temp;              /* temporary storage      */
    int pass;                 /* pass number            */
    int i;                    /* counter for inner loop */
    int is_sorted=FALSE ;     /* flag to indicate if array is
sorted */

    while (!is_sorted)
      {
      for (pass = 0; pass < n-1; ++pass)
        {
        is_sorted = TRUE;    /* set flag at beginning of pass */
        for (i = 0; i < n-1 ; ++i)
           {
           if (x[i] > x[i+1])
             {
             temp = x[i];
             x[i] = x[i+1];
             x[i+1] = temp;
             is_sorted = FALSE;  /* reset flag */
             }
           }
        }
      }
}
```

Figure 9.23   Modified bubble-sort program.

The *Shell sort*, named after its inventor Donald Shell, is more efficient than the bubble sort since it makes comparisons and exchanges over larger distances. The Shell sort essentially consists of a series of bubble sorts, but instead of comparing adjacent elements, it compares elements at some distances. Initially, the distance between the elements being compared is large; for example, the first element in the array is compared to one in the middle. At each subsequent stage the distance between elements is decreased until, in the last stage, adjacent elements are compared.

As an example of the Shell sort procedure, consider the following 12-element array shown:

8	5	2	13	1	17	6	4	9	15	7	3

During the first pass through the array, the interval over which the comparison is made is taken as $n/2$. Thus, in the first pass, the first and seventh elements are compared, then the second and eighth elements, then the third and ninth elements, and so on. Since the seventh element (6) is smaller than the first element (8), they are interchanged. Also, since the eighth element (4) is smaller than the second element (5), they are swapped. The third and ninth elements are not swapped since the third element (2) is smaller than the ninth element (9). The process is continued until the end of the list is reached. This completes the first step of pass 1. Figure 9.24b shows the arrangement of the array at the end of the first step of pass 1. For each step, these comparisons are repeated until no exchanges have been made. Since exchanges were made during the first step of pass 1, the process is repeated with the same comparison interval $(n/2 = 6)$. Figure 9.24c shows the arrangement of the array at the end of the second step of the first pass. No exchanges were made during the second step of the first pass.

The second pass is now implemented. For the second pass, the comparison interval is again halved. Thus, the comparison interval is now three. Figure 9.25a shows the array at the beginning of the first step of the second pass. During the first step of the second pass, the first and fourth elements are compared, then the second and fifth elements are compared, followed by the third and sixth elements, and so on. The first element (6) is smaller than the fourth element (13), so no exchange takes place. The second element (4) is larger than the fifth element (1), so the two are interchanged. The third element (2) is smaller than the sixth element (3), and so the two are not exchanged. This process is continued until all the elements in the

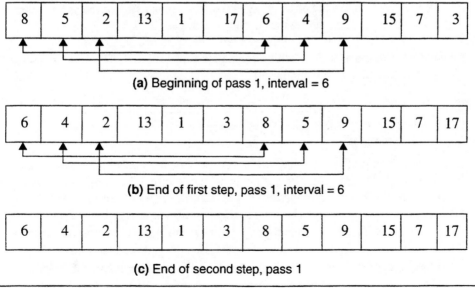

(a) Beginning of pass 1, interval = 6

(b) End of first step, pass 1, interval = 6

(c) End of second step, pass 1

Figure 9.24   Shell sort, pass 1.

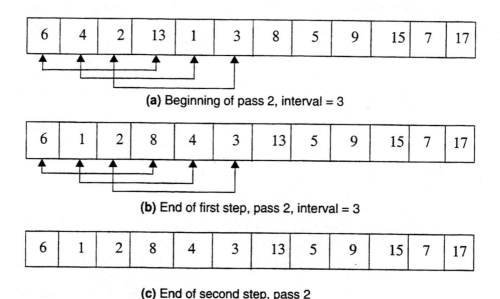

(a) Beginning of pass 2, interval = 3

(b) End of first step, pass 2, interval = 3

(c) End of second step, pass 2

Figure 9.25   Shell sort, pass 2.

array have been examined. Figure 9.25b shows the array at the end of the first step of pass 2. Since elements were interchanged in the first step, the step is repeated. Figure 9.25c shows the array at the end of the second step of the second pass. No exchanges are made during the second step of pass 2.

The third pass is now implemented. The comparison interval is again halved and the third pass is done with a comparison interval of 1. This pass is essentially similar to a pass in the bubble sort.

Example 9.8   A Shell-Sort Program

A program that uses the Shell sort to sort an array **x[]** containing *n* elements is shown in Figure 9.26. The sorting is done in the function **shell_sort()**. This function expects two parameters: **x[]** is the array to be sorted and **n** is the number of elements in the array. The sorted array is returned in **x[]**.

In function **shell_sort()** the variable **jump** is the comparison interval. It is initially set equal to *n*/2. There are two nested **while** loops in function **shell_sort()**. The outer **while** loop implements each pass of the Shell sort algorithm. The statements that form the body of the loop are executed as long as **jump** is greater than or equal to 1. The inner loop implements each step of each

```
/**************************************************************/
/*    shelsort.c -- Shell Sort                              */
/*                                                          */
/*    This program sorts an array using the Shell sort      */
/*    algorithm.                                            */
/**************************************************************/
#include <stdio.h>

#define MAX_SIZE 50
#define TRUE 1
#define FALSE 0

void main(void);
void shell_sort(double x[], int n);

void main(void)
{
    double x[MAX_SIZE];     /* array to be sorted           */
    int num_items;          /* number of elements in array */
    int i;                  /* loop counter                 */

    printf("\n Shell sort");
    printf("\n Enter number of element in list:");
    scanf("%d",&num_items);
    for (i = 0; i < num_items; ++i)
    {
        printf("Enter x(%d): ", i);
        scanf("%lf",&x[i]);
    }

    /* call Shell sort function */
    shell_sort(x,num_items);
    /* print sorted array */
    printf("\n\nSorted array\n");
    for (i = 0; i < num_items; ++i)
        printf(" %lf ", x[i]);
}

/*----------------------------------------------------------*/
/*    Function: shell_sort                                  */
/*                                                          */
/*    Purpose:                                              */
/*        This function sorts an array in ascending order   */
/*        using the Shell sort algorithm.                   */
/*                                                          */
/*    Input Parameters:                                     */
/*        x[]  - array to be sorted                         */
/*        n    - number of items in the array               */
/*----------------------------------------------------------*/
void shell_sort(double x[], int n)
{
    double temp;           /* temporary storage                      */
    int i;                 /* counter                                */
    int last;              /* last element in unsorted list          */
    int is_sorted;         /* flag to indicate if array is sorted   */
    int jump=n/2;          /* distance over which to compare         */
```

Figure 9.26 The Shell-sort program.

```
while (jump >= 1)
    {
    last = n - jump;
    is_sorted = FALSE;

    while (!is_sorted)
        {
        is_sorted = TRUE;       /* initialize flag */
        for (i = 0; i < last; ++i)
            {
            if (x[i] >= x[i + jump])
                {
                temp = x[i];
                x[i] = x[i+jump];
                x[i+jump] = temp;
                is_sorted = FALSE;  /* reset flag */
                }
            }
        }
    jump = jump/2;              /* reduce interval */
    }
}
```

FIGURE 9.26 (*continued*)

pass. The integer variable `is_sorted` serves as a flag. It is initially set to **TRUE** at the beginning of each step. If exchanges are made, then it is set to **FALSE**, which results in the inner loop being executed again. At the end of each pass the comparison interval is halved in the following statement

```
jump = jump/2;    /* reduce interval */
```

Since `jump` is a variable of type `int`, the result of the division is an integer variable that has been truncated, not rounded. Thus, if `jump` is equal to 3, the result of the division will be 1, since 1.5 is truncated to give 1. Thus the last pass is always done with a value of `jump` equal to 1.

The Shell sort is much faster than the bubble sort. For small lists of fewer than 20 items, the difference between the two methods is not significant. However, as the number of items in the list increases, the difference in execution times increases quite dramatically.

9.14 THE QUICK SORT

The last sorting algorithm we will consider is known as the *quick sort*. This method is more complicated than the Shell-sort algorithm, but it is one of the fastest sorting algorithms. It is generally faster than both the bubble-sort and the Shell sort algorithms.

In the quick-sort algorithm, one element of the list is selected as the pivot element. It does not make much difference which element is selected as the pivot element, although it is usually the first element in the list. The elements in the list are arranged into two partitions. If we are sorting the list in ascending order from left to right, then all elements in the list that are smaller than the pivot element are moved into the left partition. All elements that are larger than the pivot element are moved into the right partition. The pivot element is then placed in between the two partitions. This places the pivot element in its proper position when the list is in final sorted order. Next the two partitions are further subdivided into two additional partitions, and the quick-sort algorithm is applied recursively to each partition. This process of subdivision is continued until all the partitions have only one element each, at which point the array is sorted.

Example 9.9   A C Program for Quick Sort

The quick sort algorithm is usually written as a recursive function, which means that the function calls itself. The quick-sort program is shown in Figure 9.27. The function that implements the quick-sort algorithm is called **quick_sort()** and is written as a recursive function. The function expects three arguments: **x[]** is the array that is to be sorted, **first** is the index of the first element in the list, and **last** is the index of the last element in the list. The function is called from **main()** as follows:

```
quick_sort(x,0,num_items-1);
```

Since array subscripts in C start at 0, the first element in the list has a subscript of 0, and the last element has a subscript of **num_items-1**.

The **quick_sort()** function itself is very simple. All it does is call the function **partition()** and then calls itself twice. The following statements make recursive calls in **quick_sort()**

```
quick_sort(x,first,pivot-1);
quick_sort(x,pivot+1, last);
```

The first call causes the left partition to be sorted, and the second call causes the right partition to be sorted.

Most of the work is done by the function **partition()**. This function divides the list into two partitions and rearranges the elements in the list so that the left partition contains elements that are less than the pivot element and the right partition contains elements that are greater than the pivot element. It also moves the pivot element to its proper position in the list so that it is in between the two partitions. The function returns a value of type **int**, which represents the new position of the pivot element.

In function **partition()** the integer variable **pivot** represents the current position of the pivot element. The variable **pivot_value** is the value of the pivot element. Note the distinction between the value of the pivot element and the position of the pivot element. The value of the pivot element does not change in function **partition()**. The position of the pivot element, however, changes as the pivot element is moved to the right to its proper position in the list.

The function begins by choosing the first element as the pivot element. The statements

```
pivot = first;
pivot_value = x[first];
```

assign the index of the first element to pivot and the value of the first element **x[first]** to the variable **pivot_value**. In the **for** loop beginning with

```
for (i = first; i <= last; ++i)
```

each element in the list (starting with the second element) is compared with the value of the pivot element **pivot_value**. If the value of **x[i]** is less than **pivot_value**, then the index of the pivot element, represented by the variable **pivot**, is incremented, thus moving the current position of the pivot element to the right. Then the values of the element **x[i]** and the element in the current position of the pivot element **x[pivot]** are interchanged. This places **x[i]** before or to the left of the current position of the pivot element. No interchange takes place if the element **x[i]** is larger than the element in the current pivot position and the position of the current pivot element remains unchanged.

At the end of the **for** loop, the variable pivot contains the current position of the pivot element which marks the division between the two partitions. All elements to the right have a value larger than **pivot_value**.

The last task performed by **partition()** is to interchange **x[pivot]** and **x[first]**. This places the original pivot element in its proper position in the list. The function returns the current value of pivot which is subsequently used in further subdivision of the list.

9.15 COMPARISON OF SORTING ROUTINES

Table 9.1 compares execution times for the sorting algorithms described in this chapter for arrays sizes ranging from 1000 to 6000 elements. The arrays were generated randomly using the C library **rand()** function (see Chapter 23 for a description of the **rand()** function). From Table 9.1 we see that the quick-sort algorithms is the fastest of the four algorithms, while the bubble sort algorithm is the slowest. For small lists ($n = 1000$) the quick-sort algorithm is approximately 50

```
/*************************************************************/
/*     quicksrt.c -- Quick Sort                              */
/*                                                           */
/*     This program sorts an array using the quick sort      */
/*     algorithm.                                            */
/*************************************************************/
#include <stdio.h>
#define MAX_SIZE 50
#define TRUE 1
#define FALSE 0

void main(void);
void quick_sort(double x[], int first, int last);
int partition(double x[],int first, int last);

void main(void)
{
    double x[MAX_SIZE];    /* array to be sorted          */
    int num_items;         /* number of elements in array */
    int i;                 /* loop counter                */

    /* read in array */
    printf("\n Quick sort");
    printf("\n Enter number of element in list:");
    scanf("%d",&num_items);
    for (i = 0; i < num_items; ++i)
        {
        printf(" Enter x(%d): ", i);
        scanf("%lf",&x[i]);
        }

    /* call quick sort function */
    quick_sort(x,0, num_items - 1);

    /* print sorted array */
    printf("\n\nSorted array\n");
    for (i = 0; i < num_items; ++i)
        printf(" %lf ", x[i]);
}

/*-----------------------------------------------------------*/
/*     Function: quick_sort                                  */
/*                                                           */
/*     Purpose:                                              */
/*         This function sorts an array in ascending order using */
/*         the quick sort algorithm.                         */
/*         Note: This is a recursive function                */
/*                                                           */
/*     Input Parameters:                                     */
/*         x[]   - array to be sorted                        */
/*         first - position of first element in the list     */
/*         last  - position of last element in the list      */
/*-----------------------------------------------------------*/
void quick_sort(double x[], int first, int last)
{

    int pivot;            /* pivot element */

    if (first < last)
        {
        pivot = partition(x, first, last);

        quick_sort(x,first,pivot-1);
        quick_sort(x,pivot+1, last);
        }
}
```

```
/*----------------------------------------------------------------*/
/*    Function: partition                                         */
/*                                                                */
/*    Purpose:                                                    */
/*       This function partitions an array into two parts         */
/*       based on the value of a pivot element. All elements      */
/*       that are smaller than the pivot element are placed       */
/*       placed on the left. All elements that are larger         */
/*       larger than the pivot value are placed on the right.     */
/*       The pivot element is taken to be the first element in    */
/*       the list.                                                */
/*                                                                */
/*    Input Parameters:                                           */
/*       x[]    - array to be sorted                              */
/*       first  - position of first element in the list           */
/*       last   - position of the last element in the list        */
/*                                                                */
/*    Returns                                                     */
/*       pivot - position of the pivot element                    */
/*----------------------------------------------------------------*/
int partition(double x[],int first,int last)
{
   int pivot;              /* position of pivot element */
   double pivot_value;     /* value of pivot element    */
   double temp;            /* temporary storage         */
   int i;                  /* loop counter              */

   pivot = first;
   pivot_value = x[first];

   for (i = first; i <= last; ++i)
      {
      /* compare element with pivot element */
      if (x[i] < pivot_value)
         {
         ++pivot;            /* adjust index of pivot element */
         if (i != pivot)
            {
            /* interchange element with pivot element */
            temp = x[pivot];
            x[pivot] = x[i];
            x[i] = temp;
            }
         }
      }

   /* move pivot element to point in list that separates the  */
   /* smaller elements from the larger elements               */
   temp = x[pivot];
   x[pivot] = x[first];
   x[first] = temp;

   return (pivot);
}
```

FIGURE 9.27 (continued)

Table 9.5: Comparison of execution times (in seconds) for sorting routines

	Number of Elements in Array					
Algorithm	1000	2000	3000	4000	5000	6000
quick sort	0.06	0.11	0.16	0.22	0.27	0.38
shell sort	0.11	0.39	0.60	0.93	1.43	1.48
bubble sort	3.07	12.41	27.67	49.40	77.36	108.95
selection sort	0.93	3.73	8.46	15.06	23.46	33.79

times faster than the bubble sort. The difference in execution times between the quick sort and bubble-sort algorithms increases as the number of elements in the array increases. For $n = 6000$, the ratio of execution times for the bubble-sort and quick-sort algorithms is approximately 300. The Shell-sort algorithm is second in terms of execution times. For $n = 1000$ the ratio of execution times for the Shell-sort and quick sort algorithms is around 2, while for $n = 6000$ the ratio is around 4. The ratio of execution times for the selection sort and the quick sort is approximately 15 for $n = 1000$ and around 90 for $n = 6000$.

9.16 SUMMARY

In this chapter we presented the C language features for creating and manipulating one-dimensional arrays. An array is a collection of variables of the same data type that are referenced by the same name. The individual elements of an array are referenced by appending a subscript to the array name. The array subscript is enclosed in square brackets that appear after the array name. In C, all array subscripts begin with zero. Arrays having a single subscript are called one-dimensional arrays. We can also create arrays that have more than one subscript. Arrays having two or more dimensions are called multidimensional arrays. The elements of an array are stored in contiguous memory locations. The total number of bytes of storage allocated for an array is equal to the size of the array times the number of bytes of storage required for the type of data being stored in the array.

The individual elements of an array can be used anywhere that an ordinary variable can be. An array element can be used in assignment statements and in arithmetic expressions and as an argument to a function. Also, passing an individual element of an array to a function is no different than passing an ordinary variable or value to a function.

An entire array can also be passed to a function. This is done by simply stating the array's name without the subscript in the function call. All arrays are passed call by reference; this means that the actual array is passed and not a copy of the array.

The name of an array is a constant that contains the address of the first element of the array. When we pass the array name to the function, we are actually passing the address of the array in memory. The function can then use this address to modify the elements of the array.

In this chapter we also presented four sorting algorithms: the selection sort, the bubble sort, the Shell sort, and quick sort. The implementation of these sorting algorithms in C was also presented. The selection-sort and the bubble-sort algorithms are simple, but they are inefficient. The Shell sort is a more efficient algorithm since it makes comparisons and exchanges over large distances unlike the selection sort and the bubble sort, which compare adjacent elements. The quick sort is one of the fastest sorting algorithms and is usually written as a recursive function.

Key Terms Presented in This Chapter

array	bubble sort
array declaration	multidimensional array
array dimensions	one-dimensional array
array elements	quick sort
array initialization	selection sort
array index	sorting
array name	Shell sort
array subscript	two-dimensional array
arrays as arguments	vectors

PROGRAM STYLE, COMMON ERRORS, AND DEBUGGING GUIDE

1. When passing an array to a function you should also pass the number of elements in the array. This makes the function more general. General functions can often be used in other programs.
2. You should use symbolic constants to define the size of your arrays. This makes it easier to change the size of the arrays.
3. You should be consistent with the choice of variable names used for array subscripts. A common practice is to use `i` for the first subscript of an array and the variables `j` and `k` for the second and third subscripts.
4. The most common error when working with an array is attempting to access elements that are outside the array. You should always keep in mind that C does not do any bounds checking and that it is your respon-

sibility to make sure that you do not exceed the bounds of an array.

5. A common error is forgetting that array subscripts in C start at 0. The subscript of the last element of an array is *size*-1 and not *size*, where *size* is the number of elements in the array.

6. Another consequence of arrays beginning with a subscript 0 is that **x[i]** represents the (*i* +1) element of the array **x[]** and not the *i*th element of the array. It is a very common error to be "off by one" when referencing elements of an array.

7. When using a loop to access elements in an array, the array subscripts should never be less than 0 and should always be less than *size*-1. The following **for** statement

    ```
    for (i = 0; i <= n; ++i)    /* Error! */
    ```

    will result in an error. The correct for statement is

    ```
    for (i = 0; i < n; ++i)
    ```

8. Only static and global arrays are initialized to zero. Local or automatic arrays are not initialized. Thus you should always initialize the elements of those local arrays whose elements need to be initialized.

9. The elements of a static array are initialized to zero only once. If the function in which the static array is declared is executed more than once the elements of the static array are not reinitialized. Thus you should not assume that the elements will be initialized to zero each time the function is called.

10. It is a syntax error to provide more initializers than there are elements in the array.

11. If the number of initializers in the list of initializers is less than the number of elements of the array, the remaining elements of the array are initialized to zero.

12. The name of the array represents the address of the first element of the array.

13. The name of an array is a constant and cannot appear on the left-hand side of an assignment statement.

    ```
    float x[10];
    x[0] = 345.67;    /* correct */
    x = 345.67;       /* wrong   */
    ```

    The second assignment statement shown here is wrong because it attempts to assign a value to the array name.

14. When an array is passed to a function, the address of the first element of the array is passed to the function. The function can use this address to change the contents of the array. For reasons of efficiency, C passes the actual array and not a copy of the array, so any changes made in the

function are made to the actual array.

15. You should use the **const** type qualifier in the function definition if you do not want the function to change the original array.

16. Since it is difficult to debug a program with many large arrays, you should test your program by reducing the size of the arrays to make it more manageable to trace. After you have isolated the source of errors, you can restore the arrays to their original size. You can do this very easily if you use symbolic constants to define the size of your arrays.

17. If you get strange results in a program that uses arrays, it is very likely that you are accessing elements in an array that do not exist. This error is difficult to track down. You should check each subscript and make sure that it falls with the proper range of values for that array. One technique you can use is to print the array subscripts and the corresponding values of the array element. You should always remember that array subscripts begin with zero and not one.

EXERCISES

Review Questions

1. Consider the following declaration

   ```
   float x[20];
   ```

   a. What is the name of the array?

   b. How many elements does the array have?

   c. What is the range of subscripts that this array can have?

   d. Write a **printf()** statement to print the second element of the array.

   e. Write a **scanf()** statement to read the third element of the array.

2. Write declaration statements for each of the following:

   a. An array **x_coord[]** having 10 elements of type **float**

   b. An array **letters[]** having 200 elements of type **char**

3. The following array declarations have several errors. Identify each of them:

   ```
   #define MAXSIZE 5
      ...
      main()
      {
         int x[MAXSIZE] = {0,1,1,2,4,5};
         int y[2 * MAXSIZE];
         int z[4.0];
         ...
         ...
      }
   ```

4. Draw the array and indicate the contents of each element of the array after the following set of statements have been executed:

a.

```
int a[10],i;
for (i=0; i < 10; ++i)
    a[i] = i + 1;
```

b.

```
int x[8],i,j;
for (i=0; i < 6; ++i)
    {
    j = 7 - i;
    x[j] = i;
    }
```

c.

```
int a[10],i;
for (i=0; i < 10; ++i)
    {
    if (i < 5)
        a[i] = i;
    else
        a[i] = 10 - i;
    }
```

d.

```
int x[10];
for (i=0; i < 10; ++i)
    {
    if (i < 5)
        x[i] = -1;
    else
        if (i == 5)
            x[i] = 0;
        else
            x[i] = 1;
    }
```

e.

```
int x[10];
for (i=2; i < 10; +=i)
    x[i-2] = i;
```

5. For the array a[] shown here

a[0]	a[1]	a[2]	a[3]	a[4]	a[5]
20	10	50	30	40	60

give the value of the element referenced by the following expressions if $i = 2$ and $j = 1$:

a.   `a[i]`

b.   `a[i+j]`

c.   `a[2*i + j - 3]`

d.   `a[i+j-3]`

e.   `a[i+2-j]`

6.   Suppose we have the following declaration:

```
float x[10],z = 10.5;
```

With this declaration in effect, some of the following statements are invalid. Identify each of them

a.   `x[2] = z;`

b.   `x[12] = 4.5;`

c.   `x = z;`

d.   `x[2] = 5.3;`

7.   State whether the following statements are true or false.

a.   An array is a collection of variables of the same data type placed next to each other in memory.

b.   An array declaration specifies the type and size of an array.

c.   When you pass an array to a function, the compiler makes a copy of the array and passes this copy to the function.

d.   If you do not initialize a local array, all elements of the array are set to zero.

e.   If you do not initialize a static array, all elements of the array are set to zero.

8.   An array `x[]` of type **double** contains *n* elements. Write program segments to create a new array `y[]` such that the following are true:

a.   Each element of `y[]` contains the absolute value of the corresponding element in `x[]`.

b.   Each element of `y[]` contains the sign of the corresponding element of `x[]`. Thus,

if `x[i]` $= 0$, then `y[i]` $= 0$

if `x[i]` < 0, then `y[i]` $= -1$

if `x[i]` > 0, then `y[i]` $= 1$

c.   The element `y[i]` contains the sum of `x[i]` and `x[i+1]`, and the last element `y[n-1]` contains the sum of `x[n-1]` and `x[0]`.

9.   Translate the following into C **for** loops:

a. $$S = \sum_{i=1}^{n-1} (a_i - a_{i+i})$$

b. $\quad S = \displaystyle\sum_{i=1}^{10} a_i x_i$

(Remember that array subscripts in C begin with 0.)

Programming Exercises

10. An integer array **x[]** contains 50 elements. Write C statements to do the following:
  a. Print the last 10 elements of the array.
  b. Count the number of positive values, zero values, and negative values in **x[]**.
  c. Determine the largest absolute value in the array.
  d. Divide each element by the largest absolute value and store the result in the original element.

11. An array **x[]** contains n elements. Write separate program segments to do the following:
  a. Compute the sum of all the even elements.
  b. Compute the sum of all odd elements.
  c. Compute the sum of all elements that are less than zero.

12. Write a program to read N numbers, store these in an array, and print them in the reverse order from which they were read.

13. An array **x[]** contains n data values obtained from experiments. Write a program to determine the number of data values that are less than **xlow** and the number of values that are greater than **xhigh**.

14. Two arrays **a[]** and **b[]** have m and n elements, respectively. The elements in each array are arranged in ascending sequence. Write a program to read in the two arrays and merge the two sets into a third array **c[]** so that the elements in **c[]** are in ascending order.

15. A one-dimensional array consists of 50 elements. Write a C program to interchange the 1st and 50th elements, the 2nd and 49th elements, and so on.

16. Write a function to evaluate the scalar triple product of three vectors **A**, **B**, and **C**. The scalar triple product is defined as

$$[ABC] = A \ (B \times C)$$

Use your program to show that **[ABC]** is also equal to **B(C×A)** and **C(A×B)**.

17. An array **x[]** consists of n elements **x[0]**, **x[1]**, ... , **x[n-1]**. Write a program to determine the maximum and minimum values, **xmax** and **xmin**, and then scale each element **x[i]** so that

```
x[i] = (x[i] - xmin) / (xmax-xmin);
```

Print the scaled array.

18. For purposes for evaluating a polynomial for a given value of x, the polynomial can be written as

$$a_0 + (a_1 + (a_2 + \cdots + (a_{n-1} + a_n x)x) \cdots x)x$$

For example, the polynomial

$$3 + 4x + 5x^2 + 6x^3 + 7x^4$$

can be written as

$$3 + (4 + (5 + (6 + 7x)x)x)x$$

This is known as Horner's method of evaluating a polynomial. Write a program to read in an array $a[]$ containing the coefficients a_i of the polynomial and compute the value of the polynomial for a given value of x.

19. Given two vectors A and B such that

$$\mathbf{A} = \mathbf{A}_x i + \mathbf{A}_y j + \mathbf{A}_z k$$
$$\mathbf{B} = \mathbf{B}_x i + \mathbf{B}_y j + \mathbf{B}_z k$$

The cross product $\mathbf{A} \times \mathbf{B} = \mathbf{C}$ is given by

$$\mathbf{C} = (\mathbf{A}_y \mathbf{B}_z - \mathbf{A}_z \mathbf{B}_y)i + (\mathbf{A}_z \mathbf{B}_x - \mathbf{A}_x \mathbf{B}_z)j + (\mathbf{A}_x \mathbf{B}_y - \mathbf{A}_y \mathbf{B}_x)k$$

Write a function to compute the cross product $\mathbf{C}$. Use three arrays $a[]$, $b[]$, and $c[]$, each containing three elements, to represent the vectors. For example,

$$\mathbf{A}_x = a[0], \mathbf{A}_y = a[1], \text{ and } \mathbf{A}_z = a[2]$$

Write a **main()** program to test your function.

20. An array $x[]$ contains coordinates of n points in three-dimensional space. Since each point in three-dimensional space is represented by three coordinates (x, y, z), there is a total of $3n$ elements in the array.

Write a program to print a table consisting of the coordinates, the distance of the point from the origin, and the direction cosines of the line connecting the point to the origin. The distance of a point from the origin is given by

$$r_i = \sqrt{x_i^2 + y_i^2 + z_i^2}$$

and the direction cosines are

$$\cos \alpha_i = \frac{x_i}{r_i}$$

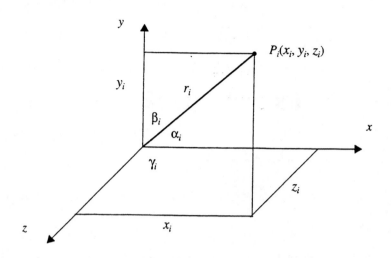

$$\cos \beta_i = \frac{y_i}{r_i}$$

$$\cos \gamma_i = \frac{z_i}{r_i}$$

			Direction Cosines		
Point	Coordinates	Distance	$\cos\alpha$	$\cos\beta$	$\cos\gamma$
1	$x_1\ y_1\ z_1$				
2	$x_2\ y_2\ z_2$				
.					
.					
N	$x_n\ y_n\ z_n$				

10

POINTERS

One of the more important and distinguishing characteristics of C as a programing language is its sophisticated use of pointers. A pointer is a variable whose value is the address or memory location of another data object. The power and flexibility that C provides in handling pointers is what sets it apart from other programming languages such as Pascal, BASIC, and FORTRAN. Pointers provide C programmers with the ability to manipulate memory addresses with the same power that is provided by assembly language. Since every real-world C program uses pointers, the correct understanding and use of pointers is critical to successful C programming. Some of the reasons for using pointers in our programs include

1. Ability to pass addresses of variables to functions so that functions can change the value of these variables
2. Capability to work with memory that has been allocated dynamically
3. Processing and manipulation of strings using C library string functions
4. Passing the address of a function to another function
5. Improved efficiency of certain functions
6. Direct access to the computer's hardware

In addition to being one of the more powerful features of C, pointers are also its most dangerous feature. Since pointers can point to any location in memory, incorrect use of pointers can cause changes in our programs or even in some important operating system parameters, resulting in a system crash. Incorrect use of pointers can also result in subtle bugs in a program that are very difficult to detect.

In this chapter we explain how to use pointers with various data types. We describe how pointers are used with arrays and the close relationship between pointers and arrays. We also describe how we can use pointers as arguments to functions since this allows our functions to change the value of the function's arguments and hence return more that one value.

10.1 ADDRESSES AND THE ADDRESS-OF OPERATOR

All objects in a C program, such as variables, arrays, and even functions, reside at a physical location in the computer's memory. The location of an object in memory is called its *address*. The representation of addresses in a machine is hardware dependent. The most commonly used unit of storage is a byte, and most computers represent addresses in terms of bytes.

We have used memory addresses in some of our previous programs. For example, all arguments passed to the **scanf()** function were preceded by the address-of operator (**&**). In the statement

```
scanf("%f", &x);
```

the address of the **float** variable **x** is passed to the **scanf()** function. We also used addresses when working with arrays. Recall that in Chapter 9 we mentioned that the name of an array without the subscript represents the address of the first element of the array. Thus, when we pass an array to a function, we are actually passing the address of the array. For example, if **a[]** is defined as

```
float a[10];
```

then the function call

```
sum_array(a);
```

passes the address of the array **a[]** rather than the individual elements of the array.

To determine the address of an object in memory we use the address-of operator (**&**). The address-of operator when placed to the left of a variable name returns the address of the data object.

Example 10.1 Addresses

The program shown in Figure 10.1 prints the values of four variables and their addresses. The variables **i** and **j** are of type **int**, and the variables **x** and **y** are of type **float**. The first **printf()** statement prints the contents of the variables. The second **printf()** statement

```
printf("\n &i = %u &j = %u &x = %u &y = %u",&i,&j,&x,&y);
```

prints the address of each variable. Each variable is preceded by the address-of operator. Since on our system machine addresses are represented by unsigned integers, we use the **%u** type specifier in the format string to print addresses.

The value **i** is stored at location 65488, the value **j** is stored at location 65490, the value **x** is stored at location 65492, and the value **y** is stored at location 65496. On our system, a variable of type **int** requires 2 bytes of storage, and a variable of type **float** requires 4 bytes of storage. Notice that the address returned by the **address-of** operator is the address of the first byte. Figure 10.2 shows these variables and their addresses. The specific memory addresses at which the values of the variables are stored are machine and implementation dependent and will vary from system to system. These addresses may vary even on the same system depending on the operating system and whether or not you have other memory resident software loaded.

The address-of operator is a unary operator; that is, it has one operand. It associates from right to left and has the same precedence as the other unary operators. The address-of operator can also be applied to array elements. For example, if **a[]** is an array then the expressions

```
&a[0];
&a[3];
```

give the address of the first and fourth elements of the array.

```
/****************************************************************/
/*  address.c -- Addresses of Variables                        */
/*                                                              */
/*  Displays addresses of several variables                    */
/****************************************************************/
#include <stdio.h>

main()
{
   int i=10, j = 20;
   float x = 2.5, y = 6.5;
   printf("\n i=%d, j=%d, x=%f, y=%f", i,j,x,y);
   printf("\n &i=%u, &j=%u, &x = %u, &y = %u", &i,&j,&x,&y);
}
```

Program output:

```
i=10, j=20, x=2.500000, y=6.500000
&i=65488, &j=65490, &x = 65492, &y = 65496
```

Figure 10.1   Addresses of variables.

Variable	Value	Address
i	10	65488
j	20	65490
x	2.5	65492
y	6.5	65496

Figure 10.2   Addresses and values stored at addresses.

The address-of operator cannot be applied to the following C expressions since they do not point to meaningful addresses:

1. We cannot obtain the address of a constant. The following statement is illegal since it attempts to obtain the address of a constant.

    &4

2. We cannot use the address-of operator with an ordinary expression. For example, the statement

    ```
    &(i + j * 2)
    ```

    is illegal since it attempts to obtain the address of an expression

3. The address-of operator cannot be applied to **register** variables. Thus the following statement

    ```
    register int i;
    ...
    ptr = &i;
    ```

    is illegal.

10.2 POINTER VARIABLES

C provides a special type of variable called a *pointer* that allows us to work with memory addresses. A pointer is a variable that contains the address of a data object. Thus a pointer is a variable that refers indirectly or "points to" another variable or data object. For example, if **x** is a variable of type **float** and **ptr_x** is a pointer variable, then the expression

```
ptr_x = &x;
```

causes the address of the variable **x** to be placed in the pointer variable **ptr_x** (see Figure 10.3).

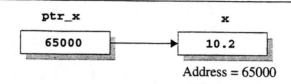

Address = 65000

Figure 10.3   Pointer variables and address.

Declaring Pointer Variables

Like all other variables in a C program, a pointer variable must be declared before it can be used. The syntax for declaring a pointer variable is

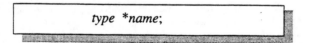

type **name*;

where *type* is a valid C data type (such as **int, float, char,** or **double**) and *name* is the name of the pointer variable. The type specifier indicates the type of variable pointed to, and the asterisk (*) preceding the variable name indicates that the variable is a pointer. A pointer variable can have any legal variable name. Thus, to define a pointer variable **ptr** that points to a variable of type **int**, we can write

```
int *ptr;
```

The declaration states that **ptr** is a pointer variable that points to a data object of type **int**. The asterisk (*) in the declaration is the *indirection* or dereferencing operator. The indirection operator when placed immediately before a pointer variable refers to the value stored at the address pointed to by the pointer variable. Thus in the foregoing declaration **ptr** is a pointer variable that points to a variable of type **int**, and ***ptr** is the integer value.

It is important to note that a pointer variable itself does not have a type in the same sense as, say, an **int** or **float** variable. In the declaration for an ordinary variable, the type specifier indicates the type of value that will be stored in the variable. However, in the declaration for a pointer variable, the type specifier indicates the type of value of the data object that the pointer variable points to rather than the type of value of the pointer variable itself. In fact, we need not be concerned with the type of value of a pointer variable, since this is hardware dependent and different systems use different schemes for representing memory addresses. On our system, addresses are represented by unsigned integers, while on other systems addresses may be represented by long integers.

When declaring pointer variables, we must indicate what type of data object the pointer variable points to. For example, to declare a pointer variable that points to a **float**, we can use the declaration

```
float *ptr_fl;   /* pointer to float variable */
```

The variable **ptr_fl** is a pointer variable that points to a data object of type **float**. We can also define pointers to variables of type **double** and **char** as follows:

```
double *ptr_db;  /* pointer to double variable */
char *ptrc;      /* pointer to char variable   */
```

A pointer variable in C holds the address of a particular data type. The compiler has to know what type of value is stored at the address pointed to by the pointer variable for it to able to retrieve correctly the value stored at that address. The different data types are stored differently and require different amounts of storage, and so a knowledge of the data type is needed to retrieve the value stored at a given address. Also, since all pointer arithmetic is done relative to the type of value that the pointer points to, it is important to declare our pointers correctly. This means, that we cannot declare a pointer to point to a variable of type **int** and then later use it to store the address of a variable of type **float**.

When declaring more than one pointer variable on the same line, each variable should be preceded by the indirection (*) operator. For example, the statement

```
float *ptr1, *ptr2;
```

declares two pointer variables, **ptr1** and **ptr2**. Each can point to a variable of type **float**. In the statement

```
float *ptr1, ptr2;
```

the second indirection operator (*) is omitted. This statement declares a pointer variable **ptr1** and an ordinary **float** variable **ptr2**.

Initializing Pointers

After a pointer has been declared, it must be initialized so that it points to a meaningful address in memory. To initialize a pointer, we assign it the address of a variable of the same type that the pointer points to. For example, the statements

```
int x = 25;
int *ptr_x;
ptr_x = &x;
```

create an integer variable **x** and a pointer variable **ptr_x** that points to a variable of type **int**. The third statement

```
ptr_x = &x;
```

uses the address-of operator (**&**) to obtain the address of **x** and then assigns this address to the pointer variable **ptr_x**. Thus **ptr_x** now contains the address (not the value) of **x**. We can combine the declaration and initialization in one statement as in

```
int x = 25;
int *ptr_x = &x;
```

Suppose that the address of the integer variable **x** is 65500. Then the value of **ptr_x** will be 65500. Figure 10.4 illustrates this.

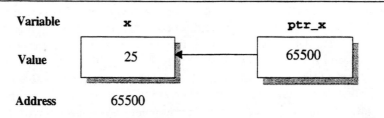

Figure 10.4   Pointer initialization.

It is important that we initialize pointers before using them in our programs. A pointer that has not been initialized can point anywhere in memory. Using a pointer that has not been initialized or using an incorrectly initialized pointer will most likely cause your program or the operating system to crash. A common example of incorrect pointer initialization is

```
int x = 25;
int *ptr;
ptr = x;    /* incorrect initialization! */
```

In the statement

```
ptr = x;    /* incorrect initialization! */
```

the value of the variable **x** is assigned to the pointer variable **ptr** rather than the address of **x**. Thus the variable **ptr** points to memory location 25 rather than the address of variable **x**. Figure 10.5 illustrates this.

A pointer variable may be initialized to null (or zero). In C, the value zero is

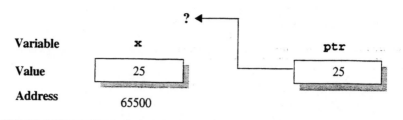

Figure 10.5   Incorrect pointer assignment.

not a valid memory address and so a pointer that is initialized to null means that the
pointer is not pointing to anything. Null pointers are typically used by functions
that return pointers to signal that an error has occurred. For example, the library
functions **malloc()** and **calloc()** that perform dynamic memory allocation
return null pointers if they are not able to allocate the requested amount of memory.
These library functions are described in Chapter 17.

10.3   THE INDIRECTION OPERATOR (*)

Once a pointer has been initialized to point to the address of a variable, we can
access the value stored in the variable using the *indirection* or dereferencing
operator (*). If **ptr** is a pointer variable, then the expression

```
*ptr
```

gives the value stored at the address pointed to by **ptr**. When the indirection
operator (*) appears in front of a pointer variable, the expression states that we
want the value stored at the address pointed to by the pointer variable rather than
the value of the pointer variable itself. Thus pointers provide an alternative means
of accessing and even changing the values of variables. The next example
illustrates some of the basic features of pointers.

Example 10.2   Basic Pointer Operations

The program shown in Figure 10.6 demonstrates some of the basic pointer
operations. The program creates a variable **x** of type **float** and assigns it a value
of 25. It also creates a pointer variable **ptr**, which is a pointer to type **float**. The
statement

```
float *ptr;
```

creates the pointer variable **ptr**, and the statement

```
ptr = &x
```

```
/*************************************************************/
/*  pointers.c  -- Basic Pointer Operations                 */
/*                                                           */
/*  Illustrates the basic features of pointers              */
/*                                                           */
/*************************************************************/
#include <stdio.h>

main()
{
    float x = 25.0;
    float *ptr;         /* pointer to type float */

    ptr = &x;           /* initialize ptr so it points to x */

    printf("\n Value of x = %f", x);
    printf("\n Address of x = %u", &x);
    printf("\n Value of ptr = %u", ptr);
    printf("\n Value stored at location pointed to by ptr = %f",
      *ptr);

    *ptr = 10.0;        /* change x indirectly */
    printf("\n \n New value of x = %f", x);
}
```

Program output

```
Value of x = 25.000000
Address of x = 65496
Value of ptr = 65496
Value stored at location pointed to by ptr = 25.000000

New value of x = 10.000000
```

Figure 10.6   Basic pointer operations.

assigns the address of **x** to **ptr**:

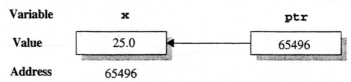

The first **printf()** statement prints the value of **x**. The second **printf()** statement prints the address of **x**. The third **printf()** statement prints the value of **ptr**. Since **ptr** was assigned the address of **x** using the address-of operator (**&**), the value contained in **ptr** is the address of **x**. The fourth **printf()** statement

```
printf("\n Value stored at location pointed to by ptr = %f",*ptr);
```

illustrates how we can obtain the value of **x** indirectly by using the indirection operator **. Since `ptr` points to **x**, the expression

```
*ptr;
```

returns the value of **x**.

The next statement demonstrates how we can indirectly change the value of **x** using `ptr`. The statement

```
*ptr = 10.0;        /* change x indirectly */
```

assigns the value 10.0 to **x**. This statement has the same effect as the statement

```
x = 10.0;
```

since `ptr` points to the address of **x**. Thus the contents of **x** are changed indirectly through the pointer `ptr`.

The indirection operator is a unary operator, which means that it has one operand. It has the same precedence as the other unary operators and "right to left" associativity. The indirection operator is the complement of the address-of operator. Suppose we declare

```
float a=10., b=20., *ptr;
```

Then the two statements

```
ptr = &a;
b = *ptr;
```

are equivalent to

```
b = *&a;
```

which in turn is equivalent to

```
b = a;
```

Figure 10.7 illustrates these operations assuming that the address of **a** is 65500.

Like other variables, pointers may appear on the right side of an assignment statement. For example, the statements

```
int x = 30;
int *ptr1, *ptr2;
ptr1 = &x;
ptr2 = ptr1;
```

create an integer variable **x** and two pointer variables `ptr1` and `ptr2`. The statement

```
ptr1 = &x;
```

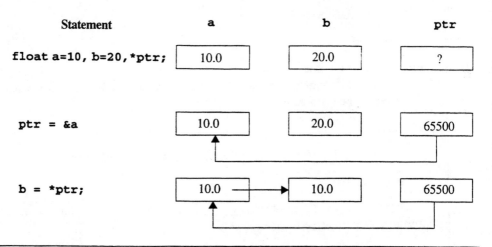

Figure 10.7   Using indirection to reassign the value of a variable.

assigns the address of **x** to **ptr1**. The statement

    ptr2 = ptr1;

assigns the value of **ptr1** to **ptr2**. Since **ptr1** points to **x**, the effect of the assignment is to make **ptr2** also point to **x**. The effect of these statements is shown in Figure 10.8, assuming that **x** has the address 65000.

Statement	x	ptr1	ptr2
int x = 30;	30		
int *ptr1, *ptr2;	30	?	?
ptr1 = &x;	30	65000	?
ptr2 = ptr1;	30	65000	65000

Figure 10.8   Pointer assignment.

Example 10.3   Interchanging Values of Variables with Pointers

PROBLEM STATEMENT: Write a program that uses pointers to interchange the values of two variables.

SOLUTION: The program shown in Figure 10.9 uses the pointers `ptr_i` and `ptr_j` to indirectly interchange the values of the variables `i` and `j`. The program creates two integer variables `i` and `j` and assigns the value 10 to `i` and 20 to `j`. The program also creates a third integer variable called **temp**. The statement

```
int *ptr_i, *ptr_j;        /* pointers to i and j   */
```

creates two pointer variables `prt_i` and `ptr_j`. The pointers are initialized in the statements

```
ptr_i = &i;                /* ptr_i points to i     */
ptr_j = &j;                /* ptr_j points to j     */
```

so that `ptr_i` points to `i` and `ptr_j` points to `j`. The statement

```
temp = *ptr_j;             /* save value of j in temp */
```

uses the indirection operator (`*`) to save the value of `j` in the temporary variable **temp** so that it is not lost in the interchange. This statement is equivalent to

```
temp = j;
```

The statement

```
*ptr_j = *ptr_i;           /* set j equal to i        */
```

indirectly assigns the value of `i` to `j`. Since `ptr_j` points to `j`, the expression `*ptr_j` returns the value stored in `j`. Also, since `ptr_i` points to `i` the value is saved at the address pointed to by `ptr_i`, which is the address of the variable `i`. Thus the statement

```
*ptr_j = *ptr_i ;          /* set j equal to i        */
```

is equivalent to

```
j = i;
```

The statement

```
*ptr_i = temp;             /* set i equal to temp     */
```

assigns the value stored in **temp** to `i`.

    Table 10.1 shows the value of the variables after each statement has been executed. We are assuming that the address of `i` is 65000 and the address of `j` is 65002.

```
/****************************************************************/
/*  swap.c                                                    */
/*  Interchanges two variables indirectly using pointers      */
/****************************************************************/
#include <stdio.h>

main()
{
    int i=10, j = 20, temp;
    int *ptr_i, *ptr_j;          /* pointers to i and j    */

    ptr_i = &i;                  /* ptr_i points to i      */
    ptr_j = &j;                  /* ptr_j points to j      */

    printf("\n Initial values: i = %d, j = %d", i,j);

    temp = *ptr_j;               /* save value of j in temp */
    *ptr_j = *ptr_i;             /* set j equal to i       */
    *ptr_i = temp;               /* set i equal to temp    */

    printf("\n Final values:   i = %d, j = %d", i,j);
}
```

```
Initial values: i = 10, j = 20
Final values:   i = 20, j = 10
```

Figure 10.9   Interchanging values of variables using pointers.

Table 10.1: Trace table for Example 10.3

Statement	i	j	temp	ptr_i	ptr_j
int i = 10,j=20,temp	10	20	?		
int *ptr_i, *ptr_j	10	20	?	?	?
ptr_i = &i	10	20	?	65000	?
ptr_j = &j	10	20	?	65000	65002
temp = *ptr_j	10	20	20	65000	65002
*ptr_j = *ptr_i	10	10	20	65000	65002
*ptr_i = temp;	20	10	20	65000	65002

10.4 POINTERS AND ARRAYS

There is a very close relationship between pointers and arrays in C. The name of an array (without subscripts) is actually a pointer constant whose value is the address of the first element of the array. Whenever we create an array, C creates a pointer constant which has the same name as the name of the array. This pointer constant always points to the first element of the array. For example, if **x[]** is an array of integers that has been defined as

```
static int x[5] = {1, 2, 4, 8, 16};
```

then the array name **x** holds the address of the first element of the array, that is

```
x == &x[0];
```

If the first element of the array **x[]** is stored at address 404, then the value of **x** is 404. The value of **&x[0]** is also 404. This is illustrated in the next example.

Example 10.4   Array Name and Array Address

The program shown in Figure 10.10 prints the addresses of all the elements of an array **x[]** if type **int**. The array consists of five elements. The program prints the value of each element and the address of each element of the array. The program also prints the value stored in the array name **x**. The output from the program is also shown in Figure 10.10. The value of **x** is 404, which corresponds to the address of the first element of the array. Notice that the elements of the array are stored in contiguous memory locations and the difference between the addresses of consecutive elements is two. Thus the address of the first element **x[0]** is 404, the address of the second element **x[1]** is 406, and so on. On our system a variable of type **int** requires 2 bytes of storage so the difference in the addresses of successive elements is two.

The relationship between the array name and the address of the array of the previous example is as follows.

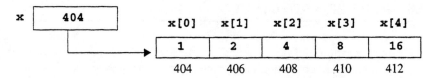

Since the array name contains the address of the first element of the array, the array

```
/****************************************************************/
/*  ary_name.c    - Array names and addresses                  */
/*                                                              */
/*  Prints the address of each element of an array and the     */
/*  value stored in the array name.                            */
/*                                                              */
/****************************************************************/
#include <stdio.h>

main()
   {
   static int x[5] = {1,2,4,8,16};
   int i;
   printf("\n Element  Address  Value ");

   for (i = 0; i < 5; ++i)
      printf("\n %d          %u       %d", i+1, &x[i], x[i]);

   printf("\n The value stored in the array name x is %u", x);
   }
```

Program output

```
Element   Address   Value
1         404       1
2         406       2
3         408       4
4         410       8
5         412       16
The value stored in the array name x is 404
```

Figure 10.10   Array name and array address.

name is a pointer to the first element of the array. There is, however, one important difference between a pointer variable and an array name. The array name is a *pointer constant* and *not* a pointer variable, which means that the value of **x** cannot be changed by an assignment statement or any other statement. The following statements are illegal:

```
x = &x[2];        /* illegal! */
x = x + 2;        /* illegal! */
++x;              /* illegal! */
```

since they all attempt to change the value of **x** which is a constant.

10.5 POINTER ARITHMETIC

C supports only a few basic operations on pointers. These include incrementing and decremeting pointers, adding or subtracting an integer from a pointer, and subtracting two pointers. It is also possible to compare two pointers using a relational operator. It is illegal to add two pointers, to multiply two pointers, or to divide one pointer by another. Pointers represent addresses, so operations such as multiplication and division are illegal since they do not yield meaningful addresses.

Example 10.5 Pointer Arithmetic

Consider the following statements:

```
int x[5] = {1, 2, 4, 8, 16};
int *ptr;
ptr = x;
```

The first statement creates an array **x[]** containing five elements of type **int**. The second statement creates a pointer variable called **ptr**. The third statement assigns the address of the first element of the array to **ptr**. If the address of the first element of the array is 404 then the expression **ptr=x** will result in **ptr** being assigned the value 404. This is shown as follows:

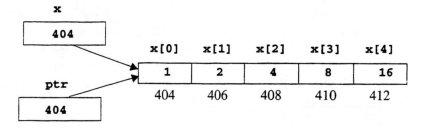

The expression

```
ptr++
```

increments the pointer variable **ptr**. The effect of this operation is that **ptr** now points to the *next* element of the array, which is **x[1]**. Thus **ptr** will be assigned the value 406. The variable **ptr** was defined to point to a variable of type **int**, so the increment operation actually adds 2 bytes to the address stored in **ptr** (since on our system an int requires 2 bytes of storage), as follows:

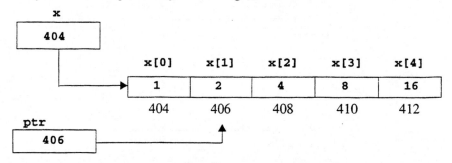

We can also add or subtract an integer value from a pointer. For example, the statement

```
    ptr +=2;
```

moves **ptr** forward *two elements*. Thus, if **ptr** were pointing at the second element of the array **x[]**, the expression would cause it to point to the fourth element, **x[3]**, of the array. The value stored in **ptr** after the operation is 408 + 4 = 412, or 408 + 2 * **sizeof**(int).

Decremeting a pointer is similar to incrementing. The expression

```
    --ptr;
```

moves **ptr** back one element in the array, so that if it were pointing to the fourth element **x[3]**, it will now point to the third element **x[3]**. Again, the compiler automatically adjusts the address so that **ptr** is pointing to the previous element. Figure 10.11 illustrates the foregoing sequence of operations.

When performing pointer arithmetic we should always keep in mind that pointer arithmetic is scaled to the size of the data object that the pointer references. If **ptr** had been declared as a pointer to a variable of type **float**, then the increment operation would have resulted in 4 bytes being added to the address stored in **ptr**. Since the compiler knows the size of the data object that the pointer

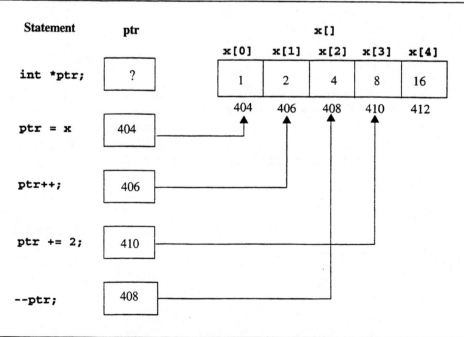

Figure 10.11   Pointer arithmetic

is pointing to, it adjusts the value of pointer accordingly. It is precisely for this reason, that when we declare a pointer variable, we have to also tell the compiler what type of value the pointer will point to.

Example 10.6   Pointer Arithmetic

Consider the following code fragment:

```
double y[5] = {1.0, 6.0, 10.5, 12.8, 30.6};
double ptr_dbl;
ptr_dbl = y;
```

The first statement creates an array **y[]** of type **double** containing four elements and initializes the elements of the array. The second statement creates a pointer to type **double** called **ptr_dbl**. The third statement initializes the pointer variable so that it points to the first element of the array, **y[0]**. If we assume that the first element **y[0]** is stored at address 500, then the third statement will assign the value 500 to **ptr_dbl**.

The statement

```
++ptr_dbl;
```

will result in **ptr_dbl** pointing to the next element in the array **y[1]**. Since on our system a value of type **double** requires 8 bytes of storage, this will result in **ptr_dbl** being assigned the value 508. Thus, in this case, the increment operation results in 8 bytes being added to the address stored in **ptr_dbl**.

The expression

```
ptr_dbl=+3;
```

will cause **ptr_dbl** to point to the fifth element of the array, **y[4]**. The value stored in **ptr_dbl** after the preceding statement has been executed will by 508 + 3(8) = 532. The expression

```
ptr_dbl -=2;
```

will result in **ptr_dbl** pointing to the third element of the array, **y[2]**. The value stored in **ptr_dbl** will now be 532 - 2(8) = 516. Figure 10.12 illustrates the sequence of operations.

When using pointers to access array elements, we should be careful not to exceed the bounds of the array. C does not perform any bounds checking on arrays, and it is the programmer's responsibility to make sure that all pointer operations result in addresses that are within the bounds of an array.

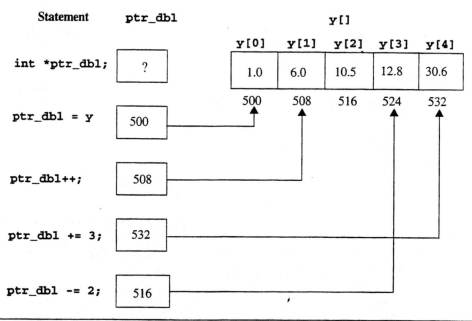

Figure 10.12   Pointer arithmetic.

We can subtract one pointer from another. If **ptr1** and **ptr2** are two pointers that point to elements within the same array then the expression

        ptr1 - ptr2

can be used to determine how far the two pointers are in the array. If **ptr1 - ptr2** is positive, then **ptr1** points to an element beyond the element pointed to by **ptr2**. If **ptr1 - ptr2** is negative, then **ptr2** points to an element beyond the element pointed to by **ptr1**. The result gives the offset in *elements* between the two pointers. For example, if **ptr1** points to the fourth element of an array and **ptr2** points to the second element of the array, then the value of **ptr1 - ptr2** will be 2.

One of the conveniences of pointer arithmetic is that the C compiler automatically performs the scaling needed for the different data types. This frees the programmer from having to think about actual addresses or the size of a particular data object. It also makes pointer expressions portable from one system to another.

10.6   ARRAY NOTATION AND POINTER NOTATION

In all the examples in Chapter 9, we used the array name followed by a subscript in square brackets to access the individual elements of an array. We call this method of representing array elements *array notation*. Because of the close relationship between arrays and pointers, we can use an alternative notation that uses pointer variables to access the individual elements of an array. We will call this *pointer notation* to distinguish it from array notation in which we used subscripts to access individual array elements.

Given the definition

```
int y[10];
```

we reference the fifth element of the array `y[]` using array notation by writing

```
y[4]
```

We can also use pointer notation to reference the fifth element of the array by writing

```
*(y + 4)
```

Since `y` is the address of the first element of the array, `y + 4` is the address of the fifth element of the array. The indirection operator (`*`) gives the value stored at the address indicated by `y + 4`.

Example 10.7   Pointer and Array Notation

PROBLEM STATEMENT: Write two versions of a program that lists the elements of an array and computes the sum of all the elements of the array. The first version of the program should use array notation. The second version of the program should use pointer notation.

SOLUTION: The two versions of a program are shown in Figures 10.13 and 10.14. The first version, (Figure 10.13) uses the familiar array notation presented in Chapter 9. The second version (Figure 10.14) uses pointer notation. Both programs use a **for** loop to compute the sum of all elements of the array. The sum is stored in the variable **sum.**

In the array version of the program, the value contained in element `x[i]` is added to the variable **sum** in the statement

```
sum +=x[i];
```

In the pointer version of the program the following statement adds the value of element *i* to the variable **sum.**

```
sum += *(x + i);
```

The expression

```
*(x + i)
```

gives the value stored at the address given by `(x + i)`.

```
/***********************************************************/
/*   sum_ary1.c - Sum of Elements of Array Using Array Notation */
/*                                                         */
/*   Lists the elements and computes the sum of all elements  */
/*   of an array using array notation.                     */
/***********************************************************/
#include <stdio.h>

main()
{
    static int x[5] = {1, 2, 4, 8, 16};
    int i, sum=0;

    for (i = 0; i < 5; ++i)
        {
        printf("\n x[%d] = %d", i, x[i]);
        sum += x[i];
        }

    printf("\n Sum of all elements is %d", sum);
}
```

Figure 10.13   A program to compute the sum of the elements of an array using array notation.

```
/****************************************************************/
/*   sum_ary2.c -- Sum of Elements of Array Using Pointer Notation */
/*                                                            */
/*   Lists the elements and computes the sum of all elements   */
/*   of an array using pointer notation                       */
/****************************************************************/
#include <stdio.h>

main()
{
    static int x[5] = {1, 2, 4, 8, 16};
    int i, sum=0;

    for (i = 0; i < 5; ++i)
        {
        printf("\n x[%d] = %d", i, *(x + i));
        sum += *(x + i);
        }

    printf("\n Sum of all elements is %d", sum);
}
```

Figure 10.14   A program to compute the sum of the elements of using pointer notation.

Although an array name is a constant that points to the first element of an array and its value cannot be changed, we can assign its value to another pointer variable, which we can then alter. For example, the statements

```
int x[5] = {1, 2, 4, 8, 16};
int *ptr = x;
```

create an array `x[]` and a pointer variable `ptr`. The pointer variable is initialized so that it contains the address of the first element of the array. Since `ptr` is a pointer variable we can change its value. The next example illustrates this.

Example 10.8   Sum Elements of Array Using a Pointer Variable

The program shown in Figure 10.15 is a variation of the pointer version of the program of the previous example that was presented in Figure 10.14. The program lists the elements of the array `x[]` and computes the sum of all elements. However, it uses a pointer variable, `ptr`, to access each element of the array.

The statement

```
ptr = x ;
```

initializes the pointer variable `ptr` so it points to the first element of the array, `x[0]`. The program uses `ptr` in a **for** loop to access each element of the array. The statement

```
sum += *ptr;
```

adds the value stored at the address pointed to by `ptr` to `sum`, and the statement

```
++ptr;
```

increments `ptr` by 1, so that it now points to the next element of the array. Notice that since `ptr` is a pointer variable, we can change its value during program execution.

The equivalence of pointer notation and array notation is one of the chief strengths of C since it allows us to use pointers to access individual elements of an array. In many situations it does not matter whether you use pointer notation or array notation. The use of pointer notation does, however, result in more efficient processing. Many C programmers prefer to use pointer notation when working with arrays, especially strings, so you need to be familiar with both notations.

```
/****************************************************************/
/*  sum_ary3.c                                                  */
/*  Lists the elements and computes the sum of all elements     */
/*  of an array using a pointer variable                        */
/****************************************************************/
#include <stdio.h>

main()
{
    static int x[5] = {1, 2, 4, 8, 16};
    int *ptr, i, sum=0;

    ptr = x;

    for (i = 0; i < 5; ++i)
        {
        printf("\n x[%d] = %d", i, *ptr);
        sum += *ptr;
        ++ptr;
        }

    printf("\n Sum of all elements is %d", sum);
}
```

Figure 10.15   Computing the sum of the elements of an array using a
                    pointer variable.

10.7 POINTERS AS FUNCTION ARGUMENTS

The arguments in a C function are passed by value which means that the
function receives copies of the arguments. Any changes made to the function
arguments affect the copies of the arguments passed to the function and not the
original arguments. Until now, the only way in which our functions could return
information back to the calling program was through the **return** statement. A
major limitation of the **return** statement is that it can return only a single value.
There are many situations in which a function must return more than one value. We
can accomplish this through the use of pointers. In fact, one of the more common
uses of pointers is as arguments to functions since this allows a function to return
multiple values.

When we pass a pointer to a function as an argument, we are passing the
address of the variable to the function. The function can use this address to access
or to change the variable stored at the address. To illustrate the basic concept
involved in passing a pointer to a function, we will write a simple function that
doubles its argument. We cannot write the function as follows:

```
void double_it(float x)
{
    x *= 2.0;
}
```

Since the function receives a copy of the argument and not the original argument, any changes made to **x** are made to the copy of **x** passed to the function **double_it()** and not to the original variable and are thus not visible to the calling function. We could, of course, write the function using a **return** statement

```
float double_it(float x)
{
    return (2.0 * x);
}
```

We could then call the function as

```
x = double_it(x);
```

which would result in the value returned by the function **double_it()** being stored in **x**, hence **x** would now have the value **2. * x**.

A second approach is to use a pointer variable as the argument to the function. The function definition for **double_it()** using a pointer as the argument is as follows:

```
void double_it(float *ptr_x)
{
    *ptr_x *= 2.0;
}
```

The argument to the function is a pointer variable **ptr_x**. Thus the function now receives the address of a variable of type **float**.

To call this function we use the statement

```
double_it(&x);
```

In the function call, the variable **x** is preceded by the address-of operator (**&**) since we are now passing the address of the variable **x** to the function and not the value of **x**. The function can use this address to gain access to the variable stored at this address and change the value of the variable if it needs to do so. This address in the formal parameter **ptr_x** in the function definition. The statement in the function **double_it()**

```
*ptr_x = *= 2.0;
```

uses the indirection operator to change the value stored at the address **ptr_x** that was passed to the function by the invoking function.

Example 10.9   Exchanging Values Using Pointer Arguments

PROBLEM DEFINITION: Write a function to exchange the value of two variables. The function should have two parameters, both of type pointer to **float** containing the address of the two variables whose values are to be interchanged. The function header for the function is

```
void exchange(float *ptr_x, *ptr_y)
```

SOLUTION: The function **exchange()** is shown in Figure 10.16. The function exchanges the values of the variables **x** and **y**. The function receives two arguments. Both arguments are pointers to type **float**. In the function call

```
exchange(&x, &y);
```

the addresses of the variables **x** and **y** are passed to the to the function **exchange()**. The function declares a variable called **temp** of type **float** for temporary storage. The values of **x** and **y** are changed by the following statements:

```
temp = *ptr_x;
*ptr_x = *ptr_y;
*ptr_y = temp;
```

The statement

```
temp = *ptr_x;
```

uses the indirection operator to save the value of the variable that is stored at the address indicated by **ptr_x** in the variable **temp**. The statement

```
*ptr_x = *ptr_y;
```

assigns the value of **y** to **x**. The expression ***ptr_y** represents the value stored at the address indicated by **ptr_x**, and the expression ***ptr_x** represents the value stored at the address contained in **ptr_x**. Thus the foregoing statement results in the value of **y** being stored in **x**. The statement

```
*ptr_y = temp;
```

assigns the value stored in **temp** to **y**. Again the indirection operator is used to access the variable stored at the address contained in **ptr_y**. The expression ***ptr_y** represents the value stored in **y**. Since the value of **x** was stored in **temp**, the foregoing statement results in the value of **x** being stored in the variable **y**. Table 10.2 shows the trace table for function **exchange()**. We are assuming that the address of **x** is 2000 and the address of **y** is 2004.

```
/******************************************************************/
/*   exchange.c   - Exchange Values of Two Variables            */
/*                                                              */
/*   Exchanges the values of two variables using pointers as    */
/*   arguments to a function.                                   */
/******************************************************************/
#include <stdio.h>

void main(void);
void exchange(float *ptr_x,float *ptr_y);

void main(void)
{
   float x = 10.0, y = 20.0;

   printf("\n Initial values: x = %f, y = %f", x,y);
   exchange(&x,&y);
   printf("\n Final values:   x = %f, y = %f", x,y);
}

void exchange(float *ptr_x,float *ptr_y)
{
   float temp;

   temp = *ptr_x;
   *ptr_x = *ptr_y;
   *ptr_y = temp;
}
```

Program output

```
Initial values: x = 10.000000, y = 20.000000
Final values:   x = 20.000000, y = 10.000000
```

Figure 10.16   A program to interchange the values of two variables using pointers as function arguments.

Table 10.2: Trace table for function `exchange()`

Variable	x	y	ptr_x	ptr_y	temp
float temp	10.0	20.0	2000	2004	?
temp = *ptr_x	10	20	2000	2004	10.0
*ptr_x = *ptr_y	20.0	20.0	2000	2004	10.0
*ptr_y = temp	20.0	10.0	2000	2004	10.0

10.8   PROGRAMMING PROJECT: SOLUTION OF SIMULTANEOUS EQUATIONS

The linear system of equations

$$a_1 x + b_1 y = c_1 \tag{10.1}$$

$$a_2 x + b_2 y = c_2 \tag{10.2}$$

when solved for x and y yields

$$x = \frac{c_1 b_2 - c_2 b_1}{a_1 b_2 - a_2 b_1} \tag{10.3}$$

$$y = \frac{a_1 c_2 - a_2 c_1}{a_1 b_2 - a_2 b_1} \tag{10.4}$$

This system is said to be *undefined* if

$$a_1 b_2 - a_2 b_1 = 0$$

and

$$c_1 b_2 - c_2 b_1 \neq 0$$

$$a_1 c_2 - a_2 c_1 \neq 0$$

and is said to be *indeterminate* if

$$a_1 b_2 - a_2 b_1 = 0$$

and

$$c_1 b_2 - c_2 b_1 = 0$$

$$a_1 c_2 - a_2 c_1 = 0$$

Problem Statement

Write a C function called **simult_comp()** that when given a_1, b_1, c_1, a_2, b_2, and c_2, solves the preceding system of equations. The function should return the values of x and y using pointers. The function should also return a value of type **int**, indicating the existence of a solution as follows:

value returned = 0, solution exists

value returned = 1, the system is undefined

value returned = 2, the system is indeterminate

Write a separate function called **get_data()** to read in the input data and a **main()** function. Function **main()** should call **get_data()** and **simult_comp()**. It should also test for the existence of a solution by examining the value returned by **simult_comp()** and display the result.

Problem Analysis

The important variables are as follows:

Input Variables

coefficients a_1, b_1, and c_1 of first equation (**double a1, b1, c1**)

coefficients a_2, b_2, and c_2 of second equation (**double a2, b2, c2**)

Output Variables

result — flag returned from computational function (**int result**)

solution — x and y (**double x, y**)

Algorithm

The major task performed by the program are the following:

1. Read input data.
2. Compute roots.
3. Print results.

The first task is handled by the function **get_input()**, the second by the function **simult_comp()**, and the last by **main()** itself. The structure chart is as follows:

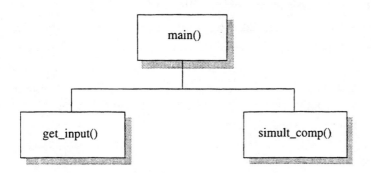

Algorithm for `main()`

1. Call `get_input()` to read in a_1, b_1, c_1 a_2, b_2, and c_2.
2. Call `simult_comp()` to determine the type of solution and to compute x and y.
3. If `result` = 1 then
    3.1 Print "System is undefined"
4. else if `result` = 2 then
    4.1 Print "System is indeterminate"
5. else
    5.1 Print x and y.

Algorithm for `get_input()`

1. Read `a1`, `b1`, and `c1` and store these at the addresses indicated by `ptr_a1`, `ptr_b1`, and `ptr_c1`.
2. Read `a2`, `b2`, and `c2` and store that at the addresses indicated by `ptr_a2`, `ptr_b2`, and `ptr_c2`.

Algorithm for `simult_comp()`

1. Compute the numerator in Equation (10.3) `numer1` from
    ```
    numer1 = c1 * b1 - c2 * b1;
    ```
2. Compute the numerator in Equation (10.4) `numer2` from
    ```
    numer2 = a1 * c2 - a2 * c1;
    ```
3. Compute the denominator `denom` from
    ```
    denom = a1 * b2 - a2 * b1;
    ```
4. If (`denom`, `numer1`, and `numer2` are all zero) then
    4.1 the system is indeterminate so return a value of 2
5. Else if (denom is `zero` and `numer1` and `numer2` are not `zero`) then
    5.1 the system is undefined so return a value of 1
6. Else
    6.1 compute x and y from Equations (10.3) and (10.4) and store the result at the addresses indicated by `ptr_x` and `ptr_y`.
    6.2 return a value of 0.

Program

The program is shown in Figure 10.17. The program consists of three functions, `main()`, `get_data()`, and `simult_comp()`. Function `main()` first calls **get_data()** to obtain the necessary input. It then calls **simult_comp()**. Based on the value returned by **simult_comp()**, it then prints the result of the computation.

Function **get_data()** obtains user input. The function header for **get_data()** is

```
void get_input(double *ptr_a1,double *ptr_b1,double
        *ptr_c1,double *ptr_a2,double *ptr_b2,double *ptr_c2)
```

The function has six arguments, all of which are pointers to type **double**. The function returns the values of a_1, b_1, c_1, a_2, b_2, and c_2 through these pointers. In the call to **get_data()** the address of the variables **a1**, **b1**, **c1**, **a2**, **b2**, and **c2** is passed. The call statement is

```
get_input(&a1,&b1,&c1,&a2,&b2,&c2);
```

The address of operator (**&**) in front of each argument indicates that it is the address of the variable that is being passed to **get_data()**. Notice also that there is no address-of operator (**&**) in front of the variables in the **scanf()** statements in function **get_data()**. For example, in the statement

```
scanf("%lf %lf %lf", ptr_a1,ptr_b1,ptr_c1);
```

there is no address-of operator in front of the variables **ptr_a1**, **ptr_b1**, and **ptr_c1**. This is because these variables are pointers and represent addresses.

The computations are performed in the function **simult_comp()**. The function header for **simult_comp()** is

```
int simult_comp(double a1, double b1,double c1,double a2,
        double b2,double c2,double *ptr_x, double *ptr_y)
```

The function has eight parameters. The first six are variables of type **double** and represent input parameters. The last two are pointers to type **double**. The values of x and y are returned though these pointers. The function also returns a value of type **int** that represents the status of the solution. The function is called by **main()** as follows:

```
result = simult_comp(a1,b1,c1,a2,b2,c2,&x,&y);
```

In the function call the address of **x** and **y** is passed to **simult_comp()**. The function **simult_comp()** uses these addresses to modify the values of **x** and **y**. In the statement

```
*ptr_x = numer1 / denom;
```

the expression ***ptr_x** represents the value stored at the address contained in

```
/*****************************************************************/
/*    simult2.c  -- Linear Simultaneous Equations              */
/*                                                             */
/*    This program solves the system of linear equations       */
/*              a1x + b1y = c1                                  */
/*              a2x + b2y = c2                                  */
/*    for x and y. It also checks the equations to determine if */
/*    the system is undefined or indeterminate and prints the  */
/*    appropriate error message.                               */
/*****************************************************************/
#include <stdio.h>
#include <math.h>

#define NEARLY_ZERO  1e-40        /* a small value close to zero */

/* function prototypes */
void get_input(double *ptr_a1,double *ptr_b1,double *ptr_c1,
               double *ptr_a2,double *ptr_b2, double *ptr_c2);
int solve(double a1,double b1,double c1,double a2, double b2,
          double c2,double *ptr_x, double *ptr_y);

main()
{
    double a1,b1,c1,a2,b2,c2;      /* coefficients */
    double x,y;                    /* solution     */
    int result;                    /* status flag  */

    /* get input data */
    get_input(&a1,&b1,&c1,&a2,&b2,&c2);

    /* solve equations */
    result = solve(a1,b1,c1,a2,b2,c2,&x,&y);

    /* display results */
    if (result == 1)
      printf("\n The system is undefined");
    else if (result == 2)
      printf("\n The system is indeterminate");
    else
      {
      printf("\n The solution is: ");
      printf("\n x = %lf y = %lf",x,y);
      }
}


/*----------------------------------------------------------------*/
/* Obtains input data                                            */
/*                                                               */
/* Input Parameters                                              */
/*    None                                                       */
/*                                                               */
/* Output Parameters                                             */
/*   *ptr_a1, *ptr_b1, *ptr_c1 - coefficients of first equation */
/*   *ptr_a2, *ptr_b2, *ptr_c2 - coefficients of second equation*/
/*----------------------------------------------------------------*/
```

Figure 10.17   A program for solving simultaneous equations.

```
void get_input(double *ptr_a1,double *ptr_b1,double *ptr_c1,
               double *ptr_a2,double *ptr_b2,double *ptr_c2)
{
   printf("\n Enter a1 b1 and c1: ");
   scanf("%lf %lf %lf", ptr_a1,ptr_b1,ptr_c1);

   printf("\n Enter a2 b2 and c2: ");
   scanf("%lf %lf %lf", ptr_a2,ptr_b2,ptr_c2);
}


/*-------------------------------------------------------------------*/
/* Solves the system of equations                                    */
/*    a1x + b1y = c1                                                  */
/*    a2x + b2y = c2                                                  */
/*                                                                   */
/*   Input Parameters                                                */
/*    a1, b1, c1 - coefficients of first equation                    */
/*    a2, b2, c2 - coefficients of second equation                   */
/*                                                                   */
/*   Output Parameters                                               */
/*    *ptr_x, *ptr_y - solution:  x, y                               */
/*                                                                   */
/*   Returns                                                         */
/*     0 - if solution exists                                        */
/*     1 - is system is undefined                                    */
/*     2 - if system is indeterminate                                */
/*-------------------------------------------------------------------*/
int solve(double a1, double b1,double c1,double a2, double b2,
          double c2,double *ptr_x, double *ptr_y)
{
   double numer1,numer2,denom;

   numer1 = c1 * b2 - c2 * b1;
   numer2 = a1 * c2 - a2 * c1;
   denom = a1 * b2 - a2 * b1;
   printf("Numer1 =%lf numer2= %lf, denom = %lf",numer1,numer2,denom);
   if ( fabs(denom) <= NEARLY_ZERO)
      {
      if ( fabs(numer1) <= NEARLY_ZERO &&
           fabs(numer2) <= NEARLY_ZERO )
         return(2);                        /* indeterminate  */
      else
         return(1);                        /* undefined      */
      }

   *ptr_x = numer1 / denom;
   *ptr_y = numer2 / denom;
   return(0);                              /*  solution exists */
}
```

FIGURE 10.17 (*continued*)

ptr_x. Since the address of x was passed as an argument to simult_comp() the value stored in the formal parameter ptr_x is the address of x. Thus the foregoing statement causes the result of the expression on the right hand side of the assignment operator to be assigned to **x**. Similarly, the statement

```
*ptr_y = numer2 / denom;
```

results in the value of the expression on the right hand side of the assignment
operator being assigned to **y**. The relationship between the variables **x, y** and the
pointers **ptr_x** and **ptr_y** is shown as follows:

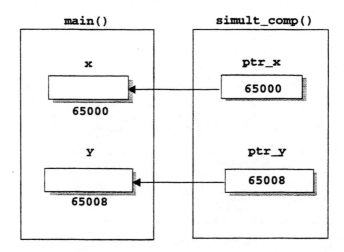

The function **comp_simult()** returns a value of type **int** representing the
status of the computation. The value returned is as follows:

1. System is indeterminate.
2. System is undefined.
3. Solution exists.

To test for a zero value of the denominator and the numerator, the function uses a
symbolic constant called **NEARLY_ZERO**, which is defined to be a very small value
in the preprocessor directive

```
#define NEARLY_ZERO 1e-40
```

which appears near the beginning of the program. For example, the **if** statement

```
if (fabs(denom) <= NEARLY_ZERO)
    return(2);
```

tests the value of **denom** to see if it is close to zero. We cannot use the statement of
the form

```
if (fabs(denom) <= 0.0)
    return(2)
```

because we need to allow for round-off errors that occur during computations involving floating point numbers.

Testing

To test the program we will consider three cases. For the first case;

$a_1 = 1, b_1 = 3, c_1 = -3$ and $a_2 = 2, b_2 = 6$ and $c_2 = -6$.

The system is indeterminate since

$$a_1 b_2 - a_2 b_1 = (1)(6) - (2)(3) = 6 - 6 = 0$$

$$c_1 b_2 - c_2 b_1 = (-3)(6) - (-6)(3) = -18 + 18 = 0$$

$$a_1 c_2 - a_2 c_1 = (1)(-6) - (2)(-3) = -6 + 6 = 0$$

For the second case;

$a_1 = 1, b_1 = 3, c_1 = -3$ and $a_2 = 2, b_2 = 6$ and $c_2 = -4$.

The system is undefined since

$$a_1 b_2 - a_2 b_1 = (1)(6) - (2)(3) = 6 - 6 = 0$$

$$c_1 b_2 - c_2 b_1 = (-3)(6) - (-6)(3) = -18 + 18 = 0$$

$$a_1 c_2 - a_2 c_1 = (1)(-4) - (2)(-3) = -4 + 6 = -4$$

For the third case;

$a_1 = 1, b_1 = 3, c_1 = -3$ and $a_2 = 2, b_2 = 6$ and $c_2 = -6$

$$a_1 b_2 - a_2 b_1 = (1)(-6) - (2)(3) = -6 - 6 = -12$$

$$c_1 b_2 - c_2 b_1 = (-3)(-6) - (-6)(3) = 18 + 18 = 36$$

$$a_1 c_2 - a_2 c_1 = (1)(-6) - (2)(-3) = -6 + 6 = 0$$

The solution for this case is

$x = 36/-12 = -3$

and

$y = 0/-12 = 0$

The output from the program for the three cases is shown in Figure 10.18.

```
Enter a1 b1 and c1: 1. 3. -3.

Enter a2 b2 and c2: 2. 6. -6.

The system is indeterminate


Enter a1 b1 and c1: 1. 3. -3.

Enter a2 b2 and c2: 2. 6. -4.

The system is undefined


Enter a1 b1 and c1: 1. 3. -3.

Enter a2 b2 and c2: 2. -6. -6.

The solution is:
x = -3.000000 y = -0.000000
```

Figure 10.18   Output from program *simulteq.c* for several cases.

10.9   PROGRAMMING PROJECT: REAL ROOTS OF A CUBIC EQUATION

The general form of a cubic equation is

$$x^3 + ax^2 + bx + c = 0 \tag{10.5}$$

Let $q = (3b - a^2)/3$ and $r = (2a^3 - 9ab + 27c)/27$. The real roots of the equation can be determined as follows. The solution falls into one of three classes depending on the value of $\Delta = q^3/27 + r^2/4$.

(a)   When $\Delta = 0$, all roots are real and at least two roots are equal

$$x_1 = 2(-r/2)^{1/3} - a/3 \tag{10.6}$$

$$x_2 = -(-r/2)^{1/3} - a/3 \tag{10.7}$$

$$x_3 = x_2 \tag{10.8}$$

(b)   When $q^3/27 + r^2/4 > 0$, there is one real root, and a pair of complex conjugate roots. The real root is given by

$$x_1 = (-r/2 + \Delta^{1/2})^{1/3} + (-r/2 - \Delta^{1/2})^{1/3} - a/3 \qquad \textbf{(10.9)}$$

(c)   When $q^3/27 + r^2/4 < 0$, all roots are real

$$x_1 = 2(-\theta/3)^{1/2} \cos(\theta/3) - a/3 \qquad \textbf{(10.10)}$$

$$x_2 = 2(-\theta/3)^{1/2} \cos(\theta/3 + 2\pi/3) - a/3 \qquad \textbf{(10.11)}$$

$$x_3 = 2(-\theta/3)^{1/2} \cos(\theta/3 + 4\pi/3) - a/3 \qquad \textbf{(10.12)}$$

where

$$\cos \theta = (3r/2q)(-3/q)^{1/2} \qquad \textbf{(10.13)}$$

Problem Statement

Write a C program to compute the real roots of a cubic equation. The program should consist of a **main()** function and two additional functions, one for obtaining user input and the one for computing the roots of the equation. The program should echo the input values and print the real roots of the equation.   ·

Problem Analysis

The important variables are as follows:

Input Variables
coefficients a, b, and c of the cubic equation (**double a, b, c**)

Output Variables
roots of equation (**double x1, x2, x3**)
result — variable representing the nature of the equation (**int result**)

Other Variables
The following variables are used in the function that computes the roots:
q, r, Δ, θ — variables used to compute roots (**double q, r, delta, theta**)
temporary variables (**double temp1, temp2**)

Algorithm

The major tasks performed by the program are the following:
1.   Read input data.

2.   Compute roots of cubic equation.

3.   Print results.

The first task is handled by the function **cubic_input()**, the second by the function **solve_cubic**, and the third by **main()**. Function **main()** is also responsible for calling the **cubic_input()** and **solve_cubic()** functions. The structure chart is

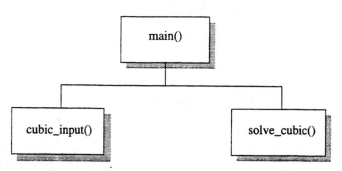

Algorithm for **main()**

1.   Call **cubic_input()** to read in *a*, *b*, and *c*.

2.   Call **cubic_solve()** to determine the type of roots and to compute the roots of the equation. Save value returned by **cubic_solve()** in **result**.

3.   If **result** = 1 then

     3.1 Print "All roots are real and there are at least two equal roots".

     3.2 Print **x1**, **x2**, and **x3**

4.   Else if **result** = 2 then

     4.1 Print "There is one real root and a pair of complex conjugate roots".

     4.2 Print **x1**.

5.   Else

     5.1 Print "All roots are real ".

     5.2 Print **x1**, **x2**, and **x3**.

Algorithm for **cubic_input()**

1.   Read **a**, **b**, and **c** and store these at the addresses indicated by **ptr_a**, **ptr_b**, and **ptr_c**.

Algorithm for `simult_comp()`

1. Compute `q`
2. Compute `r`
3. Compute `delta` from
4. If |`delta`| < `NEARLY_ZERO` then
    4.1 Compute `x1` from Equation (10.6) and store at the address given by `ptr_x1`.
    4.2 Compute `x2` from Equation (10.7) and store at the address given by `ptr_x2`.
    4.3 Compute `x3` from Equation (10.8) and store at address given by `ptr_x3`.
    4.4 Return a value of 1.
5. Else if (`delta` < 0) then
    5.1 Compute `x1` from Equation (10.9) and store at the address given by `ptr_x1`.
    5.2 Return a value of 2 .
6. Else
    6.1 Compute `theta` from Equation (10.13).
    6.2 Compute `x1` from Equation (10.10) and store at the address given by `ptr_x1`.
    6.3 Compute `x2` from Equation (10.11) and store at the address given by `ptr_x2`.
    6.4 Compute `x3` from Equation (10.12) and store at the address given by `ptr_x3`.
    6.5 Return a value of 0.

Program

The program is shown in Figure 10.19. The program consists of three functions, `main()`, `cubic_input()`, and `solve_cubic()`. The function `cubic_input()` obtains the values of a, b, and c.

The function `solve_cubic()` computes the roots of the cubic equation. Its header is

```
int solve_cubic(double a,double b,double c,double *ptr_x1,
                double *ptr_x2,double *ptr_x3)
```

The function has six formal parameters. The first three are of type **double**, and the last three are pointers to type **double**. Depending on the nature of the problem, the

```
/******************************************************************/
/*    cubic.c -- Real Roots of a Cubic Equation                  */
/*                                                                */
/*    This program determines the real roots of a cubic equation */
/*    of the form                                                 */
/*              x*x*x + a*x*x + b*x + c = 0                       */
/*                                                                */
/******************************************************************/

#define PI 3.141593
#define NEARLY_ZERO 1e-40

#include <stdio.h>
#include <math.h>

/* function prototypes */
void main(void);
void get_input(double *ptr_a,double *ptr_b,double *ptr_c);
int solve_cubic(double a, double b,double c,double * ptr_x1,
                double *ptr_x2,double *ptr_x3);

void main(void)
{
   double a,b,c,x1,x2,x3;
   int result;
   printf("\n Real roots of a cubic equation \n");

   /* get input */
   cubic_input(&a,&b,&c);

   /* solve for the real roots */
   result = solve_cubic(a,b,c,&x1,&x2,&x3);

   if (result == 1)
      {
      printf("\n All roots are real and there are at least two
              equal roots");
      printf("\n x1 = %lf, x2 = %lf, x3 = %lf", x1,x2,x3);
      }
   else if (result == 2)
      {
      printf("\n There is one real root and a pair of complex
              conjugate roots");
      printf("\n x1 = %lf",x1);
      }
    else
      {
      printf("\n All roots are real ");
      printf("\n x1 = %lf x2 = %lf x3 = %lf",x1,x2,x3);
      }
}
```

Figure 10.19   A program to determine the real roots of a cubic equation.

```
/*---------------------------------------------------------*/
/* Function: cubic_input()                                 */
/* Obtains input data                                      */
/*                                                         */
/*   Input Parameters                                      */
/*     None                                                */
/*                                                         */
/*   Output Parameters                                     */
/*     *ptr_a, *ptr_b, *ptr_c - coefficients of cubic equation */
/*---------------------------------------------------------*/
 void cubic_input(double *ptr_a,double *ptr_b,double *ptr_c)
 {
    printf("\n Enter a b and c: ");
    scanf("%lf %lf %lf", ptr_a,ptr_b,ptr_c);
 }


/*---------------------------------------------------------*/
/* Computes the real roots of a cubic equation             */
/*      x*x*x + a*x*x + b*x +c = 0                          */
/*   a2x + b2y = c2                                         */
/*                                                         */
/*   Input Parameters                                      */
/*     a, b, c - coefficients of cubic equation            */
/*                                                         */
/*   Output Parameters                                     */
/*    *ptr_x1, *ptr_x2, ptr_x3   real roots                */
/*                                                         */
/*   Returns                                               */
/*      0 - if all roots are real                          */
/*      1 - is all roots are real and at least two are equal */
/*      2 - if only one root is real                       */
/*---------------------------------------------------------*/
 int solve_cubic(double a,double b,double c,double *ptr_x1,
                 double *ptr_x2,double *ptr_x3)
 {
    double q, r, delta,temp1,temp2,theta;

    q = (3. * b - a * a) / 3. ;
    r = (2. * a * a * a - 9. * a * b + 27. * c) / 27. ;
    delta = q * q * q / 27. + r * r / 4. ;
    if ( fabs(delta) < NEARLY_ZERO )
       {
       *ptr_x1 = 2. * pow(-r/2., 1./3.) - a/3. ;
       *ptr_x2 = - pow(-r/2, 1./3.) - a/3. ;
       *ptr_x3 = *ptr_x2;
        return(1);
       }
    else if ( delta > 0.)
       {
       temp1 = -r/2. + sqrt(delta);
       if (temp1 < 0.)
           temp2 = (-1.) * pow(fabs(temp1),1./3.);
```

FIGURE 10.19   (continued)

```
       else
          temp2 = pow(temp1,1./3.);
       *ptr_x1 = temp2;
       temp1 = -r/2. - sqrt(delta) ;
       if (temp1 < 0.)
          temp2 = (-1.) * pow(fabs(temp1),1./3.);
       else temp2 = pow(temp1,1./3.);
       *ptr_x1 += (temp2 - a/3.);
       return(2);
       }
   else
       {
       theta = acos( (1.5 * r/q) * sqrt(-3.0/q) ) ;
       *ptr_x1 = 2.0 * sqrt(-q/3.0) * cos(theta/3.0) - a/3.0 ;
       *ptr_x2 = 2.0 * sqrt(-q/3.0) *
                 cos(theta/3.0 + 2.0*PI/3.0) - a/3.0 ;
       *ptr_x3 = 2.0 * sqrt(-q/3.0) *
                 cos(theta/3.0 + 4.0*PI/3.0) - a/3.0 ;
       return(3);
       }
}
```

FIGURE 10.19 (*continued*)

three roots are returned through the pointers **ptr_x1**, **ptr_x2**, and **ptr_x3**. The function also returns a value of type **int** using a return statement. The value returned depends on the value of Δ.

Function **main()** calls **cubic_input()** to obtain user input. It then calls **solve_cubic()** with the following statement:

```
   result = solve_cubic(a,b,c,&x1,&x2,&x3);
```

The addresses of the variables **x1**, **x2**, and **x3** are passed to **solve_cubic()**, which uses these addresses to return the roots of the equation.

Testing

To test the program we need to select input data such that the code for each three cases is exercised. Table 10.3 shows the results obtained by hand calculation for the following three cases:

Case 1: $a = -1, b = -2, c = -4$

Case 2: $a = 3, b = 3, c = 1$

Case 3: $a = -1, b = -9, c = 9$

The output from the program for the three cases is shown in Figure 10.20. The program results agree those obtained by hand calculations for all three cases.

```
Real roots of a cubic equation

Enter a b and c: -1. -2. -4.

There is one real root and a pair of complex conjugate roots
x1 = 2.467504


Real roots of a cubic equation

Enter a b and c: 3. 3. 1.

All roots are real and there are at least two equal roots
x1 = -1.000000, x2 = -1.000000, x3 = -1.000000


Real roots of a cubic equation

Enter a b and c: -1. -9. 9.

All roots are real
     x1 = 3.000000 x2 = -3.000000 x3 = 1.000002
```

Figure 10.20   Output from program *cubic.c.*

Table 10.3: Computations for three test cases

Case	q	r	Δ	x_1	x_2	x_3
1	-2.333	-4.741	5.148	2.467	-	-
2	0.0	0.0	0.0	-1.000	-1.000	-1.000
3	-9.333	5.926	-21.141	3.000	-3.000	1.000

10.10 SUMMARY

In this chapter we presented the C language features for handling pointers. A pointer is a variable that contains the address of another variable. Pointers are one of the more important elements of the C language and probably one of the most misunderstood. You cannot avoid pointers if you program in C. There are two operators that are associated with pointers. The address of operator (&) when placed in front of a variable name gives the address of the variable in memory. The second operator is the indirection operator (*). This operator when placed in front of a pointer returns the value stored at the address pointed to by the pointer. When declaring pointers, we must indicate the type of value that the pointer will be pointing to. Also we must always initialize any pointers that we use in our programs. Pointers that have not been initialized are the most common cause of errors in programs.

In this chapter we also discussed the close relationship between pointers and arrays. The name of an array is a pointer constant that points to the first element of the array. When we create the array, C automatically creates a pointer constant whose name is the name of the array and assigns it the address of the first element of the array. Since the name of an array is a pointer constant and not a pointer variable, we cannot change its value. When we pass an array to a function, we pass the name of the array as an argument to the function. We are thus passing the address of the array to the function. The function can use this address to modify the array. Unlike ordinary variables, the function does not receive a copy of the array since this would be inefficient, especially for large arrays. We also presented the difference between using pointer notation and array notation for accessing the elements of an array and presented several examples of using both techniques.

The C programming language supports only a few basic operations on pointers such as incrementing and decremeting pointers, adding or subtracting an integer from a pointer, and subtracting two pointers. When using pointer arithmetic, it is important to remember that all arithmetic operations are scaled to the type of data that the pointer references. Thus, when a pointer that is pointing to an element of an array is incremented, it points to the next element of the array regardless of the type of array.

Pointers are frequently used in functions that need to change more than one value. This is because it is only possible to return one value with the return statement. To change the value of more than one variable, we have to use pointers as function parameters, and we have to pass the addresses of the variables to be modified as function arguments. The function can then use these addresses to modify the value of the variables stored at these addresses. In this chapter we presented several applications that use this approach to modify variables.

Key Terms Presented in This Chapter

addresses	pointers
address of operator (&)	pointer arguments
array address	pointer arithmetic
array name as an address	pointer constant
array notation	pointer initialization
call by reference	pointer notation
indirection operator (*)	pointer variable

PROGRAM STYLE, COMMON ERRORS AND DEBUGGING GUIDE

1. When declaring pointer variables, you should include the letters `ptr` or `p` to help you remember that these are pointers and need to the treated differently from ordinary variables.

2. You should always initialize pointers before using them.

3. When writing functions, you should use call by value to pass arguments to the function. You should use pointers only for those variables whose values must be modified by the function.

4. You should use array notation instead of pointer notation when manipulating arrays. This makes your program easier to read.

5. When using functions, you should check the function prototype to see which arguments are being passed by value and which are being passed by reference.

6. When passing an array to a function, keep in mind that you are actually passing a pointer to the function. The function can use the pointer to change the elements of the array.

7. It is an error to apply the address of (`&`) operator to a constant or an expression. For example the expressions

```
&786        /* illegal */
&(x + 5)    /* illegal */
```

are illegal.

8. You can only assign an address to a pointer variable.

```
float x, y;
float *ptr;
...
ptr = &y;      /* legal    */
y = &x;        /* illegal */
```

The last statement is illegal since it attempts to assign the address of **x** to **y** which is not a pointer variable.

9. The dereferencing operator (`*`) has higher precedence than the arithmetic operator. You should note the difference between the expressions

```
*(x+2)
*x + 2
```

where x is the name of an array. The first expression represents the value of the third element of the array, while the second expression which is equivalent to

```
(*x ) + 2
```

represents 2 added to the first element of the array.

10. When declaring pointers more than one pointer variable on the same line each variable must be declared with the * prefixed to the variable name. The statement

```
float *ptr1, ptr2;   /* wrong */
```

declares only one pointer variable, **ptr1**. The variable **ptr2** is a not a pointer but a variable of type **float**. To declare both **ptr1** and **ptr2** to be pointers, we must use the statement

```
float *ptr1, *ptr2;   /* correct */
```

11. It is an error to assign a pointer of one type to a pointer of another type. For example, in the code segment

```
float *ptr1;
int *ptr2;
..
...
prt1 = ptr2;      /* WRONG */
```

a pointer to type **float** (**ptr1**) is assigned to a pointer to type **int**.

12. An array's name is a pointer *constant* whose value is the address of the first element of the array. The value of the array cannot be changed by an assignment statement or any other statement and remains fixed for the duration of the program.

```
float x[10];
...
...
x = 12.4;   /* illegal */
```

The foregoing statement is in error because it attempts to change the value of **x**, which is a pointer constant. The fact that an array name is a pointer constant is not clearly understood by many beginning C programmers and is a frequent source of errors.

13. One of the most common example of a pointer error is the use of uninitialized pointers. In the code fragment shown here

```
float x, y, *ptr;

x = 10;
*ptr = y;      /* ptr has not been initialized */
```

the pointer variable **ptr** is not initialized. It is your responsibility to make sure that all pointer variables used in your program point to a valid address and that a valid value is stored at that address.

14. A pointer to an array must point to an element in the array. For example, given the definition

    ```
    float x[5],y,*ptr_x;
    ptr_x = x;
    ```

    The statements

    ```
    y = *(ptr_x - 1);
    y = *(ptr_x + 5);
    ```

    are in error because they attempt to access data that is beyond the limits of the array.

15. The only legal pointer arithmetic operations are addition and subtraction of whole numbers. You cannot perform any other operations on pointers.

16. Pointer arithmetic operations are meaningful only if the pointer refers to an array.

17. When performing pointer arithmetic you should always keep in mind that pointer arithmetic is scaled to the size of the data object that the pointer references. Thus, if a pointer points to an array element of any type, then incrementing the pointer will result in the pointer pointing to the next array element, and decrementing the pointer will result in the pointer pointing to the previous array element.

18. Although pointers give us tremendous capabilities they are also a source of many errors. Tracking down a pointer that contains an erroneous value is one of the most difficult bugs to track down. This is due to the fact that when you use the pointer you are reading or writing to some unknown address. If you read data from the wrong address, you will end up getting garbage. If you write data to the wrong address you will overwrite other data or code. If your program gives strange results you should check all pointers to make sure that they have been initialized and are pointing to the correct address.

19. C guarantees the a pointer to a valid address will never be zero. You can use this fact by when writing functions that return pointers. Your function should return a null value to signal that an error has occurred.

EXERCISES

Review Questions

1. Identify the following statements as true or false:

   a. Every variable in memory has a unique address.

    b.   The name of an array is a pointer constant.

    c.   For a function to return more than one value, it must be passed the address o
the variables to be returned.

    d.   A pointer is a variable that contains the address of another variable.

2.   Consider the following declaration:

```
static int iarray[6] = {10,15,30,-10,-15,-30};
int *ptr_i;
ptr_i = iarray;
```

Assuming that the starting address of **iarray[]** is 2000 and that it requires 2 byte
of storage for type **int** on the system, give the values of the following expressions

    a.   `iarray`

    b.   `ptr_i`

    c.   `&iarray[0]`

    d.   `&iarray[2]`

    e.   `iarray[4]`

    f.   `iarray+3`

    g.   `prt_i + 4`

    h.   `*ptr_i`

    i.   `*(ptr_i+4)`

    j.   `&*ptr_i`

3.   Consider the following declarations:

```
int i,j;
int *p, *q;
```

Which of the following assignment expressions are illegal?

    a.   `p = &i;`

    b.   `p = &q;`

    c.   `q = i;`

    d.   `*q = &j;`

    e.   `i = *p;`

    f.   `q = (int) p;`

    g.   `i = *p + *q;`

    h.   `q = p;`

4.   Explain the difference between a pointer variable and a pointer constant.

5.   Is the name of an array a pointer variable or a pointer constant?

6.   Consider the following declarations:

```
int x[10];
int *p;
```

Which of the following statements is incorrect?

a. `x = p;`

b. `p = &x;`

c. `p = x;`

d. `p = x +2;`

7. Find the errors in the following code segments:

    a.
    ```
    int x, ptr;
    x = 10;
    ptr = &x;
    ```

    b.
    ```
    int a = 15;
    int *ptr;
    ptr = a;
    ```

    c.
    ```
    int num = 5;
    int *ptr;
    ptr = &(num+5);
    ```

    d.
    ```
    int x=5, y =10;
    int *ptr1, *ptr2;
    ptr1 = &x;
    ptr2 = &y;
    *ptr1 = &ptr2;
    ```

8. Consider the following declarations:
    ```
    float x[10],y[6][5],z=5.4,*ptr;
    int i=4;
    ```

    Identify each of the following statements as valid or invalid:

    a. `x[3] = z;`

    b. `y[3][4] = x[2];`

    c. `scanf("%f",&x[9]);`

    d. `printf("%f",x);`

    e. `y[6] = x;`

    f. `ptr = z;`

    g. `ptr = y;`

    h. `ptr = x;`

    i. `x = ptr;`

9. Consider the following declarations:
    ```
    float num, *ptr_num;
    prt_num = &num;
    ```

Which of the following expressions are true?

a. `num == *ptr_num;`

b. `num == &ptr_num;`

c. `ptr_num == *num;`

d. `ptr_num == &num;`

10. What is the output from the following program?

```
#include <stdio.h>
main()
{
    int a[4][5];
    int i,j, *ptr;

    ptr = a;
    for (i = 0; i < 4; ++i)
        for (j=0; j < 5; ++j)
            a[i][j] = i*5 + j;

    for (i=0; i < 15; ++i)
    {
        if (i %5 == 0)
            printf("\n");
        printf("%10d", *(ptr+i));
    }
}
```

11. What is the output produced by the following code fragment?

```
int a=10,b=20;
int *ptr1,*ptr2;

ptr1 = &a;
ptr2 = &b;
printf("%d %d \n",*ptr1, *ptr2);
ptr2 = ptr1;
printf("%d %d \n", *ptr1, *ptr2);
*ptr2 = 25;
*ptr1 = *ptr2;
printf(" %d %d \n",*ptr1, *ptr2);
```

12. What is the output from the following code fragments?

a.

```
int x=10, y = 20;
int *ptr1, *ptr2;
ptr1 = &x;
ptr2 = &y;
*ptr1 = *ptr2;
printf(%d %d %d %d", *ptr1,*ptr2,x,y);
```

b.

```
int x = 10;
int *ptr1, **ptr2;
ptr1 = &x;
ptr2 = &ptr1;
```

```
                 printf("\n %d %d %d",x,*ptr1,**ptr2);

     c.

                 float c[2];
                 *(c+1) = 120.5;
                 *c = *(c+1);
                 printf("\n %f %f", c[0],c[1]);


     d.

                 float b[10];
                 float *ptr;
                 b[0] = 110.0;
                 b[1] = 253.0;
                 b[2] = 3456.0;
                 ptr = &b;
                 printf("%f", *ptr);
```

13. If **fltarray[]** is a one-dimensional array of type **float** having eight elements, write expressions to refer to the following elements of the array using pointer notation:

   a.   first element
   b.   last element
   c.   third element
   d.   fifth element

14. Given the following array declaration

```
     static float x[3][4] = {
                             {1.0, 4.0, 3.0, 6.0},
                             {5.0, 5.5, 6.5, 8.5},
                             {4.2, 12.8, 16.7, 18.9}
                             };
```

   Write expressions to refer to the elements having the following values in array notation and then in pointer notation:

   a. 1.0   b. 18.9
   c. 5.5   d. 12.8
   e. 6.0   f. 8.5

15. Write a general expression to represent the element **x[i][j]** of the two-dimensional array **x[][]** of the previous problem.

16. What is the output from the following programs?

   a.
```
     #include <stdio.h>
         main()
     {
         static float x[] = {2.0,4.0,6.0};
         int j;
         for (j=0; j < 3; ++j)
```

```
                            printf("%f \n",*(x+j));
                }
```

b.

```
        #include <stdio.h>
        main()
        {
                static float x[]={2.0,4.0,6.0};
                int j;
                float *ptr;
                ptr = x;
                for (j = 0; j < 3; j++)
                        printf("%f \n", *ptr++);
        }
```

c.

```
        #include <stdio.h>
        main()
        {
                static float x[]={2.0,4.0,6.0,8.0,10.0,12.0};
                printf("%f \n",*x);
                printf("%f \n", *(x+3));
                printf("%f \n", *(x+5));
        }
```

d.

```
        #include <stdio.h>
        main()
        {
                float y[] = {10.5,20.3,11.67,18.54,13.27};
                float *ptr1, *ptr2;
                ptr1 = y;
                ptr2 = y;
                ++ptr2;
                printf("\n %f %f *(ptr1+1), *ptr2);
        }
```

Programming Exercises

17.   Write a function that accepts two arrays **x[]** and **y[]** having n elements each, adds each element of the first array to the corresponding element of the second array, and places the result in a third array **z[]**. Your function should use pointer notation and pointer arithmetic. The function header for the function is

```
        void add_two_arrays(float x[], float y[] float z[], int n)
```

Write a main program to test your function

18.   Write a function to compute the average, minimum value and maximum value for a set of observations x_1, x_2, ..., x_n. The input to the function will be the array **x[]** containing the observations, and the number of observations, **n**. The function should return the average, minimum value, and maximum value. Since the function will return more than one value, you will need to use pointers. The function header is

```
void average(double x[],int n, double *ptr_mean,
             double *ptr_min,double *ptr_max);
```

The following statement can be used to call the function

```
average(x,n,&mean,&min,&max);
```

Write a main program to read in the observations, call the function **average()**, and print the results.

11

CHARACTER STRINGS

Computers can handle both numeric and alphabetic information. Engineeri
programs for the most part contain numeric information, but there are times wh
it becomes necessary to work with alphabetic data. Alphabetic information
useful for applications such as word processing, labeling graphs, generati
mailing lists, and data processing.

In this chapter we present the C language features for working with strings.
string is a sequence of characters. Unlike some other programming languages su
as BASIC and Pascal, C does not have a string data type. Instead, a string
considered to be an array of type **char**. The individual characters in a string a
stored in adjacent memory cells, one character per cell. The C library contain
large number of functions for performing various operations on strings. In t
chapter we describe some of the more commonly used string handling functions
the C library.

11.1 CHARACTER STRING CONSTANTS

A character string constant is a sequence of characters enclosed in dou
quotation marks. Examples of character string constants are

```
"C for Engineers"
"Programming is fun"
```

The quotation marks are not part of the string but simply serve to define the start and end of the string. Whenever the compiler encounters a sequence of characters enclosed in double quotes, it recognizes it as a character string constant. It stores the individual characters of the string in adjacent memory locations with each character occupying one cell. The compiler also adds a terminating null ('\0') character at the end of the string. Figure 11.1 shows how string constants are stored in memory.

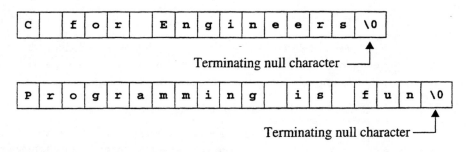

Figure 11.1 Representation of strings in C.

All strings in C are by convention stored with a terminating null character. The null character is a nonprinting character whose ASCII code is 0. Notice that each string in Figure 11.1 is terminated by the special character '\0'. The null character marks the end of the string. It is important that you end your strings with the null character since most functions that work with strings check for this terminating null character to determine whether the end of the string has been reached. A consequence of using the null character to mark the end of a string is that a string constant actually has one more character than the number of characters within the double quotation marks.

It is important to understand the difference between a constant of type and a character string constant. The character string constant **"a"** is not the same as the character **'a'**. The difference between the two is shown below.

Character constant, **'a'** | a |

Character string, **"a"** | a | \0 |

The character constant **'a'** consists of one character. The character string constant **"a"** consists of two characters, the character **'a'** and the null character **'\0'**. Also, the character **'a'** is a basic data type (**char**) while the string **"a"** is an array of type **char**.

11.2   DECLARING AND INITIALIZING STRINGS

A character string in C is an array of type **char**. As with arrays of other data types, all character strings have to be declared. In addition to the name of the string, we have to tell the compiler how many characters there will be in the string so that the compiler can provide the necessary storage to hold the characters. There are two ways in which we can declare a character string:

1. Array notation,
2. Pointer notation

The Array Form

When we declare a character string using array notation, we have to tell the compiler how many characters there will be in the string and also the name of the array. Examples of character string declarations using array notation are

```
char name[20], address[40];
```

This statement creates two arrays of type **char**. The array **name[]** consists of 20 elements, while the array **address[]** has 40 elements. Thus the array **name[]** can store a string of 19 characters, while the array **address[]** can store up to 39 characters. Recall that we have to allocate one element for the terminating null character.

The statement

```
char buffer[11];
```

creates an array of type **char** called **buffer[]**. We can use this array to store a sequence of up to 10 characters (the last character is used for storing the terminating null).

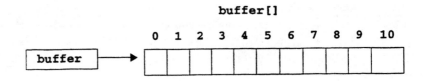

As with arrays of other data types, the name of an array of type **char** is also a pointer constant that points to the first element of the array. Thus, after the foregoing declaration, C will recognize **buffer** as a pointer constant containing the address of the first element of the character array **buffer[]**; that is

```
buffer == &buffer[0]
```

Since buffer is a pointer constant, we cannot change its value with operations such as **++buffer** and **--buffer**.

Static and external arrays can be initialized. For example, the statement

```
static char material[6] = {'s','t','e','e','l','\0'};
```

creates an array **material[]** containing six elements as shown:

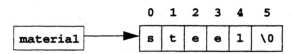

We can omit the size of the array as in the following statement:

```
static char material[] = {'s','t','e','e','l','\0'};
```

The compiler counts the number of characters and sizes the array accordingly. For our example, the compiler creates an array **material[]** containing six elements.

An alternative and more convenient format for initializing strings is to enclose the text in double quotation marks as in the declaration

```
static char material[] = {"steel"};
```

When the C compiler encounters text enclosed in double quotation marks, it automatically adds the terminating null character.

On most compilers, only static and external strings can be initialized. However, many of the newer compilers also allow initialization of automatic arrays.

The Pointer Form

Character strings can also be declared using pointers as in the statement

```
static char *planet = "Jupiter";
```

The C compiler stores this as a string of eight characters. In addition, the C compiler will also creates a pointer to type **char** called **planet**. The pointer **planet** initially points to the first character of the string "**Jupiter**", that is, it contains the address in memory of the character '**J**'. However, **planet** is a variable and can be changed in the program. For example, we can use the increment operator as in

```
++planet
```

to change its value. Now, **planet** points to the second character in the string "**Jupiter**".

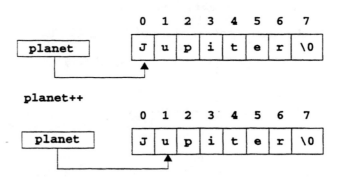

The statement

```
char *str_ptr = "This is a string constant";
```

initializes the pointer variable **str_ptr** so that it contains the address of the first character of the string constant on the right-hand side of the assignment (=) operator. Since **str_ptr** is a pointer to a character, **str_ptr** contains the address of the first character ('**T**') of the string.

There is an important difference between the two forms (array and pointer) for declaring character strings. Consider the following declarations:

```
char str_array[] = "A character array";
char *str_ptr = "A pointer to type char";
```

The first creates an array of type **char**. The array has 18 elements. The array is initialized to the string constant on the right of the assignment operator (=). The compiler also creates a pointer constant called **str_array**. The pointer constant **str_array** is initialized so that it points to the first element of the array **str_array[0]**. The second declaration creates a pointer to type **char**. The pointer is initialized so that it points to the first character of the character string on the right of the assignment operator (=). Both **str_array** and **str_ptr** are pointers, which means that both contain an address. However, the important difference between **str_array** and **str_ptr** is that **str_array** is a pointer *constant* which means that its value cannot be changed, while **str_ptr** is a pointer *variable*. We can change the value of **str_ptr**, but we cannot change the value of **str_array**. For example, we can increment **str_ptr** as follows:

```
++str_ptr;
```

Now **str_ptr** points to the second character in the string. We cannot, however, change the value of **str_array**, and **str_array** always points to the first element, **str_array[0]** of the array. Thus the following expression

```
++str_array;     /* wrong! */
```

will result in a syntax error.

Example 11.1   Array and Pointer Forms of String Declaration

The two programs shown in Figures 11.2 and 11.3 illustrate the difference between array and pointer notation as it applies to character strings. The first program (Figure 11.2) uses array notation, while the second program (Figure 11.3) uses pointer notation. Both programs print a string of characters one character at a time.

In the array version of the program (Figure 11.2), the declaration

```
static char str_array[] = "Character string to be printed";
```

creates an array of type **char** called **str_array[]** containing 31 elements. The elements of this array contain the individual characters of the string constant on the right of the assignment (=) operator. The C compiler also adds a terminating null at the end of the array. The characters in the array are printed using a **while** loop. The statement

```
while (str_array[i])
```

checks for the null character. If **str_array[i] == '\0'**, then the condition is false and the **while** loop is exited; otherwise, the statements within the body of the **while** loop are executed. The condition in the **while** loop could also have been written as

```
while (str_array[i] != '\0')
```

The **printf()** statement

```
printf("%c", str_array[i]);
```

prints one element of the array.

The second version of the program (Figure 11.3) uses pointer notation to print the string. In the declaration

```
char *str_ptr = "Character string to be printed";
```

```
/*************************************************************/
/*    string1.c  -- Array Form for Character Strings         */
/*    This program uses array notation to print a string.    */
/*************************************************************/
#include <stdio.h>

void main(void);

void main(void)
{
    static char str_array[] = "Character string to be printed";
    int i = 0;

    while (str_array[i])
        {
        printf("%c", str_array[i]);
        ++i;
        }
}
```

Figure 11.2   Array form of string declaration.

the pointer variable **str_ptr** is initialized so that it points to the first character c
the string. The statement

while (*str_ptr)

checks for the terminating null character. The expression ***str_ptr** retrieves th
character stored at the address contained in **str_ptr**. For any character other tha
the null character, the condition will be true (nonzero), and the statements withi
the body of the **while** loop will be executed. The statement

printf("%c", *str_ptr);

prints one character of the string, and the statement

++str_ptr;

increments **str_ptr** so it points to the next character of the string.

The standard C library provides many functions for working with string
These include functions for string input and output, computing the length of string
comparing strings, copying strings, searching for the presence of a character withi
a string, and converting strings to numbers. Many of these functions requir
pointers to strings as arguments. Some of these string handling functions ar
described in the sections that follow.

```
/*****************************************************************/
/*    string2.c  -- Pointer Form for Character Strings          */
/*    This program uses pointer notation to print a string.     */
/*****************************************************************/
    #include <stdio.h>

    void main(void);

    void main(void)
    {
        char *str_ptr = "Character string to be printed";

        while (*str_ptr)
           {
           printf("%c", *str_ptr);
           ++str_ptr;
           }
    }
```

Figure 11.3 Pointer form of string declaration.

11.3 STRING INPUT AND OUTPUT

Two steps are involved in reading a string into a program. First, we must create a character array and set aside sufficient space to store the string. Second, we must use a string input function to read in the string. We create space for the string by including an explicit size in the array declaration. For example, the statement

```
char buffer[81];
```

creates a character array **buffer[]** consisting of 81 elements.

We can use the **scanf()** function with the **%s** format specifier to read in a string as in

```
scanf("%s", buffer);
```

There is no address-of (**&**) operator preceding the name of the array. This is because the name of the array is also the address of the first element of the array. The **scanf()** function automatically adds a null ('**\0**') character at the end of the string. The following example reads in a string from the standard input device using the **scanf()** function and prints it along with a greeting.

```
#include <stdio.h>
void main(void)
{
  char name[81];
  printf("\n Enter name:");
  scanf("%s", name);
  printf("Hello %s", name);
}
```

Since C does not perform any bounds checking on arrays, we should allocate sufficient space to hold the string we expect to read. If more characters are entered than the space allocated for the character array that receives the string, the additional characters will be written in adjacent memory locations with the result that other data, and possibly the program itself will be overwritten. A common mistake made by beginning C programmers when reading strings is forgetting to allocate space for the string. For example, consider the following

```
static char *name;
scanf("%s", name);
```

These statements will not result in a compiler error. However, they will not work for several reasons. The declaration

```
static char *name;
```

simply creates a pointer to type **char**. *It does not allocate any storage for the string.* Also, since **name** has not been initialized, it is initialized to zero, which means that it is not pointing to anything.

Another common but more subtle error is as follows:

```
char *name = "Some name";
scanf("%s", name);
```

Here we are creating a pointer to type **char** that contains the address of the first character of the string constant **"Some name"**. The compiler allocates 10 bytes of storage for the string constant. If the string entered using the **scanf()** function has more that 10 characters, then the adjacent memory locations will be overwritten. When using pointers we should use the C library memory allocation functions such as **malloc()** and **calloc()** to allocate sufficient storage for the strings to be entered. These functions are described in Chapter 17.

The **printf()** function may be used to print a string. The **%s** format specifier in the **printf()** function is used to print the string. The **printf()** function prints all characters in the string up to the terminating null character.

Although we can use **scanf()** and **printf()** for string input and output, the C library has several other functions such as **gets()** and **puts()** that are specially designed for reading and writing strings. One of the problems with using **scanf()** for reading strings is that **scanf()** stops reading at the first white space (such as blank, tab or newline) it encounters. Thus, **scanf()** reads single words rather than whole phrases.

The gets() and puts() Functions

The **gets()** library function (for get string) reads in a line of text from the standard input device. A line of text is any string that is terminated by a newline

('\n'). A newline character is generated when you type Enter or Return. The gets() function reads all typed characters up to and including the newline and places them in the string whose address is passed as the argument to the function. The function replaces the newline character at the end of the string with a null character.

The function prototype for the gets() function is

```
char *gets(char *str);
```

The gets() function returns the same pointer that was passed to it. If an error occurs, gets() returns a null pointer. The header file *stdio.h* defines the symbolic constant **NULL** to be equal to a null pointer. You should note the difference between a null pointer and a null character. A null pointer contains an address, whereas the null character is a data object of type char. A null pointer indicates that the pointer is not pointing to any object, while the null character is a character that has an ASCII value of 0.

The following example reads in a string and prints a greeting.

```
#include <stdio.h>
void main(void);

void main(void)
{
char name[81];
printf("\n What is your name? ");
gets(name);
printf("\n Greetings %s", name);
}
```

As with the scanf() function, it is the responsibility of the programmer to provide adequate storage for the string being read in with the gets() function. If the string entered is larger than the number of characters allocated for the array, the excess characters will overflow into adjacent memory cells. The standard C library provides another function called fgets() that does allow us to limit the number of characters read. The fgets() function is described in Chapter 12.

The puts() function (for *put* string) prints a string on the screen. It automatically adds a newline character to the end of the string. For example, the statement

```
puts("Greetings");
```

prints the string enclosed in double quotation marks on the standard output device. It is also possible to add escape sequences to the string as in

```
puts("Greetings \n");
```

Here, a newline character is included in the string. Since the puts() function adds a newline at the end of the string enclosed in double quotes, the statement will result in two newline characters being printed.

Example 11.2   Names and Addresses

The program shown in Figure 11.4 illustrates the use of the **gets()** a**
puts() functions. It reads in names and addresses entered from the standard inp**
device (keyboard) and prints these on the standard output device (console).
The statement

```
char name[81],addr1[81],addr2[81],city[81],state[81],zip[81'
```

creates six arrays of type **char**. Each array has a size of 81. Although we do n**
need 81 characters to store the information contained in each array, the size of t**
arrays was selected so that there would be adequate storage for one line of text **
a standard console (80 characters). Alternately, we could have created a tempora**
buffer to store a line of input and then transferred the information to the appropri**
array using the C library **strcpy()** function to copy the string. The **strcpy**
function is described in Section 11.6. The program also creates a variable of ty**
int called **exit_flag** and a temporary array called **temp[]**. The variab**
exit_flag is initially assigned a value of **FALSE** (0).

Names and addresses are read in until the condition in the **while** statemen**

```
while (exit_flag == FALSE)
```

is true, that is, the value of **exit_flag** is **FALSE**. The **puts()** function prints **
various prompts and the **gets()** function obtains the input. For example, **
statement

```
puts("\n \nEnter name: ");
```

prompts, for the name and the statement

```
gets(name);
```

stores the value entered in the array **name[]**. The statements

```
puts(name);
puts(addr1);
puts(addr2);
```

print the name and the first two address lines.

Program execution is terminated when a **"N"** or **"n"** is entered in response**
the prompt **"Continue - (Y/N)?"**. The program checks the value of **
character stored in the first element of the array **temp[]**. The **if** statement

```
if (temp[0] == 'N' || temp[0] == 'n')
    exit_flag = TRUE
```

assigns a value of **TRUE** to the variable **exit_flag** if the condition in the **
statement is true. This causes an exit from the **while** loop.

```
/***********************************************************/
/*   nameaddr.c  -- Name and Address List                 */
/*   This program reads in names and addresses and prints */
/*   these on the standard output device. It illustrates  */
/*   the use of the C library gets() and puts() functions. */
/***********************************************************/
#include <stdio.h>
#define TRUE 1
#define FALSE 0

void main(void);

void main(void)
{
    char name[81],addr1[81],addr2[81],city[81],
        state[81],zip[81];
    char temp[21];
    int exit_flag=FALSE;

    while (exit_flag == FALSE)
        {
        puts("\n \nEnter name: ");
        gets(name);
        puts("Enter first address line: ");
        gets(addr1);
        puts("Enter second address line: ");
        gets(addr2);
        puts("Enter city: ");
        gets(city);
        puts("Enter state: ");
        gets(state);
        puts("Enter zip code: ");
        gets(zip);
        /* print information */
        puts("\n");
        puts(name);
        puts(addr1);
        puts(addr2);
        printf("%s  %s  %s \n\n", city, state, zip);
        puts("Continue - Y/N?");
        gets(temp);
        if (temp[0] == 'N' || temp[0] == 'n')
            exit_flag = TRUE;
        }
}
```

Figure 11.4   A program to print names and addresses.

11.4   THE C LIBRARY STRING HANDLING FUNCTIONS

The C library provides a large number of functions for performing string operations. Some of the functions contained in the library include functions for determining the length of strings, comparing strings, copying strings, combining

strings, and searching for specific characters in a string. The function prototypes
these strings are contained in the header file *string.h*. You should include this
in any programs that make use of any of the C library string handling functions.
suggest that you take a look at this file and the documentation accompanying y
compiler to get an idea of what string handling functions are provided with y
compiler.

The C library string functions are very useful when writing programs
make extensive use of strings. You should use these functions rather t
"reinventing the wheel" and writing your own functions. In fact, we recomm
that you use the standard C library function whenever possible. Most experien
programmers use commercially available libraries for various tasks rather t
writing their own functions since this can save a vast amount of time and eff
Examples of commercially available libraries include libraries for graphics, se
communications, printer control, data base management, input and output, ma
manipulation, and statistical analysis and numerical analysis. These libra
provide many features beyond those contained in the standard C library.
example, the input and output libraries allow a program to output informa
anywhere on the screen. However, these libraries are typically implementation
hardware dependent.

In the sections that follow we will describe some of the more frequently u
C library functions and explain how we can use these functions in our progra
We will also present examples of how you can write our own string hand
functions. This will provide a better understanding of how some of the C lib
string functions work. Table 11.1 lists some of the more commonly used C lib
string functions.

11.5   DETERMINING THE LENGTH OF STRINGS

The C library `strlen()` function returns the length of a string. The argun
to the function is the address of a null terminated string. The function counts
number of characters in the string. The null character is not included in the cc
The function prototype for the `strlen()` function is

```
unsigned strlen(const char *str);
```

the argument to the function is a pointer to type **char**.

We can also determine the number of characters in a string using the **siz**
operator. The **sizeof** operator includes the null character in its count.

Table 11.1: C library string handling functions

Function	Description
strcat	appends one string to another
strchr	locates the first occurrence of a character in a string
strcmp	compares two strings
strcmpi	compares two strings but ignores differences in the case of letters
strcpy	copies contents of one string to another
strcspn	returns the position of the first letter in a string that is also in a second string
strdup	allocates memory and makes a duplicate of a string
stricomp	compares two strings without regard to the case of the letters
strlen	returns the number of characters in a string
strlwr	converts all characters in a string to lowercase
strncat	appends n characters of one string to another
strncmp	compares the first n characters of two strings
strncpy	copies the first n characters of one string to another
strnicmp	compares the first n characters of two strings without regard to case
strnset	initializes the first n characters of a string to the specified character
strpbrk	locates the first occurrence of any character that is in both strings
strrchr	locates the last occurrence of the specified character in a string
strrev	reverses the order of characters in a string
strset	initializes all characters in a string to the specified character
strspn	returns the position of the first character in the string that is not in a given set of characters
strstr	returns the position of the first occurrence of one string in another
strtod	converts a string to a floating point value
strtol	converts a string to a long value
strupr	converts all characters in a string to uppercase

Example 11.3   The strlen() Function

The program shown in Figure 11.5 reads several character strings and prints the string and the length of the string. It uses the **strlen()** function to determine the length of each string.

The program creates a character array called **buffer[]** to store the string entered from the keyboard. It also initializes **buffer[]** to the character string constant **"A string"**. The body of the **while** loop is executed as long as the condition in the **while** statement

```
/***************************************************************/
/*    strlen.c  -- Length of Character Strings               */
/*    Reads a string and prints the number of characters     */
/*    in the string.                                         */
/***************************************************************/
#include <stdio.h>
#include <string.h>

void main(void);

void main(void)
{
   static char buffer[81] = "A string";

   while (buffer[0])
      {
      printf("\n\n Enter a character string: ");
      gets(buffer);
      printf(" You entered:%s \n",buffer);
      printf(" The length of the string is: %d",strlen(buffer));
      }
}
```

Program output

```
Enter a character string: First string
You entered:First string
The length of the string is: 12

Enter a character string: Another string
You entered:Another string
The length of the string is: 14

Enter a character string:
You entered:
The length of the string is: 0
```

Figure 11.5   The strlen() function.

```
while (buffer[0])
```

is true. The program prints a prompt and then obtains user input with the following call to the **gets()** function

```
gets(buffer);
```

It then prints the string and the length of the string with the following **printf()** statement

```
printf(" The length of the string is: %d",strlen(buffer));
```

The output from the program is also shown in Figure 11.5.

The **strlen()** function is a fairly simple function. In fact, we could write our own version of **strlen()** as shown in the next example.

Example 11.4 Functions for Computing the Length of a String

PROBLEM STATEMENT: Write two functions for computing the length of a string. The first function should use a **for** loop, while the second function should use a **while** loop to count the number of characters in the string.

SOLUTION: The first version is shown in Figure 11.6 and is called **strlen1()**. The second version of the function is shown in Figure 11.7 and is called **strlen2()**. The difference between the two versions is that **strlen1()** uses a **for** loop to count the number of characters in the string and **strlen2()** uses a **while** loop. As with the C library **strlen()** function, both functions count the number of characters in a null terminated string. The terminating null character is not included in the count.

The function prototype for **strlen1()** is similar to the C library **strlen()** function

```
unsigned strlen1(const char *ptr_str);
```

The function accepts a pointer to a string and returns a value of type unsigned int which represents the number of characters in the string. The length of the string is computed in the **for** loop

```
for (count = 0; *ptr_str !='\0'; ++ptr_str)
    ++count;
```

The variable **count** is initialized to zero at the beginning of the loop. It is then incremented with each iteration until the terminating null character is found. The

```
/*****************************************************************/
/*    strlen1.c                                                */
/*    Returns the length of a string           .              */
/*****************************************************************/
#include <stdio.h>
#include <string.h>

void main(void);
unsigned strlen1(const char *ptr_str);

void main(void)
{
    static char test[] = { "1234567890"};
    unsigned length;

    length = strlen1(test);
    printf ("\n The length of the string is %d", length);

    length = strlen(test);
    printf("\n The value returned from strlen() is %d",length);
}

unsigned strlen1(const char *ptr_str)
{
    unsigned count;

    for (count = 0; *ptr_str != '\0'; ++ptr_str)
        ++count;
    return (count);
}
```

Figure 11.6   A function for computing the lengths of strings.

pointer **ptr_str** initially points to the first character of the string. With each iteration, the increment operation, **++ptr_str**, advances the pointer **ptr_str** so that it points to the next character in the string. The condition in the **for** loop could also have been written as

```
for (count = 0; *ptr_str; ++ptr_str)
```

The second version of a function to compute the length of a string is shown in Figure 11.7. The function **strlen2()** is similar to **strlen1()** in that it accepts a null terminated string as the argument and returns a value of type **unsigned int** representing the number of characters in the string. However, it uses a **while** loop to count the number of characters in the string. The statements in the body of the **while** loop are executed as long as the condition

```
while (*ptr_str)
```

is true. The condition will be false when **ptr_str** points to the terminating null character. Within the **while** loop, the variable **count** that contains the number o

```
/**************************************************************/
/*    strlen2.c                                             */
/*    Returns the length of a string                        */
/**************************************************************/
#include <stdio.h>
#include <string.h>

void main(void);
unsigned strlen2(const char *str_ptr);

void main(void)
{
    static char test[] = { "1234567"};
    unsigned length;

    length = strlen2(test);
    printf ("\n The length of the string is %d", length);

    length = strlen(test);
    printf("\n The value returned from strlen() is %d",length);
}

unsigned strlen2(const char *ptr_str)
{
    unsigned count=0;

    while (*ptr_str )
        {
        ++count;
        ++ptr_str;
        }
    return (count);
}
```

Figure 11.7   A function for computing the length of a string.

characters in the string is incremented by the statement

    ++count;

and the pointer is advanced by one character in

    ++ptr_str;

The **strlen()** function is useful for several programming tasks involving strings, as we shall see in the later sections of this chapter.

11.6 COPYING STRINGS

The C library **strcpy()** function copies one string over another. It takes two arguments of type pointer to **char**. The two arguments are pointers that point to null terminated strings. The first string is the target string, and the second string is the source string for the copy operation. The function copies all characters in the source string (including the terminating null character) on to the target string. Thus the target string is overwritten, but the source string remains unchanged. The source string can be a string constant.

The function prototype for the **strcpy()** function is

```
char * strcpy(char *target, const char *source);
```

The return type for the function is a pointer to type **char**. The function returns the address of the target string.

Example 11.5   Copying Strings

The program shown in Figure 11.8 demonstrates the use of the **strcpy()** function. The program creates a character array **source_str[]** having a size of 50 and a pointer to type **char** called **target_str** with the declarations

```
static char target_str[50] = { "The first string"};
static char *source_str = "Second string";
```

The program then prints the two strings. The statement

```
strcpy(target_str,source_str);
```

calls the **strcpy()** function to copy the contents of **source_str** on to **target_str**. The program then prints the strings a second time. The output from the program is also shown in Figure 11.8. After the call to **strcpy()**, the contents of **target_str[]** are replaced with **source_str**, but **source_str** itself is not changed.

Since C does not perform any bounds checking, it is the programmer's responsibility to ensure that the first string has enough storage space for all the characters in the second string. In the previous example, the string **target_str** is allocated storage for a total of 50 characters. If we allow for the terminating null character, **target_str** can contain a maximum of 49 characters. Note that it would be wrong to declare **target_str** as

```
static char *target_str;
```

This declaration simply creates a pointer to type **char** but does not actually allocate any storage.

We can also write our own version of the **strcpy()** function as shown in the next example.

```
/****************************************************************/
/*    strcopy.c  - Copies One String to Another String         */
/*    Copies a string using the C library strcpy() function.    */
/****************************************************************/
#include <stdio.h>
#include <string.h>

void main(void);

void main(void)
{
    static char tarrget_str[50] = { "The first string"};
    static char *source_str = "Second string";

    printf("Before strcpy(): \n");
    printf("Target string =  |%s|\n",tarrget_str);
    printf("Source string =  |%s|\n\n",source_str);

    strcpy(tarrget_str,source_str);

    printf("After strcpy(): \n");
    printf("Target string =  |%s|\n",tarrget_str);
    printf("Source string =  |%s|\n",source_str);
}
```

Program output

```
Before strcpy():
Target string =  |The first string|
Source string =  |Second string|

After strcpy():
Target string =  |Second string|
Source string =  |Second string|
```

Figure 11.8   The C library **strcpy()** function.

Example 11.6   Our Version of the **strcpy()** Function

PROBLEM STATEMENT: Write two versions of a function for copying a string. The first should use array notation and the second should use pointer notation.

SOLUTION: The two versions of the function are shown in Figures 11.9 and 11.10. The first version **strcpy1()** uses array notation; the second version **strcpy2()** uses pointer notation.   The bulk of the work is done within a **for** loop. In **strcopy1()**, the **for** loop is written as

```
for (i = 0; source[i]; ++i)
    target[i] = source[i];
```

```
/**************************************************************/
/*    strcpy1.c                                              */
/*    Copies a string. Uses array notation.                  */
/**************************************************************/
#include <stdio.h>
#include <string.h>

void main(void);
void strcpy1(char target[],char source[]);

void main(void)
{
   static char original[] = { "1234567890"};
   char copy[81];

   printf ("\n The original string is |%s|", original);
   strcpy1(copy,original);
   printf("\n The copied string is |%s|",copy);
}

void strcpy1(char target[],char source[])
{
   int i;

   for (i = 0; source[i]; ++i)
      target[i] = source[i];

   /* add a '\0' at the end of the copy */
   target[i] = '\0';
}
```

Figure 11.9 A function for copy strings using array notation.

In `strcpy2()` (Figure 11.10), the `for` loop is written as

```
for ( ; *source ; ++source, ++destination)
   *target = *source;
```

Notice that there is no initial condition in the above `for` loop. Also, the pointers to the source string and the destination string are both incremented within the for loop. Both `strcpy1()` and `strcpy2()` add a terminating null at the end of the destination string.

You should note that in both the `strcpy1()` and the `strcpy2()` function we have included a statement that adds a null character at the end of the target string. In the `strcpy1()` function we use the statement

```
target[i] = '\0';
```

and in the `strcpy2()` function we use the statement

```
*target = '\0';
```

```
/*****************************************************************/
/*    strcpy2.c                                                 */
/*    Copies a string. Uses pointer notation.                   */
/*****************************************************************/
#include <stdio.h>
#include <string.h>

void main(void);
void strcpy2(char *target,char *source);

void main(void)
{
    static char original[] = { "1234567890"};
    char copy[81];

    printf ("\n The original string is |%s|", original);
    strcpy2(copy,original);
    printf("\n The copied string is |%s|",copy);
}

void strcpy2(char *target,char *source)
{

   for ( ; *source ; ++source, ++target)
       *target = *source;

   /* add a '\0' at the end of the copy */
   *target = '\0';
}
```

Figure 11.10   A function for copying strings using pointer notation.

to add this null character. Beginning programmers sometimes forget to add the null character at the end of a string. This can lead to errors in your programs that are difficult to trace. You should always be careful to add the null character when writing any functions for creating or manipulating strings.

The C library **strncpy()** function copies a specified number of characters from one string to another string. The **strncpy()** function has three arguments. The first two arguments are the same as **strcpy()**. The third argument, which is of type **int**, specifies the number of characters of the second string that are to be copied to the first string. The following statement

```
strncpy(target,source,10);
```

copies the first 10 characters of **source** on to **target**.

You should be careful when using the **strncpy()** function. If the number of characters in the second string is less than the number of characters to be copied, the function will add null characters to fill the first string. If, however, the number of characters in the second string is larger than the number of characters to be copied, the function will not terminate the first string with a null character. Thus, if you are copying fewer characters than the length of the second string, you should add a null character to the resulting string.

11.7 CONCATENATING STRINGS

The **strcat()** function adds or concatenates two strings **str1** and **str2** to form a single string. The result is stored in **str1**. The function removes the null character at the end of the first string and adds a new null character at the end of the concatenated string. Thus **str1** is changed, but **str2** remains unchanged.

The **strcat()** function expects two arguments. Both arguments are pointers to type **char**. Each argument is the address of a null-terminated string. The return type for the **strcat()** function is pointer to type **char**. The function returns the address of the first string. An example of using **strcat()** is given in Example 11.7.

Example 11.7   String Concatenation

PROBLEM STATEMENT: Write a program that combines two strings to form a single string.

SOLUTION: The program shown in Figure 11.11. The program creates two strings using the declaration

```
char str1[11] = "12345";
char *str2 = "67890";
```

The first string **str1[]** is declared as an array of type **char**, while the second string **str2** is declared as a pointer to type **char**. The program prints the two strings and then calls the **strcat()** function

```
strcat(str1,str2);
```

The **strcat()** function takes the contents of **str2**, adds this at the end of **str1[]**, and places the result in **str1[]**. The program then prints the contents of both strings a second time. The output from the program is also shown in Figure 11.11.

The **strcat()** function does not check to see if the expanded string will fit in the first string. Thus, if you do not allocate enough space for the first string, you will undoubtedly experience problems with your program since the excess characters will be written into adjacent memory locations and corrupt other program variables.

```
/*****************************************************************/
/*    strcat.c - String Concatenation                          */
/*    Adds two strings, to form a single string.               */
/*****************************************************************/
#include <stdio.h>
#include <string.h>

void main(void);

void main(void)
{
    char str1[11] = "12345";
    char *str2 = "67890";

    printf("\n String Concatenation");
    printf("\n Before call to strcat():");
    printf("\n First string = |%s|", str1);
    printf("\n Second string = |%s|", str2);

    strcat(str1,str2);

    printf("\n\n After call to strcat():");
    printf("\n First string = |%s|",str1);
    printf("\n Second string = |%s|",str2);
}
```

Program output

```
String Concatenation
Before call to strcat():
First string = |12345|
Second string = |67890|

After call to strcat():
First string = |1234567890|
Second string = |67890|
```

Figure 11.11 The strcat() function.

The strncat() function is similar to strcat() but accepts a third argument which specifies the number of characters to be included from str2. The function prototype for strncat() is

```
char *strncat(char *str1, const char *str2, int n);
```

The function copies n characters of str2 and adds these at the end of str1.

11.8   COMPARING STRINGS

· Since strings are represented by character arrays in C, we cannot compare tw⸱ strings using the relational operators such as ==, !=, and >=. Thus, if **str1** an⸱ **str2** are two strings, then we cannot use the following statement

```
if (str1 == str2)       /* wrong!!! */
```

to determine if the two strings are equal.

The C library provides a function called **strcmp()** for comparin⸱ th⸱ contents of two strings. The **strcmp()** function accepts two pointers as argumen⸱ and returns the following values:

0   if the two strings are equal

\> 0 if the first string is larger, that is, it follows the second
       string alphabetically

< 0 if the first string is smaller, that is, it precedes the
       second string alphabetically

Comparisons of strings are based on the ASCII codes for the characters. Strir⸱ comparison takes place as follows: The function first looks at the first character ⸱ each string. If they are different, the string with the character that has the high⸱ ASCII code is considered to be the larger of the two strings. If the first character the same for both strings, the function compares the second character of each strin⸱ It they are also the same, the third characters are compared, and so on.

A look at the ASCII codes shows that this procedure would result in the strin⸱ being sorted alphabetically, since the ASCII codes have been chosen so that

```
A < B < C < D ... < Z
```

Also, the digits 0 to 9 come before the letters since they have ASCII codes that a⸱ numerically lower than the ASCII codes for the letters A to Z. Uppercase characte⸱ come before lowercase characters, since lowercase characters have higher ASC⸱ codes. For example, the ASCII code for lowercase "a" is 97, whereas the ASC⸱ code for uppercase "A" is 65, as noted earlier.

It is also interesting to note that strings containing the digits 0 to 9 do not s⸱ in numerical order. For example, the string "2" is larger than the string "12" ev⸱ though 2 is numerically smaller than 12. This is because the ASCII code for the fir⸱ character of the string "2" is higher than the ASCII code of the first character of t⸱ string "12." If we want to sort strings containing numbers in numerical order ⸱ have to use one of the string conversion functions such as **atoi()** and **atof()** convert the strings into numeric data prior to performing the sort. The **atoi()** a⸱ **atof()** functions are described in Section 11.10.

Table 11.2 lists some strings and the value returned by the **strcmp** function. The value returned by the **strcmp()** function is the difference in the ASCII codes of the first character in the first string and the corresponding character in the second string that is not in agreement. If the first string precedes the second string alphabetically, the number returned is negative. It the second string precedes the first, then a positive number is returned. We are usually not interested in the actual value returned by **strcmp()** since, typically, we want to know only whether or not the two strings are equal.

Table 11.2: String comparison

First String	Second String	Value Returned by strcmp()
"AA"	"AB"	-1
"AA"	"AA"	0
"AA"	"AB"	-1
"Aa"	"AA"	32
"BA"	"CA"	-1
"1A"	"A1"	-16
"123"	"134"	-1
"01"	"1"	-1
"AB"	"ab"	-32
"Zaa"	"zz:	-7

Example 11.8 String Comparisons

PROBLEM STATEMENT: Write a program to read in two strings and compare these string using the **strcmp()** functions and print the result.

SOLUTION: The program is shown in Figure 11.12. The program creates two arrays of type **char**, **first_str[]** and **second_str[]**, to store the two strings entered from the keyboard. Both arrays have a size of **MAX_CHARS**. The **#define** statement

```
#define MAX_CHARS 81
```

defines **MAX_CHARS** to be 81. The program reads in the two strings using the **gets()** function and then prints these. It then calls **strcmp()** to compare the two strings

```
/*************************************************************/
/*    strcomp.c  -- String Comparison                        */
/*    Reads two strings and compares them and prints the     */
/*    result of the comparison.                              */
/*************************************************************/
#include <stdio.h>
#include <string.h>
#define MAX_LENGTH 81

void main(void);

void main(void)
{
  char first_str[MAX_LENGTH], second_str[MAX_LENGTH];
  int result;

  first_str[0] = 'A';    /* initialize */
  printf("\n String comparison ");

  while (first_str[0])
      {
      printf("\n Enter first string: ");
      gets(first_str);
      printf(" Enter second string: ");
      gets(second_str);

      printf("\n first string:  |%s|",first_str);
      printf("\n Second string: |%s|",second_str);

      result = strcmp(first_str,second_str);

      if (result == 0)
         printf("\n Strings are equal");
      else if (result < 0)
         printf("\n First string precedes the second alphabetically");
      else
         printf("\n First string follows the second alphabetically");
         printf("\n Value returned by strcmp() is: %d", result);
      }
}
```

Figure 11.12 A program for comparing two strings.

```
    result = strcmp(first_str,second_str);
```

The value returned by `strcmp()` is saved in the variable **result**. By examining the value of result, the program can determine whether or not the strings are equal and print an appropriate message. The output from the program is shown in Figure 11.13.

The C library has several other functions for comparing strings. These include `strncmp()`, `stricmp()`, and `strincmp()`. The `strncmp()` function compares two strings but looks only at the first *n* characters of each string. It takes three

```
Enter first string: AA
Enter second string: AB

First string:    |AA|
Second string:   |AB|
First string precedes the second alphabetically
Value returned by strcmp() is: -1
Enter first string: Aa
Enter second string: AA

First string:    |Aa|
Second string:   |AA|
First string follows the second alphabetically
Value returned by strcmp() is: 32
Enter first string: 01
Enter second string: 1

First string:    |01|
Second string:   |1|
First string precedes the second alphabetically
Value returned by strcmp() is: -1
```

Figure 11.13 Output from program *strcomp.c.*

arguments. The first two arguments are pointers to the strings to be compared. The
third argument is an integer that specifies the number of characters to compare. The
strncmp() function is useful for comparing portions of strings.

The code segment shown here illustrates the use of the **strncmp()** function
to obtain a "yes" or "no" type response.

```
printf("\n Enter Yes or No");
gets(str1);
if ( (strncmp(str1,"Yes",1)) == 0 )
   {
   ...
   }
if ( (strncmp(str1,"No",1)) ==0 )
   {
   ...
   }
```

The **stricmp()** function is a case insensitive version of the **strcmp()**
function. This function compares two strings, but treats uppercase and lowercase
of the same characters as equal. The **strnicmp()** is a case-insensitive version of
the **strncmp()** function.

11.9   SEARCHING FOR A CHARACTER IN A STRING

The **strchr()** function searches for a character in a string. If it finds the character, it returns the address of the character. It returns a null pointer if it does not find the character. The **strchr()** function requires two arguments, the string to search and the character to look for in the string. Consider the following statements:

```
char buffer[] = "C for Engineers";
char *ptr;
ptr = strchr(buffer, 'E');
```

The statement

```
ptr = strchr(buffer,'E');
```

assigns the address of the character **'E'** in the string **buffer[]** to the pointer variable **ptr**. We can test for the presence of a character in a string as follows:

```
if ( (ptr = strchr(buffer, 'z' )) == NULL)
```

If **ptr** is **NULL** then the string buffer does not contain the character **'z'**.

A related function is **strrchr()**. This function returns the address of the last occurrence of a character in a string. It scans the string in reverse direction, looking for a specific character. In the code segment

```
char buffer[] = "C for Engineers";
char *ptr;
ptr = strrchr(buffer, 'e');
```

the pointer variable **ptr** contains the address of the last occurrence of the character **'e'** in the string buffer after the call to **strrchr()**. The function **strrchr()** returns a null pointer if the character does not occur in the string.

11.10 STRING TO NUMBER CONVERSIONS

Almost all engineering applications require that we enter numeric data in the program. Although we can use the **scanf()** function to input numeric data, this is not necessarily the most suitable approach. The **scanf()** function can be easily mislead by errors in entering numeric data. A better approach is to read in the numerical data as a string and then convert the string to the appropriate numerical value. For example, the number 123 can be stored in a character array as the digits **'1'**, **'2'**, and **'3'** and a **'\0'** for the terminating null.

C provides several functions for converting strings into numbers. The **atoi()** function takes a character string as an argument and returns the corresponding integer value. The header for the **atoi()** function is

```
int atoi(const char *str)
```

The **atoi()** function processes all digits in the string up to the first nondigit character. It ignores leading blanks, but it does recognize a leading algebraic sign (+, −). Processing is terminated when the first nondigit character is encountered. The **atol()** converts a string to a type **long** value. Its operation is similar to the **atoi()** function.

The **atof()** function takes a character string as an argument and returns a value of type **double**. This function recognizes the character representations of a floating point number, which means that it recognizes any leading plus and minus sign, the characters **'e'** and **'E'** used to represent exponents in floating point numbers and any also plus and minus signs preceding the exponent. As with the **atoi()** and **atol()** functions, the first unrecognized character ends the conversion. The C library has another function called **strtod()** that converts a string to a value of type **double**.

To use the string to number conversion functions you must have the following **#include** statement in your program

```
#include <stdlib.h>
```

The header file *stdlib.h* includes the declarations for the **atoi()**, **atol()**, and **atof()** functions.

Example 11.9 String to Number Conversions

The program shown in Figure 11.14 illustrates the conversion of strings to type **int**, **long**, and **double** values. It makes use of the C library **atoi()**, **atol()** and **atof()** functions to convert strings to numbers. The program prints several strings and the corresponding numeric value returned by the three functions. You should study the output from the program. The program includes the header file *stdlib.h* since the file contains the function prototypes for the string to number conversion functions. Note that these functions stop processing the string when the first nondigit character is encountered, and they ignore all leading blank characters.

```
/*****************************************************************/
/*    StrToNum.c  - String to Number Conversions                */
/*    Converts strings to numbers using the C library atoi(),    */
/*    atol() and atof() functions.                               */
/*****************************************************************/
#include <stdio.h>
#include <stdlib.h>
void main(void);

void main(void)
{
  printf("\n String to Integer Conversion");
  printf("\n string = |%s| \t number = %d","123",atoi("123"));
  printf("\n string = |%s| \t number = %d","-123",atoi("-123"));
  printf("\n string = |%s| \t number = %d"," 123",atoi(" 123"));
  printf("\n string = |%s| \t number = %d","123 ",atoi("123 "));
  printf("\n string = |%s| \t number = %d","1.23",atoi("1.23"));

  printf("\n\n String to Long Conversion");
  printf("\n string = |%s| \t number = %ld","890345",atol("890345"));
  printf("\n string = |%s| \t number = %ld","-890345",atol("-890345"));
  printf("\n string = |%s| \t number = %ld"," 890345",atol(" 890345"));
  printf("\n string = |%s| \t number = %ld","890345 ",atol("890345 "));
  printf("\n string = |%s| \t number = %ld","8903.45",atol("8903.45"));

  printf("\n\n String to Float Conversion");
  printf("\n string = |%s| \t number = %lf","8903.45",atof("8903.45"));
  printf("\n string = |%s| \t number = %lf","890345e2",atof("-890345e2"));
  printf("\n string = |%s| \t number = %lf"," 890345E-2",atof("890345E-02"));
  printf("\n string = |%s| \t number = %lf","-8903.45 ",atof("-8903.45 "));
}
```

Program Output:

```
String to Integer Conversion
    string = |123|          number = 123
    string = |-123|         number = -123
    string = | 123|         number = 123
    string = |123 |         number = 123
    string = |1.23|         number = 1

String to Long Conversion
    string = |890345|       number = 890345
    string = |-890345|      number = -890345
    string = | 890345|      number = 890345
    string = |890345 |      number = 890345
    string = |8903.45|      number = 8903

String to Float Conversion
    string = |8903.45|      number = 8903.450000
    string = |890345e2|     number = -89034500.000000
    string = | 890345E-2|   number = 8903.450000
```

Figure 11.14 String to number conversions.

11.11 PROGRAMMING PROJECT: AZIMUTH AND BEARING CONVERSIONS

Surveyors and civil engineers employ two angular measurements. Angular measurements called azimuths are measured clockwise from north from 0 to 360 degrees. Azimuths are also called compass headings. Another form of angular measurement is the compass bearing. A bearing angle is measured from either the north or south in an east or west direction. Thus a compass bearing consists of three items: north or south, an angle between 0 and 90 degrees, and east or west. For example, the bearing angle N 30° E means a 30-degree angle measured from the north to the east.

Figure 11.15 shows the relationship between an azimuth and bearing angle for the four quadrants. A common problem in involves conversions from azimuths to bearings, and vice versa.

Problem Statement

Write a C program that will perform that will convert an azimuth to a bearing and a bearing to an azimuth. The program should read in the azimuth in decimal degrees . The bearing angle should be read in the form *N/S degrees E/W*. The program should display the result in the same format as the input format.

Problem Analysis

The important variables are as follows:

Input Variables
azimuth angle (**char azimuth_str[]**)
bearing angle (**char bearing_str[]**)
type of conversion required (**char choice**)
    1 = azimuth to bearing, 2 = bearing to azimuth

Output Variables
azimuth angle (**double azimuth**)
north-south (**char ns**)
bearing angle (**double bearing**)
east-west (**char ew**)

Algorithm

The basic algorithm for the problem is the following:

1. Read desired conversion.
2. If conversion is from azimuth to bearing,

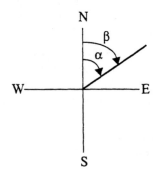
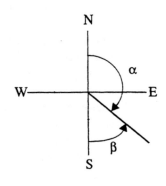

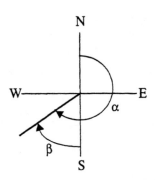
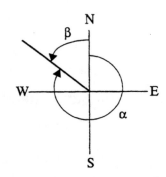

Conversion from Azimuth to Bearing

Quadrant	Bearing
I	N α W
II	S(180 − α) E
III	S(α − 180) W
IV	N(360 − α) W

Conversion from Bearing to Azimuth

Quadrant	Bearing
I	β
II	180 − β
III	180 + β
IV	360 − β

Figure 11.15 Conversions between azimuths and bearings.

    2.1 Read azimuth angle.

    2.2 Convert to bearing angle.

    2.3 Print bearing angle.

3.   Otherwise,

    3.1 Read bearing angle.

    3.2 Convert to azimuth angle.

    3.3 Print azimuth angle.

The input and output tasks that consist of reading in the desired type of conversion, reading in the azimuth or bearing angle, and printing the result are handled by the main program. Separate functions are used to perform the conversion for bearings to azimuths and azimuths to bearings.

Algorithm for `main()`

1.   Input **choice**.

2.   If **choice** is equal to 1 then

    2.1 Read in azimuth angle.

    2.1 Call **azimuth_to_bearing()** function.

    2.1 Print bearing angle.

3.   If **choice** is equal to 2

    3.1 Read in bearing angle.

    3.2 Call **bearing_to_azimuth()** function.

    3.3 Print azimuth angle.

Algorithm for `azimuth_to_bearing()`

1.   If azimuth < 0 or azimuth > 360 THEN

    1.1 bearing is undefined.

2.   Else if azimuth $<= 90$

    2.1 bearing is N azimuth E.

3.   Else if azimuth $<= 180$

    3.1 bearing is S (azimuth $- 180$) E.

4.   Else if azimuth is $>= 270$

    4.1 bearing is S (azimuth $- 180$) W.

5.   Else

    5.1 bearing is N (360 $-$ azimuth) W.

Algorithm for `bearing_to_azimuth()`

1. If first direction of bearing is N

    1.1 If second direction of bearing is E then

    1.1.1 azimuth is equal to bearing.

    1.2 Else

    1.2.1 azimuth is equal to 360 – bearing.

2. Else

    2.1 If second direction is E then

    2.1.1 azimuth is equal to 180 – bearing

    2.2 Else

    2.2.1 azimuth is equal to 180 + bearing.

Program

The program is shown in Figure 11.16. The program consists of three functions: **main()** which performs all the input and output operations and calls the other two functions, **azimuth_to_bearing()** which converts and azimuth angle to a bearing angle, and **bearing_to_azimuth()** which converts a bearing angle to an azimuth angle.

The type of conversion to be performed is determined by the value contained in the character variable **choice**. The statement

```
choice = getche();
```

calls the C library function **getche()** to read in a character and echo it to the display terminal. The character is assigned to the variable **choice**. Based on the value of **choice**, the switch statement transfers control to the appropriate case statements. The azimuth and bearing angle is read in as a character string. Since the bearing angle contains blank spaces, we cannot use the **scanf()** function to read in the string. The statement

```
gets(bearing_str);
```

uses the **gets()** function to read in the string.

Depending on the type of conversion selected, **main()** calls the **azimuth_to_bearing()** or the **bearing_to_azimuth()** function to perform the conversion and then prints the results.

The function header for **azimuth_to_bearing()** is

```
void azimuth_to_bearing(double azimuth_str,char *p_ns,
    double *p_bearing, char *p_ew);
```

```
/**********************************************************/
/*  bearing.c -- Azimuth And Bearing Conversion           */
/*                                                         */
/*  Converts an azimuth angle to a bearing angle.          */
/*  Also converts a bearing angle to an azimuth.           */
/**********************************************************/
#include <stdio.h>
#include <string.h>
#include <conio.h>
#include <stdlib.h>

void azimuth_to_bearing(double azimuth, char *ns,
          double *bearing, char *ew);
double bearing_to_azimuth(char *p_bearing_str);

main()
{
  double azimuth;      /* azimuth angle          */
  double bearing;      /* bearing angle          */

  /* character strings containing */
  /* bearing and azimuth angles   */
  char bearing_str[31], azimuth_str[31];
  char ns;             /* north-south */
  char ew;             /* east-west   */
  char choice;

  /* display menu  and obtain selection */
  printf("\n AZIMUTH AND BEARING CONVERSIONS");
  printf("\n 1 - Azimuth to bearing");
  printf("\n 2 - Bearing to azimuth");
  printf("\n Enter 1 or 2: ");
  choice = getche();

  switch (choice)
     {
     /* azimuth to bearing */
     case '1':
        printf("\n Enter azimuth angle: ");
        scanf("%lf",&azimuth);
        azimuth_to_bearing(azimuth_str,&ns,&bearing,&ew);
        printf("\n The bearing is: %c %lf %c",
               ns,bearing,ew);
     break;

     /* bearing to azimuth */
     case '2':
        printf("\n Enter bearing angle: ");
        gets(bearing_str);
        azimuth = bearing_to_azimuth(bearing_str);
        printf("\n The azimuth is:   %.4lf \n \n",azimuth);
        break;
     }
}
```

Figure 11.16 A program for converting azimuths to bearings, and vice versa.

```
/*---------------------------------------------------------*/
/*  Converts an azimuth angle to a bearing angle and       */
/*  prints the result.                                     */
/*                                                         */
/*  Input Parameters                                       */
/*    azimuth_str - azimuth angle                          */
/*                                                         */
/*  Output Parameters                                      */
/*    *p_ns       - north or south                         */
/*    *p_bearing - bearing angle                           */
/*    *p_ew       - east or west                           */
/*---------------------------------------------------------*/
void azimuth_to_bearing(char *p_azimuth_str,char *p_ns,
      double *p_bearing, char *p_ew)
{
   double azimuth;

   /* get angle */
   azimuth = atof(p_azimuth_str);

   if (azimuth < 0 || azimuth > 360.0)
      {
      *p_ns = '*';
      *p_ew = '*';
      *p_bearing = 0.0;
      }
   else if (azimuth <= 90.0)
      {
      *p_bearing = azimuth;
      *p_ns = 'N';
      *p_ew = 'E';
      }
   else if (azimuth <= 180)
      {
      *p_bearing = 180. - azimuth;
      *p_ns = 'S';
      *p_ew = 'E';
      }
   else if (azimuth <= 270)
      {
      *p_bearing = azimuth - 180.;
      *p_ns = 'S';
      *p_ew = 'W';
      }
   else
      {
      *p_bearing = 360. - azimuth;
      *p_ns = 'N';
      *p_ew = 'W';
      }
}
```

FIGURE 11.16   (continued)

```
/*----------------------------------------------------------*/
/*   Converts a bearing to an azimuth                       */
/*                                                          */
/*   Input Parameters                                       */
/*    p_bearing_str - compass bearing                       */
/*                                                          */
/*   Output Parameters                                      */
/*     None                                                 */
/*                                                          */
/*   Returns:                                               */
/*     azimuth - azimuth angle                              */
/*----------------------------------------------------------*/
double bearing_to_azimuth(char *p_bearing_str)
{
    double azimuth;
    double bearing;
    char ns,ew;

    /* read N/S from bearing string */
    if (strchr(p_bearing_str,'N') != NULL )
        ns = 'N';
        else
        ns = 'S';
        p_bearing_str += 2;

        /* get bearing angle  */
        bearing = atof( (p_bearing_str));

        /* read E/W from bearing string */
        while ( strchr(p_bearing_str, 32 ) == NULL)
            ++p_bearing_str;
        ++p_bearing_str;
        if (strchr(p_bearing_str,'E') != NULL )
            ew = 'E';
        else
            ns = 'W';

        /* convert to azimuth */
        if (ns == 'N')
            {
            if (ew == 'E')                     /* NE */
                azimuth = bearing;
            else
                azimuth = 360. - bearing;      /* NW */
            }
        else    /* must be 'S' */
            {
            if (ew == 'E' )                    /* SE */
                azimuth = 180. - bearing;
            else
                azimuth = 180. + bearing;      /* SW */
            }

    return (azimuth);
}
```

FIGURE 11.16   *(continued)*

The function has four parameters. The first parameter is a variable of type **double** that contains the azimuth angle. The remaining three parameters are pointers to type **char**. The variables that these pointers point to are assigned values upon return from the function based on the value of the azimuth angle, as for example in the following block of statements

```
else if (azimuth <= 90.0)
    {
    *p_bearing = azimuth;
    *p_ns = 'N';
    *p_ew = 'E';
    }
```

which assign values to ***p_ns**, ***p_ew**, and ***p_bearing** when the azimuth angle is less then 90 degrees.

The function **bearing_to_azimuth()** accepts one string argument containing the string representation of the bearing angle and returns a double value containing the azimuth angle. The function uses the **strchr()** library function to parse through the string and skips over any blank characters. The pointer variable **ptr_bearing_str** points to the current location in the string. After the north-south, east-west, and degrees components have been extracted from the string, these are stored in the variables **ns, degrees**, and **ew**. The function then uses these variables to determine the quadrant of the angle and computes the azimuth based on the algorithm presented earlier.

Testing

Testing this program is fairly straightforward since all we have to do is enter four azimuth angles for each of the four quadrants. We can then use the resulting bearing angles returned by the program as input and have the program convert these back to azimuth angles. If both sets of results are the same, then is means that the program is producing correct results. Table 11.3 lists the four azimuth angles used for testing the program and the corresponding bearing angles. The results from the program agree with the values given in Table 11.3.

Table 11.3: Azimuth and bearing angles for test runs

Quadrant	Azimuth	Bearing
I	30.0	N 30.0 E
II	120.0	S 60.0 E
III	210.0	S 30.0 W
IV	330.0	N 30.0 W

11.12 ARRAYS OF STRINGS

Since strings are arrays of type **char** we can use a two-dimensional array of type **char** to represent an array of strings. Consider the following declaration

```
static char materials[4][10];
```

This declaration creates a two-dimensional array of type **char**. The array has four rows, and each row has room for 10 characters. We can now use this two-dimensional array to store a list of materials as in the following:

```
static char materials[4][10] = {"Steel",
                                 "Concrete",
                                 "Aluminum",
                                 "Wood"};
```

Figure 11.17 shows the array after it has been initialized. Since the array **materials[][]** was declared as a static array, all elements of the array that have not been assigned a value are set to null.

S	t	e	e	l	\0	\0	\0	\0	\0
C	o	n	c	r	e	t	e	\0	\0
A	l	u	m	i	n	u	m	\0	\0
W	o	o	d	\0	\0	\0	\0	\0	\0

Figure 11.17 A two-dimensional array containing a list of materials.

To access a string in the array, we can simply provide the name of the array followed by the row index in square brackets. For example, to print the string **"Concrete"**, we can use the following **printf()** statement

```
printf("%s", material[1]);
```

We can also access an individual character. For example, to print the '**n**' in the string "**Concrete**", we can use the following **printf()** statement

```
printf("%c", material[1][2]);
```

Thus, to access an individual character, we specify the row index and then the column index. We should keep in mind that row and column numbers being at 0 and not 1.

11.13 ARRAYS OF POINTERS

The C language provides the programmer with another means of storing a collection of strings. Instead of using a two-dimensional array of characters, we can use one-dimensional array of pointers to type **char**. The declaration

```
static char *ptr_material[4];
```

creates an array of pointers to type **char**. The array contains four elements. We can combine the declaration and initialization in one statement by writing

```
static char *ptr_materials[4] = {"Steel","Concrete","Aluminum","Wood"};
```

This statement creates an array of four pointers to type **char**. It also initializes these pointers so that each element points to the first character of the corresponding string on the right-hand side of the equal sign. Figure 11.18 shows the array after it has been initialized assuming that the strings are stored in contiguous memory locations beginning at address 2001. The first element of the array **ptr_material[0]** points to the first character in the string **"Steel"**, the second element of the array **ptr_material[1]** points to the first character of the string **"Concrete"**, and so on.

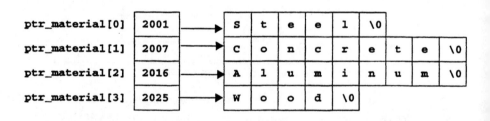

Figure 11.18 An array of pointers to type **char**.

To access an individual string in the array of strings, we have to specify the corresponding element of the array **ptr_material[]**. For example, to print the string **"Concrete"**, we can use the following **printf()** statement

```
printf("%s", ptr_material[2]);
```

Here, we are passing the address of the first character of the string **"Concrete"**. We can also access an individual character by applying the indirection operator. For example, to print the character **'n'** in the string **"Concrete"**, we can use the following statement

```
printf("%c", *(ptr_material[2] + 2));
```

The second element of the array of pointers **ptr_material[2]** contains the address of the first character of the string **"Concrete"**. We obtain the address of the third character **'n'** by adding two to this address, that is, **ptr_material[2] + 2** is the address of the third character in the string **"Concrete"**. Finally, we use the indirection operator ***(ptr_material[2]+2)** to obtain the value that is stored at this address.

It is important to recognize that the strings pointed to by the elements of the array **ptr_material[]**, may not be changed because they are constants. Thus, if we wanted the fourth element **ptr_material[3]** to point to the string **"Composite"** instead of **"Wood"**, we cannot simply overwrite **"Wood"** with **"Composite"**. Instead we have to assign a new value to **ptr_material[3]** as in

```
ptr_material[3] = "Composite"
```

Thus we can modify a pointer to a string so that it points to a different string, but we cannot change the string itself.

The difference between the two forms for representing arrays of strings is that **ptr_material[]** is a one-dimensional array of pointers while **material[][]** is a two-dimensional array of type **char**. The array **ptr_material[]** has the data type pointer to type **char**. You should also note that the elements of **ptr_material[]** contain addresses, more specifically, the addresses of the first character of each string.

C programmers prefer to use arrays of pointers to strings rather than two-dimensional arrays of characters for several reasons. Pointers are faster and easier to use and most of the C library string handling functions work with pointers. Also, in a conventional two-dimensional array of characters, each row of the array has the same number of elements. If we allocate enough storage to hold the longest string, some space will be wasted since the strings in the other rows will not completely fill the row. With an array of pointers to strings, no space is wasted. Arrays of pointers to strings are thus used quite frequently in C programs for displaying a list of items that do not change during the course of a program, such as a list of error messages, or a list of choices from which a user can make a selection.

11.14 COMMAND LINE ARGUMENTS

When a C program is executed the function **main()** is passed two arguments by the operating system. The first argument, which is called **argc** (for argument count) by convention, is an integer value. This argument indicates the number of arguments entered on the command line plus one. The command line is the line that you type to run the program. The second argument which is called **argv** (for argument vector) is a pointer to an array of strings. Each string in the array contains one of the command line arguments. The number of pointers in **argv** is equal to **argc**. The first string in the **argv[]** array, **argv[0]**, contains the complete name of the program. The exact string contained in **argv[0]** is implementation dependent. However, in most cases **argv[0]** is the complete name of the program. The remaining strings on the command line are assigned in succession to the other elements of the argument vector **argv[]**. Thus for the command line

C> cmdline first second third fourth

the value of **argc** is 5, since four strings were entered on the command line, **arg[0]** points to the name of the program (on our system this is **"C:\cmdline.exe"**), **arg[1]** points to **"first"**, **argv[2]** points to **"second"**, **argv[3]** points to **"third"**, and **argc[4]** points to **"fourth"**, as show in Figure 11.19.

For a C program to access the command line arguments, we need to modify the declaration of function **main()** as follows:

void main(int argc, char *argv[]);

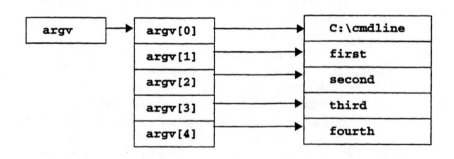

Figure 11.19 Command line arguments.

Example 11.10   Command Line Arguments

PROBLEM STATEMENT: Write a program to read in command line arguments and print the number of arguments and the value of each argument.

SOLUTION: The program shown in Figure 11.20 reads the command line arguments and prints the number of arguments and the value of each argument. The output from the program is also shown in Figure 11.20.

The number of arguments is printed in the **printf()** statement

```
printf("Number of pointers in argv[] = %d \n", arg_c);
```

A **for** loop is used to print the strings pointed to by the array of pointers, **arg_g[]**

```
for (i = 0; i < arg_c; ++i)
    printf("Argument: arg_v[%d] = %s \n", i, arg_v[i]);
```

```
/*********************************************************/
/*    cmdline.c   - Command Line Arguments              */
/*    Reads arguments from the command line and prints them. */
/*********************************************************/
#include <stdio.h>

void main(int arg_c, char *arg_v[]);

void main(int arg_c, char *arg_v[])
{
    int i;

    printf("Number of pointers in argv[] = %d \n", arg_c);
    for (i = 0; i < arg_c; ++i)
        printf("Argument: arg_v[%d] = %s \n", i, arg_v[i]);
}
```

Program output

```
C:\CBOOK\CHAP11>cmdline first second third fourth
Number of pointers in argv[] = 5
Argument: arg_vector[0] = C:\CMDLINE.EXE
Argument: arg_vector[1] = first
Argument: arg_vector[2] = second
Argument: arg_vector[3] = third
Argument: arg_vector[4] = fourth
```

Figure 11.20 A program to read command line arguments.

A common use of command line arguments is to pass file names and other parameters to a program. Note that on our system **argv[0]** points to the complete name of the program file. This is useful since it tells you the directory in which the program file resides. It is very likely that any files associated with the program will also be in the same directory as the program file.

11.15 SUMMARY

In this chapter we presented the C language features for working with character strings. C does not have a string data type. A string is considered to be an array of characters. The individual characters in the string are stored in adjacent memory cells.

A character string constant is a sequence of characters enclosed in double quotation marks. The quotation marks are not part of the string but serve to define the start and end of the string. All strings in C are by convention stored with a terminating null ('\0') character. The null character is a nonprinting character and has the ASCII code 0. The null character marks the end of the string and most string functions check for this terminating null character to determine whether the end of the string has been reached.

Since a string is an array of characters, we can use either array notation or pointer notation when working with strings. In this chapter we presented examples of using both approaches to access the individual elements of a string. To read and write strings we can use the %s format specifier in the **scanf()** and **printf()** functions. To read in a string we need to pass the name of the string as an argument since in C the name of an array represents the address of the first element of the array. When reading in a string we always need to make sure that we have allocated sufficient space to hold the string we expect to read. We can also use the C library **gets()** and **puts()** function for reading and writing strings. These functions are specially designed for reading and writing strings and work better than the generic **scanf()** and **printf()** functions.

In this chapter we also described some of the more commonly used C library string handling functions. Some of the functions contained in the C library include functions for determining the length of a string, copying, comparing and combining strings, and searching for specific characters in a string.

Since strings are arrays of type **char** we can use two-dimensional arrays to represent an array of strings. Another means of storing a collection of strings is to use an one-dimensional array of pointers to type **char**. One-dimensional arrays of pointers are used more frequently to represent an array of strings since pointers are faster and easier to use than two-dimensional arrays and there is no wasted storage.

Key Terms Presented in This Chapter

arrays of pointers	**atol()** function
arrays of type **char**	character strings
atof() function	command line arguments
atoi() function	concatenating strings

gets() function	**strlen()** function
null terminating character	strings
puts() function	string comparison
strcat() function	string constants
strcmp() function	string initialization
strcpy() function	**strchr()** function

PROGRAM STYLE, COMMON ERRORS, AND DEBUGGING GUIDE

1. When working with strings you should always be aware of the difference between a array of characters and a pointer to type **char**. The following two statements are not the same

   ```
   char string[5];    /* array of characters  */
   char *string;      /* pointer to type char */
   ```

   The first statement creates an array that can store five characters. The name of the array is a pointer constant and contains the address of the first element in the array. The second statement creates a pointer variable.

2. You should always include the header file *string.h* when using any of the C library string handling functions.

3. You cannot assign a character string to a character variable. The following is an error

   ```
   char ch;
   ch = "T";    /* illegal */
   ```

   In the foregoing, **"T"** is an array consisting of the character **'T'** and the terminating null character. The correct assignment statement is

   ```
   ch = 'T';    /* correct */
   ```

   Here, 'T' is a single character.

4. The most common and also the most frequent error when working with strings is not allocating memory for storing the string.

   ```
   char *ptr_str;
   printf("Enter a string");
   scanf("%s", ptr_str);    /* no storage allocated */
   ```

   In this example, no storage was allocated to hold the string. The first statement

```
char *ptr_str;
```

simply creates a pointer variable.

5. When using **scanf()** to read in a string you should make sure that you provide **scanf()** with an array that is large enough to hold the largest string that will be entered.

```
char array[21];
printf("Enter a string");
scanf("%s", array);
```

A run-time error will occur if more than 20 characters are entered.

6. When allocating storage for a string, always remember to allocate storage for the terminating null character.

7. When copying a string, you should always make sure that the null character is copied.

8. If you build a string yourself, you need to add the null character at the end of the string as shown in the following example.

```
char year[5];
string[0] = '1';
string[1] = '9';
string[2] = '9';
string[3] = '9';
string[4] = '\0';    /* null character at end */
```

9. It is an error to print a string that does not contain a terminating null character.

10. When using the **strncpy()** function, you need to append a null character to **str1** (the first argument) if **str2** (the second argument) has more characters than the number of characters specified in the third argument.

11. Given the declaration

```
char * str;
```

the statement

```
*ptr = "Programming is fun";   /* cannot do this!! */
```

is wrong. The statement attempts to assign the address of the string to the memory location to which **str** points rather than to the variable **str**. The correct statement is

```
ptr = "Programming is fun";   /* can do this */
```

12. Another example of an incorrect assignment statement is the following:

```
char str[20];
str = "Programming is fun"; /* cannot do this either */
```

The second statement attempts to assign the address of the sting into
str. However, **str** is a pointer constant since it is the name of the
string array (**str** points to the first element of the array) whose value
cannot be changed.

EXERCISES

Review Questions

1. For the following pairs of strings, indicate whether the value returned by the
   strcmp() function is 0 (the two strings are equal), less than zero (the first string
   follows the second string alphabeticaily), or greater than zero (the first string precedes
   the second string alphabetically).

   a. **"123"**, **"ABC"**

   b. **"ABCD"**, **"aBCD"**

   c. **"ABC1"**, **"ABC2"**

   d. **"ABCD"**, **"abcd"**

   e. **"41"**, **"21"**

   f. **"X*Y"**, **"X/Y"**

2. Consider the following declaration:

   ```
   static char *ptr_numbers[6] =
           {"one","two","three","four","five","six"};
   ```

   a. Show the array after it has been initialized.

   b. Write a **printf()** statement to print the third string.

   c. Write a **printf()** statement to print the letter **x** in the string "**six**".

3. Consider the following declaration:

   ```
   static char numbers[6][6] =
           {"one","two","three","four","five","six"};
   ```

   a. Show the array after it has been initialized.

   b. Write a **printf()** statement to print the third string.

   c. Write a **printf()** statement to print the letter **x** in the string "**six**".

4. What is the output from the following program:

   ```
   #include <stdio.h>
   main()
   {
       static char str[] = "Professional Engineer";
       ptr_str = str;
   ```

```
       puts(ptr_str++);
       puts(ptr_str);
       str[13] = '\0';
       puts(str);
   }
```

5. What will be printed by the following:

```
    #include <stdio.h>
    char str[] = "0123456789";
    main()
    {
        char *ptr_str;
        ptr_str = str;
        while (*ptr_str)
            {
            printf("%s\n", ptr_str);
            ptr_str++;
            }
    }
```

Programming Problems

6. Write your own version of the **strcat()** function. Recall that the **strcat()** function concatenates two strings, **str1** and **str2**, to form a single string. The result is stored in **str1**. The function removes the null character at the end of the first string and adds a new null character at the end of **str1**.

7. Write a recursive function that returns the length of a string.

8. Write a recursive function that copies a string.

9. Write a function called **string_index()** that returns the location of the first occurrence of a character **c** in a string **str**. If the character does not exist in the string, the function should return **NULL**. The function will be called as follows:

```
    int result;
    char str[] = "Programming for Engineers"
    char c = 'e';
    result = str_index(str,'c');
```

10. Write a function to extract a substring from a string. The function is called as follows:

```
    sub_string(source,start,count,destination);
```

where **source** is the character string from which the substring is to be extracted, **start** is an index indicating the position of the first character of in the substring in the source, **count** is the number of characters to be extracted, and **destination** is the array of characters to which the substring will be written. For example, the call

```
    sub_string("Professional Engineer",14,8,dest);
```

will extract the substring "**Engineer**" from the string "**Professional Engineer**" and place the result in **dest**.

Your function should insert a null character at the end of the substring in